A Pictorial History of
Blackamericans

Fifth Revised Edition of
A Pictorial History of the Negro in America

A Pictorial History of
Blackamericans

Langston Hughes,
Milton Meltzer,
and C. Eric Lincoln

Crown Publishers, Inc., New York

This book was originally published as *A Pictorial History of the Negro in America.*

© 1956, 1963 by Langston Hughes and Milton Meltzer. © 1968 by Milton Meltzer and the Estate of Langston Hughes. © 1973 by Milton Meltzer, C. Eric Lincoln, and the Estate of Langston Hughes. © 1983 by Milton Meltzer and the Estate of Langston Hughes. All rights reserved. No part of this book may be reproduced or transmitted in any form or by any means, electronic or mechanical, including photocopying, recording, or by any information storage and retrieval system, without permission in writing from the publisher. Published by Crown Publishers, Inc., One Park Avenue, New York, New York 10016 and simultaneously in Canada by General Publishing Company Limited.

Library of Congress Cataloging in Publication Data: Hughes, Langston, 1902–1967. A pictorial history of Blackamericans. Includes index. 1. Afro-Americans—History. I. Meltzer, Milton, 1915–   . II. Lincoln, C. Eric (Charles Eric), 1924–   . III. Title. E185.H83 1983 973'.0496 83–7742
ISBN 0-517-55072-5

10 9 8 7 6 5 4 3 2
Manufactured in the United States of America.

Part Five:
The Souls of Black Folk, 1900–1920

Part Six:
The New Negro, 1920–1941

Part Seven:
Searching for Freedom, 1940–1956

Part Eight:
The Range of Resistance

Part Nine:
Sharing the Power . . .

Preface

Heracleitus, one of the great philosophers of ancient Greece, taught that "You can't step into the same river twice." Since the waters are ever rushing onward in their part of the divine scheme, nothing remains to the second invasion that was part of the first. Therefore, each step is a distinct experience. When one looks at change in the abstract, the argument seems convincing enough. Certainly, when the last edition of this book was published a mere ten years ago, dozens of black experiences that are commonplace today could not even be imagined then. So perhaps Heracleitus was right: where political and civil history in the United States is concerned, we're wading in a new river; we're playing a new ball game!

But are we? We've seen changes, yes. *Many changes indeed!* Are they *generative* changes, though? Or do they tend to be remedial, incidental, and cosmetic? If generative, then the reasons for the old behavior are no longer felt to be compelling, and the life which includes the new kinds of relationships that constitute "change" is now acceptable to all concerned. Remedial change tends to be *ad hoc*—a bit of balm spread where the fly bites, as often as it bites, but with no real concern for eliminating the sources of corruption. Cosmetic change is all a matter of make-believe; it is the denial through cleverness and deceit of what is patently undeniable.

The decade just past has brought both substantial and part-illusory change. It is not always easy to distinguish the one from the other, for the sources from which they derive are not always infallible indexes of their value or intention. Only time will tell. It is not the best of all possible times; neither is it the worst. We will take what we have and make of it what we need. If ever we have what we need, then will we be properly equipped for aspiration. There is no need to walk in waters that are old; new floods are created everyday—if we can but manage them.

Blackamericans, Wherever in America

Who or what is a Negro? For America the issue has never been settled with finality, for at various times black people have been known as "colored people," "people of color," "Negroes," "Afro-Americans," "Aframericans," "Black Anglo-Saxons," "Black Americans," and by a number of other appellations. Most southern states have laws to the effect that any person having any Negro blood whatever is a Negro. The United States Bureau of the Census declares:

A person of mixed white and Negro blood should be returned as a Negro, no matter how small the percentage of Negro blood. Black and mulatto persons are to be returned as Negroes, without distinction. A person of mixed Indian and Negro blood should be returned as a Negro, unless the Indian blood very definitely predominates and he is universally accepted in the community as an Indian. Mixtures of nonwhite races should be reported according to race of the father, except that Negro-Indian should be reported as Negro.

The problem is that the reasoning behind the state and federal pronouncements about "Negroes" seems to imply that somewhere at some time there existed a race or a nation of "Negroes," and that all of the people in the United States who are not 100 percent white and who are not distinctively Indian belong to the Negro race or nationality. Such reasoning does not help much in identifying people by race, if that is important. Many Americans who are called "Negroes" are "whiter" than tens of thousands of other Americans who are classified as "white." For three hundred years and more, runaway slaves (and later freedmen) intermarried with the Indians of nearby tribes so frequently as to have produced in some sections of the country a distinctive physical subtype. The Blackamerican of pure African descent is quite rare, and recent computer studies show that millions of "white" Americans have to varying degrees African ancestry of varying degrees of remoteness.

Who then, is a "Negro" and what difference does it make? It is far easier to answer the second question than the first. As long ago as 1819, the South Carolina courts held that a Negro was a slave, or subject to becoming a slave, and that a slave was *ipso facto* a Negro. The Mississippi Supreme Court said that in the eyes of the law "a Negro is *prima facie* a slave." The courts seemed to be trying to provide a simple rule of thumb for the complex problem of deciding who should have what rights in a society in which all men were held "created equal," but some, by common agreement among their fellows, were to be treated as though they were not.

Now that slavery has been officially abolished for more than a hundred years, it would seem that our efforts to get on with making this a free and equal society could be enhanced by avoiding the use of words which because of past associations are likely to be weighted with meanings we no longer intend to convey. The problem is that in their subconscious understanding most Americans still associate "Negroes" with cotton fields and cakewalks and a debased status in society. It is probable that all Americans are descendants of people who were slaves at some point in their history, but "Negroes" and "slaves" still have such a vivid association with our recent past that the use of the word Negro is not now an effective way to express the highest level of appreciation for people who consider themselves the equals of any other.

The black people of America are African by derivation, American by nationality, and *Blackamerican* in terms of the rich, distinctive subculture they have developed here in the West. As Malcolm X once said, *"We are all black, different shades of black."* Some Blackamericans have fair skin and blond hair. Some are as black as the African night their fathers knew. But being black in the contemporary world is not so much a matter of skin color as it is a state of mind— an attitude about the value of persons and their rights as human beings without regard to such physical accidents as color. To be "black" is to adopt a cultural response which denies and negates the traditional implications of being "white," or "nonwhite," or "Negro," as the case may be. It is an assertion that we are what we are without reference to what others may name us or name themselves.

Black people consider themselves American, not because national status was conferred upon them gratuitously, but because they were here in the beginning— before there *was* an America, and because their blood and sweat and tears are forever mingled with those of others whose struggles and triumphs made this country great. Blacks cleared the forests and dug the canals and laid the tracks and fought to keep the country free— shoulder to shoulder and back to back with other Americans who happened to be white. *They are Blackamericans*, proud of their heritage and confident of their future. And wherever you look you will find them working, playing, worshipping, dreaming, creating, and expressing their cherished freedom in the spirit of the country they would like to help make a model for democratic peoples everywhere.

Part One
THE PECULIAR INSTITUTION
1619-1863

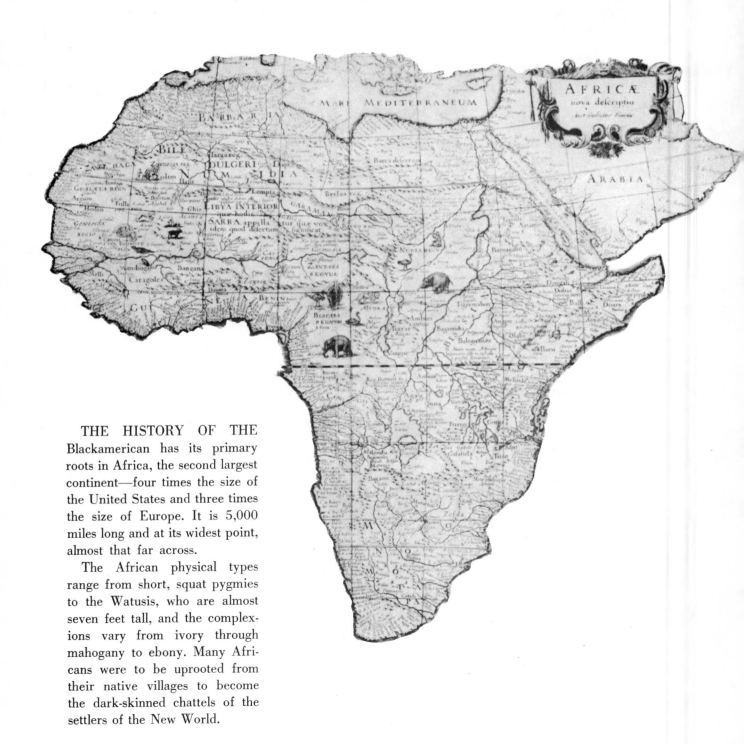

THE HISTORY OF THE Blackamerican has its primary roots in Africa, the second largest continent—four times the size of the United States and three times the size of Europe. It is 5,000 miles long and at its widest point, almost that far across.

The African physical types range from short, squat pygmies to the Watusis, who are almost seven feet tall, and the complexions vary from ivory through mahogany to ebony. Many Africans were to be uprooted from their native villages to become the dark-skinned chattels of the settlers of the New World.

Secret society mask, sculptured in wood, Nigeria.

Bronze leopard head, from seventeenth-century Court of Benin, Nigeria.

First, We Were Africans

Africa is an ancient land. For thousands of years before history was reduced to writing, generations upon generations of black men were locked in an unremitting struggle with their environment in the determination that life should have meaning and purpose beyond mere survival. There are many "cradles of civilization" in the ancient river valleys of the world, where because of a unique balance of ecological factors, survival-plus made possible the emergence of cultures. But increasingly the careful reading of nature's own records seems to show that Africa not only gave the world its earliest civilizations, she gave the world *man*. The evidence is there under the patterned layers of earth in the Olduvai Gorge in East Africa, preserved by the hot dry sands of the Sahara, and beneath the mud and silt of centuries in the valley of the Nile.

Meaningful survival. That is the essence of civilization. That is the stuff of culture. The Africans survived; they learned to cope with the rivers and the forests, the lion, the leopard, and the crocodile; they learned the names and the characters of the gods. They flourished and built civilizations. Great civilizations.

In Egypt they labored to build the pyramids and the temples thousands of years before Europe developed a stable civilization. Black Pharaohs ruled Egypt for centuries and black Queen Nefretete, one of the most beautiful women of all time, graced the Egyptian throne as the wife of Aahmes I, to become cofounder of the great Eighteenth Dynasty.

The Greeks and the Romans knew of and wrote about the black peoples of Egypt and Ethiopia. Secular history and the Holy Scriptures of three great religions bear irrefutable testimony to the African influence on the development of Judaism, Christianity, and Islam. If Hagar had not borne a child for Abraham; if Ebedmelech had not rescued the prophet Jeremiah from the dungeon; if the Queen of Sheba had not captured the admiration of Solomon; if Abdul Hasan Ali, black sultan of Morocco, had not befriended Mohammed, the course of religious history would have been changed for countless millions of believers.

A number of superior civilizations rose and fell in West Africa before the coming of the white man. Ancient Ghana was flourishing about the time of the

7

Male figure carved in wood, the Ivory Coast.

Female figure in wood, Baluba, the Congo.

Ghana's splendor was succeeded by Mali, a small state whose history antedated that of Ghana by two hundred years, but which did not attain importance until the twelfth century when, through a series of conquests under Sundiata Keita, it became a great empire. By the fourteenth century it was described as a rich, well-ordered state. Mali was a Moslem state, and in 1324 its ruler, Mansa Musa, made a pilgrimage to Mecca. It was undoubtedly one of the most regal pilgrimages of all time, involving an entourage of 60,000 persons. There were 12,000 servants, 500 slaves (each carrying a golden staff), and eighty camels laden with more than two tons of gold to be distributed among the poor. On his return from Mecca, Mansa Musa brought with him master architects and builders who, among other things, were assigned to build the libraries and other public buildings in the fabled city of Timbuktu.

Mali waxed and waned as civilizations do, and was in time eclipsed by the kingdom of Songhay under Askia Mohammed Askia who came to power about the time Columbus was reporting his "discovery" of America to Queen Isabella of Spain. Remarkably, Askia's kingdom covered most of West Africa and was greater than all of the European states combined. Historians acclaim his rule as one of great plenty and absolute peace. Under Askia, Timbuktu became a thriving commercial cross-roads of 100,000 people, where the merchants from distant lands came in endless caravans to exchange their exotic wares for gold. Timbuktu was an intellectual center unrivaled at the time. To its famous University of Sankore came the ambitious youth from the Moslem world to study law and medicine. Medieval Europe sent its best scholars there to see the great libraries with manuscripts in Greek and Latin as well as in Arabic, and to consult with the learned mathematicians, astronomers, physicians, and jurists whose intellectual endeavors were paid for out of the king's own treasury.

The decline of Songhay and Timbuktu in the seventeenth century signaled the end of an epoch of the great civilizations of West Africa. But the glory of Africa, that most ancient of ancient lands, must not sleep for long. There is a biblical tradition which promises that "Ethiopia shall stretch forth her wings." The fortunes of Africa will be reversed. Her greatness will be restored.

Roman invasion of Britain, and did not begin its decline until the eleventh century. At the height of its glory, Ghana boasted a standing army of 20,000 men, their horses caparisoned in cloth made of gold. An honor guard, bearing golden shields and gold-mounted swords, with gold plaited into their hair, waited upon the king. The king's splendidly attired attendants were seconded by dogs of an excellent breed, wearing collars of gold and silver, who never left the king's seat.

Greek warriors escort a woman captive to the slave market.

Arab traders of the late nineteenth century on a slaving expedition in East Africa.

How We Came to America

Out of Africa, from ancient times through the Middle Ages, almost to yesterday, to the rest of the known world came gold and silver, ivory, and human beings exported as slaves. At first, African slaves were prizes of war. The more beautiful women were carried off by armed conquerors to become concubines, and both men and women became servants. Triumphant armies made slaves of conquered peoples, regardless of color.

Slavery is as old as civilization. In ancient Greece and Rome there were thousands of slaves, black as well as white. Slavery was a pronounced feature of European civilization. In fact, the word "slave" is a literal reminder of the time when the Slavs of Eastern Europe were sold by the Germans for whatever they would bring in the slave markets of Western Europe. Tacitus, the celebrated historian, recounting the Roman occupation of England during the ninth century, wrote that the Britons were "too stupid" to make efficient slaves. Nevertheless, the sale of Englishmen as slaves continued unabated until the Norman Conquest of 1066, after

which William the Conqueror decided that slavery could be continued locally, but that no more Britons could be sold in the international markets. Ironically, the English were later to become the master slavers of all time, plundering Africa and its peoples. By the mid-eighteenth century, more than three hundred slave ships sailed out of Liverpool alone. Over the entire period of this traffic in human bodies, English ships hauled away four times as many Africans as all the competing nations of Europe combined.

Slavery was customary throughout Asia. When the Moslems came to Africa, they sold Africans by the thousands to traders in Arabia and Persia. During the fourteenth and fifteenth centuries, fashionable Venetians, Spaniards, and Portuguese kept black page boys and dusky slave girls in attendance. But it was not until commercial expansion led to the exploration and colonization of the New World that African slavery became a profitable institution. Eventually it was to develop into a monstrous enterprise, regulated by international

A French slave galley of the late seventeenth century.

agreement among the "civilized" nations of the world; an enterprise which depopulated the towns and villages of West Africa as effectively as some dreadful plague. Torn from their homes and their families, bound to each other in chains, the men and women of Africa were brought to America.

But that all began a hundred years after America was discovered, and long after the first Africans came to America, not in bondage, but accompanying the early explorers. Pedro Alonzo Niño, navigator of the flagship on which Columbus sailed to the New World, was the first man of African descent, of whom there remains any record, to see America. When Balboa discovered the Pacific Ocean in 1513, there were in his party thirty black men who helped clear the first road across the isthmus between the two oceans. Narváez's expedition to Florida in 1528—following in Ponce de Leon's foot-steps—lost all but a handful of men in attacks by the Indians. Two soldiers, Cabeza de Vaca and his black companion, Esteban, escaped and wandered on the North American continent for six and a half years. In 1539, another Black, Esteban Dorantes, or "Little Steven," set out from Mexico City in the party of Friar Marcos de Niza, in search of the fabled Seven Cities of Cibola. When the others wearied, Esteban went on ahead alone, except for his Indian guides, and opened up to European settlers the rich area that is now Arizona and New Mexico.

A century later, Africans were being marketed like cattle in black market trading in Spanish-controlled American waters. The practice, although illegal, was widely engaged in by some unscrupulous ship captains. One, the famous British buccaneer, Sir John Hawkins, accompanied by Sir Francis Drake, another British pirate, shipped slaves aboard their vessel, called the *Jesus of Lubeck*. In 1619, a Dutch ship dropped anchor at Jamestown, Virginia, with a cargo of twenty Africans,

In the New World, slaves, called "money-making machines," worked in mines and shops, on ranches and plantations, on docks and in homes.

which they bartered to the settlers for fresh provisions. These twenty "negars" were destined to become the first black slaves in English America.

The Guinea Coast—known as the Slave Coast—of West Africa, about 1700.

TO BE SOLD on board the Ship *Bance-Island*, on tuesday the 6th of *May* next, at *Afhley-Ferry*; a choice cargo of about 250 fine healthy

NEGROES,

juft arrived from the Windward & Rice Coaft. —The utmoft care has already been taken, and fhall be continued, to keep them free from the leaft danger of being infected with the SMALL-POX, no boat having been on board, and all other communication with people from *Charles-Town* prevented.

Auftin, Laurens, & Appleby.

N. B. Full one Half of the above Negroes have had the SMALL-POX in their own Country.

An advertisement of a cargo of slaves aboard the *Bance-Island*, anchored off Charleston, during a plague of smallpox.

An artist's conception (*c.* 1796) of a group of Negroes just landed from Surinam to be sold as slaves.

11

"Slave Traffic on the Coast of Africa."

"Black Gold"

By the middle of the sixteenth century more than 10,000 Africans a year were being sold to the European colonists in the West Indies. Portuguese ships were the first to engage in the slave traffic, but it was not long before Spanish, French, Dutch and English slavers took it up.

The English colonists in the New World imported white indentured workers at first, but found there weren't enough of them. The Indians in the Americas refused to work or, in the main, proved to be poorly fitted for long hours of hard labor. In the long run, the Europeans found it easier and cheaper to import Africans as slaves. Thus, by the seventeenth century, the African slave trade was booming in the Americas. To compete with the Dutch and French, the King of England in 1672 chartered the Royal African Company, which soon dominated the entire slave trade. The slave dealers made so much money from their human cargoes that soon Africans came to be known as "black gold."

The sea lane across the Atlantic which the slave ships followed from the Gulf of Guinea to New England, Chesapeake Bay, the Gulf of Mexico or the Spanish Main was known as the Middle Passage. Sailing vessels took many weeks to traverse the Western Ocean. During the long voyages many slaves died, for they were stacked like logwood in dank holds, chained together and allowed on deck only a few minutes per day for fresh air and exercise. In bad weather they got neither. The food was often spoiled, the water stagnant, their quarters filthy. For each five slaves delivered safely to the Americas, historians estimate that one perished on the way. Some slaves committed suicide by jumping into the water, or even by swallowing their own tongues. Those who rebelled were often shot down or beaten to death on shipboard.

Most of the Africans imported to the Americas came from Gambia, the Gold Coast, Guinea or Senegal. The natives

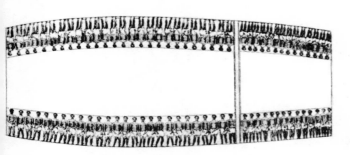

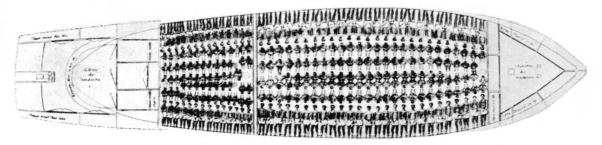

Loading plan of a slave ship, with the irons used for shackling the cargo.

of Senegal, who were often skilled artisans, brought the highest prices. On the other hand, the Eboes from Calabar were rated as undesirable merchandise, as they frequently preferred suicide to bondage. Those from the Gaboons were considered weaklings.

By the seventeenth century slaves could be secured in Africa for about $25 a head, or the equivalent in merchandise, and sold in the Americas for about $150. But later, when the slave trade was declared illegal, Africans brought much higher prices. Many slave-ship captains could not resist cramming their black cargo into every foot of space, even though they might lose from 15 to 20 per cent of the lot on the way across the ocean. It is estimated that 7,000,-000 Africans were abducted during the eighteenth century alone, when the slave trade became one of the world's great businesses.

Section of a vessel, showing the way in which slaves were stowed on board.

Slaves in the New World

Whenever a slave ship sailed into a colonial port on the American mainland, its arrival was announced by a town crier or by an advertisement in the local newspaper. Householders and planters, as well as professional slave dealers, came down to the docks to select house servants and field hands.

To the slaves, Boston, or Baltimore, or Charleston, were unfriendly cities in an unfriendly new world, cold to their half-naked bodies and bare feet and peopled with mysterious white people who spoke a language they could not comprehend. But at least the seasickness and cramped quarters on shipboard were over. What lay ahead, the Africans—strangers in a strange land—did not know. But soon they learned what their lot might include: a lifetime of hard work without pay, meager food, the lash of the whip.

Families might be ruthlessly scattered, sold away from each other, never to meet again, for slaves had no control over their destinies. They could not understand their masters' language. In their new homes the fellow slaves with whom they worked might be from diverse parts of Africa, with no common language. Indeed, as a safeguard against rebellion, it

was customary to separate Africans of the same tribe and to disperse relatives. From a single African family arriving in the colonies, the father might be sold to Maryland, the mother to the Carolinas and the children scattered from Virginia to the Gulf, never to see each other again.

In the New England colonies, where the colonists themselves were industrious and where white artisans and small farmers were prevalent, there was no demand for large numbers of slave workers. But from Maryland to the Carolinas, and later as far west as Louisiana, where vast stretches of fertile land had to be cleared for ever-increasing plantations of tobacco, rice and sugar cane, manpower was sorely needed. So it was that the colonies in the South became the greatest purchasers of slaves.

In the early days many of these slaves were brought from the West Indies, rather than directly from Africa. But by the late 1700's an increasing number of slave ships were sailing directly into North American ports. By this time busy markets had been established at Philadelphia, Richmond, Charleston and New Orleans. In Maryland and Virginia a thriving domestic business in the breeding of slaves for Southern plantations developed after the colonial period.

The American settlers soon found tobacco to be a profitable export crop and many slaves were put to work in the tobacco fields. Columbus found the Caribs on Hispaniola using tobacco. The white explorers took to it with enjoyment and early in the sixteenth century carried it back to Europe, where tobacco-smoking and snuff-taking had become fashionable. As the export business increased, more and more slaves were imported to cultivate its tall stalks with the pink, red or white flowers, to dry its wide leaves and to pack them for shipping. In Maryland, the Piedmont section of Virginia and in North Carolina, vast acreages were given over to tobacco. In North Carolina, field hands were so urgently needed at one time that the governor offered grants of land to importers of slave workers over fourteen years old. But by the mid-1600's so much tobacco had

been grown that the European market was glutted and prices fell.

The colonial planters then turned their attention to the cultivation of rice, sugar cane and indigo. These, too, required many hard-working laborers to clear the land, to plant and harvest the crops, so there was no let-up in the importation of Africans. By the end of the seventeenth century there were twice as many Africans as whites on the American continents and in the West Indies.

Gradually, in the Southern colonies, sugar cane became an important source of revenue. The cane fields were tended almost entirely by slaves, from the planting and cutting to the crushing of the stalks for juice. The crushed cane was used for fuel and molasses, for food and as a base for rum. Molasses and rum, in turn, were often used as barter in the triangular trade linking Africa, the West Indies and North America.

Slaves extracting and boiling the juice of sugar cane.

Negroes testing tobacco in Virginia.

Housing, airing and vending tobacco in Virginia.

Picking cotton on a Georgia plantation where the rows stretched as far as the eye could see.

Invention of the Cotton Gin

In early colonial days cotton was not a major crop. Converting the white bolls into clean lint for the making of thread was slow and tedious, for human hands were then the only means of separating the lint from the seeds. To clean by hand enough cotton for a few yards of cloth was a long-drawn-out process. A whole family, with the help of the house servants, might gather before the fireplace in the evening to remove the white fluff from the seeds, fiber by fiber, to acquire by bedtime only a few pounds of lint.

Yet, since cotton cloth was highly valued, the colonies grew a little cotton for their own use and colonial housewives mixed it with wool for their spinning wheels. King George III accepted cotton in payment of rent on crown lands. Some American cotton was grown for export to English mills. But not until Eli Whitney invented his famous gin did cotton become a major crop.

Eli Whitney received his diploma from Yale in 1792 and took ship for the South to fill a position as tutor in a Carolina planter's home. He was invited by the widow of a leading Revolutionary War general, Mrs. Nathanael Greene, to break his journey by spending a few days on her plantation near Savannah. "During this time," Whitney later wrote his father, "I heard much said of the extreme difficulty of ginning cotton — that is, separating it from its seed. There were a number of very respectable gentlemen at Mrs. Greene's, who all agreed that if a machine could be invented which would clean the cotton with expedition, it would be a great thing both for the country and for the inventor."

In a few days the young Yankee worked out a plan for such a machine. Ten days later, he made a successful model. Within six months he had built a contraption that enabled a man to seed ten times as much cotton as before and to clean it more efficiently. With the aid of a horse to turn the gin, a man could clean fifty times as much cotton as before. Whitney's cotton gin was a major contribution to the industrial revolution which was then taking place, and within a few years it had changed the economy of the entire South. Cotton quickly became a leading crop and a chief export commodity.

To grow cotton and to pick, gin and bale it took a great deal of hard work. For example, if one man alone were to bring one acre of cotton to fruition, that man would have to walk almost a thousand miles, from spring to fall, up and down the rows of his single acre, plowing, planting, chopping and picking, then piling his bags into a wagon to haul them to the gin.

In the South, this labor was delegated to the slaves. Thus, in the single year of 1803, less than ten years after the invention of the cotton gin, more than 20,000 Negroes, many of them supplied by New England slave traders, were brought into Georgia and South Carolina to work in the cotton fields. Whitney's gin, which made cotton big business, also riveted the chains of slavery tighter than ever about the ankles of black men and women.

A model of Eli Whitney's cotton gin.

Cleaning cotton before the invention of the gin.

Eli Whitney at the age of fifty-five. Never able to patent his gin or to profit greatly from its manufacture, he turned to the making of firearms and became wealthy.

Negro female slaves helped to gin cotton. Mechanical ginning freed many hands for work in the fields.

King Cotton

In search of new lands for growing cotton, many colonists pushed farther and farther inland away from the coast. The wilderness first had to be cleared—the trees and brush cut away, the swamps drained, the roots and rocks removed—before the plowshares could be sunk into virgin earth. For this heavy preliminary labor, black hands were most useful, indeed necessary, for there were not enough white men to do it.

As the colonists penetrated deeper and deeper into the American interior—to the Mississippi, then across it—with the settlers went African black men and black women. Thus slavery, in time, extended as far as Texas and, eventually, California. From the Carolinas, through Georgia, across Alabama, into the rich black soil of the Mississippi Valley spread the cotton belt. Land was still plentiful, so that when older land became unproductive, planters and slaves simply cleared new acreage farther west to plant new crops.

After a series of industrial inventions—the spinning jenny in 1765, the water frame in 1769 and the power loom in 1785—mechanized the British textile industry and made possible more rapid manufacture of textiles, the demand for raw cotton rose from English mill-owners.

In America, Whitney's gin had made the removal of seeds from the lint so much easier that more and more cotton was being baled and shipped abroad. More and more slaves were needed to work the fields and resourceful Southern planters instituted large-scale methods of cultivation.

In the port towns ships brought cargoes of slaves from Africa and carried bales of cotton to England. From the time of the signing of the Declaration of Independence, American cotton production jumped to more than half a million bales a year in the first quarter of the nineteenth century, and by 1850, to more than 3,000,000 bales. Three-fourths of the world's cotton was being supplied by the Gulf States. Vast fortunes were made and slavery became a vital element of the South's economy.

Thus it was that for more than a hundred years the story of the South—and the Southern Negro—was the saga of King Cotton.

Scene on the Alabama River, loading cotton.

GANG OF 25 SEA ISLAND
COTTON AND RICE NEGROES,
By LOUIS DE SAUSSURE.

On THURSDAY the 25th Sept., 1852, at 11 o'clock, A.M., will be sold at RYAN'S MART, in Chalmers Street, in the City of Charleston,

A prime gang of 25 Negroes, accustomed to the culture of Sea Island Cotton and Rice.

CONDITIONS.—One-half Cash, balance by Bond, bearing interest from day of sale, payable in one and two years, to be secured by a mortgage of the negroes and approved personal security. Purchasers to pay for papers.

Cleaning cotton with one of the early gins.

"The Best Friend," the first locomotive built in the United States for actual service on a railroad, was fired by Negro firemen. One of them once caused the boiler to explode when, to stop the annoying hiss of escaping steam, he sat on the lever of the escape valve.

Slaves as Skilled Workers

Not all slaves, however, were relegated to the fields. There were houses and docks to be built, bridges to be constructed, gates and fences to be made and mended. For these and similar purposes skilled artisans were developed among the Negroes, especially in urban communities. The custom of hiring out bondsmen to others became a pattern, and some masters encouraged their slaves to learn a trade, since their wages went to their masters and skilled slaves fetched a better rate of hire. Some slaves became expert brickmasons, carpenters and workers in iron, building many a stately Southern mansion and moulding the beautiful iron grillwork of the gates and balconies of old New Orleans and Charleston. Owners of foundries, tobacco factories, textile mills and contractors employed slaves in skilled and semi-skilled capacities.

As railroads were developed, thousands of Negroes were employed in the laying of roadbeds. The first fireman on the first locomotive built in America (in 1830) was a slave. In the construction of the Muscle Shoals Canal, the contractors gave special compensation to the masters of any slaves who were injured or killed by explosions or cave-ins. Similar arrangements were made in the case of slaves employed in coal, copper and gold mines. Although at that time white workers, no matter how dangerous their occupation, were not covered by any sort of accident insurance, slave-holders could secure protection for their investment in human chattels.

In some parts of the South more slaves than whites were engaged in skilled trades. Soon the competition between slave labor, controlled by the slave-owners, and free white labor developed to such an extent that bitterness sometimes flared into violence against the Negroes, who had no part in the creation of the system. White workers began to protest against the custom of hiring out slaves as artisans, thus forcing white labor to compete with bondsmen for a low wage scale.

In Virginia, where white seamen out of work protested, a law was passed as early as 1784 limiting the number of slaves in each ship's crew.

Adam Perry, a slave, was hired out in 1834 to the South Carolina Railroad. In 1852 he became the fireman for engineer Henry G. Raworth. For nineteen years they worked together without an accident, their engine requiring no repairs but replacement of parts.

A horse-propelled car of about 1829 which could carry a dozen passengers. A slave with a whip kept the horse going twelve miles an hour.

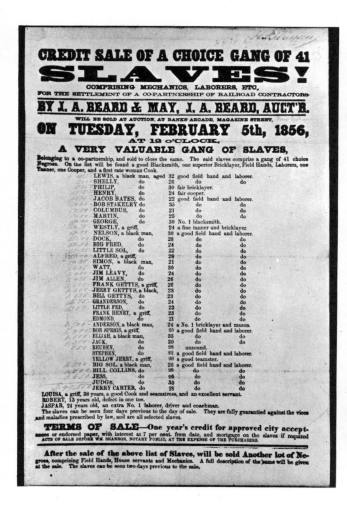

Negro slaves mining gold about 1852 at Spanish Flat near Placerville, California.

Pierre Toussaint, a hairdresser from Santo Domingo (1776-1853).

Madame Pierre Toussaint.

Euphemia Toussaint, their adopted daughter.

Slave Domestics

House servants were generally much better off than field hands. Being nearer the master's kitchen, they often ate better and the white family's cast-off clothing usually became theirs. In some houses of quality, slaves could acquire good manners and grammatical English. The living quarters for favored Negro servants were sometimes far more comfortable than the housing poor whites could afford. In New England, but rarely in the South, where there were laws against it, a slave might be taught to read and write. But, even in the South, slave companions of white children often learned to read from them.

The privileges enjoyed by house slaves created between domestic servants and field hands a gulf of suspicion and envy. The latter, whose lives were barren of delicacies, cast-off finery or creature com-forts, did not trust the slaves in the Big House. On the other hand, between the black domestics and the white families whom they served, close bonds of affection and friendship often developed. The Negro "mammy" of the South, caring for generations of white offspring, is a classic picture of devotion.

There are many examples of affection between bondservants and their masters. Pierre Toussaint and his family, slaves of Jean Bérard in Santo Domingo, were brought by their owner to New York during the turmoil of the Haitian Revolution. Poverty overtook the master there, but at his death the Negro Pierre Toussaint assumed the family burden and, earning a living as a hairdresser, supported his master's widow, Madame Berard, in luxury until she married again. She later freed Toussaint.

An Omission
from the Declaration

Thomas Jefferson, who in 1801 became the third President of the United States, was born in Virginia of a slave-holding family and himself owned slaves. But he was a cultivated man whose political convictions were influenced by his study of the great liberal philosophers, Rousseau, Locke and Montesquieu.

As chairman of the committee which drafted the Declaration of Independence, Thomas Jefferson wrote into his first rough draft a paragraph condemning human bondage in which he denounced George III for his propagation of slavery in the colonies and said of the English sovereign:

"He has waged cruel war against human nature itself, violating its most sacred rights of life and liberty in the persons of a distant people who never offended him, captivating and carrying them into slavery in another hemisphere, or to incur miserable death in their transportation thither. This piratical warfare, the opprobrium of *infidel* powers, is the warfare of the *Christian* king of Great Britain. Determined to keep open a market where MEN should be bought and sold, he has prostituted his negative for suppressing every legislative attempt to prohibit or to restrain this execrable commerce; and that this assemblage of horrors might want no face of distinguished die, he is now exciting those very people to rise in arms among us, and to purchase that liberty of which *He* deprived them, by murdering the people upon whom *He* also obtruded them; thus paying off former crimes committed against the liberties of one people, with crimes which he urges them to commit against the *lives* of another."

But slavery was too profitable a business in the colonies, and this paragraph was not acceptable to the Southern delegation. It was omitted from the final version of the Declaration as adopted by the Continental Congress of the United States on July 4, 1776. So, from the beginnings of the new nation's history, the voteless Negro bondsman influenced the policies and documents of the new republic.

RAFFLE

Mr. Joseph Jennings respectfully informs his friends and the public that, at the request of many acquaintances, he has been induced to purchase from Mr. Osborne, of Missouri, the celebrated

DARK BAY HORSE, "STAR,"

Aged five years, square trotter and warranted sound; with a new light Trotting Buggy and Harness; also, the dark, stout

MULATTO GIRL, "SARAH,"

Aged about twenty years, general house servant, valued at *nine hundred dollars*, and guaranteed, and

Will be Raffled for

At 4 o'clock P. M., February first, at the selection hotel of the subscribers. The above is as represented, and those persons who may wish to engage in the usual practice of raffling, will, I assure them, be perfectly satisfied with their destiny in this affair.

The whole is valued at its just worth, fifteen hundred dollars; fifteen hundred

CHANCES AT ONE DOLLAR EACH.

The Raffle will be conducted by gentlemen selected by the interested subscribers present. Five nights will be allowed to complete the Raffle. BOTH OF THE ABOVE DESCRIBED CAN BE SEEN AT MY STORE, No. 78 Common St., second door from Camp, at from 9 o'clock A. M. to 2 P. M.

Highest throw to take the first choice; the lowest throw the remaining prize, and the fortunate winners will pay twenty dollars each for the refreshments furnished on the occasion.

N. B. No chances recognized unless paid for previous to the commencement.

JOSEPH JENNINGS.

Slavery and the Law

When the first Constitutional Convention met in Philadelphia in 1787, the Northern delegates contended that slaves were property, therefore should not be counted in apportioning representation. A compromise—the first of many which slavery was to bring about—was reached: "Representatives and direct taxes shall be apportioned among the several states . . . according to their respective numbers, which shall be determined by adding to the whole number of free persons . . . three-fifths of all other persons." These "other persons" were slaves.

The slave trade was then extended for twenty years and Article XI, Section 9, of the new Constitution of the United States read: "The migration or importation of such persons as any of the States now existing shall think proper to admit, shall not be prohibited by the Congress prior to the year one thousand eight hundred and eight, but a tax or duty may be imposed on such importation." And Article IV, Section 2, provided for the return of runaway slaves: "No person held to Service or Labour in one State, under the Laws thereof, escaping into another, shall . . . be discharged from such Service or Labour, but shall be delivered up on Claim of the Party to whom such Service or Labour may be due." This extradition of fugitive slaves was further strengthened by the Fugitive Slave Law of 1793.

When the United States bought Louisiana from France in 1803, the institution of slavery was still further entrenched by the establishment of many great sugar cane and cotton plantations there. In 1807, Congress passed a law prohibiting the importation of African slaves, but its enforcement was lax and violations were many, as the soaring price of Negroes and the demand for slave labor led to the spread of slave smuggling. As late as 1859 the yacht *Wanderer* landed more than 300 Negroes on a Georgia dock, but no one was punished. Over a quarter of a million slaves were smuggled into the United States this way.

A slave auction at Richmond, Virginia, in 1856.

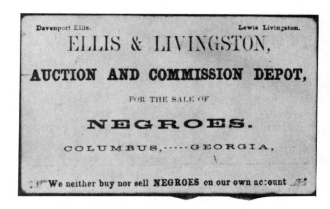

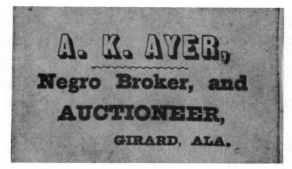

Types of business cards used by slave dealers.

The Entrenchment of Bondage

$1200 TO 1250 DOLLARS! FOR NEGROES!!

THE undersigned wishes to purchase a large lot of NEGROES for the New Orleans market. I will pay $1200 to $1250 for No. 1 young men, and $850 to $1000 for No. 1 young women. In fact I will pay more for likely

NEGROES,

Than any other trader in Kentucky. My office is adjoining the Broadway Hotel, on Broadway, Lexington, Ky., where I or my Agent can always be found.

WM. F. TALBOTT.

LEXINGTON, JULY 2, 1853.

The New Orleans slave market, one of the busiest in the South, often sent traders to other cities for new stock.

NEGROES FOR SALE.

I will sell by Public Auction, on Tuesday of next Court, being the 29th of November, *Eight Valuable Family Servants*, consisting of one Negro Man, a first-rate field hand, one No. 1 Boy, 17 years of age, a trusty house servant, one excellent Cook, one House-Maid, and one Seamstress. The balance are under 12 years of age. They are sold for no fault, but in consequence of my going to reside North. Also a quantity of Household and Kitchen Furniture, Stable Lot, &c. Terms accommodating, and made known on day of sale.

Jacob August.
P. J. TURNBULL, *Auctioneer.*

Warrenton, October 28, 1859.

Printed at the *News* office, Warrenton, North Carolina.

As pioneer settlers streamed westward across the Mississippi, those who had slaves took them along into the new lands. In the West both the natural resources of the frontier and the human resources of slavery were ruthlessly exploited. The new freedom of the frontier did not mean freedom for the Negro. Men were desperately needed to clear the land and cultivate the crops, so the price of slaves went up and trading in slaves in the newly settled regions became a major enterprise. In 1821 Missouri entered the Union as a slave state, as did Texas in 1845. Interstate slave trading firms developed and soon offered thousands of Negroes for sale. Some companies which sold dry goods, furniture and agricultural implements also handled slaves, for blacks were considered as goods, or chattels, not human beings.

Since newly imported Africans were heathens, the colony of Virginia in 1670 passed a law declaring that all persons not believing in Christ, *i.e.*, Africans, might, in good Christian conscience, be held as slaves for the duration of their lives. For more than a century thereafter, ministers of Southern churches continued to defend human bondage on the grounds that Africans were barbarians. Planters claimed that the prosperity of the South depended on slave labor. Southern politicians running for office championed the system. In 1835 Governor McDuffie of South Carolina declared that domestic slavery, instead of being a political evil, "was the cornerstone of our political edifice."

In 1858 the *Southern Literary Messenger* said: "We assert that in all countries and at all times there must be a class of hewers of wood and drawers of water who must always of necessity be the substratum of society. We affirm that it is best for all that this class should be formed of a race upon whom God himself has placed a mark of physical and mental inferiority."

From defending and apologizing for it, the South had turned to asserting that slavery was a positive good and liberty a threat to humankind.

Typical descriptions of slaves *(opposite page)* and handbill *(left)* announcing a sale of Negroes.

BY

HEWLETT & BRIGHT.

SALE OF

VALUABLE

SLAVES,

(On account of departure)

The Owner of the following named and valuable Slaves, being on the eve of departure for Europe, will cause the same to be offered for sale, at the NEW EXCHANGE, corner of St. Louis and Chartres streets, on *Saturday,* May 16, at Twelve o'Clock, *viz.*

1. **SARAH,** a mulatress, aged 45 years, a good cook and accustomed to house work in general, is an excellent and faithful nurse for sick persons, and in every respect a first rate character.

2. **DENNIS,** her son, a mulatto, aged 24 years, a first rate cook and steward for a vessel, having been in that capacity for many years on board one of the Mobile packets; is strictly honest, temperate, and a first rate subject.

3. **CHOLE,** a mulatress, aged 36 years, she is, without execption, one of the most competent servants in the country, a first rate washer and ironer, does up lace, a good cook, and for a bachelor who wishes a house-keeper she would be invaluable; she is also a good ladies' maid, having travelled to the North in that capacity.

4. **FANNY,** her daughter, a mulatress, aged 16 years, speaks French and English, is a superior hair-dresser, (pupil of Guilliac,) a good seamstress and ladies' maid, is smart, intelligent, and a first rate character.

5. **DANDRIDGE,** a mulatoo, aged 26 years, a first rate dining-room servant, a good painter and rough carpenter, and has but few equals for honesty and sobriety.

6. **NANCY,** his wife, aged about 24 years, a confidential house servant, good seamstress, mantuamaker and tailoress, a good cook, washer and ironer, etc.

7. **MARY ANN,** her child, a creole, aged 7 years, speaks French and English, is smart, active and intelligent.

8. **FANNY or FRANCES,** a mulatress, aged 22 years, is a first rate washer and ironer, good cook and house servant, and has an excellent character.

9. **EMMA,** an orphan, aged 10 or 11 years, speaks French and English, has been in the country 7 years, has been accustomed to waiting on table, sewing etc.; is intelligent and active.

10. **FRANK,** a mulatto, aged about 32 years speaks French and English, is a first rate hostler and coachman, understands perfectly well the management of horses, and is, in every respect, a first rate character, with the exception that he will occasionally drink, though not an habitual drunkard.

☞ All the above named Slaves are acclimated and excellent subjects; they were purchased by their present vendor many years ago, and will, therefore, be severally warranted against all vices and maladies prescribed by law, save and except FRANK, who is fully guaranteed in every other respect but the one above mentioned.

TERMS:—One-half Cash, and the other half in notes at Six months, drawn and endorsed to the satisfaction of the Vendor, with special mortgage on the Slaves until final payment. The Acts of Sale to be passed before WILLIAM BOSWELL, *Notary Public,* at the expense of the Purchaser.

New-Orleans, May 13, 1835.

Corn Shucks, Fat Back and Malaria

As plantations grew larger and the business of slavery bigger, the condition of slaves generally worsened. About 88 per cent of the country's slaveholders owned twenty slaves or less. Most plantations were owner-operated and managed and the planters themselves often worked in the fields. Such planters, in the main, were reasonably decent to their slaves, though there was some harshness and cruelty. But cruelty was more often the case where an overseer, employed by an absentee owner or by a planter whose holdings were too extensive to handle alone, managed the plantation. The quarters provided for field hands usually consisted of crudely-built shacks with dirt floors. Slaves slept on beds made of corn shucks; their standard food was corn-meal, fat back and molasses—the diet also of many poor whites.

Because Africans were believed to be immune to malaria, they were considered especially valuable for work in the rice swamps and turpentine camps, where mosquitoes were legion. Profit-sharing overseers too often were interested only in getting as many hours of work and as large a crop out of the slaves as they could. To this end they used the whip and occasionally various forms of torture. Even minor infractions might be punished by nailing a slave to the side of the barn by his ear, or by stringing him up by his wrists and flogging him. Severe discipline was generally thought necessary to keep the slaves in check and prevent rebellion.

A Currier & Ives print, "The Old Plantation Home."

A slave family in front of their cabin.

Westover, the Byrd family mansion in Charles City, Virginia.

The Montgomery House, New Orleans in 1867.

Slave

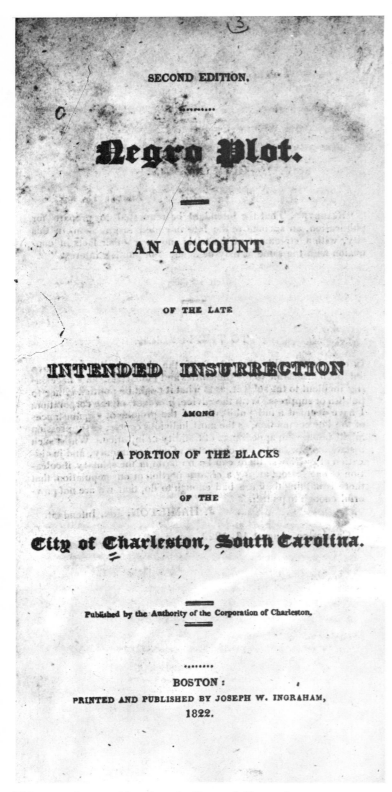

SECOND EDITION.

....

Negro Plot.

——

AN ACCOUNT

OF THE LATE

INTENDED INSURRECTION

AMONG

A PORTION OF THE BLACKS

OF THE

City of Charleston, South Carolina.

═══

Published by the Authority of the Corporation of Charleston.

═══

....

BOSTON:
PRINTED AND PUBLISHED BY JOSEPH W. INGRAHAM,
1822.

Title page of a pamphlet about the Denmark Vesey plot.

The earliest slave rebellions go back to the seventeenth century, when there were several instances of rebellion aboard ship before the slave cargoes reached America. On the *Kentucky*, more than forty slaves were once put to death for staging an uprising in mid-ocean. Such slave revolts occurred so often during the Middle Passage that they were rated an occupational hazard by the traders. Once ashore, the danger did not cease.

In Gloucester County, Virginia, as early as 1663—less than fifty years after the first Africans reached Jamestown—slaves had joined with white indentured servants to plan a rebellion. But the plot was nipped and the heads of the black ringleaders were impaled in the public square. In New York, in 1712, rebel slaves killed nine whites in street-fighting. In the same city, in 1741, a rumor spread that some hundred slaves were to join with white indentured servants to strike back at their masters. Eighteen of these Negroes were hanged, thirteen burned at the stake and seventy sold into the South. Four white persons, including two women, were hanged.

Throughout the colonies slave codes became more stringent. A master's control over his slaves was unquestioned, even to the meting out of torture or death. Restlessness among the slaves was intensified by the Revolutionary War and its proclaimed ideals of liberty and independence. Some slaves, too, took the Christian version of the Bible literally and believed that God meant all men and women to be free. Such a slave was Gabriel Prosser of Virginia, who felt he was divinely "called" to deliver his people. Carefully, Gabriel made plans for months and swore to secrecy his black followers, who were thought to include most of the 40,000 slaves then living in the region. Gathering his followers in Old Brook Swamp, Gabriel planned to attack Richmond on August 30, 1800. But he was betrayed, and on the very evening set for the outbreak, a great storm came up, with torrential floods and gales, and the doomed rebellion was washed away. Richmond by then was under martial law. Scores of slaves were imprisoned or hanged on the spot. Several weeks later their leader was captured. On October 7, after refusing to talk, Gabriel Prosser was publicly hanged.

In 1822, in Charleston, South Carolina, the carpenter Denmark Vesey, who had bought his own

Revolts

freedom the year of Gabriel Prosser's conspiracy, planned one of the most extensive revolts against slavery ever recorded. But he was betrayed by a frightened house slave and, with thirty-six others, was put to death. Vesey used his knowledge of the French and Haitian Revolutions and the congressional debates on the Missouri Compromise to foster among the slaves adherence to the principle of equality and the realization of their common power.

In Virginia, in 1831, the greatest revolt of all occurred, led by Nat Turner, a plowman and a preacher, whose father had escaped to freedom. Deeply religious, like many of the other black rebels, Turner felt that he was called by God to lead "the children of Egypt" out of bondage. With five others, Turner swore to massacre all the whites on the nearest plantations and then gather followers as he advanced. Some sixty whites were killed in Southampton County and the whole South was thrown into a panic. In retaliation, more than one hundred Negroes, innocent and guilty, were struck down before the rebellion was quelled.

Making a tour of the slave states a few years before the Civil War, Frederick Law Olmsted reported that he found "no part of the South where the slave population is felt to be quite safe from a contagion of insurrectionary excitement." The South had become a powder keg. Slavery was the powder.

The discovery of Nat Turner in hiding after the failure of his rebellion.

An extract from the *Liberator* in 1831 concerning the Nat Turner uprising.

Osceola, the Seminole chief who was imprisoned but managed to escape.

Abraham, a Negro interpreter who lived with the Seminoles.

Caocoochee, or "Wild Cat," a friend of fugitive slaves.

Refuge among the Indians

Many slaves seeking freedom simply ran away. Sometimes they joined the Indians. The Indians, who had been conquered or harassed by the early settlers, were not averse to aiding discontented slaves to strike back. In Connecticut, in 1658, Indians and Negroes together burned the homes of a number of slave masters. Runaway Negroes often found shelter among the Indians and frequently intermarried with them. In 1690 in Massachusetts a similar group planned a revolt. In 1786 an "idle set of free Negroes" was said to be inhabiting an Indian reservation in Virginia.

During the War of 1812 one of the charges against the British was that they encouraged slaves to escape to Indian territory, where they fought with the British and the Indians against the United States. When a British commander abandoned a fort in western Florida just south of the Georgia line, about a thousand runaway slaves living among the Creek and Seminole Indians took it over. In 1816 General Andrew Jackson was ordered to "destroy the fort and return the stolen Negroes and property to their rightful owners." United States troops invaded Florida. Thus began the first of the Seminole Wars. In part, this warfare was a slave-catching expedition by the government. The "Negro Fort" was blown up by a cannon which exploded the powder magazine, killing almost 300 men, women and children within the fort, among them some Indians. All the survivors were sent into slavery in Georgia.

After this incident, the Southern leaders continued to accuse the Seminoles of harboring fugitive slaves and urged the government to remove the Indians forci-

Osman, a fugitive slave who was found living in the Dismal Swamp of Virginia in 1856. Many bands of runaways lived in maroon communities in the swamps, mountains and forests of the South.

bly to the West. This led to the Second Seminole War in 1835. In this war, Osceola, the son of an Indian chief's daughter by a white trader, played a prominent part. Osceola had married a girl whose father was an Indian and whose mother was a fugitive slave. A government agent kidnapped Osceola's wife and took her into slavery, and Osceola himself was imprisoned. But he escaped and, with his Indian troops, ambushed and killed the government agent in revenge. More than 500 captured Negro exiles were seized and enslaved in the course of the Second Seminole War, which did not end until 1843. The two wars, which resulted in the re-enslavement of these Negroes, cost the United States from $10,000,000 to $20,000,000.

Political cartoon of 1840 caricaturing Secretary of War Joel Poinsett, who imported bloodhounds from Cuba to track down fugitive slaves during the Seminole Wars.

Slaves, like other property, could be insured. This policy is dated September 3, 1852.

George Washington with a Negro miner on a surveying expedition.

Anthony Benezet, anti-slavery author of some of America's first textbooks.

Reading, Writing—and Thinking

Because of the dangers of uprisings, most of the Southern states had laws requiring free Negroes to carry passes, prohibiting all Negroes from congregating in large numbers and from holding church services, unless supervised, for fear such services might be used for the plotting of rebellions. It was also generally against the law for a slave to be exposed to book-learning, since knowledge was thought to lead to a desire for freedom. Nevertheless, some slaves acquired an education and some few owners encouraged slaves in rudimentary studies.

As a youngster in Baltimore, the slave Frederick Douglass was fortunate in having, for a short time, a mistress who taught him his ABC's. But her husband said, "If you teach him how to read, he'll want to know how to write, and this accomplished, he'll be running away with himself." Mr. Auld's prediction proved correct, for young Douglass soon bought a copy of the *Columbian Orator,* which included a great many speeches about liberty. By copying these speeches over and over Douglass learned to write and, when he was twenty-one, he did run away to freedom. He become a spokesman for the Negro.

When the English actress Fanny Kemble came to America and married a Georgia plantation owner, she wrote of a sixteen-year-old slave boy who had asked her to teach him to read, "I will do it . . . and yet it is simply breaking laws of the government under which I am living." Then she decided, "Unrighteous laws are made to be broken . . . I'll teach every other creature that wants to learn."

George Washington, who himself owned slaves, was sympathetic to their education and in his will he provided for the manumission of his bondsmen. In Philadelphia, Benjamin Franklin, who did not believe in slavery, was president of the Abolitionist Society, which in 1774 founded a school for Negro children. Anthony Benezet, an immigrant from France in 1731 and a Philadelphia Quaker, devoted much time to the teaching of colored youth and became an advocate not only of their education but of their emancipation. In Philadelphia, during the yellow fever epidemic of 1793, Dr. Benjamin Rush enlisted two Negroes, Richard Allen and Absalom

John Woolman, a member of the Society of Friends, who treated slaves as brethren.

Benjamin Franklin founded a Negro school that lasted a century.

Dr. Benjamin Rush was an early advocate of the Negro's right to an education.

Mrs. Auld of Baltimore teaching her slave Frederick Douglass to read.

The British actress Fanny Kemble, who taught a slave to read.

Jones, as his special assistants, instructing them in administering medicines and caring for the sick. And in New Jersey, John Woolman, a Quaker contemporary of Benezet, not only was active in aiding the education of slaves but himself refused to use any of the products of slave labor, as his individual protest against the system.

As early as 1790 in Charleston, free men of color had established a school, but in 1834 South Carolina passed a law prohibiting the teaching of Negro children, slave or free. Daniel Payne, a free Negro who had studied and later taught in the Charleston school for free Negroes founded in 1810, became a famous bishop of the African Methodist Episcopal Church. Another free Negro who gained his early education in the slave state of South Carolina—Francis L. Cardozo—eventually went to the University of Glasgow and studied law in London. Cardozo later returned to South Carolina and held various high offices during the Reconstruction era.

Thus, even in the South, despite the slave system, some Negroes achieved an education.

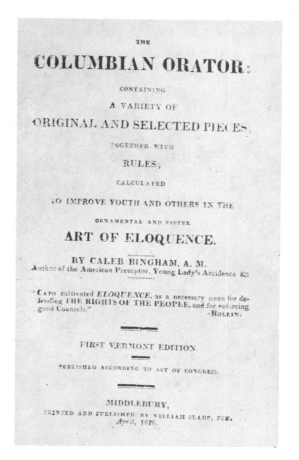

THE

COLUMBIAN ORATOR:

CONTAINING

A VARIETY OF

ORIGINAL AND SELECTED PIECES,

TOGETHER WITH

RULES;

CALCULATED

TO IMPROVE YOUTH AND OTHERS IN THE

ORNAMENTAL AND USEFUL

ART OF ELOQUENCE.

BY CALEB BINGHAM, A. M.

Author of the American Preceptor, Young Lady's Accidence &c

"CATO cultivated ELOQUENCE, as a necessary mean for defending THE RIGHTS OF THE PEOPLE, and for enforcing good Counsels."
—ROLLIN.

FIRST VERMONT EDITION.

PUBLISHED ACCORDING TO ACT OF CONGRESS.

MIDDLEBURY,
PRINTED AND PUBLISHED BY WILLIAM SLADE, JUN.
April, 1816.

Famous Bondsmen

Phillis Wheatley to whom General George Washington wrote a letter of commendation for her verses.

Through a combination of personal talents and fortuitous circumstances, a few slaves were able to become outstanding individuals. Such a slave was Phillis Wheatley, brought from Senegal as a child and sold on the docks at Boston in 1761 to John Wheatley, a tailor. He gave the girl the family name and his wife taught her to read and write. Before she was twenty Phillis achieved some renown as a poet. She was eventually given her freedom and a trip to London, where she read her poems before the nobility. Her fame grew and she became one of the best known poets of New England.

As early as 1746 Lucy Terry of Deerfield, Massachusetts, a slave, had published poetry. Later the writer-preacher Jupiter Hammon circulated his poems as broadsides and in 1787 published *An Address to Negroes in the State of New York,* which went into three editions. He hoped to buy his freedom from the proceeds, but was not successful.

In 1789 there appeared in England an autobiography, *The Interesting Narrative of the Life of Oloudah Equiano, or Gustavus Vassa,* written by a former slave in Virginia who had purchased his freedom and made his home in England. A half-century later at Chapel Hill, North Carolina, a slave poet, George Moses Horton, published his first book, *The Hope of Liberty.* A sightless Georgia slave boy known as Blind Tom displayed such astonishing musical talent as a composer-pianist that he played his way to fame. Tom Molineux, born a slave in Virginia, became America's first champion pugilist. The first American athlete ever to compete abroad, he won even greater fame in England, where he fought forty rounds with Tom Cribb in 1810.

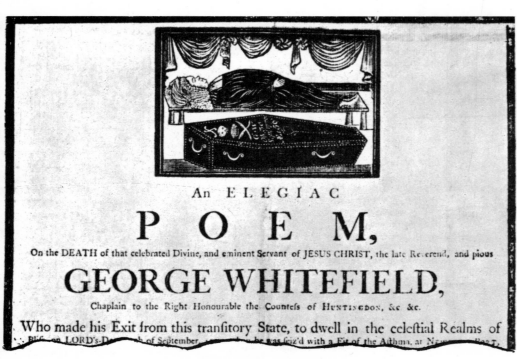

An elegiac poem written by Phillis Wheatley at the age of seventeen.

Onesimus, a slave owned by Cotton Mather, encouraged inoculation for smallpox in America by describing its successful use in Africa.

Tom Molineux in the ring.

The explorers Lewis and Clark on the Columbia River in 1806, with Captain Clark's slave York.

A New York handbill of 1868 announcing a concert by Blind Tom. His former master, Colonel Bethune, became his concert manager.

WALNUT STREET
THEATRE,

Box 50 cents—Pit 25 cents—Gallery 18 3-4 cents.
Doors will be opened at half after 6, and the Curtain
rise at a quarter after 7 o'clock, precisely.

On this occasion

Mr. J. R. SCOTT
AND
MR. HOWARD,
WILL APPEAR.
Mr. RICE
As the Far Famed

Jim Crow

Will also appear, and discuss
10 New Subjects,
In his Fashionable Lyric Style.

Monday Evening,
JUNE 3, 1833.

Will be presented, (1st time these 5 year) Macklin's admirable Comedy of the

Man
OF THE
WORLD.

Sir Pertinax M'Sycophant, ...Mr. Maywood.
Egerton, ...Mr. Wood.
Lord Lumbercourt, ...Mr. Faulkner.
Sidney, ...Mr. Murdoch.
Melville, ...Mr. Walstein.
Plausible, ...Mr. Hadaway.
Eitherside, ...Mr. Darley.
Sam, ...Mr. Eberle.
John, ...Mr. Crutar.
Tomlins, ...Mr. Watson.
Lady M'Sycophant, ...Mrs. Turner.
Lady Rodolpha, ...Mrs. Maywood.
Constantia, ...Mrs. Roper.
Betty Hint, ...Mrs. Thayer.
Nanny, ...Mrs. Walstein.

AFTER WHICH,
Mr. RICE
Will appear and discuss in Lyric Style, the following

10 NEW SUBJECTS.

1—Important News from Washington,
2—Interview with the President,
3—Benefit of Temperence Societies,
4—Reformation of Jim Crow.
5—Trip from Baltimore,
6—Description of the various passengers; and
7—Every one for himself.
8—News of Massa Randolph.
9—De general turn out in de Department, and
10—De Wonder of JIM CROW.

To conclude with the Nautical Drama of

Black Eyed
SUSAN.

WILLIAM, - - - Mr. J. R. SCOTT.
Captain Crosstree, ...Mr. Murdoch.
Gnatbrain, ...Mr. Hadaway.
Doggrass, ...Mr. Walstein.
Raker, ...Mr. Jervis.
Hatchet, ...Mr. Drummond.
Jacob Twig, ...Mr. Whiting.
Quid, ...Mr. Eberle.
Seaweed, ...Mr. Watson.
BLUE PETER, ...Mr. HOWARD.
In which he will sing THREE STANZAS of
Black Eyed Susan.
AND
"TELL HER I LOVE HER."

"Daddy" Dan Rice, who introduced "Jim Crow," was followed by other famous white minstrel-men such as Dan Emmett, who wrote "Dixie," and George Primrose, who popularized "Carry Me Back to Old Virginny," written by James Bland, a Negro.

J. D. B. De Bow, editor of *De Bow's Review*, in 1867. George Fitzhugh, a leading theoretician of the slave system, who often engaged in debates with abolitionists on Northern platforms.

Slave songs, juba dances and the playing of the *bonja*, made by the slaves from a hollow gourd, were a standard part of American entertainment for more than half a century.

The Roots of Jim Crow

On a Cincinnati street in 1830, Dan Rice, a famous white "blackface" minstrel, saw a ragged little Negro boy singing "Jump, Jim Crow." Rice then copied the urchin's lively song-and-dance and for years performed the act to great applause. Gradually, the words "Jim Crow"—from this song—came to be applied to the legal segregation of Negroes from whites in everyday life. The blackface minstrels, by their stage portrayal, helped to establish the stereotype of Negro inferiority and the desirability of segregation.

That Negroes were biologically and mentally inferior to whites was a basic argument employed in every way to bolster the slave system. Senator John C. Calhoun of South Carolina contended that blacks could never absorb education and that bondage was good for the slaves. The Southern press was nearly unanimous in its support of slavery. In New Orleans the propaganda medium for the African slave trade, *De Bow's Review*, featured the writings of George Fitzhugh, author of *The Sociology of the South*. Fitzhugh declared that "slavery, black or white," was necessary and the proper condition of the working man. He called for the ousting of Northern teachers in the South and urged that all textbooks used in the schools be written by Southerners.

The rift between the North and the South over the issue of slavery began to widen rapidly and was expressed in bitterly opposite opinions in both politics and literature. While white minstrels in blackface entertained the nation with burlesques of the Negro, the increasing presence of black men—more of whom were receiving some sort of an education—on American soil began to split the United States into two camps, one for the continuance of slavery and one for its abolition.

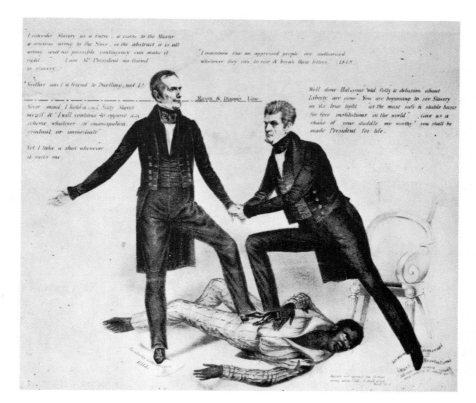

A cartoon of 1839 showing Henry Clay (*left*) and John C. Calhoun (*right*) standing upon a prostrate Negro.

"Firebell in the Night"

A long and stormy debate over the extension of slavery into the territories and new states of the Union was stilled for a time by the passage of the Missouri Compromise in 1820. Missouri was admitted to the Union as a slave state, and Maine as a free state, thus making a sectional balance of twelve states each. The informal line barring slavery from all new states north of the Ohio River—which had been recognized and respected from the founding of the Republic—had now been advanced to the lands west of the Mississippi River. By law, slavery was now to be prohibited "forever" in any new United States territories north of Missouri. To old Thomas Jefferson news of the bitterness and fiery passion of the debate came "like a firebell in the night," tolling the "knell of the Union."

In the North, immigrants were pouring into the industrialized towns and cities, swelling their population and wealth. In the South, cotton's rising value and the search for new lands on which to grow it pushed the frontiers ever westward. Fearing that the Northern states might dominate the new territories, John C. Calhoun tried to cement a political alliance between the cotton-growers of the South and the farmers of the West, both hungry for more land. Their eyes turned toward Texas, a vast empire that might be conquered for slavery.

The North protested against the annexation movement as well as any movement designed to extend slavery. Petitions flooded Congress. In reply, the Southerners pushed through the gag rule, which tabled all anti-slavery petitions. But soon the entire country became a debating society with a single question on everyone's lips. On John Quincy Adams' motion, the gag rule was finally abolished in 1844. But the problem of slavery continued to plague the nation and it reached a new climax in the war with Mexico over the annexation of Texas.

The prospect of adding more territories as a result of this war led to another heated debate in Congress over the slavery issue. The Democrats defended the war as a just one, while the Whigs denounced it as a drive for new slave lands. The House passed the Wilmot Proviso to bar slavery from any of the domains taken in the Mexican War, but the bill was lost in the Senate, where Calhoun attacked it as a threat to Southern rights and power. To Calhoun the writing on the wall was clear: the industrial North was outstripping the agrarian South. He warned that if Southern domination of the Supreme Court, the foreign service, the armed forces and the administrative offices—a power that had been held since the turn of the century—should be broken, it would mean political revolution, anarchy, civil war and widespread disaster.

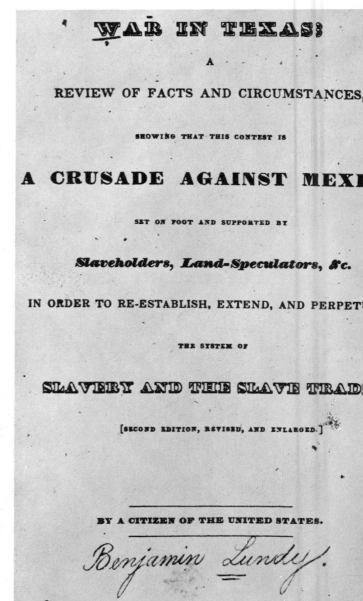

WAR IN TEXAS;

A

REVIEW OF FACTS AND CIRCUMSTANCES,

SHOWING THAT THIS CONTEST IS

A CRUSADE AGAINST MEXI

SET ON FOOT AND SUPPORTED BY

Slaveholders, Land-Speculators, &c.

IN ORDER TO RE-ESTABLISH, EXTEND, AND PERPET

THE SYSTEM OF

SLAVERY AND THE SLAVE TRAD

[SECOND EDITION, REVISED, AND ENLARGED.]

BY A CITIZEN OF THE UNITED STATES.

Benjamin Lundy.

PHILADELPHIA:

ECCLESIASTICAL ROLL OF INFAMY.

No public act of any ecclesiastical body in America was ever so infamous as the passage of the following resolution by the General Conference of the Methodist Episcopal Church, May 28, 1840.—

"Resolved, That it is inexpedient and unjustifiable for any preacher to permit colored persons to give testimony against white persons in any state where they are denied that privilege in trials at law."

This resolution is outrageously unjust, unless the colored Methodists in Ohio and the slave states are unworthy of belief. Let those who recognise 80,000 slaves as members of Christ's body, while they thrust a gag into their mouths, tell us if they fellowship liars, or if they have robbed their Savior's brethren of a right to testify against their plunderers, because state laws had done so before.

NORTHERN PREACHERS WHO VOTED FOR W. A. SMITH'S GAG.

Pittsburg Conference.
Robert Hopkins,
J. C. Sansom,
George S. Holmes.
Erie Conference.
J. C. Ayres,
David Preston.
Michigan Conference.
Adam Poe,
J. McMahan.
Ohio Conference.
William H. Raper,
W. B. Christie,
J. Young,
Leonidas L. Hamline,

S. Hamilton,
J. F. Wright.
Illinois Conference.
Peter Akers,
P. Cartwright,
S. H. Thompson,
Hooper Crews,
John Clark,
John T. Mitchell.
Indiana Conference.
E. R. Ames,
Augustus Eddy.
Philadelphia Conference.
Henry White.

CONGRESSIONAL ROLL OF INFAMY.

...on of W. C. Johns... of Maryland... was

This blacklist of Northern congressmen who had voted in 1840 for the gag rule was published in the *Anti-Slavery Almanac.*

A painting by Alfred Jones, "Mexican News—1848," shows a group of small-town people reading the war news on the steps of the post office.

ANTI-SLAVERY PEACE PLEDGE.

WE, the undersigned,

hereby solemnly pledge ourselves not to countenance or aid the United States Government in any war which may be occasioned by the annexation of Texas, or in any other war, foreign or domestic, designed to strengthen or perpetuate slavery.

Name.	Residence.

A peace pledge circulated by the abolitionists.

...njamin Lundy's pamphlet *(left)* de-...red the "War in Texas" was a crusade ...ainst Mexico on behalf of slave-holders.

Compromise and Crisis

With the decade of the 1850's about to begin, the political pot came to a boil. At the door of the Union stood California, seeking admission as a free state. The western lands were filling rapidly with Southern highlanders, settlers from the middle Atlantic seaboard, New Englanders and immigrants from foreign shores. Which way would the new territories go? What would be done about the outright refusal of many free-staters to return fugitive slaves to their masters? What about the renewed insistence upon the adoption of the Wilmot Proviso in the new lands of the Southwest?

Congress met in December, 1849, with both Democrats and Whigs divided into warring factions over slavery and with the minority Free Soilers holding the balance of power. It took more than sixty ballots to elect a Speaker of the House. Disunion talk erupted from Northern abolitionists and Southern secessionists alike.

The great debate opened with Henry Clay's attempt to find a middle ground that would unite the nation. Let the territories carved from Mexico decide the slavery question for themselves, he proposed. Allow California to enter the Union as a free state. Kill the slave trade, but not slavery in the District of Columbia. And write a new and harsher fugitive slave law that would force the North to return runaways to their owners. The dying Calhoun opposed Clay's compromise and again threatened secession. On March 7, 1850, Daniel Webster—reaching once more for the Presidency—stood up in the Senate, faced the South, supported Clay's compromise and urged the North to carry out the fugitive slave clause "with all its provisions, to the furthest extent."

"Was there nothing better," asked Emerson, "for the foremost American man to tell his countrymen than that slavery was now at that strength that they must beat down their consciences and become kidnappers for it?"

Thaddeus Stevens of Pennsylvania, risking his seat in the House, voted against the bill, predicting the compromise would be "the fruitful mother of future rebellions, disunion and civil war." But "the godlike Daniel's" voice was to carry the measure. By September it was law—to the liking of neither North nor South. An uneasy truce prevailed.

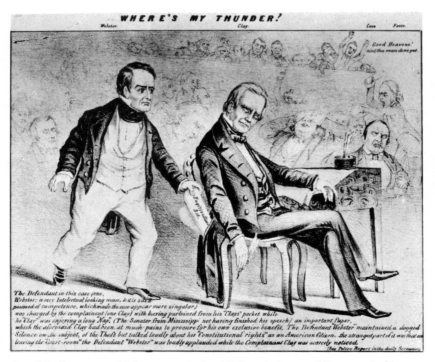

A political cartoon which appeared after Webster's famous "Compromise" speech in which he stole Clay's thunder.

CONQUERING PREJUDICE TO SAVE THE UNION.

PRACTICAL ILLUSTRATION OF THE FUGITIVE SLAVE LAW.

DECLARATION OF SENTIMENTS
—OF THE—
COLORED CITIZENS OF BOSTON,
ON THE FUGITIVE SLAVE BILL!!!

A broadside expressing the reactions of Boston Negroes to the Fugitive Slave Law, including a statement by William Lloyd Garrison, "though himself a non-resistant."

Daniel Webster.

THE BLACK LIST.
Total vote from free States in favor of the Fugitive Slave bill.

DEMOCRATS.—*Maine*—Messrs. Fuller, Gerry, Littlefield—3.

New Hampshire.—Messrs. **HIBBARD** and **PEASLEE**—2.

New York—Mr Walden—1.

New Jersey—Mr Wildrick—1.

Pennsylvania—Messrs Dimmick, Job Mann, McLanahan, Robbins, Ross and James Thompson—6.

Ohio—Messrs. Hayland and Miller—2.

Indiana—Messrs. Alberston, William J. Brown, Dunham, Gorman, McDonald—5.

Illinois—Messrs. Bissel, T. L. Harris, McClernand, Richardson, Young—5.

Michigan—Mr A. W. Buel—1.

Iowa—Mr Leffier—1.

California—Mr Gilbert—1. Total 27.

WHIGS.—Messrs. Elliot, of *Mass.*; McGaughey, of *Ind.*; John L. Taylor, of *Ohio*—Total, 3.

Total Ayes from free states, 30.

The blacklist of free-state Congressmen who voted for the Fugitive Slave Law (from a broadside distributed in 1850).

The Fugitive Slave Law

The new Fugitive Slave Law signed by President Millard Fillmore on September 18, 1850, provided that any federal marshal who did not arrest on demand an alleged runaway might be fined $1,000. Fugitive slaves or suspects could be arrested on request without a warrant and turned over to a claimant on nothing more that the claimant's sworn testimony of ownership, with no need for further proof. A black fugitive or captured free man could not ask for a jury trial nor testify in his own behalf. Any person aiding a runaway slave by giving him shelter, food or any sort of assistance was liable to six months' imprisonment and a $1,000 fine. Officers capturing a fugitive slave were entitled to a fee. This last provision caused unscrupulous officers to become kidnappers of even free Negroes, for it was easy to find greedy claimants who would falsely swear to ownership and gladly pay a bribe for a new slave.

At the passage of this bill, despair and panic swept over the colored population of the North. It was estimated that more than 50,000 fugitives had found shelter above the Mason-Dixon line. Many had married free Negroes. Now no Negro felt safe. As their leader Frederick Douglass said, "Under this law the oaths of any two villains (the capturer and the claimant) are sufficient to confine a free man to slavery for life."

Thousands of Negroes in the North fled overnight to Canada. Some of the more active colored abolitionists went to England. For free Negroes a reign of terror had come. Armed clashes frequently developed between the zealous slave-catchers and Negro and white abolitionists. In deliberate defiance of the law, abolitionists made many attempts to rescue fugitives. Some attempts succeeded, some failed.

Northern writers such as Wendell Phillips, Lowell, Whittier, Emerson and Thoreau thundered denunciations of the Fugitive Slave Law, while Southerners continually complained that it was not being adequately enforced. Threatening secession and a boycott of Northern industries and trade, the South demanded that both federal and state officers enforce the Fugitive Slave Law to the fullest. But it could not exact full cooperation from the citizenry.

ANTI-SLAVE-CATCHERS' MASS CONVENTION!

All the People of this State, who are opposed to being made SLAVES or SLAVE-CATCHERS, and to having the Free Soil of Wisconsin made the hunting-ground for *Human Kidnappers*, and all who are willing to unite in a

☞ STATE LEAGUE, ☜

to defend our State Sovereignty, our State Courts, and our State and National Constitutions, against the flagrant usurpations of U. S. Judges, Commissioners, and Marshals, and their Attorneys; and to maintain inviolate those great Constitutional Safeguards of Freedom—the WRIT OF HABEAS CORPUS, and the RIGHT OF TRIAL BY JURY—as old and sacred as Constitutional Liberty itself; and all who are willing to sustain the cause of those who are prosecuted, and to be prosecuted in Wisconsin, by the agents and executors of the Kidnapping Act of 1850, for the alleged crime of rescuing a human being from the hands of kidnappers, and restoring him to himself and to Freedom, are invited to meet at

Broadside of a call to a convention in Milwaukee, April 7, 1854.

A poster showing fleeing Negroes pursued by armed white slave-catchers.

The Kansas-Nebraska Bill

The original Kansas and Nebraska territories.

An 1860 cartoon caricaturing Stephen Douglas as a "squatter sovereign" prepared to defend slavery in Kansas.

Four years after the great debate which many believed had settled the question of slavery's extension, Stephen A. Douglas of Illinois introduced his Kansas-Nebraska bill to the Senate. The "Little Giant" proposed, in effect, to repeal the Missouri Compromise, and, under the principle of "squatter," or "popular sovereignty," to permit the new territories to come into the Union with or without slavery. Again protests flooded Congress from the North, this time from conservatives, too, who had supported the 1850 Compromise in the hope that it would bring peace and halt the spread of slavery.

In Ripon, Wisconsin, angry men met to resolve that if the Douglas bill went through, they would organize a new party dedicated to oppose the extension of slavery. This coalition of Northerners and Westerners who bolted from the Whig, Free Soil and Democratic parties wrote the name "Republican" on their new political banner.

In May, 1854, the Kansas-Nebraska bill became law. Frederick Douglass called it "an open invitation to a fierce and bitter strife." The race to settle Kansas began. Southerners took their slaves along, and Northerners, their militant opposition to slavery. John Brown went to Kansas—with guns. From his pulpit in Brooklyn, Henry Ward Beecher hurled invectives at all slave-holders, shouting that a gun was a greater moral agency in Kansas than a Bible. The rifles supplied the Free Soilers in Kansas by sympathizers in the East were soon called "Beecher's Bibles."

When Kansas elected its first territorial legislature in March, 1855, armed Missouri slave-owners, fearful that their slaves might escape into Kansas if it remained free soil, poured over the borders to vote. Although less than 2,000 qualified voters were enrolled, the number of votes cast that day exceeded 6,000, most of them on the side of slavery. The new legislature, illegally elected, set up a code of laws providing prison sentences for those who contended slavery was not legal in Kansas. It imposed the death penalty for anyone helping a slave to escape and two years in jail for possessing abolitionist literature. This so angered the anti-slavery party that it called a new convention in Topeka, drafted a new constitution and set up a separate government.

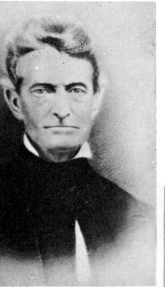

A letter *(below)* written by John Brown *(left)* to George Stearns, a Boston businessman, asking for money to buy firearms.

Albany N.Y. 28th April, 1857.

My Dear Sir

The Worcester Gun Factory cannot supply me with Revolvers in time; but the Mass, Arms, Co; (whose Revolvers I have used, & which are much the same as Colts) offer to let me have what I need being 2 oo for $13 oo, Thirteen Hundred Dollars.

* * * * * *

He did not want the thing to be made public. Now if Rev I Parker, & other good people at Boston, would make up that amount; I might at least be well armed. Please write Watson My best wishes to yourself and Family. very Respectfully Your Friend

John Brown

A broadside calling for delegates to a free-state convention at Big Springs, Kansas.

The Reverend Henry Ward Beecher.

SOUTHERN CHIVALRY — ARGUMENT VERSUS CLUB'S.

An 1856 lithograph showing Representative Preston S. Brooks of South Carolina striking Senator Charles Sumner of Massachusetts for his "crime against Kansas" speech attacking the pro-slavery forces.

"Bleeding Kansas"

The little town of Lawrence, settled largely by Easterners, became the center of free-soil sentiment in Kansas. Armed Missourians attempted to drive the early settlers of Lawrence away, but they refused to leave. However, on May 21, 1856, a posse of several hundred men, mostly from Missouri and led by a United States marshal, entered Lawrence with a number of warrants accusing various citizens of treason against the government. In the course of attempting to serve these warrants, the posse turned into a lawless mob which burned the Free State Hotel, wrecked the newspaper office and ransacked a number of homes. In retaliation, on May 24, John Brown, with his abolitionist sons and followers, attacked a group of slave-holding settlers on Pottawatomie Creek. They shot five of these to death—as a free state lesson of "an eye for

an eye and a tooth for a tooth." Two days before thi incident, Senator Charles Sumner of Massachusetts ha been caned into insensibility after making a speech in th Senate attacking the pro-slavery elements in Kansas. South Carolina Congressman, Preston S. Brooks, injure Sumner so badly that the Senator was out of public lif for three years. Brooks resigned, but was triumphantly r elected to Congress.

Violence, from Kansas to the Capitol, warned how da gerously close to open warfare were the two opposin forces in the United States—those who believed in slav ery and those who did not. Meanwhile, the politically dis franchised Negroes, around whose status this conflic raged, could themselves do little to stem the flood swirlin at the very roots of the Republic.

Voting at Kickapoo, Kansas, where many fraudulent names were found in the ballot boxes, more than a thousand of them allegedly copied alphabetically from a Cincinnati business directory.

The Marais des Cygnes massacre in Kansas, May 19, 1858, in which five free staters were killed and six were wounded.

The people of Lawrence (*left*) were prepared to defend their homes from invasion. A Missouri posse which entered Lawrence with warrants for the arrest of various citizens left the Free State Hotel (*above*) a charred ruin.

The Dred Scott Decision

With "Bleeding Kansas" the chief campaign issue in the 1856 presidential election, the battle over slavery shifted to the ballot boxes. The Democrats nominated James Buchanan; the Republicans chose John C. Frémont, the explorer-hero; and the disintegrating Whigs endorsed the ticket of the Know-Nothings, who had picked Millard Fillmore. Buchanan won, with 1,800,000 votes to Frémont's 1,300,000 and Fillmore's 875,000. The Republicans had gained great strength. On March 6, 1857, two days after Buchanan's inauguration, the Supreme Court handed down a decision that made Dred Scott the best-known Negro in America.

Dred Scott was a Virginia-born slave who had been carried by his master, an Army doctor, from Missouri into the free state of Illinois and then into the free territory of Minnesota. He remained away from Missouri for four years before being returned to that state.

On the grounds that he had become a free man by virtue of residence on free soil, Dred Scott in 1846 sued for his liberty. A St. Louis court upheld his contention but was overruled by the Missouri Supreme Court. Meanwhile Scott was sold to another master but, with help from various sources, he carried his fight for freedom to a still higher court. In 1856 the final disposition of his case came before the highest court of the land in Washington.

Of the nine justices composing the Supreme Court, five, including seventy-year-old Chief Justice Roger B. Taney, were Southerners. At first the judges tried to avoid the crucial issue. But eventually Taney announced that the questions of "peace and harmony" of the country required a settlement by judicial decision.

When Taney read his opinion, only one judge concurred with him; five others read separate and varied concurring opinions and two dissented head-on. The Chief Justice ruled that from the founding of the country Negroes had been "considered as a subordinate and inferior class of beings" who therefore "had no rights which the white man was bound to respect." Taney further declared that Negroes could not rightfully become citizens of the United States, since the words of the Declaration of Independence and the Constitution were never meant to include Negroes.

The first page of the argument of Montgomery Blair, counsel for Dred Scott.

Dred Scott therefore had no right even to bring suit. Furthermore, Congress could not legally deprive slaveholders of their right to take human "articles of merchandise" into any part of the Union, North or South. In effect, the Supreme Court declared the Missouri Compromise and all other anti-slavery laws to be unconstitutional.

Taney's decree made the slave-holders and slave-catchers jubilant. But in the North and the West great mass meetings were held in furious protest against this decision. White voters in ever greater numbers were driven toward the anti-slavery movement. Many friends of freedom lost hope. But Frederick Douglass declared, "My hopes were never brighter than now. . . The Supreme Court is not the only power in this world. . . Judge Taney cannot bail out the ocean, annihilate the firm old earth or pluck the silvery star of liberty from our Northern sky."

A caricature of President James Buchanan at the time of the Dred Scott decision.

Chief Justice Roger B. Taney.

Dred Scott, from a daguerreotype made by Fitzgibbon in St. Louis, 1851.

A PUBLIC MEETING

WILL BE HELD ON

THURSDAY EVENING, 2D INSTANT,

t 7½ o'clock, in ISRAEL CHURCH, to consider the atrocious decision of th Supreme Court in the

DRED SCOTT CASE,

nd other outrages to which the colored people are subject under the Constitu ion of the United States.

C. L. REMOND,
ROBERT PURVIS

nd others will be speakers on the occasion. Mrs. MOTT, Mr. M'KIM an . S. JONES of Ohio, have also accepted invitations to be present.
All persons are invited to attend. Admittance free.

Philadelphia Negroes call for protest meeting against the Dred Scott decision.

Part Two

FREE MEN OF COLOR

1619-1863

FREDERICK DOUGLASS, who was to become an outstanding spokesman for his people, ran away to freedom. But in both the South and the North there were numerous Negroes who acquired their freedom in other ways. Some were born free, some purchased their freedom, others were granted manumission by their masters. Free Negro men marrying slave women sometimes bought the freedom of their wives. In New Orleans in 1767, François Ricou, himself free, agreed to serve his master for seven years without pay in order to purchase his wife's freedom. This he was permitted to do that they might live happily together. But in Charleston a free Negro shoemaker who had purchased his wife from her white master for $700 but later found very hard to please, sold her at a profit of $50.

Some free Negroes of means purchased slaves and permitted them to work their way out of bondage within a specified time. As early as 1651 there were free Negroes in Virginia who owned their own farms, and some even had white indentured servants. Of the 1,000,000 Negroes in the United States in 1800, about ten per cent were free. When the Civil War began, there were a half-million Negroes listed by the census as non-slaves. About half of these free men of color lived in the South and half in the North. Charleston and New Orleans particularly were centers of free

Negro workers in skilled trades, and both cities had a considerable number of well-educated persons.

Life in the cities of the South was more favorable than in the country for the free Negroes. In the Northern cities free Negroes often aroused the animosity of competing white workers and so did not fare so well in the trades. Free Negroes were taxed the same as whites but were denied most of the privileges of citizenship. As the crisis mounted between the "slaveocracy" and the North, free Negroes were increasingly hemmed in with laws and regulations which diminished their liberty almost to the vanishing point.

John Jones was born free in North Carolina in 1817 and died in Chicago in 1879, one of the country's wealthiest Negroes. An apprentice tailor, he taught himself to read and write and waged a relentless struggle against slavery. A friend of John Brown and Frederick Douglass, Jones made his home in Chicago an Underground Railroad station. He led the fight to repeal the Illinois Black Laws (under which Negroes could not vote or testify in court), by making speeches, writing pamphlets, organizing Negroes and whites and lobbying in the state legislature. Jones was twice voted Cook County Commissioner, the first of his race in the North to win so important an elective post, and while in office helped secure the law that abolished local segregated schools.

Mrs. John Jones, who
was also free-born.

John Jones, a free-born
Negro of Chicago

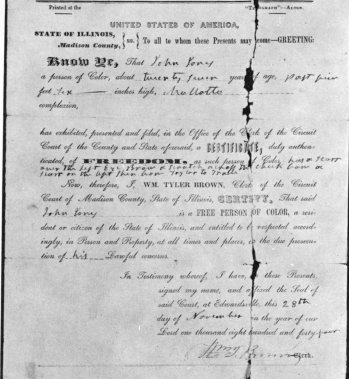

Printed at the   "TELEGRAPH"--ALTON.

UNITED STATES OF AMERICA,

STATE OF ILLINOIS, } ss. { To all to whom these Presents may come—GREETING:

Madison County,

Know Ye, *That John Jones*

a person of Color, about twenty seven years of age, post five

feet six —— inches high. Mulatto

complexion,

has exhibited, presented and filed, in the Office of the Clerk of the Circuit

Court of the County and State aforesaid, a **CERTIFICATE,** *duly authen-*

ticated, of **FREEDOM,** *as such person of Color, has a scar*

over the left Eye Brow a scratch across the cheek bow a

scar on the left hand from Toy low to Wrist

Now, therefore, I, WM. TYLER BROWN, Clerk of the Circuit

Court of Madison County, State of Illinois, **CERTIFY,** *That said*

John Jones —— is a FREE PERSON OF COLOR, a resi-

dent or citizen of the State of Illinois, and entitled to be respected accord-

ingly, in Person and Property, at all times and places, in the due prosecu-

tion of his —— Lawful concerns.

In Testimony whereof, I have, to these Presents,

signed my name, and affixed the Seal of

said Court, at Edwardsville, this 28th

day of November in the year of our

Lord one thousand eight hundred and forty-four

Wm. T. Brown, Clerk.

John Jones' certificate of freedom, filed in Alton, Illinois, in 1844.

The 29th Regiment have already left us, and the 14th Regiment are following them, so that we expect the Town will soon be clear of all the Troops. The Wisdom and true Policy of his Majesty's Council and Col. Dalrymple the Commander appear in this Measure. Two Regiments in the midst of this populous City; and the Inhabitants justly incensed: Those of the neighbouring Towns actually under Arms upon the first Report of the Massacre, and the Signal only wanting to bring in a few Hours to the Gates of this City many Thousands of our brave Brethren in the Country, deeply affected with our Distresses, and to whom we are greatly obliged on this Occasion—No one knows where this would have ended, and what important Consequences even to the whole British Empire might have followed, which our Moderation and Loyalty upon so trying an Occasion, and our Faith in the Commander's Assurances have happily prevented.

Last Thursday, agreeable to a general Request of the Inhabitants, and by the Consent of Parents and Friends, were carried to their Grave in Succession, the Bodies of Samuel Gray, Samuel Maverick, James Caldwell, and Crispus Attucks, the unhappy Victims who fell in the bloody Massacre of the Monday Evening preceding!

On this Occasion most of the Shops in Town were shut, all the Bells were ordered to toll a solemn Peal, as were also those in the neighboring Towns of Charlestown Roxbury, &c. The Procession began to move between the Hours of 4 and 5 in the Afternoon; two of the unfortunate Sufferers, viz. Mess. James Caldwell and Crispus Attucks, who were Strangers, borne from Faneuil-Hall, attended by a numerous Train of Persons of all Ranks; and the other two, viz. Mr. Samuel Gray, from the House of Mr. Benjamin Gray, (his Brother) on the North-side the Exchange, and Mr. Maverick, from the House of his distressed Mother Mrs. Mary Maverick, in Union-Street, each followed by their respective Relations and Friends: The several Hearses forming a Junction in King-Street, the Theatre of that inhuman Tragedy! proceeded from thence thro' the Main-Street, lengthened by an immense Concourse of People, so numerous as to be obliged to follow in Ranks of six, and brought up by a long Train of Carriages belonging to the principal Gentry of the Town. The Bodies were deposited in one Vault in the middle Burying-ground: The aggravated Circumstances of their Death, the Distress and Sorrow visible in every Countenance, together with the peculiar Solemnity with which the whole Funeral was conducted, surpass Description.

An account of the burial of the victims of the Boston Massacre published in the Boston *Gazette and Country Journal.*

First to Fall

In the North American colonies there was much chafing and muttering and talk of freedom from English tyranny. Since Britain's colonies existed chiefly for the purpose of enriching the mother country, they were heavily taxed. Their products could seldom be sold to other countries except by way of England, and they could be shipped only in English ships. The British stamp had to be affixed to most items sold in the colonies, imports were taxed, British officials were sent to enforce these regulations and the colonists were required to support the royal troops.

"Taxation without representation" and the presence of British redcoats in the streets of Boston so angered the citizens that on March 5, 1770, a group of them threatened the British soldiers with sticks and stones. The troops, in turn, fired upon the rebellious colonists, and the first to be shot down was a former slave, Crispus Attucks, who had run away from his master twenty years earlier to become a seaman. Two other men fell dead that night, and two more lay mortally wounded. Several were less seriously injured. The people of Boston were so incensed at this attack that the British troops thought it best to withdraw to Castle Island. The body of the slain Crispus Attucks lay in state in Faneuil Hall until, along with three of the other victims of the Boston Massacre, he was entombed in a common sepulchre as thousands bared their heads at the cemetery.

RAN-away from his Master William Brown of Framingham, on the 30th of Sept. last, a Molatto Fellow, about 27 Years of Age, named Crispas, 6 Feet two Inches high, short curl'd Hair, his Knees nearer together than common; had on a light colour'd Bearskin Coat, plain brown Fustian Jacket, or brown all-Wool one, new Buckskin Breeches, blue Yarn Stockings, and a check'd woollen Shirt. Whoever shall take up said Run-away, and convey him to his abovesaid Master, shall have ten Pounds, old Tenor Reward, and all necessary Charges paid. And all Masters of Vessels and others, are hereby caution'd against concealing or carrying off said Servant on Penalty of the Law. Boston, October 2. 1750.

TO be Let, a convenient Dwelling-House suitable for a small Family, scituate in ——— Street at the South-End. Inquire

An advertisement offering a reward for the return of a runaway slave, Crispus Attucks, who was to be the first to fall in the Boston Massacre twenty years later. From the Boston *Gazette*, October, 1750.

Paul Revere's broadside, which was published in the Boston *Gazette*, March 12, 1770.

Negroes in the American Revolution

From the earliest battles at Lexington and Concord, in the spring of 1775, to the proclamation of victory at Yorktown eight years later, Negroes fought for American independence. Some 5,000, both slave and free, served under Washington's command. When the Continental armies were formed, Negroes were not welcomed and soon were officially barred. But when it was learned that the British had declared free all slaves who joined their side, the colonies, in order to offset the possible wholesale desertion of slaves to the enemy, adopted various policies regarding the use of Negroes. Some masters sent their slaves to war instead of going themselves.

In 1776, New York passed a law allowing white men who had been drafted to send free Negroes to enlist. By 1778, Massachusetts and Rhode Island allowed slaves to enroll in the services, and the Bucks of America, an all-Negro company from Massachusetts, had a Negro commander. Except for the four all-Negro units from these two states and Connecticut, most Negroes were integrated into the fighting groups with whites, in both the North and the South. The Marquis de Lafayette, who aided the colonists, praised the valor of Negro soldiers and credited a Negro spy, James Armistead, with having helped to save his forces from defeat by Cornwallis. On the British side, the Hessian officer Schloezer declared Negro soldiers to be "able-bodied, strong and brave fellows."

In the Continental Navy many black sailors served on Revolutionary gunboats. A Negro, Captain Mark Starlin of the Virginia Navy, was commander of the *Patriot*. At war's end, despite his battle record, Starlin was re-enslaved by his old master.

Only Georgia and South Carolina resisted to the end of the war the enlistment of Negro soldiers. But they paid dearly for, between 1775 and 1783, some 25,000 Negro slaves in South Carolina escaped to the British lines, and an equally large number ran away from Georgia soil to join the enemy.

One of the first to write about the black role in the American Revolution was the fugitive slave J. W. C. Pennington, whose *Textbook of the Origin and History of the Colored People* appeared in 1841. William C. Nell's book followed in 1852.

The Stamp Act of 1765—a British revenue measure which taxed the colonists for newspapers, licenses, legal documents, even dice and cards—resulted in the public burning of stamps in Boston and universal refusal to use them.

Resenting the British tax on tea, a party of citizens disguised as Mohawk Indians, in 1773 threw overboard into Boston harbor 342 chests of tea imported by the East India Company of London.

When General George Washington crossed the Delaware on Christmas Day, 1776, with him were two Negroes, Oliver Cromwell and Prince Whipple.

The Marquis de Lafayette, French soldier and statesman, joined Washington's staff and later became a founder of the Society of Friends of Negroes.

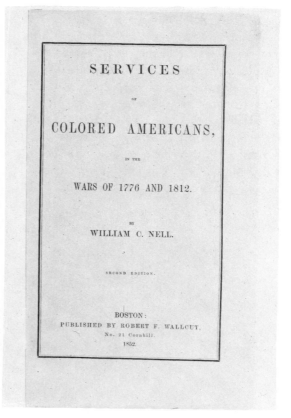

SERVICES

OF

COLORED AMERICANS,

IN THE

WARS OF 1776 AND 1812.

BY

WILLIAM C. NELL.

SECOND EDITION.

BOSTON:
PUBLISHED BY ROBERT F. WALLCUT,
No. 21 Cornhill.
1852.

Title page of the first edition of a history of the black fighters in the American Revolution and the War of 1812. Nell was a pioneer black historian.

Black Fighters for Freedom

Even Georgia and South Carolina, while refusing to recruit Negroes as soldiers, used slaves in the Continental forces as builders of fortifications, tenders of horses and as body servants to the officers. South Carolina Negroes accompanied "the old swamp fox" Francis Marion on his campaigns. On the other hand, in Georgia, at the siege of Augusta, about a third of the men manning Fort Cornwallis for the British were runaway slaves who were not acceptable as troops on the American side. For several years after the war a group of escaped Negroes, who called themselves "the King of England's soldiers," conducted raids on white settlements along the shores of the Savannah River. Some captured slaves taken from the colonists were freed by the British if they would fight. Others were shipped off to the British West Indies.

As indicated, the announced policy of the British to liberate all slaves who freely joined their services was one of the factors that caused a change in the colonists' early policy of refusing Negro enlistments. Washington revoked an order prohibiting Negroes from serving in the ranks. Alexander Hamilton and James Madison not only urged enlistment of the slaves but argued in favor of their freedom in return for service under arms. Maryland inducted 750 slaves on a promise of liberation after the war, with payment to their masters. New York passed a bill giving freedom to all slaves who served until honorably discharged. Virginia in 1783 granted freedom to all slaves who had fought in the Continental Army. At Valley Forge, George Washington enlisted the aid of a black battalion from Rhode Island, all of whose men were promised their freedom at the end of hostilities.

At the battle of Bunker Hill in 1775, Peter Salem became an outstanding hero when he shot a British Major Pitcairn. And another Negro, Salem Poor, won official commendation as a "brave and gallant soldier." At the battle of Brandywine in 1777, Black Sampson, "a giant Negro armed with a scythe," performed "great deeds of valor." That same year at Newport, Tack Sisson, a black soldier, aided in the capture of a General Prescott. In 1778, at the battle of Rhode Island, a Negro regiment thrice drove back Hessian troops who charged against them. In 1779 a black spy called Pompey supplied the information leading to the victory of Stony Point. That year, too, during the siege of Savannah, several hundred Haitian Negroes fought with the French troops against the British. In 1781 an entire unit of Negro soldiers was wiped out in defense of Colonel Greene at Points Bridge, New York.

But gallantry under fire notwithstanding, many masters sought to retain their slaves after the war. But many a British ship had left America with fleeing Negroes aboard. George Washington thought that some of his own slaves, still missing at the end of the war, might have sought refuge abroad. At the close of the Revolution freedom had not yet brought freedom for black Americans.

British troops sending captured slaves to the West Indies.

Peter Salem, a Negro *(left,* with rifle) at the battle of Bunker Hill.

Marion's brigade crossing the Pedee River, South Carolina, 1778.

Bethel African Methodist Episcopal Church was founded in Philadelphia in 1794.

"Upon This Rock"

Lemuel Haynes, who fought in the Continental Army at Ticonderoga, later became one of the first Negroes in the United States to serve as a pastor for a white congregation, heading various churches in Vermont for more than twenty years. In the early days of slavery, some Negroes, particularly in New England, were permitted to belong to otherwise white churches, but few preached in them. If Negroes attended church services with whites, they were duly segregated.

It might be said that Negroes in the colonies became Christians almost in spite of Christianity as it was practiced by their owners. Other than the Quakers, all sects sanctioned slavery, and "Servants, obey your masters" was a familiar text in many pulpits. In some communities where serious attempts were made to Christianize slaves, balconies were set aside for them in white churches. But in many communities, slaves were forbidden to assemble at all for worship.

African religious rituals were forbidden and drums were banned, since in Africa drums had been employed not only for religious ceremonies but also to send messages. Colonial planters feared the drums might be used on American plantations to signal a revolt. Slave rebellions that might flare up beyond control were a constant threat. The planters feared, too, that the Christian Bible might be interpreted to slaves as proving the brotherhood and therefore the equality of all

Peter Williams, once the sexton of John Street Methodist Church in New York, is shown standing in the doorway.

men, not excluding Negroes. Besides, the Bible was a book, and if slaves learned to read the Bible, they might come to read books with really dangerous thoughts in them. Religion had hard going in the Southern states and, after the great slave revolts of the early nineteenth century, Negroes almost everywhere in the South were prohibited from preaching or gathering for any purpose whatsoever.

Among the free Negroes of the North, conditions were somewhat different. They began to build their own places of worship. A favorite text among them was: "Upon this rock I will build my church and the gates of hell shall not prevail against it." One of their favorite songs became "Go down, Moses, 'way down in Egypt land, and tell old Pharaoh to let my people go."

Pulled from his knees one Sunday while at prayer by a white usher in the St. George Methodist Episcopal Church in Philadelphia, Richard Allen made a firm resolution. A few years later he founded the African Methodist Episcopal denomination. Allen established in Philadelphia its first meeting house—Bethel —dedicated in 1794, and became its first bishop. In New York, Peter Williams, sexton of the John Street Methodist Church, finding his own people unwelcome there, led in the founding of the A. M. E. Zion Church in 1796. And, from his earnings as a tobacco merchant, he financed the building of its first temple.

The Reverend Richard Allen, like thousands of slaves, bought his own freedom

Separate Churches

During the American Revolution, and prior to the great slave rebellions which later caused Southern whites to prohibit the formation of Negro churches, several large Baptist colored congregations came into being in the South. In Virginia, churches were organized for Negro Baptists in Petersburg in 1776, in Richmond in 1780 and in Williamsburg in 1786. In Savannah, Georgia, George Liele founded a Baptist congregation for Negroes in 1779. Under the pastorship there of Andrew Bryan, a slave, the first Baptist Church for colored worshippers was built in 1796. Though white men sought to abolish this church by whipping its members and jailing Bryan it continued to function, and in 1799 a second colored Baptist church was erected in Savannah.

Negroes seldom formed separate churches until they had been forced to withdraw from, or were denied access to, existing churches. But, in setting up their own houses of worship, they developed initiative and encouraged capacities for leadership among their own people. Unable to take part in politics or to attend schools and possessing no social centers, the Negroes made their churches focal points for community activities, and from the churches emerged many distinguished leaders. One such leader was the Reverend Absalom Jones who, with Richard Allen, founded the Free African Society in Philadelphia. A civic and religious organization, it was of great help to the city during the devastating yellow fever epidemic of 1793.

Early in the nineteenth century an increasing number of separate Baptist churches began to spring up. In 1805 a free Negro, Joseph Willis, founded such a church at Mound Bayou, Mississippi. The Reverend Thomas Paul in 1809 established in Boston the first African Baptist Church and later aided in the organization of the Abyssinian Baptist Church in New York, which was to become the largest church of the Baptist denomination in the world. Meanwhile, the separate Methodist sects continued to spread. In 1817, the African Methodist Church, under the leadership of the Reverend Morris Brown, listed more than a thousand members in

The Reverend Andrew Bryan preached in Georgia.

Charleston. But, after the Denmark Vesey rebellion of 1822, this church was forced to suspend services and Morris Brown fled to the North, where he later became a bishop.

When white Methodists refused to ordain Negro elders, the Negro Zionites, under the leadership of Charles Anderson, George Collins, Christopher Rush and James Varick, themselves elected and ordained a number of colored elders, and in 1822 James Varick became their first bishop. Christopher Rush later became a bishop of the A. M. E. Zion Church. Separatism first appeared in the Presbyterian sect in 1807, when John Gloucester organized the First African Presbyterian Church in Philadelphia. In 1818 St. Philip's Episcopal Church was opened for Negroes in New York City, with Peter Williams, Jr. as its first rector. And in 1829 the colored Dixwell Avenue Congregational Church was established in New Haven.

Traveling Negro evangelists of various faiths preached to large groups of both white and Negroes, South as well as North. One known as Uncle Jack preached to both masters and slaves from plantation to plantation in Virginia. In the early 1800's Black Harry, sometimes singly and at other times accompanying the white Bishop Asbury, attracted large audiences. And Harry Evans so stirred up the people of both races in Fayetteville, North Carolina, that the city officials tried to stop him from preaching. At Upper Sandusky, Ohio, John Stewart, a free Negro, became the first Methodist Episcopal missionary working among the Wyandot Indians.

James Varick, the first bishop of the ...onist Church.

A meeting in the African Church, Cincinnati, Ohio, 1853.

The Reverend Thomas Paul led the congregation of the first Negro Baptist Church in Boston.

The Reverend Absalom Jones, a Philadelphia church leader.

The first Negro Baptist Church, Savannah, Georgia.

General Andrew Jackson called Negro
troops to his aid in the War of 1812.

The War of 1812

When Washington City was captured by the British in the War of 1812, among the leading citizens of Philadelphia requested to help defend it from a similar fate were Bishop Richard Allen and the Reverend Absalom Jones. These Negro church leaders recruited more than 2,000 colored men, who worked continuously for forty-eight hours building fortifications at Gray's Ferry. Later a battalion of Philadelphia Negroes was formed for military service. A number of Negroes served in the Navy on the Great Lakes and, after the Battle of Lake Erie, Captain Oliver H. Perry praised them highly. Concerning "a black man by the name of Johnson," (John Johnson) who was killed in a naval battle, Nathaniel Shaler, the commander of the *Governor Tompkins* said, "When America has such tars, she has little to fear from the tyrants of the ocean."

New York State passed a bill providing for the formation of two regiments of color for the Army. General Andrew Jackson, in preparing for the battle of New Orleans, called all free Negroes to the ranks, stating, "Through a mistaken policy, you have heretofore been deprived of participation in the glorious struggle for national rights in which

our country is engaged. This no longer shall exist." On January 3, 1815, two battalions of men of color took such a valiant part in the battle of New Orleans that Andrew Jackson declared, "I expected much from you . . . but you surpass my hopes. . . Soldiers, the President of the United States shall be informed of your conduct on the present occasion; and the voice of the Representatives of the American nation shall applaud your valor, as your General now praises your ardor."

Many Negro slaves took part in the War of 1812, hoping to become free afterward. It did bring freedom to some, but others were returned to their masters at the end of hostilities. Numbers of slaves were encouraged by the British to escape to their ranks on the promise of freedom. Some earned their liberty this way. But others were sold into new bondage in the West Indies. At the end of the war the United States demanded an indemnity due them by the Treaty of Ghent, for all confiscated property, including slaves. Eventually the British paid more than a million dollars.

The gallantry shown by the Negro soldiers was forgotten, however, not long after the smoke of the battle cleared.

Negro riflemen helped the Americans to win the battle of New Orleans.

A Negro sailor at the battle of Lake Champlain. Negroes formed 10 to 20 per cent of naval crews.

John Randolph's will set his slaves free upon his death.

Back to Africa?

Shortly after the close of the War of 1812 a Negro sea captain, Paul Cuffee of Massachusetts, took thirty-eight Negroes aboard one of his own vessels and set sail for Sierra Leone in Africa, paying all of their expenses out of his own pocket. His purpose was to settle the Negroes so that they might instruct the Africans in agriculture and mechanics and themselves find a better life. It was not the first time someone had proposed taking Negroes back to Africa. Fifty years earlier, men like Thomas Jefferson had thought it feasible to combine gradual emancipation with deportation.

To many Southerners the presence of free Negroes was a threat to the institution of slavery. "A free African population," said a South Carolina judge, "is a curse to any country . . . and corrupters of the slaves." In the North, with its heavy immigration of Irish and German workers, the competition of black labor also made free Negroes unwelcome. Colonization, dramatized by Cuffee's voyage, was a way to diminish the number of free Negroes.

Captain Paul Cuffee and his brig, the *Traveller*.

Joseph Roberts, first President of Liberia.

President Andrew Jackson of Tennessee, who owned about 100 slaves, favored colonization.

Within a few years of Cuffee's experiment the American Colonization Society was formed, under the leadership of such prominent slave-holders as John C. Calhoun, Henry Clay, John Randolph and Bushrod Washington. They persuaded Congress to purchase territory in Africa, which they named Liberia after the word "Liberty," and its capital Monrovia after President Monroe. But at the very outset the Society was attacked by free Negroes and white abolitionists alike. In 1817, an audience of 3,000 Philadelphians heard two Negro leaders, Richard Allen and James Forten, brand the Society as an "outrage" formed for the benefit of slave-holding interests. The first group of black colonists set sail for Liberia in 1820. Ten years later some 1,400 Negroes had been settled in the colony. But it was a slow trickle. In New York, Martin R. Delany called the Society "anti-Christian" and "one of the Negro's worst enemies." Hartford Negroes asked, "Why should we leave this land so dearly bought by the blood, groans and tears of our fathers? This is our home; here let us live and here let us die."

Under heavy assault, colonization died. Hardly 15,000 Negroes left American shores.

Work and Freedom

Like Crispus Attucks of Boston and Paul Cuffee, many free Negroes were seamen on merchant ships, whaling boats and smaller craft. By 1859 more than half of all American seamen were Negroes. Few free Negroes were farmers. Most of them lived in urban centers, so those in Southern towns who had a knowledge of skilled trades were usually able to work at them. But in the North they often encountered opposition from competing white workers, including German and Irish immigrants, who at times resorted to violence against them.

The greater number of free Negroes, however, had no special skills. To earn a living they worked at common tasks from street-cleaning to ditch-digging. Most of the women were domestic servants, some were seamstresses, a few became teachers. Some men went into business as street vendors, barbers, sailmakers, carpenters, brickmasons, tailors and small shopkeepers. In Baltimore, in 1860, there were several colored grocers and druggists. In Atlanta there was a Negro dentist, Roderick Badger. In Creole New Orleans, where color lines were less harsh, there were even architects and lithographers of color. A young slave doctor, James Derham, worked out his freedom as an assistant to a white Dr. Dove, then, as Dr. Derham, set up his own office. Free men of color in New Orleans, by the outbreak of the Civil War, owned more than $15,000,000 worth of property.

A few free Negroes achieved considerable individual wealth. Paul Cuffee possessed several sailing ships. In Louisiana Cyprian Ricard owned almost a hundred slaves, who worked his large acreage. In North Carolina a successful Negro cabinetmaker, Thomas Day, employed white helpers. Solomon Humphries, a colored grocer in Macon, Georgia, left at his death an estate valued at $20,000, including a number of slaves. And in New Orleans Thomy Lafon was said to be worth a half-million dollars at his death.

But these men were unusual, for most free Negroes existed on meager earnings. Many had escaped to freedom with no possessions, no skills and no education. Fortunately, as more and more

A chimney sweep.

A servant.

A fruit vendor.

Negro oarsmen worked alongside white men in the whaling industry.

white men headed West during the nineteenth century, Northern urban communities began to experience a labor shortage. So Negroes could usually find some sort of work to do. Certainly only a very, very few free Negroes ever voluntarily went back into slavery, no matter how hard the bed of freedom might become. But because their families were still enslaved, or from lack of security, some few did.

A watercart man.

A porter in Wall Street.

Hardships Endured

The fear of re-enslavement shadowed free Negroes everywhere. Generally not allowed to testify in their own behalf, or to bear witness against white men in court, a Negro once taken in tow by the slave-catchers had small chance to escape. With practically no political power, men of color exercised no control over laws or lawmakers. In the South, Negroes were not permitted to possess firearms, watch-dogs, poisons or alcoholic beverages. For even the most petty crimes. courts dealt them harsh sentences. In North Carolina a free Negro boy was hanged for allegedly taking five dollars' worth of candy from the home of a white "lady of great respectability." Legally, the lash might be used on free Negroes as well as slaves in the South. And some courts even took upon themselves the sentencing of free Negroes into slavery, rather than jail, for misdemeanors. Free men of color in most communities were required to carry passes and their freedom of movement was severely restricted. In some Southern states it was against the law for a free Negro who left the state to return, no matter how many relatives he left behind. In some states they were not allowed entrance.

Lacking most of the rights of citizenship, free Negroes in most localities were nevertheless taxed equally with others. In Baltimore, Negroes paid school taxes, although colored children were not allowed to attend the city schools. Outside of some areas in New England, free Negroes could not vote because of local property qualifications or legal barriers. Ohio excluded colored men from the franchise in 1803, as did later Connecticut, Rhode Island, Illinois, Indiana, Iowa and Pennsylvania. Three times between 1827 and 1841, the free Negroes of Cincinnati were run out of town by mobs. In 1839 whites burned the Negro section of Pittsburgh. During the 1830's there were anti-Negro riots in a number of cities in New York State. And in 1834 a three-day reign of terror gripped Philadelphia. Negro homes were burned, black men were seized and beaten and the African Presbyterian Church building demolished.

Uncle Sandy, an ex-slave who mutilated himself to avoid re-enslavement.

A railway conductor expelling a Negro from a coach.

But none of these things kept Negroes from their striving to be free. Not restrictions, proscriptions, the lack of the ballot, lack of legal protection, the threat of mob lawlessness were as disturbing to free Negroes as the constant danger of being taken away into slavery. One ex-slave known as Uncle Sandy had purchased his own freedom for $3,200. When the slave-catchers tried to take him, he plunged a knife into his hip, cut the muscles of his ankle, then chopped off the fingers of one hand with a hatchet to render himself useless for work. With knife in hand, he dared the slavers to touch him.

With all its hardships, freedom was ever preferable to slavery.

THE Convention of Deputies from the Abolition Societies in the United States, assembled at Philadelphia, have undertaken to address you upon subjects highly interesting to your prosperity.

THEY wish to see you act worthily of the rank, you have acquired as freemen, and thereby to do credit to yourselves, and to justify the friends and advocates of your color in the eyes of the world.

As the result of our united reflections, we have concluded to call your attention to the following articles of advice. We trust, they are dictated by the purest regard for your welfare; for we view you as Friends and Brethren.

In the first place, WE earnestly recommend to you, a regular attention to the important duty of public worship; by which means you will evince gratitude to your CREATOR, and, at the same time, promote knowledge, union, friendship, and proper conduct amongst yourselves.

Secondly, WE advise such of you, as have not been taught reading, writing, and the first principles of arithmetic, to acquire them as early as possible. Carefully attend to the instruction of your children in the same simple and useful branches of education. Cause them, likewise, early and frequently to read the holy Scriptures; these contain, amongst other great discoveries, the precious record of the original equality of mankind, and of the obligations of universal justice and benevolence, which are derived from the relation of the human race to each other in a COMMON FATHER.

Thirdly, TEACH your children useful trades, or to labor with their hands in cultivating the earth. These employments are favorable to health and virtue. In the choice of masters, who are to instruct them in the above branches of business, prefer those who will work with them; by this means they will acquire habits of industry, and be better preserved from vice, than if they worked alone, or under the eye of persons less interested in their welfare. In forming contracts, for yourselves or children, with masters, it may be useful to consult such persons as are capable of giving you the best advice, and who are known to be your friends, in order to prevent advantages being taken of your ignorance of the laws and customs of our country.

Fourthly, BE diligent in your respective callings, and faithful in all the relations you bear in society, whether as husbands, wives, fathers, children or hired servants. Be just in all your dealings. Be simple in your dress and furniture, and frugal in your family expenses. Thus you will act like Christians as well as freemen, and, by these means, you will provide for the distresses and wants of sickness and old age.

Fifthly, REFRAIN from the use of spirituous liquors; the experience of many thousands of the citizens of the United States has proved, that these liquors are not necessary to lessen the fatigue of labor, nor to obviate the effects of heat or cold; nor can they, in any degree, add to the innocent pleasures of society.

Sixthly, AVOID frolicking, and amusements which lead to expense and idleness; they beget habits of dissipation and vice, and thus expose you to deserved reproach amongst your white neighbours.

Seventhly, WE wish to impress upon your minds the moral and religious necessity of having your marriages legally performed; also to have exact registers preserved of all the births and deaths which occur in your respective families.

Eighthly, ENDEAVOUR to lay up as much as possible of your earnings for the benefit of your children, in case you should die before they are able to maintain themselves—your money will be safest and most beneficial when laid out in lots, houses or small farms.

Ninthly, WE recommend to you, at all times and upon all occasions, to behave yourselves to all persons in a civil and respectful manner, by which you may prevent contention and remove every just occasion of complaint. We beseech you to reflect, that it is by your good conduct alone that you can refute the objections which have been made against you as rational and moral creatures, and remove many of the difficulties, which have occurred in the general emancipation of such of your brethren as are yet in bondage.

WITH hearts anxious for your welfare, we commend you to the guidance and protection of that BEING who is able to keep you from all evil, and who is the common Father and Friend of the whole family of mankind.

By order, and in behalf, of the CONVENTION,

Theodore Foster, President.

Philadelphia, January 6th. 1796.
Thomas P. Cope, Secretary.

[PHILADELPHIA: PRINTED BY ZACHARIAH POULSON, JUNIOR, NUMBER EIGHTY, CHESNUT-STREET.]

A portion of a broadside of 1797 exhorting Negroes to "refrain from the use of spirituous liquors . . . pay attention to the important duty of public worship, avoid frolicking . . . lay up as much as possible of your earnings . . . behave yourselves to all persons in a civil and respectful manner . . . by which you may prevent contention . . . and remove many of the difficulties which have occurred in the general emancipation of such of your brethren as are yet in bondage."

[1839]   *Anti-Slavery Almanac.*   19

A NORTHERN FREEMAN ENSLAVED BY NORTHERN HANDS.

Education

To acquire an education was the burning desire of most free Negroes, especially those who had formerly been slaves. Only a few Northern communities, and no Southern ones had free public schools open to Negroes. Ohio, from 1829 to 1849, excluded Negroes from the public schools and most of the other western states made little or no provision for them. In 1824 the City of New York took over the support of its seven African Free Schools. The first of these schools had been founded by the Manumission Society in 1787, with a white teacher, Cornelia Davis. Thus colored children had free education available to them in New York years before there were similar public schools for white children. And the African Free School became the precursor of the New York free public school system. Later, Manhattan's African Schools had Negro men and women teachers, and many distinguished persons were graduated from them, including Patrick Reason, Henry Highland Garnet and the actor Ira Aldridge.

In 1849 Sarah C. Roberts sued the city of Boston for its discrimination in refusing to admit a colored child to its school. Her lawyer was Charles Sumner, who was to become a noted abolitionist Senator, and Sumner's assistant was a young Negro attorney, Robert Morris. Their case was lost, but in 1855 the Massachusetts legislature declared that "no person shall be excluded from a Public School on account of race, color or religious opinions." In the South, of course, the few educational facilities which existed for free Negroes were entirely separate and often the teaching of Negroes had to be clandestine. But for almost thirty years prior to 1831 a Negro, John Chavis, conducted an excellent school in Raleigh, North Carolina, for white students by day and for Negroes by night. He had to dismiss his Negro students after 1831.

In the realm of higher education, the first colored student to graduate from an American college was John Russwurm, who received a degree from Bowdoin College in Maine in 1826. Oberlin in 1834 put to its white students a questionnaire "as to the practicability of admitting persons of color," and was one of the first colleges in the West to enroll not only Negroes, but women. It had been established by abolitionists who had withdrawn from Lane Theological Seminary in Cincinnati after free discussions of the evils of slavery had been curtailed there. In Kentucky an anti-slavery editor and an abolitionist minister in 1855 established Berea College, which freely admitted Negroes as well as whites. Its charter began with the phrase: "God hath made of one blood all nations that dwell upon the face of the earth." But, because many institutions of higher learning still had no place for free Negroes, colleges such as Wilberforce in Ohio (1856) and Ashmun Institute (later renamed Lincoln University) in Pennsylvania (1854) came into being especially for the education of Negro youth. Wilberforce was supported by the Methodist Episcopal Church and Lincoln by the Presbyterians.

The original building of the Wilberforce University.

Negro children being denied entrance to a school.

Equality before the Law.

This argument, though addressed to the Supreme Court of Massachusetts, is mainly national and universal in topics, so that it is applicable wherever, especially in our country, any discrimination in educational opportunities is founded on race or color. It is a vindication of Equal Rights in Common Schools. The term "Equality before the Law" was here for the first time introduced into our discussions. It is not found in the common law, nor until recently in the English language. It is a translation from the French, whence Mr. SUMNER took it.

Or, stating the question with more detail and with more particular application to the facts of the present case, are the Committee having superintendence of the Common Schools of Boston intrusted with *power*, under the Constitution and Laws of Massachusetts, to exclude colored children from the schools and compel them to find education at separate schools set apart for colored children only,

Charles Sumner, whose legal brief for desegregated schools in 1849 was a forerunner of the 1954 Supreme Court desegregation decision.

Robert Morris led the fight against Jim Crow schools in Boston.

An engraving made from a drawing of the New York African Free School by Patrick Reason while a pupil there.

ARGUMENT

OF

CHARLES SUMNER, ESQ.

AGAINST THE

CONSTITUTIONALITY OF SEPARATE COLORED SCHOOLS,

IN THE CASE OF

SARAH C. ROBERTS *vs.* THE CITY OF BOSTON.

Before the Supreme Court of Mass., Dec 4, 1849.

BOSTON:
PUBLISHED BY B. F. ROBERTS,
1849.

PRINTED AT NO. 3 CORNHILL.

Ira Aldridge as a young actor.

A Famous Actor

Ira Aldridge, the first internationally famous American Negro actor, was born of non-slave parentage in 1807, the state of his birth disputed as either Maryland or New York. While still a pupil in the African Free School in Manhattan, he acted as a super in Shakespearean plays presented by a group of Negro actors at the African Grove on Bleecker Street, not very far from the Negro-owned Fraunces Tavern, where George Washington had sometimes dined. When white hoodlums stoned the African Grove and several times broke up the performances, the theater was forced to close its doors. Young Aldridge then took a job as a backstage worker at the Chatham Theater, where he could at least watch the plays from the wings, although he could not take part in them.

Ira Aldridge's father, a Presbyterian minister, worried about his son's interest in the theater and sent him abroad in his teens to the University of Glasgow. But the lure of the stage took young Aldridge down to London where, before he was twenty, he was playing Othello at the Royalty Theater. With the famous Edmund Kean as Iago, Aldridge later toured England and the continent in "Othello" with great success.

For forty years thereafter he performed as a star in all the major European cities. The King of Sweden invited him for special performances in Stockholm. The King of Prussia conferred upon him the Order of Chevalier and from the Czar of Russia he received the Cross of Leopold. Théophile Gautier, once visiting in Russia, wrote of Ira Aldridge, "He is the lion of St. Petersburg. In order to obtain a seat at one of his matinées, I found it necessary to apply for tickets some days in advance." Some Moscow students were so excited by Aldridge's performances that they would await him outside the stage door, unhitch the horses of his carriage and themselves pull his vehicle through the streets.

Ira Aldridge never returned to the United States. Still a star at the age of sixty, he died on tour in 1867 in Lodz, Poland, thus ending a celebrated career which spanned more than four decades. In his memory there is an Ira Aldridge Memorial Chair in the Shakespeare Memorial Theater at Stratford-on-Avon, and there are books about him in both English and Russian.

Aldridge wearing some of his medals.

Aldridge as the singing slave, Mungo, in "The Padlock."

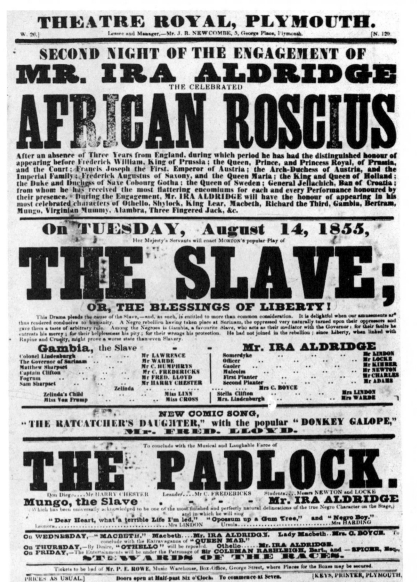

Playbill, Plymouth, England, 1855.

Ira Aldridge as Othello, his most popular role.

Aldridge with Taras Shevehenko, a Ukrainian poet.

Cover of *Benjamin Banneker's Almanac.*

Arts and

A Negro interested in mathematics, the stars, the cycle of the four seasons and the advantages of peace over war, as well as the abolition of slavery, was one Benjamin Banneker who, after the age of forty, achieved such distinction that Thomas Jefferson presented his name to President George Washington for membership on the commission to survey and plan the city of Washington. For two years Banneker carried on this work. Then, in 1791, he returned to his farm in Maryland and began writing and publishing an annual almanac which was popular in American households for the next ten years.

Banneker was born near Baltimore in 1731 and learned to read from his grandmother, an English woman who had been an indentured servant but eventually herself owned slaves and married one of them. Little Benjamin went to a private school, displayed an aptitude for mechanical sciences and, while a young man, made the first wooden clock in America. But it was not until he was forty that Banneker became absorbed in astronomy through books and astronomical instruments loaned him by a Quaker miller. In 1789 Banneker predicted a solar eclipse with astonishing accuracy. In 1793 he wrote *A Plan of Peace-Office for the United States* in which he suggested that a Secretary of Peace be ap-

A drawing of Rillieux's evaporating pan, which was patented in 1846.

N.Rillieux Evaporating Pan. Patented Dec. 10. 1846

Sciences

pointed to the Cabinet and that militia laws, military titles, parades and uniforms, which fascinate the minds of young men, be done away with, for "were there no uniforms, there would probably be no armies."

Another free Negro with a creative mind was Norbert Rillieux, born in New Orleans in 1806 and educated in France. Rillieux, while chief engineer of the Louisiana Sugar Refining Company, made a most important contribution to the advance of the sugar industry by his invention of an evaporating pan that revolutionized the refining of raw sugar in the 1840's. Rillieux established the scientific principles that form the basis of all modern industrial evaporation.

During the same period Charles L. Reason achieved distinction as an educator, heading the Institute for Colored Youth in Philadelphia and being appointed professor of belles lettres at a white institution, Central College, in McGrawville, New York. Elizabeth Taylor Greenfield, the "Black Swan," achieved considerable fame as a singer, Frances E. W. Harper as a poet and speaker, Edmonia Lewis as a sculptress and Patrick Reason as a painter and engraver. It was Patrick Reason who fashioned the massive coffin plate for Daniel Webster's funeral.

Charles L. Reason, an educator.

A painting of James Williams, a runaway slave, by Patrick Reason.

Edmonia Lewis, a sculptress.

Elizabeth Taylor Greenfield, a singer.

Frances E. W. Harper, a poet.

The Written

All of the colored writers of the ante-bellum period had a cause to plead: freedom for the slaves. The free Negro intellectuals devoted the major portion of their talents to that cause, often to the neglect of the profession for which they had trained. The physician James McCune Smith, a graduate of the University of Glasgow, who wrote a distinguished paper on the "Influence of Climate on Longevity," devoted as much time to the anti-slavery struggle, if not more, than he did to medical research. The Reverend J. W. C. Pennington, who had received a degree of Doctor of Divinity from the University of Heidelberg, preached against slavery from New England to Europe and frequently wrote about the condition of his people. Martin R. Delany, a graduate of the Harvard Medical School, also devoted his energies to publicizing the problems of his race.

The titles of many of Frances E. W. Harper's poems, such as "The Slave Auction" and "Bury Me in a Free Land," indicate clearly where her chief interest lay. And the first Negro novelist in

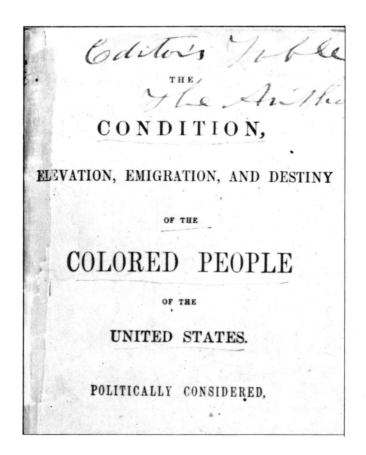

The Reverend J. W. C. Pennington, author of an early history of the Negro.

THE

CONDITION,

ELEVATION, EMIGRATION, AND DESTINY

OF THE

COLORED PEOPLE

OF THE

UNITED STATES.

POLITICALLY CONSIDERED,

CLOTEL;

OR,

THE PRESIDENT'S DAUGHTER:

A Narrative of Slave Life

IN

THE UNITED STATES.

BY

WILLIAM WELLS BROWN,

A FUGITIVE SLAVE, AUTHOR OF "THREE YEARS IN EUROPE."

With a Sketch of the Author's Life.

"We hold these truths to be self-evident: that all men are created equal; that they are endowed by their Creator with certain inalienable rights, and that among these are LIFE, LIBERTY, and the PURSUIT OF HAPPINESS." — *Declaration of American Independence.*

Word

America, William Wells Brown, who had trained as an apprentice printer with the abolitionist editor Elijah P. Lovejoy, became an agent of the Western Massachusetts Anti-Slavery Society. His *Clotel, or The President's Daughter,* was published in London in 1853 and in the United States in 1864 and was widely read.

Only the free Creole Negro writers of Louisiana, many of them educated in Paris, expressed little interest in the problems of bondage and of race. In their anthology, *Les Cenelles,* edited by Armand Lanusse and published in New Orleans in 1845, there are poems about lovely ladies, sunsets and love, but none about slavery. Included in *Les Cenelles* is the poetry of Victor Sejour, the tall dark-skinned writer of Louisiana who became the literary idol of Paris, a friend of Alexandre Dumas and Louis Napoleon. Between 1844 and the time of his death in France in 1874, twenty-one of his plays were produced in Parisian theaters, some at the great Théâtre Français.

William Wells Brown, the first Negro in America to write a play or a novel.

Dr. James McCune Smith, a physician, scientist, orator and writer on abolition.

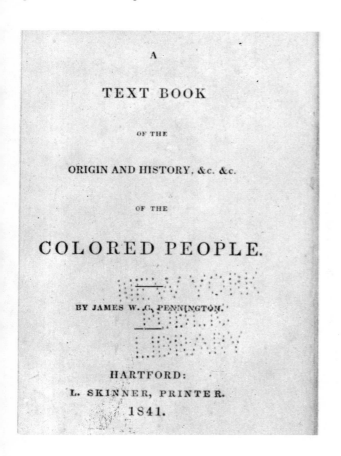

A

TEXT BOOK

OF THE

ORIGIN AND HISTORY, &c. &c.

OF THE

COLORED PEOPLE.

BY JAMES W. C. PENNINGTON.

HARTFORD:
L. SKINNER, PRINTER.
1841.

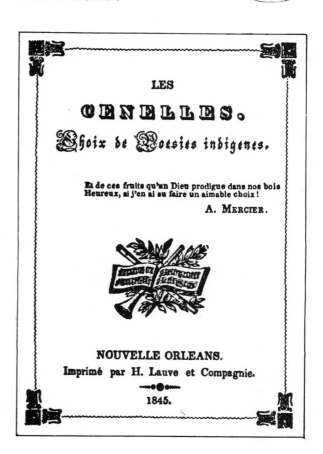

LES

CENELLES.

Choix de Poésies indigènes.

Et de ces fruits qu'un Dieu prodigue dans nos bois
Heureux, si j'en ai su faire un aimable choix!

A. MERCIER.

NOUVELLE ORLEANS.
Imprimé par H. Lauve et Compagnie.
1845.

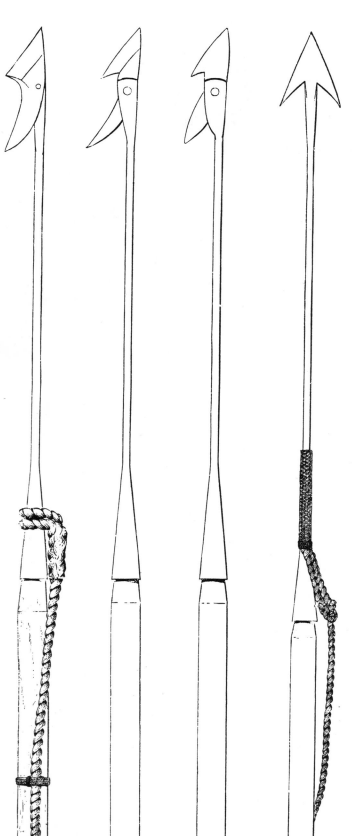

William Alexander Leidesdorff, prominent San Franciscan.

Toggle harpoons, invented by Lewis Temple.

ew of San Francisco in 1849, with the Leidesdorff home shown *(extreme left)* with a porch and a railing.

Highways and Byways

mes P. Beckworth, frontiersman.

From the highways of the East to the byways of the West some free Negroes, like other Americans, roamed at will. Their occupations varied and a few made distinct contributions to American progress. In New Bedford, Massachusetts, in 1848 a Negro blacksmith, Lewis Temple, invented a toggle harpoon, known as "Temple's Toggle," which became the standard harpoon of the American whaling industry—the "universal whale iron."

The year before, in faraway San Francisco, William Alexander Leidesdorff launched the first steamboat ever to sail on San Francisco Bay. Leidesdorff was a seaman from the Virgin Islands who had become a naturalized American citizen in 1844. He established himself as a businessman in San Francisco and built the first hotel in that city. A member of the city's first town council and of the first school board, he later became city treasurer. Leidesdorff organized the first horseracing in the state, lived well and entertained lavishly. A waterfront street there bears his name today.

James P. Beckworth, equally famous in the annals of the West, was a rugged frontiersman familiar with the wilds as well as city streets. A mulatto blacksmith from S. Louis, he joined General William H. Ashley's Rocky Mountain Fur Company. He ranged the Far West as a hunter, trapper and guerilla fighter against the Indians, acquired two Indian wives at once from the Blackfeet tribe and later a third wife from the Crow Indians, in whose nation he became a chief. In 1854 Beckworth dictated his memoirs to a writer in San Francisco and they were published by Harper & Brothers two years later. He died among the Crow Indians while on a peace mission for the government.

MINUTES

AND

PROCEEDINGS

OF THE

FIRST ANNUAL CONVENTION

OF THE

PEOPLE OF COLOUR,

HELD BY ADJOURNMENTS IN THE

CITY OF PHILADELPHIA,

FROM THE

Sixth to the Eleventh of June,

INCLUSIVE,

1831.

PHILADELPHIA:
PUBLISHED BY ORDER OF THE COMMITTEE
OF ARRANGEMENTS.

1831

The Convention

Almost all free Negroes were outspoken against slavery. Some became outstanding abolitionists, speakers and organizers of meetings and conventions. As early as 1817 at Bethel Church in Philadelphia, under the leadership of James Forten, Richard Allen and Absalom Jones, a large group of free Negroes came together in opposition to the American Colonization Society. Again at Philadelphia, in the autumn of 1830, Negroes from several states met to discuss their problems and to publish an "Address to Free People of Color of These United States." Out of this meeting grew the first Convention of Color, which convened for six days the following June and passed a number of resolutions, among them one favoring the continued settlement of Negroes in Canada, but another opposing any plans for repatriation to Africa.

From this time on, large groups of Negroes continued to hold meetings in various Northern cities to protest against slavery, to petition state legislatures and Congress for freedom for their brothers in bondage and to bolster, with oratory and resolutions, the continuing struggle for the achievement of full citizenship. As a means to that end, the conventions stressed the importance of education for Negroes and the value of training in literature, science and the mechanical arts.

Among the outstanding organizers and speakers in the colored convention movements were William Wells Brown, Samuel Cornish, John B. Vashon, Robert Purvis and the Presbyterian minister Henry Highland Garnet. At the Buffalo Convention of Colored Citizens, held in 1843, the Reverend Garnet urged Negroes to "Arise! Strike for your lives and liberties . . . Rather die free men than live to be slaves . . . Let your motto be resistance . . . No oppressed people have secured their liberty without resistance."

An 1854 convention of free Negroes ended its resolution: "We advise all oppressed to adopt the motto, *Liberty or Death*." This clause was considered so revolutionary that the convention voted it down. But everywhere it was clear that no Negro wanted slavery and few wanted colonization in Africa

Movement

rica. These colored conventions, with the aid, and some participation, of prominent white abolitionists such as Benjamin Lundy, Arthur Tappan and William Lloyd Garrison, made the entire country aware of their sentiments and did much to disprove the charge of Negro inferiority. Though methods differed as to how their goals should be achieved there was great unity among Negroes on the goals themselves: freedom and citizenship.

Henry Highland Garnet, a minister, editor and orator.

PROPERTY QUALIFICATION

OR

O PROPERTY QUALIFICATION:

A FEW FACTS

ROM THE RECORD OF PATRIOTIC SERVICES OF THE COLORED MEN OF NEW YORK,

DURING THE WARS OF 1776 AND 1812,

WITH A COMPENDIUM OF THEIR PRESENT BUSINESS, AND PROPERTY STATISTICS.

COMPILED BY

WILLIAM C. NELL,

AUTHOR OF "COLORED PATRIOTS OF THE AMERICAN REVOLUTION."

NEW YORK:

FOR SALE BY THOMAS HAMILTON, 48 BEEKMAN STREET, AND WM. H. LEONARD, 5 BEEKMAN STREET.

1860.

People's Independent Ticket.

Members to State Council.

PHILADELPHIA:
Rev. J. CLINTON,
R. PURVIS,
BENJAMIN B. MOORE,
ALPHONSO M. SUMNER,
DAVID B. BOWSER,
JAMES MAC. CRUMMILL,
ROBERT COLLINS,
J. J. G. BIAS,
SAMUEL WILLIAMS,
Rev. ADAM S. DRIVER,
JAMES H. WILSON, M. D.
FRANCIS A. DUTERTE.
S. VAN BRAKLE.
WEST PHILADELPHIA:
Rev. WILLIAM JACKSON.
HARRISBURG:
Rev. E. BENNET,
GEORGE W. CARR.
PITTSBURG:
H. WALTERS,
Rev. LEWIS WOODSON.
P. JACKSON,
Rev. A. R. GREEN.

An election leaflet listing free Negro candidates in Philadelphia.

Part Three

THE NORTH STAR

1619-1863

The struggles of Negro runaways to achieve and maintain freedom and the efforts of white abolitionists, in combination with free Negroes of the North, to destroy the institution of slavery in defiance of all the laws upholding it, constitute one of the stirring epics of American history. In the face of great obstacles and at great risk—determined slave-holders, apathetic public opinion in the North, Presidential and Congressional opposition, armed mobs, prison and even death—thousands of men and women, black and white, devoted their lives to the cause of emancipation. All of the reform movements of the first half of the nineteenth century in the United States were overshadowed by the crusade of the abolitionists, whose cause eventually merged with the tramp-tramp-tramp of the Union Armies. The Negro—whether he should be freed or not—became a crucial issue in American life.

First published as a small *Narrative* in 1845, expanded in *My Bondage and My Freedom* in 1855, further extended in 1881 and finally revised and enlarged in 1893 as the *Life and Times of Frederick Douglass,* this famous autobiography has been published in many editions in America and in Europe. The initial reason for publishing it was that when Frederick Douglass began to appear as an anti-slavery speaker before large audiences, some did not believe that so eloquent and intelligent a man had ever been a slave. To prove that his amazing career was a genuine story, Douglass wrote the first version of his *Narrative,* citing his birthplace and his master's name, which further endangered his freedom in the North and drew to the attention of slave-catchers his precarious status as a runaway.

NARRATIVE

OF THE

LIFE

OF

FREDERICK DOUGLASS,

AN

AMERICAN SLAVE.

WRITTEN BY HIMSELF.

BOSTON:

PUBLISHED AT THE ANTI-SLAVERY OFFICE,

No. 25 CORNHILL.

1846.

RULES
For the Society of
NEGROES. 1693.

WE the Miserable Children of *Adam*, and of *Noah*, thankfully Admiring and Accepting the Free-Grace of GOD, that Offers to Save us from our Miseries, by the Lord Jesus Christ, freely Resolve, with His Help, to become the Servants of that Glorious LORD.

And that we may be Assisted in the Service of our *Heavenly Master*, we now Join together in a SOCIETY, wherein the following RULES are to be observed.

I. It shall be our Endeavour, to Meet in the *Evening* after the *Sabbath*; and *Pray* together by Turns, one to Begin, and another to Conclude the Meeting; And between the two *Prayers*, a *Psalm* shall be Sung, and a *Sermon* Repeated.

II. Our coming to the Meeting, shall never be without the *Leave* of such as have Power over us: And we will be Careful, that our Meeting may Begin and Conclude between the Hours of *Seven* and *Nine*; and that we may not be *unseasonably Absent* from the Families whereto we pertain.

III. As we will, with the Help of God, at all Times avoid all *Wicked Company*, so we will Receive none into our Meeting, but such as have sensibly *Reformed* their Lives from all manner of Wickedness. And therefore, None shall be Admitted, without the Knowledge and Consent of the *Minister* of God in this Place; unto whom we will also carry every Person, that seeks for *Admission* among us; to be by Him Examined, Instructed and Exhorted.

IV. We will, as often as may be, Obtain some Wise and Good Man, of the *English* in the Neighbourhood, and especially the Officers of the Church, to look in upon us, and by their Presence and Counsil, do what they think fitting for us.

V. If any of our Number, fall into the Sin of *Drunkenness*, or *Swearing*, or *Cursing*, or *Lying*, or *Stealing*, or notorious *Disobedience* or *Unfaithfulness* unto their Masters, we will *Admonish* him of his Miscarriage, and Forbid his coming to the Meeting, for at least *one Fortnight*; And ex-

The Reverend Cotton Mather's broadside.

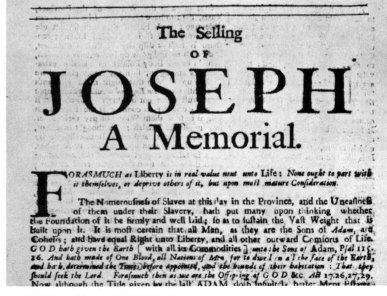

The Selling
OF
JOSEPH
A Memorial.

FORASMUCH as Liberty is in real value next unto Life: None ought to part with it themselves, or deprive others of it, but upon most mature Consideration.

The Numerousness of Slaves at this day in the Province, and the Uneasiness of them under their Slavery, hath put many upon thinking whether the Foundation of it be firmly and well laid; so as to sustain the Vast Weight that is built upon it. It is most certain that all Men, as they are the Sons of *Adam*, are Coheirs; and have equal Right unto Liberty, and all other outward Comforts of Life. GOD hath given the Earth [with all its Commodities] unto the Sons of Adam, Psal 115. 16. And hath made of One Blood, all Nations of Men, for to dwell on all the face of the Earth; and hath determined the Times before appointed, and the bounds of their habitation: That they should seek the Lord. Forasmuch then as we are the Offspring of GOD &c. Act 17. 26,27,29. Now although the Title given by the last ADAM, doth infinitely better Mens Estates,

Samuel Sewall's anti-slavery tract.

"Liberty...

When the eminent New England divine Cotton Mather drafted his rules for slave behavior in 1693 he permitted Negroes to sing, preach and pray, but he also required them to inform on runaways and to promise not to seek freedom for themselves. Almost forty years later, another citizen of Massachusetts, Samuel Sewall, who felt there could be "no progress in gospelling" until bondage was abolished, published the first anti-slavery tract printed in the Colonies. "The Selling of Joseph" began with these words: "For as much as Liberty is in real value next unto Life: None ought to part with it themselves or deprive others of it, but upon most mature Consideration." For his tract Sewall received only "frowns and hard words," but so strongly did he believe that his words were the "brest-work" of a necessary campaign that he boldly reprinted the tract six years later.

Few American Negroes could read, but they had ears. A few knew that some white citizens were on the side of freedom for the blacks. There are records as early as 1661 of individual slaves petitioning for their own manumission. In 1773, "The humble Petition of many slaves, living in the Town of Boston," praying "for such Relief as is consistent with your Wisdom, Justice and Goodness" was presented to the Governor of the Colony of Massachusetts, His Majesty's Council and the House of Representatives. Men like the New Jersey Quaker John Woolman, Benjamin Franklin and Dr. Benjamin Rush of Philadelphia openly encouraged Negroes to seek the abolition of slavery, as did the Huguenot Anthony Benezet.

Thomas Jefferson wrote that abolition, though thwarted by Britain, was a desirable objective for the colonies. Thomas Paine, whose first article, entitled "African Slavery in America," appeared in a Pennsylvania paper in 1775, was co-author of a law adopted in

Next unto Life"

Pennsylvania in 1780 which abolished slavery gradually in that state. Many colonists realized the inconsistency of fighting for colonial freedom while upholding slavery. A group of Philadelphia Quakers organized in 1775 the first American anti-slavery society.

Five years after the Revolutionary War a group of free Negroes, under the leadership of Prince Hall, who had fought in the war, presented to the Massachusetts legislature a petition against the African slave trade and the selling of free Negroes into slavery. And in 1797 the first petition to the Congress of the United States by Negroes was presented by a group of fugitive slaves living in Philadelphia, asking that their freedom be protected. Congress declined even to receive the petition.

Thomas Paine.

Dr. Benjamin Rush.

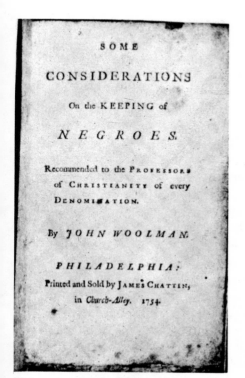

Title page of John Woolman's first essay, 1754.

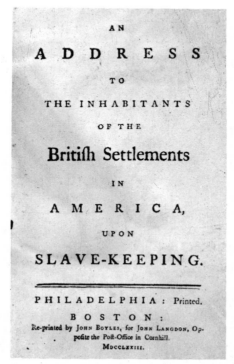

An address by Dr. Benjamin Rush, 1773.

Title page of an essay by Anthony Benezet, 1773.

Thomas Jefferson.

Mighty Words

Concerning slavery, Jefferson declared, "I tremble for my country when I reflect that God is just, that His justice cannot sleep forever." Patrick Henry, although himself owning Negroes, had said, "I will not, I cannot justify it." And in 1794 George Washington wrote, "I shall be happily mistaken if they are not found to be a very troublesome species of property ere many years have passed over our heads." Clearly slavery troubled the minds of good men.

Some slaves loved their masters—in paternal households, not the great plantations managed by overseers solely for profit—and some masters loved their slaves. When Thomas Jefferson returned to his home after two terms as President, his slaves unharnessed his horses at the gate, themselves pulled his carriage to the door and carried "their master bodily in their arms into the Monticello house." They lived well, ate well and were "the envy of Albemarle County." His slaves were freed at his death.

"We hold these Truths to be self-evident, that all Men are created equal, that they are endowed by their Creator with certain unalienable Rights; that among these are Life, Liberty, and the Pursuit of Happiness. That to secure these Rights, Governments are instituted among Men, deriving their just Powers from the Consent of the Governed. . . . " So stated the Declaration of Independence. Abolitionists used these words in their fight against slavery. In France the same sentiments were incorporated into the Dec-laration of the Rights of Man. These American words were as flame to the Spanish colonies turning against the tyranny of Spain. They were as flame to the slaves who could feel freedom in the air about them. Free Negroes and white abolitionists repeated these words over and over again for the slaves.

In January, 1777, a petition was presented to the government of Massachusetts that declared, "A Great Number of Blacks detained in a State of slavery in the Bowels of a free and Christian Country Humbly showeth that you Petitioners apprehend that they have in Common with all other men a Natural and Unalienable Right to that freedom which the Great Parent of the Universe hath bestowed equally on all mankind . . ." Two slaves who could write a little signed their names and another made his mark "in behalf of themselves and other Petitioners."

In spite of the "unalienable Rights" of the Declaration of Independence, when the Constitutional Convention met at Independence Hall in Philadelphia in 1787 slavery was strengthened greatly by the document which the delegates drew up for the approval of Congress. As finally adopted, the Constitution of the United States agreed to a compromise that allowed the South to count three-fifths of its slaves as a basis for representation in Congress, permitted the importation of Africans for another twenty years and required states to return fugitive slaves to their owners. But in the preamble of the Constitution there still remained the word *liberty*.

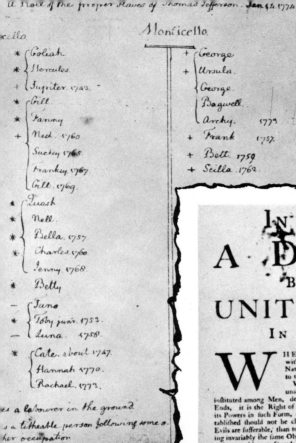

An inventory of the slaves belonging to Thomas Jefferson, 1774.

The Declaration of Independence.

WALKER'S

APPEAL,

IN FOUR ARTICLES,

TOGETHER WITH

A PREAMBLE,

TO THE

COLORED CITIZENS OF THE WORLD,

BUT IN PARTICULAR, AND VERY EXPRESSLY TO THOSE OF THE

UNITED STATES OF AMERICA.

Written in B ston, in the State of Massachusetts, Sept. 28, 1829.

SECOND EDITION, WITH CORRECTIONS, &c.

BY DAVID WALKER.

1830.

Prince Saunders was an ardent and outspoken abolitionist orator in the North.

Lunsford Lane of Raleigh, North Carolina, became an anti-slavery agent and speaker.

Charles B. Ray was a leader of the American and Foreign Anti-Slavery Society.

Robert Purvis was active in organizing the first annual convention of free colored people.

Negro Abolitionists

After the Revolutionary War, free Negroes became increasingly active in the anti-slavery movement. Some of them had fought in the war. Others had escaped to freedom during the war or had gained freedom through military service. All of them had heard the words "liberty" and "freedom" over and over and not only desired such a state for themselves but also for the black millions still in bondage. They began to speak about freedom, write about freedom and to meet among themselves and with white abolitionists dedicated to their cause. Pulpit, platform and press were turned over to their use and the demand grew for political action. Petitions were drawn up and presented to embarrassed, more often enraged, state legislatures. "Life" the free Negroes had, but "liberty" was precarious, and "the pursuit of happiness" still a far-distant goal.

Techniques for achieving freedom for all Negroes varied from preaching and praying, speaking and organizing, to outright demands for violence. David Walker, free-born but the son of a slave father, hated slavery so intensely that he moved from North Carolina to Massachusetts, where he became a leader in the Boston Colored Association and an agent for the first Negro newspaper, *Freedom's Journal.*

In 1829 Walker published the first edition of his famous *Appeal.* Within a year it went into three printings, greatly stirring all Negroes who could read and infuriating the slave forces. It asked:

"Can our condition be any worse? Can it be more mean and abject? If there are any changes, will they not be for the better, though they may appear for the worst at first? Can they get us any lower? Where can they get us? . . . The Indians of North and of South America—the Greeks—the Irish, subjected under the king of Great Britain—the Jews, that ancient people of the Lord—the inhabitants of the islands of the sea—in fine, all the inhabitants of the earth (except, however, the sons of Africa) are called *men,* and of course are, and ought to be free. But we (colored people) and our children are *brutes!* and of course are, and *ought to be slaves* to the American people and their children forever! to dig their mines and work their farms; and thus go on enriching them from one generation to another with our *blood* and our tears! . . . How would they like for us to make slaves of, and hold them in cruel slavery, and murder them as they do us? . . . I ask you, had you not rather be killed than to be a slave to a tyrant, who takes the life of your mother, wife and dear little children? . . . answer God almighty; and believe this, that it is no more harm for you to kill a man who is trying to kill you, than it is for you to take a drink of water when thirsty . . . The greatest riches in all America have arisen from our blood and tears . . . But Americans, I declare to you, while you keep us and our children in bondage, and treat us like brutes to make us support you and your families, we cannot be your friends. You do not look for it, do you? Treat us like men, and we will be your friends."

Jermain Loguen escaped from Tennessee to freedom and the ministry in New York.

Charles Lenox Remond was a delegate to the London Anti-Slavery Conference.

Charles L. Reason was a professor of belles lettres at New York Central College.

Samuel Ringgold Ward was the pastor of a New York Presbyterian church.

☞PLEASE TO READ AND CIRCULATE.

$1,50 Per Annum—$1 in advance.   Advertisements conspicuously inserted.

WEEKLY Advocate.

ESTABLISHED FOR, AND DEVOTED TO THE MORAL, MENTAL, AND POLITICAL IMPROVEMENT OF THE PEOPLE OF COLOR.

Vol. I.   New-York, Saturday, January 7, 1837.   No. 1.

PHILIP A. BELL, GENERAL AGENT.

Philip A. Bell.

FREEDOM'S JOURNAL.

" RIGHTEOUSNESS EXALTETH A NATION."

NEW-YORK, FRIDAY, MARCH 16, 1827.

The Reverend Samuel E. Cornish.

John Russwurm.

Freedom's Journals

A journal with six subscribers was one of the first anti-slavery newspapers. Benjamin Lundy was the intrepid white editor who began publishing his *Genius of Universal Emancipation* in 1812 from whatever town he happened to visit in his long effort to secure freedom for the black man. Within twenty years there were dozens of energetic editors, white and black, knitting together the abolitionist movement in thousands of towns and villages across America. The usual four-page editions carried passages from sermons, speeches in Congress and at conventions, excerpts from anti-slavery literature, quotes from the Southern press, exhortations to vote, to petition, to debate, to refute, to protest!

These journals were a power, although many of them flowered and were cut down almost overnight. Others maintained a continuing influence, such as the *National Anti-Slavery Standard*, the *National Era* and the *Anti-Slavery Bugle*. Twice mobs wrecked the Cincinnati office of the *Philanthropist* and sought the life of its editor, James Birney. A Philadelphia mob destroyed the office of Whittier's *Pennsylvania Freeman* in 1838. Cassius Clay's *True American*, launched in Lexington in 1845, had been published only three months when sixty townsmen deported the press to Cincinnati.

A white machinist named William S. Bailey moved South to Newport, Kentucky, "to carry the

abolition war into enemy territory" with a small printing press. Again and again in the 1850's his tiny *Newport News* was wrecked and his house burned down, but with the help of his wife and children he persisted in trying to make white workers see that "the system of slavery enslaves all who labor for an honest living."

Negro newspapers had an even harder time getting born and few survived the rigors of publishing without funds or advertising. *Freedom's Journal* was the earliest to appear, in 1827, edited by Samuel E. Cornish, pastor of the African Presbyterian Church in New York, and John Russwurm, a Bowdoin graduate and the first Negro in the United States to receive a college degree. When Russwurm left for Liberia, Reverend Cornish continued the paper until 1830 under the name of *Rights of All*. In 1837 he put out the *Weekly Advocate* with Philip Bell, renaming it a few months later the *Colored American*. In another year New York saw David Ruggles' *The Mirror of Liberty*. In the 1840's came Stephen Myer's *Elevator*, in Albany, and William Allen's and Henry Highland Garnet's *National Watchman*, in Troy. Westward, in Pittsburgh, Martin R. Delany, a Harvard graduate, issued the *Mystery* in 1843. The *Ram's Horn* in New York listed young Frederick Douglass as assistant editor and published contributions from John Brown.

But perhaps one of the most important abolitionist newspapers—Garrison's *Liberator*—had its roots in Baltimore, when twenty-four-year-old William Lloyd Garrison joined Benjamin Lundy's *Genius* in 1829. The young editor served seven weeks in jail for denouncing a shipowner who was busily profiting from the coastal slave trade. Released when Arthur Tappan paid the fine, Garrison made his way to Boston, announcing "I have a system to destroy, and I have no time to waste."

James G. Birney.

Benjamin Lundy.

THE LIBERATOR.

VOL. I.] WILLIAM LLOYD GARRISON AND ISAAC KNAPP, PUBLISHERS.

Boston, Massachusetts.] OUR COUNTRY IS THE WORLD—OUR COUNTRYMEN ARE MANKIND. [SATURDAY, JANUA

William Lloyd Garrison in 1846.

"Like Meets Like," a political cartoon indicating that William Lloyd Garrison *(right)*, had joined forces with Laurence M. Keitt, a South Carolina secessionist, to destroy the Union.

Garrison

When the first issue of the *Liberator* appeared in Boston on New Year's Day, 1831, the rhymed "Salutation" at the head of its first column informed the world:

To date my being from the opening year,
I come, a stranger in this busy sphere,
Where some I meet perchance may pause and ask,
What is my name, my purpose, or my task?
My name is '*Liberator*'! I propose
To hurl my shafts at freedom's deadliest foes!
My task is hard—for I am charged to save
Man from his brother!—to redeem the slave!

In "To the Public," the lead editorial which followed the "Salutation," its editor, William Lloyd Garrison, said:

"I shall strenuously contend for the immediate enfranchisement of our slave population . . . I will be as harsh as truth, and as uncompromising as justice. On this subject I do not wish to think, or speak, or write, with moderation. No! no! Tell a man whose house is on fire, to give a moderate alarm; tell him to moderately rescue his wife from the hands of the ravisher; tell the mother to gradually extricate her babe from the fire into which it has fallen—but urge me not to use moderation in a cause like the present. I am in earnest—I will not equivocate—I will not excuse—I will not retreat a single inch—*and I will be heard*."

Garrison quickly became the leading and most militant voice among the white abolitionists and was one of the founders of the New England and the American Anti-Slavery Societies. A frequent participant in Negro conventions and an opponent of African colonization, he was burned in effigy in Charleston.

and Phillips

When in 1835 a mob raided a meeting of the Boston Female Anti-Slavery Society at which Garrison was speaking and, with cries of "Lynch him!" dragged him through the streets, the scene was witnessed by a young lawyer from a leading Boston family, Wendell Phillips, who, until that time, had no particular interest in abolition. Phillips was so outraged by what he saw that he became attracted to the anti-slavery cause, gave up the practice of law because he could not support a Constitution legalizing bondage, ceased to exercise his right to vote—as a protest against a pro-slavery government—and devoted his life to the abolitionist cause. A persuasive and stirring speaker, Wendell Phillips ranked with Garrison as an anti-slavery leader, he was a delegate to the World Anti-Slavery Convention in London in 1840 and a great favorite at abolitionist meetings everywhere. To use his own phrase, he became one of the "men whose words are half battles."

By 1840 the American Anti-Slavery Society listed 250,000 members, published more than two dozen journals and had about fifteen state organizations supervising 2,000 local chapters. But differences of opinion developed within the rapidly growing movement. Garrison's followers believed moral suasion and passive resistance were the path to emancipation. They shunned political action and advocated the dissolution of the Union. They denounced churches for their support of slavery. The opposition, led by the Tappan brothers, James Birney and Gerrit Smith, split away in 1840 and formed the American and Foreign Anti-Slavery Society. It refused to support the woman's rights movement but plunged deeply into political action, forming the Liberty Party the same year.

The fight against slavery had moved from propaganda to politics.

Wendell Phillips in 1845.

Wendell Phillips speaking against slavery on Boston Common.

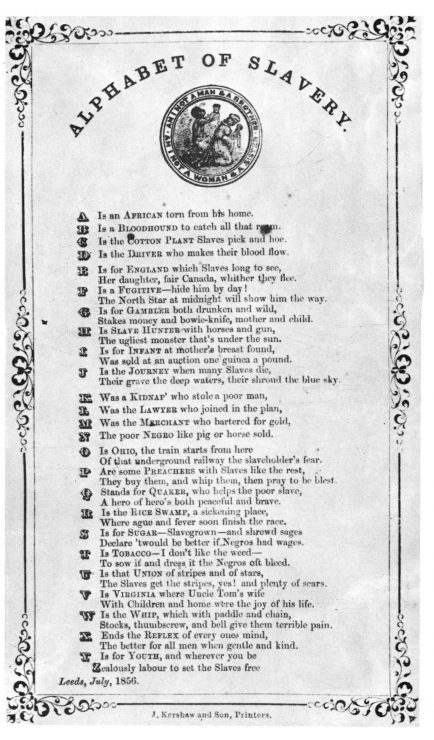

THOUGHTS

ON

AFRICAN COLONIZATION:

Garrison attacked colonization furiously for "lulling the whole country into a deep sleep."

ALPHABET OF SLAVERY.

A Is an AFRICAN torn from his home.
B Is a BLOODHOUND to catch all that roam.
C Is the COTTON PLANT Slaves pick and hoe.
D Is the DRIVER who makes their blood flow.
E Is for ENGLAND which Slaves long to see,
Her daughter, fair Canada, whither they flee.
F Is a FUGITIVE—hide him by day!
The North Star at midnight will show him the way.
G Is for GAMBLER both drunken and wild,
Stakes money and bowie-knife, mother and child.
H Is SLAVE HUNTER with horses and gun,
The ugliest monster that's under the sun.
I Is for INFANT at mother's breast found,
Was sold at an auction one guinea a pound.
J Is the JOURNEY when many Slaves die,
Their grave the deep waters, their shroud the blue sky.
K Was a KIDNAP' who stole a poor man,
L Was the LAWYER who joined in the plan,
M Was the MERCHANT who bartered for gold,
N The poor NEGRO like pig or horse sold.
O Is OHIO, the train starts from here
Of that underground railway the slaveholder's fear.
P Are some PREACHERS with Slaves like the rest,
They buy them, and whip them, then pray to be blest.
Q Stands for QUAKER, who helps the poor slave,
A hero of hero's both peaceful and brave.
R Is the RICE SWAMP, a sickening place,
Where ague and fever soon finish the race.
S Is for SUGAR—Slavegrown—and shrewd sages
Declare 'twould be better if Negros had wages.
T Is TOBACCO—I don't like the weed—
To sow it and dress it the Negros oft bleed.
U Is that UNION of stripes and of stars,
The Slaves get the stripes, yes! and plenty of scars.
V Is VIRGINIA where Uncle Tom's wife
With Children and home were the joy of his life.
W Is the WHIP, which with paddle and chain,
Stocks, thumbscrew, and bell give them terrible pain.
X Ends the REFLEX of every ones mind,
The better for all men when gentle and kind.
Y Is for YOUTH, and wherever you be
Z Zealously labour to set the Slaves free

Leeds, July, 1856.

J. Kershaw and Son, Printers.

The South Strikes Back

The abolitionists made stinging use of the printed and spoken word, but words were, after all, only "half battles." The slave forces were accustomed to using the whip and other forms of violence against whites who befriended Negroes. In Georgia a subscriber to the *Liberator* was tarred, feathered, horse-whipped and half-drowned. A number of whites in the South were killed for associating with Negroes in public. In Nashville, Tennessee, in 1835, a vendor of Bibles, Amos Dresser of Lane Seminary, was charged with being an abolitionist and whipped by a mob at midnight in the public square. By this time it had become almost impossible to speak openly against slavery in the South or to circulate printed matter concerning abolition.

Garrison's fiery editorials in the *Liberator* and his tracts such as *"Thoughts on African Colonization"* were effective in arousing anti-slavery sentiment in the North, but simply added fuel to the flames of resentment in the slave states. Disagreeing with Garrison's methods, the American Anti-Slavery Society, led by Tappan, decided to address its appeals to the non-slave-holding whites of the South, who constituted five-sixths of its population. Their magazine, the *Anti-Slavery Record*, their paper, *Human Rights*, their official organ, the *Emancipator*, and a magazine for children, the *Slave's Friend*, all mild in tone and basing objections to slavery on moral and religious grounds, were regulary posted to a selected list of Southerners. But in 1835 a grand jury in Alabama indicted Ransom G. Williams of the American Anti-Slavery Society for having mailed into that state a copy of the *Emancipator*, and his extradition was requested of the State of New York. The South wanted no interference of any sort with slavery, and no discussion, printed or otherwise, of abolition.

Broadsides such as this alphabet, which sold for a few cents, were popular at anti-slavery meetings.

ANTI-COLONIZATION
AND
Woman's Rights Ticket.
Members to State Council.

Robert Purvis,
Wm. Whipper, Columbia, Pa.
Samuel Van Brakle,
Benjamin Clark, York, Pa.
Alphonso M. Sumner,
James McCrummill,
J. J. Gould Bias,
Francis A. Duterte,
Edward Bennet, Harrisburg, Pa.
David B. Bowser,
Rev. Lewis Woodson, Pittsburg, Pa.
Rev. A. R. Green, Pittsburg, Pa.
John B. Vashon, Pittsburg, Pa.
Samuel Williams,
James M. Wilson, M. D.
Benjamin B. Moore,
Joseph Gardner, Reading, Pa.
Rev. William Jackson, West Phila.
Prof. Charles L. Reason,
Rev. Joseph Clinton.

A Pennsylvania state election ticket, linking two of the great reform movements. Many Negroes were candidates for office.

Anti-slavery fairs were a major means of fund-raising.

This illustration headed an article describing slave-breeding in the border states for sale in New Orleans.

By virtue of special compact, Shylock demanded a pound of flesh, cut nearest to the heart. Those who sell mothers separately from their children, likewise claim a legal right to human flesh; and they too cut it nearest to the *heart.—L. M. Child.*

On, woman! from thy happy hearth
Extend thy gentle hand to save
The poor and perishing of earth—
The chained and stricken slave!
Oh, plead for all the suffering of thy kind—
For the crushed body and the darkened mind. *J. G. Whittier.*

FIFTH ANNIVERSARY
OF THE
MASSACHUSETTS ANTI-SLAVERY SOCIETY,
WEDNESDAY, JANUARY 25, 1837.

[☞ The public meetings, during the day, will be held in the SPACIOUS LOFT, OVER THE STABLE OF THE MARLBOROUGH HOTEL, and in the evening, in the REPRESENTATIVES' HALL.]

HOURS OF THE MEETINGS.

Meeting for Delegates at 9 o'clock in the morning, at 46, Washington-Street.

First public meeting at 10 o'clock A. M., in the LOFT OVER THE STABLE OF THE MARLBOROUGH HOTEL.

Second public meeting at 1-2 past 2 o'clock, P. M. same place.

Evening meeting at 1-2 past 6 o'clock, in the REPRESENTATIVES' HALL.

☞ The Committee of Arrangements respectfully inform the ladies that ample accommodations have been prepared for them. The loft is spacious, clean, well warmed, and will accommodate, with ease and perfect safety, at least 1000 persons.

☞ AMOS DRESSER, a citizen of this State, who was 'Lynched' at Nashville, for the crime of being an Abolitionist, will be present, and during the meetings in the afternoon and evening, will give a history of that affair.

An announcement of a meeting at which Amos Dresser recounted his Nashville "lynching."

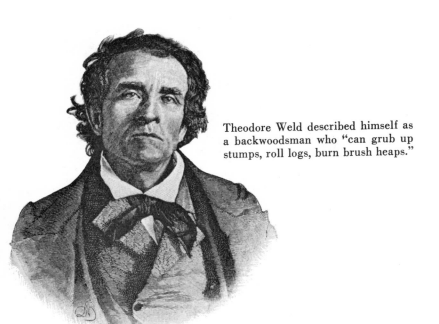

Theodore Weld described himself as a backwoodsman who "can grub up stumps, roll logs, burn brush heaps."

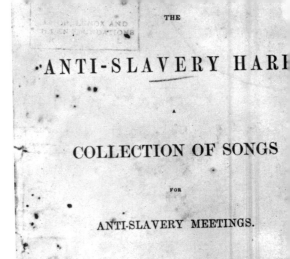

In Spite of Mobs

If it was foolhardy to oppose slavery openly in the South, it became dangerous in many parts of the North to do so. Theodore Weld, whom Lyman Beecher called "logic on fire," born in Connecticut of Puritan stock, believed the crusade against slavery should be carried to the people in rural areas, villages and small cities. He went about speaking on his own and, if local tempers permitted, living in a community long enough to make his influence felt. Weld was often threatened by mobs and his meetings broken up. In Troy, New York, he was stoned by a mob including a city official, from the hall where he had been lecturing all the way to his lodgings.

When, after hundreds of anti-slavery speeches, his voice gave out, Weld agreed to scout the New England colleges and seminaries for recruits to a special band of agents for the American Anti-Slavery Society. He spent almost a month in New York instructing and inspiring them. He had performed the same inspirational service among the students at Oberlin in Ohio early in his career, helping to make the college a center of social reform. He wanted no publicity or credit for his labor and much of his writing was published anonymously. His book, *Slavery As It Is*, was widely

circulated and because of its factual, non-sensational presentation, it shocked thousands out of their complacency. He believed in the education of the Negro and himself taught colored children. In New York he boarded with a colored family.

Like Weld, the Reverend John G. Fee, son of a slave-holder, persisted, in the face of angry mobs, in preaching, praying and speaking against slavery in the slave state of Kentucky, Those who attended Fee's abolition church, or who aided him in establishing interracial Berea College, were ostracized by the community, which finally dispersed his teachers and drove a dozen Berea families across the river into Ohio. Fee himself was warned that if he came back to Kentucky, he would be hung.

In *Anti-Slavery Melodies for the Friends of Freedom* published in 1843, Henry Wadsworth Longfellow had a song, *The Slave at Midnight*, whose final line asked, "And what earthquake's arm of might breaks his dungeon gates at night?" Some felt that it would indeed take an earthquake to destroy slavery. But abolitionists as active as Weld and Fee were certainly capable of stirring up a tempest.

The Slave at Midnight.

WORDS BY PROFESSOR LONGFELLOW.

...d he sang the psalm of David, He a negro and enslaved,

...l the voice of his devotion, Filled my soul with strange emotion,

...l and Silas, in their prison, Sang of Christ, the Lord arisen,

..., alas, what holy angel, Brings the slave this glad evangel,

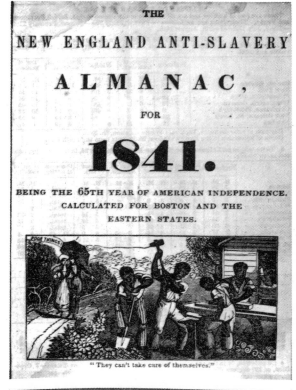

THE
NEW ENGLAND ANTI-SLAVERY
ALMANAC,
FOR
1841.
BEING THE 65TH YEAR OF AMERICAN INDEPENDENCE.
CALCULATED FOR BOSTON AND THE
EASTERN STATES.

"They can't take care of themselves."

THINGS FOR ABOLITIONISTS TO DO.

1. *Speak for the slave:* plead his cause everywhere, and make every body feel that you are in earnest. Get up anti-slavery discussions in debating societies, lyceums, and wherever you can get an opening, abroad and at home, in social circles and in public conveyances, wherever you find mind to be influenced, *speak for the slave.* Get others to speak for him, enlist as many as you can to take his part. Words from a full heart *sink deep.*

2. *Write for the slave.* Do you take a religious or a political paper? write ... article for it, ... an appeal, a slave law, testi...

"THINGS FOR THE ABOLITIONISTS TO DO"

1. *Speak for the slave*: Plead his cause everywhere, and make everybody feel that you are in earnest. . . .
2. *Write for the slave*: Do you take a religious paper? Write a short article for it, a fact, an argument, an appeal. . . .
3. *Petition for the slave*: Begin at once to circulate petitions for the immediate abolition of slavery. . . .
4. *Work for the slave:* Distribute anti-slavery publications, circulate them in your neighborhood, take them with you on journeys . . . .
5. *Work for the free people of color*: See that your schools are open to their children and that they enjoy in every respect all the rights to which as human beings they are entitled.

The Reverend John G. Fee of Kentucky, a preacher against slavery, founded Berea College in 1858.

Horace Greeley was for years the editor of the anti-slavery New York *Tribune.*

The Reverend Samuel J. May, a Harvard graduate, left the Unitarian ministry to work as an anti-slavery agent.

Songs
of
Freedom

While slaves were singing on the great plantations, "Nobody knows de trouble I've seen," or "Go down, Moses, 'way down in Egypt land, and tell old Pharaoh to let my people go," a popular troupe known as the Hutchinson Family was touring the country, including abolitionist songs in their repertoire. Jesse Hutchinson, Jr., composed "The Bereaved Slave Mother" and also one of the most famous anti-slavery songs, "Get Off the Track." Hutchinson toured Europe in 1845 to great acclaim, sometimes following Frederick Douglass' speeches there with songs on the same theme. A half century earlier songs like "Poor Black Boy," "The Desponding Negro," and "I Sold a Guiltless Negro Boy" were popular. Besides the customary hymns, abolitionist meetings were enlivened by such ballads.

The abolitionist movement attracted not only many of the leading intellectuals of the time but many ordinary people. By 1840 nearly a quarter of a million, including many women, had joined the Anti-Slavery Society. In those days women were not expected to take part in public meetings. At the National Convention of Abolition in Philadelphia in 1834, there were sixty-seven male delegates and four women observers. Of these four, one—Lucretia Mott —had the courage to stand up and speak. Six years later, women delegates to the World's Anti-Slavery Convention in London, were refused seats because of their sex. In protest, Garrison and others refused to take part in the meeting. This convention thereby became a landmark in the history of "the woman question," for Lucretia Mott returned to the United States to become a founder of the woman's rights movement.

Published in 1844, "Get Off the Track" was set to the tune of "Old Dan Tucker." Its opening lines ran:
> "Ho! the car Emancipation
> Rides majestic thro' our Nation,
> Bearing on its train the story,
> Liberty! a nation's glory."

"Ye Abolitionists in Council — Ye Orator of Ye Day Denouncing Ye Union." From a cartoon in *Harper's Weekly* of 1859.

Four of the "Singin' Yankees" of New Hampshire, "The Old Granite State" are *(left to right)* Judson, Abby, John and Asa.

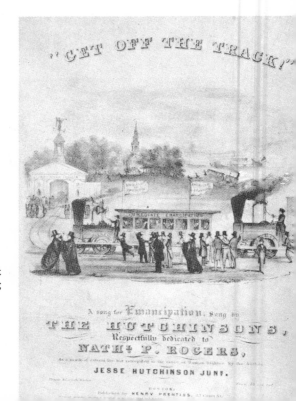

Thomas Clarkson addressing the 1840 Convention of the World Anti-Slavery Society in London. Clarkson and William Wilberforce, the foremost British abolitionists, led the campaign which ended the British slave trade by 1807. From a painting by Benjamin R. Haydon.

Executive committee of the Pennsylvania Anti-Slavery Society, 1851. (*Front row, left to right*) Oliver Johnson, Mrs. Margaret Jones Burleigh, Benjamin C. Bacon, Robert Purvis, Lucretia Mott, James Mott. (*Back row*) Mary Grew, E. W. Davis, Haworth Wetherald, Abby Kimber, J. Miller McKim and Sarah Pugh.

Lucretia Mott made her home a station on the Underground Railroad.

Abby Kelley joined Frederick Douglass on his first speaking tours.

Angelina Grimké spoke against slavery, even though her father was a slave-holding judge.

Lydia Maria Child, Lucretia Mott and Maria Weston Chapman were elected to the executive committee of the American Anti-Slavery Society in spite of great opposition. "To put a woman on the committee with men," thundered Lewis Tappan, "is contrary to the usages of civilized society," and, as a protest against Garrisonian "radicalism," both he and the president, Arthur Tappan, resigned, taking many followers with them. But Garrison and Wendell Phillips supported the right of both women and of Negroes to serve on committees and to take active part in anti-slavery organizations.

Among the outstanding women reformers who combined their interest in temperance or woman's rights with abolition were Julia Ward Howe, Lucy Stone, Susan B. Anthony, Abby Kelley and the Grimké sisters, Sarah and Angelina (who became Mrs. Theodore Weld). Lydia Child, a widely-read writer of children's stories, wrote *An Appeal In Behalf of That Class of Americans Called Africans*, which caused Southern bookstores to ban her other books. Julia Ward Howe, who later wrote the "Battle Hymn of the Republic," was a member of the Radical Club of Boston to which Longfellow, Emerson, Holmes, Phillips and other celebrities belonged and where the slave question was often discussed. Lucy Stone and Susan B. Anthony, both ardent advocates of woman suffrage, worked almost as hard in the cause of abolition in the face of male opposition on both scores. When a Massachusetts minister heard Lucy Stone was to speak in his town, he said contemptuously, "A hen will attempt to crow."

But male contempt did not keep the Grimké sisters of South Carolina from paying their own expenses to address gatherings of women on both suffrage and slavery after they left the South. Sarah Grimké and Abby Kelley were both Quakers, and each defied

Lucy Stone taught fugitive slaves how to read and write.

Lydia M. Child was the editor of the *National Anti-Slavery Standard*.

Susan B. Anthony was general agent for the Anti-Slavery Society.

Julia Ward Howe wrote the "Battle Hymn of the Republic."

Reformers

Lewis Tappan established a high school for Negro youths.

convention by appearing on public platforms. In 1836 Angelina published her *Appeal to the Christian Women of the South*, which attacked slavery's apologists and rallied more Miriams "to lead out the captive daughters of the Southern States to liberty and light."

The wealthy Tappan brothers of New York, dry goods merchants who built the Broadway Tabernacle and founded the *Journal of Commerce*, could not reconcile themselves to woman's rights, in or out of the abolition movement, but they were staunch opponents of slavery and gave huge sums to fight it. Arthur Tappan financed the legal defense of Prudence Crandall, who sought to teach Negroes in Connecticut, and also helped support Lane Seminary and Oberlin College. The Tappan store in New York was assailed by a mob in 1834, and Lewis Tappan's house was wrecked and his furniture burned in the street. When bankers pressured him to relinquish the anti-slavery cause he replied, "I will be hung first!"

It was a mob attack upon a New York State Anti-Slavery Society meeting in Utica that caused Gerrit Smith to invite all the delegates to his country home nearby, where he himself became a member of their group. Son of an ex-slave-holder, Smith collaborated with the Negro abolitionists James McCune Smith and Charles Ray in settling free Negroes on his farmlands and training them in husbandry.

Gerrit Smith, a philanthropist and an organizer of the Liberty Party.

Gerrit Smith, the Reverend Theodore Parker and Dr. Samuel Gridley Howe were militant abolitionists who believed that "No man's freedom is safe unless all men are free." Eventually they supported and aided John Brown. In 1858 Parker predicted that "the great American question of the nineteenth century" could not be settled without bloodshed. Garrison answered, "Perhaps blood will flow—God knows, I do not; but it shall not flow through any counsel of mine." Abolitionist blood did flow as a result of sporadic violence in both the North and the South. In Kentucky, Cassius M. Clay, the Southern-born publisher of the abolitionist *True American* kept two cannon loaded before his office in Lexington.

Arthur Tappan, often called the patron of emancipation.

Samuel Gridley Howe, a noted social reformer and an opponent of slavery.

Cassius M. Clay fearlessly warred with the slavery powers in his home territory.

John Greenleaf Whittier's poem, "My Countrymen in Chains!" was published in 1835 as a broadside with this drawing as its heading. At the bottom were three lines that read: "He that stealeth a man and selleth him, or if he be found in his hand, he shall surely be put to dèath. Exod. XXI: 16. England had 800,000 Slaves and she has made them FREE! AMERICA has 2,500,000!—and she HOLDS THEM FAST!!!! Sold at the Anti-Slavery Office, 130 Nassau Street, and 67 Lispenard St., New York. Price *Three Cents*."

Anti-Slavery Poets

How long have I in bondage lain,
And languished to be free!
Alas! and must I still complain —
Deprived of liberty.
    — From "On Liberty and Slavery"
      by George Moses Horton

They are slaves who fear to speak
For the fallen and the weak....
They are slaves who dare not be
In the right with two or three.
    — From "Stanzas on Freedom"
      by James Russell Lowell

Make me a grave where'er you will,
In a lowly plain, or a lofty hill;
Make it among earth's humblest graves,
But not in a land where men are slaves.
    — From "Bury Me in a Free Land"
      by Frances E. W. Harper

He did not feel the driver's whip,
Nor the burning heat of day;
For Death had illuminated the Land of Sleep,
And his lifeless body lay
A worn-out fetter that the soul
Had broken and thrown away!
    — From "The Slave's Dream"
      by Henry Wadsworth Longfellow

I am the hounded slave, I wince at the bite of
    the dogs,
Hell and despair are upon me, crack and again
    crack the marksmen,
I clutch the rails of the fence, my gore drips . . .
Agonies are one of my changes of garments.
I do not ask the wounded person how he feels,
I myself become the wounded person.
    — From "Song of Myself"
      by Walt Whitman

Frances E. W. Harper

John Greenleaf Whittier

James Russell Lowell

Henry Wadsworth Longfellow

Ralph Waldo Emerson

Henry David Thoreau

Walt Whitman

William Cullen Bryant

105

"A Printing Press Demolished at Slavery's Bidding."

Garrison and George Thompson, an English abolitionist, were mobbed in Boston in 1835.

The branding of Captain Jonathan Walker.

"The Branded

Except for Edgar Allan Poe, the major poets of the early and middle nineteenth century were either abolitionists or sympathetic to the cause of freedom and as a result were often the victims of printed, verbal and sometimes physical attacks. With Theodore Weld, John Greenleaf Whittier organized an anti-slavery library, which the American Anti-Slavery Society offered for sale, wrote scores of poems in behalf of freedom and penned powerful pamphlets such as "Justice and Expediency." Whittier faced mobs at least four times and knew the taste of terror. In a poem, "The Branded Hand," he immortalized the arrest and branding of Captain Jonathan Walker off Pensacola in an open boat while aiding seven slaves to escape to the Bahamas. Ralph Waldo Emerson, an eloquent supporter of Garrison, wrote of the Fugitive Slave Law, "This filthy enactment . . . I will not obey it, by God!" William Cullen Bryant, poet and editor of the New York *Evening Post*, defended the right of abolitionists to free speech as against "despotism and anarchy."

Abolitionist poetry, among other matter, might have been in the mails the night a mob sacked the post office in Charleston, South Carolina, in 1835.

Slave-holders raid the Charleston post office.

Hand"

It burned all anti-slavery literature awaiting delivery. Thereafter the Postmaster General of the United States excused Southern postmasters from delivering abolitionist material. Freedom of the press was greatly endangered as mobs, with increasing frequency, attacked abolitionist presses.

The offices of Birney's *Philanthropist* in Cincinnati were twice sacked. In St. Louis, when the Reverend Elijah P. Lovejoy, editor of the *Observer*, protested the lynching of a Negro, he was forced to leave town. He moved his printing press up the Mississippi to Alton, Illinois, in 1837, but it was seized on arrival and thrown into the river. A second and a third press were subsequently dumped into the water, but Lovejoy persisted in publishing and bought a fourth press. A mass meeting invited him to leave Alton. "Is not this a free state?" he replied. "Have not I the right to claim the protection of the laws? . . . Before God and you all, I here pledge myself to continue it, if need be, till death." With five bullets in his body, Lovejoy died, defending his press. The Alton tragedy fused abolitionism and freedom of the press into a common cause. To the most conservative Northerners, Lovejoy died a martyr to liberty.

The destruction of Birney's *Philanthropist* press in Cincinnati.

A mob attacking an Alton, Illinois, warehouse the night the Reverend Elijah Lovejoy was killed.

Prudence Crandall.

Miss Crandall's advertisement for Negro pupils in the *Liberator*.

View of Canterbury, showing Miss Crandall's school (*far left*).

A Crime to Teach

Mobs in some localities invaded schools, burned books and ran teachers out of town if they talked of abolition to their classes or dared instruct colored children. In 1833 a Negro girl, Sarah Harris, applied for admission as a non-resident student of a boarding school operated by Miss Prudence Crandall in Canterbury, Connecticut. She was accepted, although most of the parents withdrew their daughters in protest. Then Miss Crandall, a Quaker, opened a school expressly for colored girls. The villagers tried to burn it, they threw manure into her well, the local doctors refused to treat her students and the grocers refused to sell her food. But to her school came Negro girls from Boston, Philadelphia and New York. A vagrancy law under which outsiders might be given ten lashes on their bare backs was invoked against the young Negro students, but abolitionists put up bonds for them.

Then Connecticut passed a law against the free establishment of Negro schools—a law aimed especially at Prudence Crandall—which she refused to obey. She was

EDUCATIONAL LAWS OF VIRGINIA.

THE

PERSONAL NARRATIVE

OF

Mrs. Margaret Douglass,

A SOUTHERN WOMAN,

WHO WAS IMPRISONED FOR ONE MONTH

IN THE

COMMON JAIL OF NORFOLK,

UNDER THE LAWS OF VIRGINIA,

FOR THE CRIME OF

TEACHING FREE COLORED CHILDREN TO READ.

"Search the Scriptures!"
" How can one read unless he be taught?"
HOLY BIBLE.

BOSTON:
PUBLISHED BY JOHN P. JEWETT & CO.
CLEVELAND, OHIO:
JEWETT, PROCTOR & WORTHINGTON.
1854.

Margaret Douglass.

arrested and stayed in jail overnight, postponing acceptance of bail from her friends, in order to call attention to her persecution. Garrison's *Liberator* headlined her case and published weekly editorials in her defense. But Prudence Crandall was convicted. When, on appeal, the highest state court dismissed the conviction on a technicality, a mob broke all the windows of her school building and endangered the lives of her charges. To protect them from further harm, Prudence Crandall decided to close the school. No longer able to live in peace in Canterbury, she moved away. But several of her students were to become teachers and abolitionists. Twenty years later, another pioneer teacher of Negro children, Margaret Douglass of Norfolk, Virginia, went to jail for teaching colored children.

"Colored Schools Broken Up in the Free States," an illustration in an 1839 *Anti-Slavery Almanac.*

Mutiny on the Amistad

One day in the spring of 1839 a handsome young African whose name was Cinque was seized and carried off to be sold into slavery. The son of a Mendi chief, he soon found himself with many others chained in a sitting position in the hold of a Portuguese vessel bound for Cuba. At Havana, Cinque and some fifty blacks in his cargo were purchased by two Spaniards, who chartered the *Amistad* to carry their newly acquired slaves to Principe. At night, the Africans, seizing weapons from the sleeping sailors, killed Captain Ferrer and the cook. With Cinque now in command, they tied the two owners of the cargo to the bridge and ordered them to steer the schooner toward Africa. The white sailors were not killed but set adrift in a small boat.

But the Spaniards steered north and west instead of east and south. For sixty-three days they zig-zagged. Desperate from thirst and lack of food, ten of the Africans died before the *Amistad* arrived off Long Island one day in August. There a brig of the United States Navy sighted the strange ship and sent a party of men aboard to ascertain its business. Astonished to find only Africans in charge, at pistol point they ordered all hands below deck. The *Amistad* was convoyed to New London, and the Africans, except for three little girls, were charged before the United States Circuit Court at New Haven with the murder of the Amistad's captain. All were imprisoned to await trial.

A Mendi village in Sierra Leone, British West Africa.

Cramped quarters for slaves below decks on the *Amistad*.

A drawing of the *Amistad*.

The death of Captain Ferrer aboard the *Amistad* off the Cuban coast, July, 1839.

"God . . . Give

The Africans who had taken over the *Amistad* spoke a tongue which no one in New Haven understood. But they acquired many friends nonetheless among the townspeople and the teachers and students at Yale. They were allowed to exercise daily on the New Haven green and crowds, watching as they performed acts of physical prowess, tossed them coins which permitted the prisoners to supplement their jail diet with better food. The three little girls among the Africans began to learn English words and, through them, Professor Josiah Willard Gibbs of Yale was able to ascertain some of the quality of their language. In this way Gibbs finally located, aboard a British ship in New York harbor, a Mendi sailor who could serve as an interpreter.

Through James Covey the story of the *Amistad* captives was revealed and American newspapers were filled with articles about them and their case. Abolitionists flocked to their defense, charging that the Africans had been kidnapped from their homes and that they had the right of free people anywhere to employ whatever force was necessary to secure their freedom. When court proceedings began, there was so much excitement concerning the case that the law students at Yale were dismissed from classes to attend the trial. There were many intricate legal question involved—marine law, jurisdiction, the rights of the Spanish slavers to demand extradition, and whether or not, through their mutiny, the Africans were now free men or still slaves.

An Amistad Committee was formed, including Lewis Tappan, who contributed funds to their defense. Out of this Amistad Committee, the American Missionary Association eventually developed to combat "the sins of caste, polygamy and slave-holding." Southern politicians were opposed to the freeing of the *Amistad* Negroes and President Martin Van Buren stood ready to send them back into slavery. The court proceedings lasted all winter and public opinion became increasingly divided. A brilliant battery of lawyers was in charge of the Africans' defense.

Joseph Cinque, painted from life by Nathaniel Jocelyn in New Haven. "What a master spirit is his," wrote Whittier of the African. "What a soul for the tyrant to crush down in bondage."

Professor Josiah Willard Gibbs of Yale *(left)* theologian and linguist who found the key to Cinque's language. James Covey, *(right)* an African seaman from Mendi.

Me Utterance"

In court, young Cinque made in his native language a speech so impassioned that, although no one understood it, it helped swing the verdict in his favor. But the decision was appealed to the highest court.

John Quincy Adams, now a Congressman from Massachusetts, was so moved by the plight of the captives that, weak and almost sightless at the age of seventy-three and having been out of law practice more than thirty years, he nevertheless undertook to argue the case before the U. S. Supreme Court. "I implore," he wrote, "the mercy of Almighty God . . . to give me utterance that I may prove myself in every respect equal to the task." On March 9, 1841, after an eight-and-a-half-hour argument by "Old Man Eloquent," the Supreme Court ordered Cinque and his fellow Africans freed. Facing "the insurmountable burden of labor" yet to be encountered in putting down the slave trade, Adams wrote in his diary, "Yet my conscience presses on; let me but die upon the breach." Under the guidance of abolitionist teachers, Cinque acquired considerable learning before he and his fellows returned to Sierra Leone in 1842. They were accompanied by two missionaries, who set up its first anti-slavery mission.

In 1841 another mutiny occurred aboard the *Creole,* sailing from Virginia for New Orleans. On the high seas 130 slaves rebelled, killed a slave-owner and guided the ship into the harbor of Nassau, where, under British law, they would be free. While the blacks were held at Nassau awaiting word from London, the *Creole* case was hotly debated in Congress, Charles Sumner arguing for freedom for the mutineers in that the slave laws of Virginia did not apply beyond the borders of the state, while Daniel Webster, then Secretary of State, took an opposite position. Meanwhile, the British allowed the Negroes at Nassau to go free. Some infuriated American slave-owners called for war, and on Congressional demand, the British government eventually had to pay an indemnity for not returning the *Creole's* slave cargo to bondage.

John Quincy Adams. Sixth President of the United States, eight times a Congressman from Massachusetts, statesman, scholar, distinguished parliamentarian and tenacious orator, he was the leader of the anti-slavery debates which forced the major political parties to break their silence on the subject of slavery.

113

Frederick Douglass

Frederick Douglass was the foremost Negro abolitionist. Condensed from the opening pages of his *Narrative* is this story of his life as a slave in Maryland.

"In Talbot County, Eastern Shore, State of Maryland, near Easton, I, without any fault of my own, was born, and spent the first years of my childhood. From certain events, the dates of which I have since learned, I suppose myself to have been born in February, 1817 . . . .

My first experience of life began in the family of my grandmother. The practice of separating mothers from their children and hiring them out at distances too great to admit of their meeting, save at long intervals, was a marked feature of the slave system. My only recollections of my mother are a few hasty visits made in the night on foot, after the day's tasks were over. Of my father, I knew nothing. Grandmother belonged to a mysterious personage called "Old Master" whose name seemed ever to be mentioned with fear and shuddering, and unhappily for me, all the information I could get concerning him increased my dread of being separated from my grandmother.

But the time came when I must go. I was less than seven years old. On the plantation of Colonel Lloyd I was left to the tender mercies of Aunt Katy, a slavewoman who, ill-tempered and cruel, was often guilty of starving me and the other children. I had offended Aunt Katy and she adopted her usual mode of punishing me: namely, making me go all day without food. Sundown came, but no bread. I was too hungry to sleep, when who but my own dear mother should come in. She read Aunt Katy a lecture which was never forgotten. That night I learned as I had never learned before, that I was not only a child, but somebody's child. My mother had walked twelve miles to see me, and had the same distance to travel over before the morning sunrise. I do not remember seeing her again . . . .

On Colonel Lloyd's plantation, where one of the most heart-saddening scenes I ever witnessed was the whipping of old Barney, Mr. Gore was overseer. Gore whose very presence was fearful, undertook to flog a young colored man named Bill Denby. He broke away, plunged into the creek and, standing there with the water up to his neck, refused to come out; whereupon Gore *shot him dead!*

I hardly became a thinking being when I first learned to hate slavery. At the beginning of 1836 I took upon me a solemn vow to gain my liberty. I succeeded in winning to my scheme a company of five young men. Early on the appointed morning we went as usual to the field but I had a sudden presentiment, 'Betrayed!' The constables grabbed me. I was firmly tied. Resistance was idle. Five young men guilty of no crime save that of preferring *liberty* to *slavery* were literally dragged behind horses a distance of fifteen miles and placed in the Easton jail. I wished myself a beast, a bird, anything rather than a slave."

"The last time Fred saw his mother."

"Colonel Lloyd whipping old Barney."

"The overseer, Gore, shooting Denby."

Jesse Hutchinson, Jr., dedicated this song to Douglass, "in token of confident esteem" in 1845, and it was sung at many anti-slavery meetings.

"One Life to Lose"

As a boy of ten, in temporary service with his master's daughter, Frederick Douglass had learned to read a little from his mistress—until her husband angrily interfered. Then fences and pavements became his copy-books, as he picked up what knowledge he could from white children and copied letters and words on walls with chalk. He acquired a copy of the *Columbian Orator*, his only book, and devoured the speeches of Pitt, Fox and Burke, with their stirring words about liberty and freedom. In his early teens Fred taught at a little country Sunday School, which included insruction in spelling as well as the scriptures until white men broke it up with sticks and stones, warning him not to try "to be another Nat Turner."

Fred was sent for taming by his master to "a man named Edward Covey, who enjoyed the reputation of being a first-rate hand at breaking young Negroes." The first week under Covey he was flogged so severely that he bore forever the scars upon his back. During his first six months there, his *Narrative* relates, "I was whipped either with sticks or cowskins every week. Aching bones and a sore back were my constant companions." One day while working in the broiling sun, Frederick fainted. To revive him, Covey gave him a series of brutal kicks, then struck him on the head with a hickory slab. That night Frederick struggled seven miles through the dark to his master's house to beg to be removed from Covey's care. But his master ordered him back at once.

Then it was that Fred, now sixteen, tall and strong, decided to defend himself in the future. The next time Covey tried to hit him he flung the white man to the ground each time he approached. Covey gave up, contenting himself from then on with simply trying to work Fred to death. Thus it was that Frederick learned "when a slave cannot be flogged, he is more than half free. Men are whipped oftenest who are whipped easiest."

But, a few years later, hired out as a shipyard worker in Baltimore, Fred could not keep himself from being severely beaten by a gang of white workers, one of whom kicked him in the eye out of resentment against a slave working beside him. Frederick's master removed him from the docks, not through any sympathy, but rather because he did not wish his property damaged. All of his pay went to his master. "I worked for it, collected it . . . yet upon returning every Saturday night, this money—my own hard earnings, every cent of it—was taken from me by Master Hugh." Dreams of freedom were still in his mind. "Why am I a slave? I will run away. I will not stand it. I have only

Frederick Douglass as a young man at the beginning of his public career.

Douglass and his wife arrive in Newport after traveling on deck; Negroes were not allowed cabin accomodations aboard.

one life to lose. I had as well be killed running as die standing." On September 3, 1838, at the age of twenty-one Frederick escaped to New York disguised as a sailor. There he was joined by a free Negro girl he had courted in Baltimore. They were married and together set out for New Bedford, where in freedom they made their home.

"A Piece of Property or a Man"

William Lloyd Garrison in 1839.

The abolitionist William C. Coffin happened to hear Douglass speak before a Negro congregation in New Bedford. Coffin invited him to tell his story at an anti-slavery convention in 1841 in Nantucket. Hesitant and at a loss for words at his first appearance before a large audience made up almost entirely of white people, Douglass nevertheless so effectively told the story of his life under slavery and his escape to freedom that when he finished, William Lloyd Garrison cried, "Have we been listening to a thing, a piece of property or a man?" And the crowd answered, "A man! A man!" From that day Frederick Douglass became a public figure.

When John A. Collins persuaded him to become a speaker for the Massachussetts Anti-Slavery Society, Douglass said, "I had not been quite three years from slavery, and was honestly distrustful of my ability. Besides, publicity might discover me to my master. But I finally consented to go out for three months." Those three months were extended to a half a century of public life. He toured with Collins, with Garrison and with Wendell Phillips. He spoke at Faneuil Hall and at other great auditoriums. He was attacked by mobs in Boston, Harrisburg and in Indiana where, though his hand was broken in the melee, he spoke with his arm in a sling.

Enroute to England in 1845, some Southerners threatened to throw Douglass overboard for a talk he made aboard ship. He lectured in England for two years not only on slavery but also on woman suffrage and other subjects, and there raised enough money to purchase his freedom and to establish a newspaper on his return to the United States. But when he wished to visit France, the American minister in London refused to validate Douglass for the trip; so he had to obtain a special permit from the French minister to land on French soil.

George Latimer was a fugitive slave whose Virginia master came to Boston to claim him, but able lawyers came to the fugitive's defense. Abolitionists issued the *Latimer Journal, and North Star* thrice weekly to publicize the case, and Douglass reported his speeches in behalf of Latimer in his first letter to the press in the *Liberator*, November 18, 1842.

THE LATIMER JOURNAL, AND NORTH STAR.

" Star of the North, I look to thee   While on I press: for well I know   Thy light and truth shall set me free."

VOL. I.   BOSTON, WEDNESDAY, NOVEMBER 23, 1842.   NO. 5.

THE LATIMER JOURNAL.

TERMS.—One cent a number, tri weekly. A liberal discount to newsmen and boys. Advertisements (at discretion) one cent a line.

Edited by an association of gentlemen, and published every Monday, Wednesday and Friday mornings, at No. 15 State Street. It is not connected with the Courier.

Wm. White & H. P. Lewis, Printers.

own liberties. *We have endeavored not to say anything about Southern oppressors, but we here plainly tell them that they must never DARE come to Massachusetts to prostrate our laws to support their own institutions, as they have done in the present case.* The Latimer case was a test case, and its result has been a triumphant one. We rejoice in its bloodless termin-

dence, insulted the memories of the revolutionary heroes, violated God's laws, treated with contempt the teachings of Jesus Christ, given her professedly free soil as hunting ground to that detested human being, the human blood-hound, and invited the slave owners to seize upon our sons and daughters, and carry them into slavery, and made herself a fair mark for the scorn and con-

Grand Convention of Freemen!

At the Marlboro' Chapel, Saturday, Nov. 12.

The meeting was called to order by Dr Henry Ingersoll Bowditch, and organized by the choice of Francis Jackson, of Boston, as President, and William Bassett, of Lynn, as Vice President. In the absence of Francis

THE NORTH STAR.

RIGHT IS OF NO SEX—TRUTH IS OF NO COLOR—GOD IS THE FATHER OF US ALL, AND ALL WE ARE BRETHREN

VOL. I. NO. 1.   ROCHESTER, N. Y. FRIDAY, DECEMBER 3, 1847.   WHOLE

As a believer in equality for women, Douglass was the only male speaker at the first woman's rights convention. As a free Negro opposing all racial proscriptions, he declared, "The way to break down an unreasonable custom is to contradict it in practice." Douglass once clung so hard to his seat in a railroad coach when the conductor tried to eject him from a "white" car that the bench was torn from the floor as Douglass, bench and all were tossed off. Another time, when Douglass was refused sleeping quarters on a New York-Newport boat, and had to spend the night on deck, Wendell Phillips remained on deck with him, unwilling to allow Douglass "to bear the burden of insult and outrage alone."

But neither Phillips nor Garrison believed that Douglass should start a Negro paper, since they felt the *Liberator* and other established papers fighting the cause of abolition were enough. On this issue, and the question of political action through the ballot, which Garrison opposed, the paths of the great white abolitionist and the famous Negro began to divide. In 1847, in Rochester, Douglass founded the *North Star*. From addressing white people about Negroes, he turned to addressing Negroes themselves. Believing that "the man *struck* is the man to *cry out*"—and that "he who has endured the *cruel pangs of Slavery is the man to advocate Liberty* . . . not distinct from, but in connection with our white friends," the *North Star* was printed for all to read. Its slogan was, "Right is of no sex—Truth is of no color—God is the Father of us all, and all we are Brethren."

Douglass resisting an Indiana mob.

THE LATIMER

AND

GREAT MASSACHUSETTS PETITION.

When Latimer's freedom was bought by his master's acceptance of $400, Douglass spoke at the celebration. Some 6,300 people signed a petition that state officers be forbidden to arrest or detain fugitives, that use of state property be denied for such detentions and that federal amendments be urged, serving free states from any connection with slavery.

CLAIMS OF THE NEGRO,

ETHNOLOGICALLY CONSIDERED.

AN ADDRESS,

Before the Literary Societies

OF

WESTERN RESERVE COLLEGE,

At Commencement, July 12, 1854.

BY FREDERICK DOUGLASS.

This address by Frederick Douglass, delivered at a Western Reserve College commencement on July 12, 1854, was one of the first Negro attempts to refute racism scientifically.

A daguerreotype of John Brown on which is written "Regarded as the best picture by the family."

"All We Are

When the name of the *North Star* was changed to *Frederick Douglass' Paper*, the masthead bore this line: "Devoted to the rights of all mankind without distinction of color, class or clime." Certainly Frederick Douglass' interests were unlimited and his friends and associates were of many nationalities. In England, his friends included members of Parliament. In Ireland, the liberation leader Daniel O'Connell playfully called Douglass "the black O'Connell of the United States." When Southern friends of the Irish cause sent O'Connell contributions he returned them, saying he would "never purchase the freedom of Ireland with the price of slaves." In company with George Thompson and Garrison, in London, Douglass visited the venerable Thomas Clarkson, who seized both his hands and cried, "God bless you, Frederick Douglass! I have given sixty years of my life to the emancipation of your people, and if I had sixty years more they should all be given to the same cause."

After his return from Europe, Frederick Douglass met for the first time the militant-minded man whose name he "had heard in whispers" and spent a night at his home in Springfield, Massachusetts. Douglass described John Brown as a white man who "is in sympathy a black man, as deeply interested in our cause as though his own soul had been pierced with the iron of slavery." Brown believed "slaves had the right to gain their liberty in any way they could, did not believe that moral suasion would ever liberate the slave, or that political action would abolish the

During George Thompson's turbulent visit to America, he met Garrison and Phillips in Philadelphia to discuss an international society for the abolition of slavery.

Brethren"

system," Douglass wrote. "He was not averse to the shedding of blood, and thought the practice of carrying arms would be a good one for the Negro people to adopt, as it would give them a sense of their manhood. "No people," he said, could have self-respect, or be respected, who would not "fight for their freedom." Then Brown proceeded to outline to Douglass a plan of slave revolt to begin in Virginia, which Brown would lead, since "slavery was a state of war, and the slave had the right to anything necessary to his freedom." Brown said he himself could be killed, but he "had no better use for his life than to lay it down in the cause of the slave."

This night spent with John Brown, Douglass said, caused him to become all the less hopeful of the peaceful abolition of slavery and to draw away from "the Garrison school of non-resistants," although, contrary to Garrison and Phillips, Douglass continued to hope for favorable action under the Constitution, which he felt was "in its letter and spirit an anti-slavery instrument." Douglass was against violence but he had the "apprehension that slavery could only be destroyed by bloodshed." Meanwhile, with others, Douglass continued to apply what written, verval, moral and political pressure he could to end bondage in the United States without violence.

The *North Star*, Douglass said, "was changed to *Frederick Douglass' Paper* in order to distinguish it from the many papers with 'Stars' in their titles. There were 'North Stars,' 'Morning Stars,' 'Evening Stars.' Because some of these stars were older than my star, I felt mine, not theirs, ought to be the one to go out."

Anti-Slavery Politics

John Quincy Adams, concerned about the curtailment of constitutional rights under the "gag rule," persisted in presenting anti-slavery petitions to the House, only to be silenced by the Speaker. At one session in January, 1842, Adams, with "provoking pertinacity," introduced and spoke on almost 200 varying petitions.

Of the friends of abolition in political life Douglass wrote, "Without Adams, Giddings, Hale, Chase, Wade, Seward, Wilson and Sumner to plead our cause in the councils of the nation, the taskmasters would have remained the contented and undisturbed rulers of the Union." Certainly, no one did more in his time to disturb the complacency of the slave-owners than did John Quincy Adams, for seventeen years a member of Congress. Adams waged a running battle for eight years against the "gag rule" which prevented the consideration of petitions opposing slavery. He supported the people's right to petition.

On the day in 1848 when Adams collapsed on the floor of the House of Representatives, a young colleague who saw him was Abraham Lincoln, lately elected from Illinois. Among those who opposed the Mexican War of 1846 were Lincoln, Adams and Joshua Giddings of Ohio. Giddings had termed the conflict a "war against an unoffending people . . . with the design of extending slavery" and had declared he would "lend it no aid, no support whatever." The first militant abolitionist member of Congress, he was Lincoln's fellow boarder at Mrs. Sprigg's lodgings in Washington where, when the pros and cons of slavery generated too much heat around the dinner table, Lincoln sometimes acted as peacemaker.

Most abolitionists who participated in politics were Whigs rather than Democrats, since they believed the latter party to be dominated by slaveholders. In 1840 the Tappan wing of the American Anti-Slavery Society participated in the calling of a national third party convention at Albany. From this grew the Liberty Party, which nominated James G. Birney for President. But Birney, who believed that one active Congressman like Giddings was worth hundreds of anti-slavery lecturers, could muster but 7,000 votes for his ticket. And on a second try in 1844, the Liberty Party counted only 60,000 ballots. In 1848 the Liberty Party merged into the Free Soil Party, which nominated Van Buren. The Democrats, who had been in the saddle for twenty years, continued to win elections and cater to the slave-holders; the abolitionists alone could not swing an election.

The earliest existing photograph of Abraham Lincoln, taken about 1846 when he was a Representative in Congress.

Joshua R. Giddings of Ohio, the earliest abolitionist Congressman and Lincoln's colleague.

James G. Birney, the initial presidential candidate of the Liberty Party.

Freemen's Ticket.

At the Anti-Slavery Meeting of Lewis County, held at Martinsburgh, Sept. 22, 1840, J. A. NORTHROP, of Lowville, was called to the Chair, and HORATIO HOUGH, of Martinsburgh, appppointed Secretary.

On motion, *Resolved*, That we heartily concur, and hail with pleasure, the organization of the *Freemen's Ticket*, as based on the immutable principles of eternal right, contained in the Declaration of Independence, that all men are created " of one blood," with equal and inalienable rights.

Resolved, That we cheerfully concur, and pledge ourselves practically to support,

FOR PRESIDENT,

JAMES G. BIRNEY,

Of New-York.

FOR VICE-PRESIDENT,

THOMAS EARL,

Of Pennsylvania.

FOR GOVERNOR,

Gerrit Smith,

Of Madison County.

. FOR LIEUT. GOVERNOR,

Charles O. Shepard,

Of Genesee County.

Resolved, That we concur in the nomination of STEPHEN CROSBY, of Herkimer County, to represent the *Freemen's Ticket*, in this Congressional District, and of JAMES C. DELONG, of Oneida County, as a candidate to represent the 5th Senate District in the Senate of this State.

Resolved, That LEVI ROBBINS, of Denmark, be Member of Assembly, HORATIO HOUGH, of Martinsburgh, County Clerk, WM. C. LAWTON, of Copenhagen, Sheriff, *George W. Fowler*, of Turin, and *Adoniram Foot*, of Martinsburgh, Coroners.

A handbill of the Freemen's ticket of the Liberty Party, 1840.

Horace Mann, educator and Free Soil Congressman.

DISUNION PLEDGE.

Believing that an oath or affirmation to support the Constitution of the United States is utterly irreconcilable with the freedom of the slave,

We, the undersigned,

hereby pledge ourselves not to vote for a candidate for any office, the entrance upon which requires such oath or affirmation.

Name.	Residence.

A Garrisonian pledge form.

A Negro Resolution

Negro leaders were active in anti-slavery politics from the beginning. Ward, Garnet, Brown, Loguen and others stumped for the Liberty Party, and at its 1843 meeting in Buffalo colored men, for the first time, participated officially in a national political convention. Although still a Garrisonian believer in disunion, Douglass attended his first official party convention under a Liberty banner in 1848. A few months later he was present at the founding of the Free Soil Party in Buffalo and endorsed their candidates in his paper. Van Buren failed to carry a single state, but the Free Soilers elected two Senators and thirteen Representatives to Congress.

When the second Free Soil convention met in Pittsburgh in 1852, Douglass was elected, by acclamation, a secretary of the convention. The John P. Hale-George W. Julian ticket got only half as many votes as the Free Soil ticket of 1848, but Douglass' friend Gerrit Smith won a seat in Congress. Upon Smith's unexpected resignation, the New York *Tribune* proposed that Frederick Douglass succeed him. Cries of horror rose at the prospect of a Negro seated in Congress, but Douglass wrote prophetically that although he had not the slightest hope for his own election, he expected before the end of his life to see competent colored men in the halls of Congress.

By this time there were in Congress, in addition to those previously mentioned, such anti-slavery figures as William Henry Seward of New York, Thaddeus Stevens of Pennsylvania and Horace Mann of Massachusetts. Mann, who after serving the abolitionist cause in Congress became president of Antioch College—one of the first colleges to open its doors alike to women and Negroes—

Charles Sumner, a Massachusetts Senator from 1851 to 1874, championed equal suffrage for Negroes and whites.

Thaddeus Stevens, elected to Congress on a Whig ticket in 1848, became one of the chief anti-slavery spokesmen.

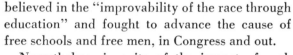

A "Barn Burner" cartoon of the 1848 campaign. The Barn Burners, the radical wing of the New York Democrats, supported the Wilmot Proviso. In 1848 they joined the "Conscience Whigs" to form the Free Soilers.

believed in the "improvability of the race through education" and fought to advance the cause of free schools and free men, in Congress and out.

Nevertheless, in spite of the impact of such men in Washington, many sincere abolitionists—followers of Garrison—continued to believe political action futile for their cause. Some even went so far as to circulate petitions against the upholding of the Constitution of the United States or voting for candidates who swore to do so. Most free Negroes, however, urged their fellows to take advantage of the ballot. Many of them flocked to the Free Soil Party. Indicative of their sentiments, a group of colored citizens in Boston passed the following resolution in 1852:

Resolved: That as the Whig and so-called Democratic parties of this country are endeavoring to crush, debase and dehumanize us as a people, any man among us voting for their respective candidates virtually recognizes the righteousness of their principles and shall be held up to public reprobation as a traitor, a hissing and a by-word, a pest and a nuisance, the off-scouring of the earth.

"The Land of Liberty," a cartoon published in *Punch* in 1847, depicting the U. S. A. as a land of warmongers, congressional ruffians, lynchers and slavers.

Owen Lovejoy, who was elected to Congress on the 1856 Republican ticket.

Henry Wilson, the Natick cobbler who became anti-slavery Senator from Massachusetts, and later, Vice-President.

Benjamin F. Wade, a Republican Senator from Ohio and Giddings' law partner.

The Republican Party

Early in 1854, aided by the Free Soilers, a number of both Whigs and Democrats, weary of the temporizing or outright opposition of their parties on the issue of the extension of slavery to the territories, created the Republican Party. In 1856 it nominated John C. Frémont and William L. Dayton as candidates for President and Vice-President, and in its platform was a strong plank supporting the exclusion of slavery for the new states. "Free Soil, Free Speech, Free Press, Free Men and Frémont" was the Republican slogan.

At the polls Buchanan and the Democrats won, sweeping the South and the West. But the Republicans elected 108 Representatives and fifteen Senators to the Thirty-fourth Congress, including the abolitionists Benjamin F. Wade of Ohio, Henry Wilson of Massachusetts and Owen Lovejoy (brother of the slain editor, Elijah Lovejoy) of Illinois. In the ranks of the new Republican Party was Abraham Lincoln who, campaigning throughout Illinois for Frémont, upheld with simple eloquence the Republican plank opposing the extension of slavery. In one of his many campaign speeches for the Republicans in 1856, on the subject of black men in bondage Lincoln was heard to say, "When I see strong hands sowing, reaping and threshing wheat into bread, I cannot refrain from wishing and believing that those hands, some way, in God's time, shall own the mouth they feed."

The newly-formed Republican Party's candidates for President and Vice-President in 1856.

A Republican poster of 1856, predicting that Fillmore and Buchanan would be crushed by the avalanche of states Frémont hoped to carry.

The former explorer, Frémont, is caricatured on a bony nag, "Abolition," which had Horace Greeley's head; Senator William Henry Seward is leading it. Behind them is the Reverend Henry Ward Beecher, carrying rifles for Kansas.

"I Think of the Great Things of God, Not the Little Things"

Sojourner Truth was not only an abolitionist but an ardent speaker for temperance, prison reform, better conditions for working people and woman's suffrage.

Two women who had been born slaves devoted all their energies to freeing others. Both were deeply religious. One, Sojourner Truth, was termed a mystic. The other, Harriet Tubman, was a woman of action, but in times of stress her favorite prayer was, "Lord, you have been with me through six troubles. Be with me in the seventh." Both women were so famous while they lived that books were written about them although neither could read or write. Both women had been married, but most of their lives each walked alone, and each covered wide areas in her travels. Each faced danger and possible death, one at mob-threatened meetings where abolitionists were stoned and the other at state boundary lines dividing freedom and slavery.

Sojourner Truth was born Isabella Baumfree about 1797, the property of a Dutch master in New York, and she spoke English with a Dutch accent all her life. Her childhood home was a hotel cellar where her parents and a number of other slaves were quartered. While still a child, Isabella's parents died, and she was sold and resold, finally becoming the property of one John Dumont in whose service she remained until New York State freed all its slaves in 1827. But Isabella's master did not want to let her go, so she ran away, leaving her children behind. When her five-year-old son Peter was sold to an Alabama owner Isabella went to court and succeeded in getting Peter back. Another time, accused of the murder of an employer by a white man who had no proof, Isabella again went to court, sued for libel and won a judgment of $125, an unusual vindication for a Negro then.

One day in 1843 Isabella decided to leave her job as a domestic servant to travel. "The Spirit calls me," she said, "I must go." With only a few coins in her purse, Isabella departed, feeling the call, although free herself, to preach and teach against slavery, under a symbolic new name. She declared, "The Lord gave me *Sojourner* because I was to travel up and down the land showin' the people their sins and bein' a sign unto them. Afterwards I told the Lord I wanted another name, cause everybody else had two names; and the Lord gave me *Truth*, because I was to declare truth unto people."

Sojourner Truth became a famous figure at antislavery meetings. Once she said about her work, "I think of the great things of God, not the little things." A very tall, very dark woman, with a deep voice like a man's, she electrified many audiences and irritated those who did not agree with her. When a man told her that he cared no more about her speeches than he would about a fleabite, "Maybe not," Sojourner replied, "but the Lord willing, I'll keep you scratchin'."

Harriet Tubman, who was born a slave on the Eastern Shore of Maryland about 1823, ran away and brought many others to freedom. During the Civil War she was a nurse, a spy and a scout. She lived until 1913.

Harriet Tubman was an even greater irritant to the slave-owners than Sojourner Truth, for not only did she make speeches in the North but time after time she went into the South and brought slaves out to freedom. At one time $40,000 was offered for her capture. When she was about twenty-five she ran away herself from a Maryland plantation, leaving her husband, parents, brothers and sisters behind. Two brothers started out with her, but became frightened and went back. Perhaps to prevent this from ever happening again Harriet Tubman carried a pistol on her freedom forays and if any slave heading North in her parties faltered, she drew her gun and said, "You'll be free or die!" Strength to go on was always forthcoming.

Up creek beds, through swamps, over hills in the dark of night, on nineteen secret trips into the dangerous South, Harriet Tubman guided more than 300 slaves to freedom, including her aged parents. Once in 1851 she took a party of eleven all the way to Canada, since the Fugitive Slave Law had, by then, made it dangerous to stop short of the border. One slave in the party, on whose head was a $1,500 reward, was so frightened he would not say a word nor, on the train crossing from Buffalo, even look out the window at the scenery. But when he found himself on free soil, he sang and shouted so much no one could shut him up. Harriet Tubman said, "You old fool, you! You might at least have looked at Niagara Falls on the way to freedom!"

Friendless and without work in Canada, Harriet herself prayed, cooked and begged for these refugees all winter. Then, in the spring she went back South to free more. She went alone, but once she got her slaves started, Harriet had help. There were secret stations of the Underground Railroad from Wilmington, Delaware, to the Great Lakes—hiding places in barns, cellars, churches, woodsheds, caves—and white friends to help with food and warm clothing and wagons with false bottoms for long trips in harsh weather. Harriet Tubman one of the most famous "conductors" on the Underground Railroad, once said, "I nebber run my train off de track, and I nebber lost a passenger."

William Still, the author of a book, *Underground Railroad*.

Levi Coffin, "President" of the Underground Railroad.

Runaways surrounded.

Slave-catchers invade an Underground barn.

A runaway protects his family from bloodhounds.

The Underground Railroad

There were also white "conductors" on the Underground Railroad; John Fairfield, of a Virginia slave-holding family, was one. Sometimes posing as a peddler or a slave-trader, sometimes as a traveling-evangelist, he brought many slaves out of the South. But the majority of slaves who escaped did not have guides to help them—at least not until they had made Northern contacts. However, some slaves knew that if they reached Wilmington, Delaware, the Quaker Thomas Garrett would feed and hide them. In Camden, John Hunn would help and in Philadelphia was William Still, the Negro secretary of the Vigilance Committee who kept a record of all the "passengers"—sometimes called "merchandise"—passing through his station. In New York City many white sympathizers and free Negroes like Charles Ray stood ready to help a refugee. In upstate towns were Gerrit Smith, Stephen Myers and the Reverend J. W. Loguen, himself an escaped slave. When runaways got as near the border as Rochester, Frederick Douglass or Susan B. Anthony would shelter them until they could make the "last jump" into Canada. On the western escape route that ran through Cincinnati, Levi Coffin helped more than 300 Negroes to continue northward.

Travel on the Underground was mostly at night, as the runaways had to remain in hiding by day. Way stations were ten to twenty miles apart. "Conductors" sometimes used covered wagons or carts with false bottoms to convey slaves from one "station" to another. Quakers did not believe in violence, but "conductors" of other faiths often secreted arms to use for defense, if need be.

With the help of more than 3,000 members of the Underground, it is estimated some 75,000 slaves escaped to freedom in the decade preceding the Civil War. By 1858 so many slaves were running away from Maryland that some masters met to see what could be done to stop them. Methods of

THE VIGILANCE COMMITTEE.

APPEAL.

NEW-YORK, JUNE, 1844.   VOL. I.

Committee of Vigilance.

An appeal by a New York Vigilance Committee to raise funds for runaways.

Will any one now say in view of these few, ... similar facts, that the slaves are ... would not have their liber- States, where formerly the minions of the slaveholder seized them and hurried them back to bondage for a paltry reward; but where now ... mittee stand ready to shield

escape for slaves varied, but generally it was on foot, wading in streams as much as possible to throw bloodhounds off the scent. But sometimes a slave "borrowed" his master's horse. Very daring ones even rode on trains. And one had himself nailed in a box with some biscuits and a "bladder" of water and shipped from Richmond to Philadelphia. When William Still opened the box, out popped Henry Brown. Still, who later wrote a book entitled *Underground Railroad* was known as a "brakeman" and his Philadelphia home was a busy "station." Many Underground Railroaders went to jail. Some, like John Fairfield, were killed.

The "resurrection" of Henry "Box" Brown, a Virginia slave who had himself shipped to freedom.

A page *(right)* from the diary of Daniel Osborn, an Ohio Quaker, recording the fugitives he aided.

344   UNDERGROUND RAILROAD

4 mo. 14 – 1844 – John Osborn and wife and two children from Maysville Kentucky — 4

5 mo 8 : A colored man and wife from Mason Co. Kentucky — 2

5 mo 10 A colored man from Winchester Kentucky

5 mo 25 = 4 colored men from Mason Co. Kentucky, one of them taken in Woodbury by the tobacco pedler — 4

5 mo. 27 3 colored men from Mason Co Kentucky — 3

6 mo 3 2 colored men from Kenton Co. Kentucky — 2

6 mo 4 3 colored men from Trimble Co. Kentucky and 1 white man from Vix burg Mississippi — 4

6 mo. 15 A colored man from Kentucky driving carriage for an Oberlin Lady — 1

3 months 21

8 mo 12 A colored man and boy from Kentucky, boy stoped at J. S. Hopkins's — 2

THIRTY DOLLARS
REWARD.

RAN away, on the 22d of Auguſt laſt, *a handſome Negro Lad*, named

A R C H,

Ignatious Davis of Frederick-Town, Maryland, advertises in 1743 for a lost slave, "Arch."

TEN DOLLARS
REWARD.

RAN away, on the 23d inſt. a handſome active *Mulatto* ſlave, named A R C H, about 21 years of age, is ſlender built and of middle ſtature, talks ſenſible and artful, but if cloſly examined is apt to tremble, has a ridge or ſcar on

An earlier advertisement inserted by Ignatious Davis in 1741 indicates that Arch had run away before.

FREDERICK CITY, MD.   185

DEAR SIR:

At the request of numerous slave-holders I have entered into arrangements for the detection of runaway servants; engaging in my service the most experienced men of the mountain, and Northern frontier of this State, throughout Pennsylvania; and also effecting tion from the county in which I live, to the Canada frontier.

The numerous plots which I have brou justice, is a g

John M. Pope of Frederick City, Maryland, announces that he has gone into the slave-catching business, requiring a fee in advance for his services.

STOCKHOLDERS
OF THE UNDERGROUND
R. R. COMPANY
Hold on to Your Stock!!

The market has an upward tendency. By the express train which arrived this morning at 3 o'clock, fifteen thousand dollars worth of human merchandise, consisting of twenty-nine able-bodied men and women, fresh and sound, from the Carolina and Kentucky plantations, have arrived safe at the depot on the other side, where all our sympathising colonization friends may have an opportunity of expressing their sympathy by bringing forward donations of ploughs, &c., farming utensils, pick axes and hoes, and not old clothes; as these emigrants all can till the soil. N. B.—Stockholders don't forget, the meeting to-day at 2 o'clock at the ferry on the Canada side. All persons desiring to take stock in this prosperous company, be sure to be on hand.

Detroit, *April 19, 1853.*   By Order of the

BOARD OF DIRECTORS.

An Underground Railroad handbill *(above)*, issued in Detroit, 1853, reports the successful passage to Canada of twenty-nine fugitives, worth $15,000, fresh from Carolina and Kentucky.

An Underground Railway map *(right)*, showing the routes to Canada used by fugitive slaves.

"The Business of Egypt"

Among those outstanding in conducting "the business of Egypt," (the Underground Railroad), were, as pictured below: (1) Isaac Hopper of Philadelphia and New York, who was active as early as 1787; (2) Calvin Fairbank, who served, all told, seventeen years in prison for his abolitionist activities; (3) John Hunn, one of the "chief engineers" of the Underground; (4) Samuel D. Burris, a daring Negro conductor; (5) Thomas Garrett, the Delaware station-master, who aided 2,700 fugitives and paid more than $8,000 in fines; (6) Salmon P. Chase, the "attorney general" for fugitive slaves, who later became Lincoln's Secretary of the Treasury; (7) Abigail Goodwin; (8) J. Miller McKim; (9) William Whipper; (10) Daniel Gibbons; and (11) Elijah F. Pennypacker.

With hundreds of other helpers, their activities covered all the escape routes from the Eastern seaboard to the Great Lakes and their ranks included men and women of all religious faiths, and of none. John B. Mahan was a Baptist, Thomas Garrett a Quaker and Lewis Paine of Georgia was said to be an atheist. But runaway slaves did not ask the religions of those who aided them on their dangerous exodus. To get out of "Egypt" into the "Promised Land" was a perilous undertaking. But once there beneath the North Star, each escaped slave must have felt as Harriet Tubman did when she said, "I looked at my hands to see if I was de same person now I was free. Dere was such a glory ober everything! De sun come like gold trou de trees and ober de fields, and I felt like I was in heaven."

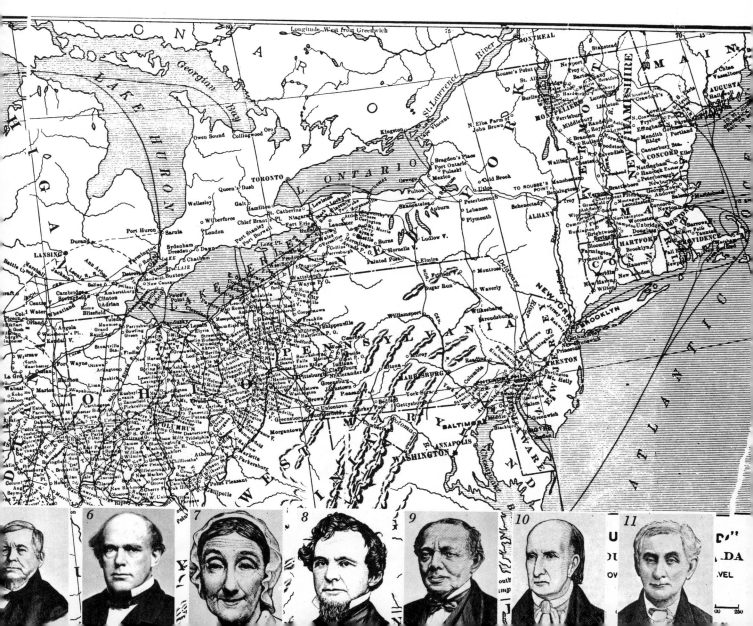

Rescue by Force

When the federal Fugitive Slave Law of 1850 offered to federal officers in the North a fee for captured slaves, Negro-catching became a profitable business. The abolitionists had the double task of rescuing slaves, first from slavery, then from Northern captors. Harriet Tubman, saying she could no longer trust Uncle Sam with her "passengers," took them all the way across the Northern states into Canada. Unfortunate refugees and free-born men, once taken by slave-catchers and unable to testify in court, had no opportunity to defend themselves legally. Their only chance to maintain freedom lay in escape or rescue by force from the clutches of avaricious constables, marshals or jailers.

In 1851 a group of Boston Negroes, led by Lewis Hayden, forcibly took a refugee, Frederick Jenkins, known as Shadrach, from federal officers. In that same city citizens had hidden William and Ellen Craft until the slave-catchers, with their federal warrants, were driven out of town. Ellen Craft, very light of complexion, had dressed as a man and posed as William's owner on the train.

In 1858 near Oberlin, Ohio, three U. S. marshals seized and escaped slave, John Price, but a group of Wellington citizens almost instantly rescued him. When thirty-seven of the rescuers were indicted by a federal grand jury, the case became front-page news throughout the country. Charles H. Langston, a Negro, and Simeon M. Bushnell, a white man, were the first of the group convicted. They served time in the county jail but on their release were greeted with a brass band and hailed as heroes. "The Fugitive Slave Law," abolitionists contended, "was made to be broken."

Ellen Craft.

Vol. III. No. VII.   JULY, 1837.   Whole No. 3

This picture of a poor fugitive is from one of the stereotype cuts manufactur in this city for the southern market, and used on handbills offering rewards runaway slaves.

THE RUNAWAY.

William Craft.

Twenty of the Wellington rescuers before the county jail.

Fugitives arriving at Levi Coffin's Indiana farm, a busy station on the Underground Railroad.

Margaret Garner, resisting capture by slavers, killed two of her children rather than see them returned to slavery. On the way back to Kentucky she drowned herself in the Ohio River.

Frederick Douglass writes in his *Life and Times*: "The thing which more than all else destroyed the Fugitive Slave Law was the resistance made to it by the fugitives themselves. A decided check was given to the execution of the law at Christiana, Pennsylvania, where three Negro men, being pursued by Mr. Gorusch and his son, slew the father, wounded the son and drove away the officers and made their escape to my house in Rochester. The work of getting these men safe into Canada was a delicate one. They were not only fugitives from slavery but charged with murder, and officers were in pursuit of them. There was no time for delay. Happily for us, the suspense was not long, for it turned out that on that very night a steamer was leaving for Toronto, Canada." Douglass himself put these free Negroes—unfairly harassed since they had never been slaves in the first place—on the north-bound boat. "This affair at Christiana," Douglass continued, "and the Jerry rescue at Syracuse inflicted fatal wounds on

the Fugitive Slave Law. It became thereafter almost a dead letter." Two white men and several Negroes at Christiana were tried for treason, but, defended by Thaddeus Stevens, they were acquitted. Abolitionists felt that they had acted rightly against the slave-catchers, kidnappers of free men.

The Jerry rescue, like that of Shadrach in Boston and of the three men at Christiana, took place in the year 1851. At the very time of a meeting of the Liberty Party in Syracuse, Jerry McHenry, a runaway Negro who had been living as a free man for several years, was seized by slavers to be returned South. But from the Journal Building, where he was being held, McHenry was rescued by an indignant group of men, led by Gerrit Smith and William Seward, in such open defiance of the law that prosecution was deemed futile.

Such open disobedience to federal law and such widespread assistance to fugitive slaves caused Southerners to lose faith in the Compromise of 1850,

"Rocking Slaves in Faneuil Hall," a Boston cartoon of 1851 commemorating the rescue of Shadrach.

1851

which included the frequently evaded Fugitive Slave Law. The government found it more and more difficult to enforce it. The cost of returning a slave to the South in some cases amounted to many times the slave's monetary value. The newspaper headlines given each sensational case and the violent partisanship engendered for and against the return of fugitives, widened the gulf between those who bought and sold human beings and those who opposed such traffic. The federal government, under President Fillmore, though hard put to uphold the Fugitive Slave Law, was yet determined to do so.

William Parker and other free Negroes rout slave-catchers at Christiana, Pennsylvania.

18

The Journal building in Syracuse.

Page from the account book of the Boston Vigilance Committee listing contributions to Underground Railroad activities.

The Vigilance Committee Dr.

1851				
April		Am't bro't forward	653	59
"	20	James ___ott fugitive passage to Canada	11	
"	"	___ver Printing 500 Billets	3	
		Prayers for Thos Sims		
		Sundries for the Committee	10	42
		Printing 1000 Placards & Posting	6	50
		caution to Colored People		
		expenses in Canada for Committee	21	
		boat in the Harbor	7	
		use of Tremont Temple	50	
		Apr 8 & 11th		
		for Sending a wounded Fugitive }	15	
		John Hatten to Canada		
		use & chaise case of Thos Sims	10	
		days watching Mr Caphart	9	
		" Bussetts fare to Canada	7	50
		'age of 3 Fugitives to		
		___ H S Jones J Brown & Wife }	21	7
		__n assisting Andrew J Burton & family	20	
		___ __n Bearse fare of Saml Ward to Plymouth __	7	72
		& Sundries		
	"	F W Bird rent of Committee room	25	
	"	Wm C Nell services for Johnson, Truett, Barnard &	1	32
		Elizth Dorsey		
	20	Loring Moody expenses to Fall River	5	
	21	Amos Baker use of Chapman Hall	12	50
		Prentiss & Sawyer Printing Petitions &c	19	
		___ewis Hayden Clothes for S Ward fugitive	7	87
		__ustin Bearse services rendered to the Committee	60	

Boston police guarding Sims.

The courthouse during Sims' trial.

Police conveying Sims to the vessel for return to Georgia, where he was publicly whipped.

The Sims Case

Thomas Sims was a "spruce-looking" young Negro of seventeen when his Georgian master came to Boston in April, 1851, and claimed him as a slave. His arrest created so much public interest that an armed guard had to be placed around the courthouse, where Sims was held in a room leased by the federal government. To prevent his rescue, the sidewalk before the courthouse was chained off. According to *Gleason's Pictorial*, "a few hot-headed people had succeeded in arousing the lower classes of the populace and the colored population to such a state of excitement that a mob was constantly anticipated and prepared for. The military were under arms at all hours, the various independent companies relieving each other at the post of duty in Faneuil Hall, where they awaited the orders of the Mayor . . . Court Street and Court Square were so thronged from morning until night, during each day of the continuance of the case, that the storekeepers in the neighborhood, many of them, were obliged to close their stores."

Placards for a meeting went up. "A large concourse of people responded to the notice, but the authorities having very properly refused to permit the 'front of the State House' to be used for any such purpose, the crowd adjourned to the head of the Commons, from the steps of which, on Beacon Street, the heated and over-excited orators harangued them . . . The language ascribed to Mr. Phillips on this occasion we should be loath to print." Meanwhile, prayers were raised for Sims in many Boston churches and two of the top lawyers in the city volunteered their services in his defense. But commissioners ruled that Sims must be returned to the South with his master. The young slave begged for a knife to stab himself through the heart in court. As he was led away, he cried, "And this is Massachusetts liberty!"

Thomas Sims in court.

Before dawn some 300 armed constables gathered at the courthouse to escort Sims to a southbound ship while a crowd of abolitionists cried shame upon the city of Boston. At the dockside they sang hymns and prayed. In many churches bells tolled as the young Negro was carried back into bondage. In a speech about the Sims case, Wendell Phillips, the non-resistant, for the first time indicated approval of the use of violence. "It is just possible that the fugitive slave, taking his defense in his own right hand, and appealing to the first principle of natural law, may . . . gain the attention of all, and force them to grapple with the problem of slavery and the Fugitive Slave Bill." And Garrison added, "Every fugitive slave is justified in arming himself for protection and defense."

A placard written by Theodore Parker.

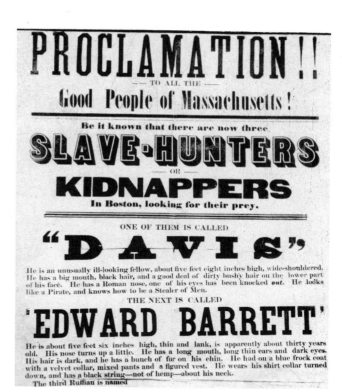

A warning proclamation posted in Boston, April 4, 1851.

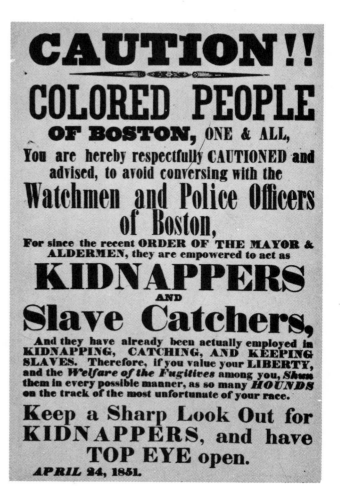

KIDNAPPING AGAIN!!

A MAN WAS STOLEN LAST NIGHT BY THE
Fugitive Slave Bill COMMISSIONER!
HE WILL HAVE HIS
MOCK TRIAL
ON SATURDAY, MAY 27, AT 9 O'CLOCK,
In the Kidnapper's 'Court,' before the Hon. Slave Bill Commissioner,
AT THE COURT HOUSE, IN COURT SQUARE.
SHALL BOSTON STEAL ANOTHER MAN?
Thursday, May 25, 1854.

A Boston poster announcing Anthony Burns' seizure.

The Reverend Thomas Higginson was wounded in the rescue attempt.

Richard H. Dana, Jr., who defended seamen and fugitive slaves.

A pamphlet tells the story of Anthony Burns, 1854. This case prompted many states to pass Personal Liberty Acts blocking enforcement of the Fugitive Slave Law.

$40,000 for a Slave

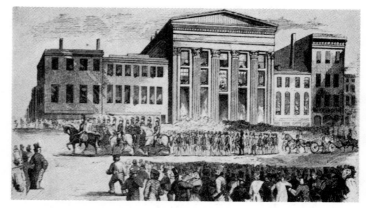

Federal and state troops returning Burns to slavery.

When on May 24, 1854, Anthony Burns was arrested and placed under guard in the federal jury room of the Boston courthouse at the behest of his former master, Colonel Charles Suttle of Alexandria, Virginia, the news spread quickly although an attempt was made to keep it secret. The next morning three distinguished lawyers were in court to defend him: Charles M. Ellis, a member of the Boston Vigilance Committee the purpose of which was to protect the rights of colored persons; Richard Henry Dana, Jr., author of *Two Years Before the Mast;* and Robert Morris, the city's most prominent colored attorney.

The following evening Faneuil Hall was filled to overflowing with citizens gathered to protest Burns' arrest and to denounce the posse sworn in as special constables to guard him, nearly a third of whom were known thugs with prison records. On the platform of Faneuil Hall that night, after Wendell Phillips and Theodore Parker had spoken, a man cried, "When we go from this Cradle of Liberty, let us go to the tomb of liberty—the courthouse!" The crowd broke for Court Square, where the Reverend Thomas Wentworth Higginson and Lewis Hayden were already leading a group of abolitionists in battering down the door of the courthouse to rescue Burns. But within, constables and deputies were ready with pistols and clubs. Reverend Higginson was wounded and in the scuffle one of the deputies was killed. Military reinforcements arrived, the abolitionists were routed and many were arrested.

Despairing of freeing Burns by force or by legal means, over the weekend the friends of freedom raised $1,200 and negotiated to purchase his freedom. But the U.S. Attorney refused to permit this transaction, insisting that in keeping with the Fugitive Slave Law the refugee must be returned to Virginia.

When Burns came to trial on Monday police and soldiers surrounded the courthouse, guarded every door and window and lined the staircase leading to the courtroom. From Washington, President Pierce wired to spare no expense in having the military protect the court "to insure execution of the law."

Lewis Hayden, the daring leader of various slave rescues.

The Reverend Theodore Parker had a part in the Burns rescue attempt.

On Friday, when Burns was sentenced to return to slavery twenty-two military units, including the entire Fifth Regiment of Artillery, were assembled in Boston to see that Burns did not escape and a cannon was set up in front of the courthouse. Besides the police of Boston, 1,500 dragoons, marines and lancers, with Burns in their midst, marched to the dockside through streets lined by a crowd of 50,000 persons hissing and crying, "Shame!" At one point, the populace tried to break through a police cordon and rescue Burns. Several were injured. As the revenue cutter *Morris* sailed for Virginia that day with Burns aboard, the Reverend Daniel Foster ordered the crowd on the dock to kneel in prayer.

Although the slave's market value was only $1,200, it had cost the government more than $40,000 to return Anthony Burns to his master. "We rejoice," wrote the Richmond *Enquirer*, "but a few more such victories and the South is undone."

FUGITIVE BLACKSMITH;

OR,

EVENTS IN THE HISTORY

OF

JAMES W. C. PENNINGTON,

PASTOR OF A PRESBYTERIAN CHURCH, NEW YORK,

FORMERLY A SLAVE IN THE STATE OF MARYLAND, UNITED STATES.

"Let mine outcasts dwell with thee, Moab; be thou a covert to them from the face of the spoiler.—ISAIAH xvi. 4.

Second Edition.

LONDON:
CHARLES GILPIN, 5, BISHOPSGATE WITHOUT.
1849.

THE

NARRATIVE

OF

LUNSFORD LANE,

FORMERLY OF

RALEIGH, N. C.

Embracing an account of his early life, the redemption by purchase of himself and family from slavery,
And his banishment from the place of his birth for the crime of wearing a colored skin.

PUBLISHED BY HIMSELF.

BOSTON:
PRINTED FOR THE PUBLISHER:
J. G. TORREY, PRINTER.
1842.

THE

LIFE AND ADVENTU

OF

ZAMBA,

AN AFRICAN NEGRO KIN

AND HIS EXPERIENCE OF

SLAVERY IN SOUTH CARO

WRITTEN BY HIMSEL

CORRECTED AND ARRANGED BY
PETER NEILSON.

LONDON:
SMITH, ELDER AND CO., 65, CO
1847.

SLAVERY

IN THE

UNITED STATES:

A NARRATIVE

OF THE

LIFE AND ADVENTURES

OF

CHARLES BALL,

A BLACK MAN,

WHO LIVED FORTY YEARS IN MARYLAND, SOUTH CAROLINA AND GEORGIA, AS A SLAVE, UNDER VARIOUS MASTERS, AND WAS ONE YEAR IN THE NAVY WITH COMMODORE BARNEY, DURING THE LATE WAR. CONTAINING AN ACCOUNT OF THE MANNERS AND USAGES OF THE PLANTERS AND SLAVEHOLDERS OF THE SOUTH—A DESCRIPTION OF THE CONDITION AND TREATMENT OF THE SLAVES, WITH OBSERVATIONS UPON THE STATE OF MORALS AMONGST THE COTTON PLANTERS, AND THE PERILS AND SUFFERINGS OF A FUGITIVE SLAVE, WHO TWICE ESCAPED FROM THE COTTON COUNTRY.

NEW-YORK:
PUBLISHED BY JOHN S. TAYLOR,

NARRATIVE

OF

SOJOURNER TRUTH,

A

NORTHERN SLAVE,

EMANCIPATED FROM BODILY SERVITUDE BY THE STATE OF NEW YORK, IN 1828.

WITH A PORTRAIT.

"SWEET is the virgin honey, though the wild bee store it in a reed;
And bright the jewelled band that circleth an Ethiop's arm;
Pure are the grains of gold in the turbid stream of the Ganges;
And fair the living flowers that spring from the dull cold sod.
Wherefore thou gentle student, bend thine ear to my speech,
For I also am as thou art; our hearts can commune together;
To unsunsel matters will I stoop, for mean is the lot of mortal;
I will rise to noblest themes, for the soul hath a heritage of glory."

NEW YORK:
PUBLISHED FOR THE AUTHOR.

THE

REV. J. W. LOG

AS

A SLAVE

AND AS

A FREEM

A NARRATIVE OF REAL

SYRACUSE, N. Y.:
J. G. K. TRUAIR & CO., STEREOTYPERS AND P

Tell Their Tales

In answer to a letter from his former master, W. H. Gatewood of Bedford, Kentucky, the Negro Henry Bibb replied:

"You may perhaps think hard of us for running away from slavery, but as to myself, I have but one apology to make, which is this: I have only to regret that I did not start at an earlier period . . . To be compelled to stand by and see you whip and slash my wife without mercy when I could afford her no protection, not even by offering myself to suffer the lash in her place, was more than I felt it to be the duty of a slave husband to endure, while the way was open to Canada. My infant child was also frequently flogged by Mrs. Gatewood, for crying, until its skin was bruised literally purple. This kind of treatment was what drove me from home and family to seek a better home for them."

— From *Life and Adventures of Henry Bibb*, 1849

"The only respite from constant labor the slave has through the whole year is during the Christmas holidays . . . It is the only time to which they look forward with any interest or pleasure. They are glad when night comes, not only because it brings them a few hours' repose but because it brings them one day nearer Christmas. It is hailed with delight by the old and the young . . . It is the time of feasting and frolicking and fiddling—the carnival season with the children of bondage. They are the only days when they are allowed a little restricted liberty, and heartily indeed do they enjoy it."

— From Solomon Northup's *Twelve Years A Slave*, 1853

ginning as early as 1837, when Charles Ball published his narrative, fugitive slaves continued to tell their stories in print for e next quarter of a century, one or more such narratives appearing ery year, some of them running into several editions and achieving nglish as well as American publication. Also widely read were the rratives of Lewis and Milton Clarke, Samuel Ringgold Ward, oses Grandy, William Wells Brown, Julius Melbourne, Josiah Hen-m and William and Ellen Craft.

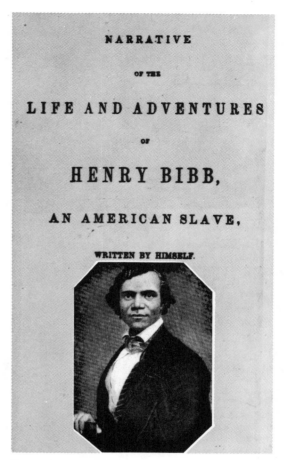

Henry Bibb organized in 1851 the Refugees' Home Colony in Canada, which purchased 1,300 acres of land for the settlement of escaped slaves.

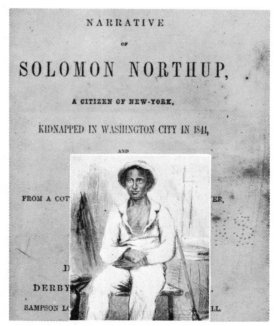

Solomon Northup's *Narrative* kept the printers busy, selling 27,000 copies within two years of its publication.

Harriet Beecher Stowe.

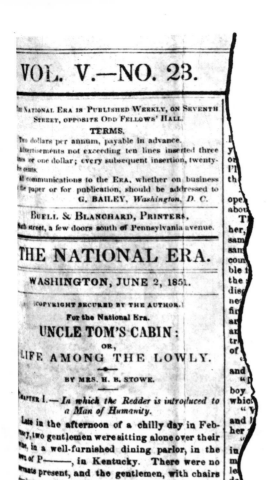

VOL. V.—NO. 23.

THE NATIONAL ERA IS PUBLISHED WEEKLY, ON SEVENTH
STREET, OPPOSITE ODD FELLOWS' HALL.

TERMS.

Two dollars per annum, payable in advance.
Advertisements not exceeding ten lines inserted three
times for one dollar; every subsequent insertion, twenty-
five cents.

All communications to the ERA, whether on business
of the paper or for publication, should be addressed to
G. BAILEY, *Washington, D. C.*

BUELL & BLANCHARD, PRINTERS,
Seventh street, a few doors south of Pennsylvania avenue.

THE NATIONAL ERA.

WASHINGTON, JUNE 2, 1851.

[COPYRIGHT SECURED BY THE AUTHOR.]

For the National Era.

UNCLE TOM'S CABIN:
OR,
LIFE AMONG THE LOWLY.

BY MRS. H. B. STOWE.

CHAPTER I.—*In which the Reader is introduced to
a Man of Humanity.*

Late in the afternoon of a chilly day in February, two gentlemen were sitting alone over their
wine, in a well-furnished dining parlor, in the
town of P——, in Kentucky. There were no
servants present, and the gentlemen, with chairs
closely approaching, seemed to be discussing some
subject with great earnestness.

For convenience sake, we have said, hitherto,
two gentlemen. One of the parties, however,

A song, "Little Eva," by John Greenleaf
Whittier.

"Uncle Tom's Cabin"

"In the midst of these fugitive slave troubles," wrote Frederick Douglass, "came the book known as *Uncle Tom's Cabin*, a work of marvelous depth and power . . . Its effect was amazing, instantaneous and universal." *Uncle Tom's Cabin* was first published in 1851 in the *National Era*, printed just as each chapter came fresh from the pen, for Mrs. Stowe had six children, including a new baby, with little time for careful writing. Her husband, a Biblical scholar, had been teaching at Lane Seminary in Cincinnati. She had seen slavery just across the Ohio River and had wanted to do something about it.

When the Stowes moved to Brunswick, Maine, after he had been asked to teach at Bowdoin College, the beginnings of a story came to her one Sunday in church. She went home and sat down to write a novel. As a book, *Uncle Tom's Cabin* was turned down by one publisher; another accepted it doubtfully. Mrs. Stowe said, "I hope it will make enough so that I may have a new silk dress." It was published in March, 1852, in Boston. Before the first week was up the whole edition of 5,000 copies had been sold. Before the summer Mrs. Stowe's royalties had amounted to $10,000. Eight printing presses, going day and night, could not supply the demand for copies; 300,000 were sold during the first year.

Though it appeared in England, France and Germany and was soon translated into many languages, its circulation was forbidden in the South. The character of Uncle Tom was based in part on the life of Josiah Henson, an escaped slave whose narrative Mrs. Stowe had read. He had described how, as a punishment, an overseer had cut off his father's ear. One day Harriet Beecher Stowe received a package. When she opened it, out fell the ear of another slave—a tribute from the South.

The escape of Eliza and her child across the Ohio.

Mary E. Webb; a free colored woman, reading from *Uncle Tom's Cabin* at the home of the Duchess of Sutherland in London, 1856.

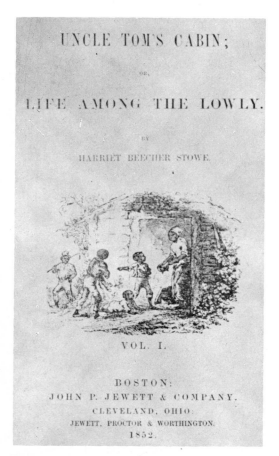

An 1853 juvenile version of *Uncle Tom's Cabin*.

UNCLE TOM'S CABIN;

OR,

LIFE AMONG THE LOWLY.

BY

HARRIET BEECHER STOWE.

VOL. I.

BOSTON:
JOHN P. JEWETT & COMPANY.
CLEVELAND, OHIO:
JEWETT, PROCTOR & WORTHINGTON.
1852.

Title page of the first edition of America's most famous novel.

"The Impending Crisis

"The object of these sketches," wrote Harriet Beecher Stowe in her preface to *Uncle Tom's Cabin*, "is to awaken sympathy and feeling for the African race, as they exist among us; to show their wrongs and sorrows, under a system so necessarily cruel and unjust as to defeat and do away with the good effects of all that can be attempted for them by their best friends."

But her book awakened more than a sympathy; according to Frederick Douglass it lighted "a million campfires in front of the embattled hosts of slavery." *Uncle Tom's Cabin* became a best-seller second only to the Bible. To Mrs. Stowe came hundreds of scurrilous letters from the South, but thousands of letters of praise from all over the world, from Heine in Germany, George Sand in France, Dickens and Macaulay in England and even one from Queen Victoria.

When in the fall of 1852 a dramatization of the book opened in Troy, New York, it ran for 100 performances. At the National Theater in New York City it remained a year. Later, four companies were performing the play nightly in Manhattan, and for more than half a century thereafter all across the country whole generations wept over Little Eva's ascension into heaven and Uncle Tom's death at the hands of Simon Legree. "The theater," Wendell

A scene from a dramatization of *Uncle Tom's Cabin*.

of the South"

Phillips said, "has preached immediate emancipation and has given us the whole of *Uncle Tom*, while the pulpit is either silent or hostile."

Meanwhile, in 1857, another book had appeared which infuriated the South, although it was written by a poor white North Carolinian, Hinton R. Helper. *The Impending Crisis of the South* attributed the backwardness of that region and the poverty of the poor whites directly to the cupidity of the slave system and the greed of a small minority of slaveholders. He quoted government statistics to prove his economic points: how cotton culture had exhausted the land, limited diversified crops and starved the masses. "There is no legislation except for the benefit of slavery, the slave-holders," he said, and of the treatment of the poor whites by wealthy slavers: "Never were the poorer classes of a people . . . so basely duped, so adroitly swindled or so damnably outraged." With his book banned in the slave states, Helper wrote, "The South can never have a literature of her own until after slavery shall have been abolished."

As the impending crisis developed, American writers devoted more and more attention to the conflict between slavery and freedom. In 1859 a man who had never written a book seized a government arsenal. His intention: to arm the slaves.

Hinton Rowan Helper.

The slave auction scene from "The Octoroon," an 1859 play by Dion Boucicault which became a hit in London.

NEW YO

FEARFUL AND EXCITING INTELLIGENCE

NEGRO INSURRECTION AT HARPER'S FERRY.

Extensive Negro Conspiracy in Virginia and Maryland.

Seizure of the United States Arsenal by the Insurrectionists.

Arms Taken and Sent into the Interior.

The Bridge Fortified and Defended by Cannon.

Trains Fired into and Stopped---Several Persons Killed---Telegraph Wires Cut---Contributions Levied on the Citizens.

Troops Despatched Against the Insurgents from Washington and Baltimore,

&c.,   &c.,   &c.

SPECIAL DESPATCHES TO THE HERALD.

WASHINGTON, Oct. 17, 1859.

A telegraph despatch has just been received by the Secretary of War from Mr. Garrett, President of the Baltimore and Ohio Railroad, stating that a serious affair has occurred at Harper's Ferry, where the United States Armory and the bridge are in possession of a large band of armed men, said to be abolitionists, but thought to be Armory men. The guns from the Armory have been taken for offensive use, and the leaders notified our men that no trains shall pass the Armory and Bridge. Our officers were fired upon, and a laborer nearly killed. The wires being cut, we got our advices from the next station. He asks the Secretary of War to get the government to allow the military of Washington and Baltimore to go on in the three o'clock train this afternoon, and render them such assistance as may be necessary. The Cabinet are now in session upon the matter.

The government immediately ordered that a company of marines from Washington barracks should leave this afternoon, under the command of Colonel Harris, for Harper's Ferry, and if necessary any further assistance that may be required.

Colonel Robert Lee, of the army, will command the United States forces. He leaves in the afternoon train with a company of marines, and will be joined on the Ohio Railroad by a company of volunteers from Maryland. Troops have been ordered from Old Point.

WASHINGTON, Oct. 17, 1859.

A passenger who has just arrived here, who left Harper's Ferry this morning, having been detained there for upwards of five hours, corroborates the statements received to-day by the Secretary of War.

This gentleman, who is an intelligent man, states that a negro insurrection of a formidable character, headed by white men, is in active operation. They are fully armed with muskets and other arms, which they had seized at the Armory. They had, when the train left, taken all of the white citizens, so my informant says, and held them as prisoners. They number one hundred and fifty, and recruits were coming in constantly from the surrounding country.

My informant says that they told him that they ——— seven hun-

), TUESDAY, OCTOBER 18, 1859.—TRIPLE SHEET.

the Un'ted States Arsena | and improbable as to cause no fears of such an | Capt. Cook has also lived
House, in which was said to | outbreak. | time
oney, and all the other pub-
y the mob.
nion that the object
ro

John Brown's Raid

When in July, 1859, under the name of Isaac Smith, John Brown rented an old house on the Kennedy farm in Maryland across the Potomac from Harper's Ferry, he began to store arms and lay careful plans. About a dozen men drilled in a secluded field. Visitors were unwelcome. In the house, Brown's sixteen-year-old daughter Annie and seventeen-year-old Martha, wife of his son Oliver, kept a lookout as they cooked and washed dishes for the men. Oliver and his brother Watson aided their father.

Meanwhile, Brown went to keep a rendezvous with Frederick Douglass in a stone quarry in Pennsylvania. There Douglass tried to discourage him and refused to join his venture because he felt the plan was bound to fail. Brown returned to his farm without Douglass, but Shields Green, a runaway slave from Charleston whom Douglass had sheltered, came with Brown. He found Dangerfield Newby, a former Virginia slave, already there. Later that summer other Negroes began to arrive at the farm: two young students from Oberlin—Lewis Sheridan Leary and his nephew, John Armstrong Copeland—and Osborn Perry Anderson from Pennsylvania.

With a group of twenty-one men, on the rainy Sunday night of October 16, 1859, John Brown attacked the federal arsenal at Harper's Ferry with the objective of taking the town, distributing arms to the slaves in the vicinity and spreading the revolt from there across the South. The arsenal was taken, but the plan failed. President Buchanan called out the marines and the cavalry under the command of Colonel Robert E. Lee; Brown, wounded, was taken prisoner. In the early fighting Brown's two sons were killed, as were Sheridan Leary, Dangerfield Newby and six others. Osborn Anderson escaped. John Copeland and Shields Green were hanged for treason.

In all, seven of the raiders died on the gallows, including John Brown. But while they were awaiting trial, the whole country was in a state of excitement. Southern cities called out troops for fear of slave uprisings, and Washington itself was patrolled by the military. Brown, lying wounded and bloodstained a few hours after his capture, warned, "You may dispose of me very easily. I am nearly disposed of now, but this question is still to be settled—this Negro question, I mean—the end of that is not yet."

The Kennedy farm, near Harper's Ferry, where such secrecy prevailed in Brown's preparations that when the raid first occurred—as the early newspaper reports indicate—it was not known who was in charge.

An attack on the insurgents at the Baltimore & Ohio bridge.

"For a Noble Cause"

Under sentence of death after the failure of the raid, the Negro John Copeland wrote his brother from prison, "It was a sense of the wrongs which we have suffered that prompted the noble but unfortunate Captain John Brown and his associates to attempt to give freedom to a small number, at least, of those who are now held by cruel and unjust laws, and by no less cruel and unjust men. To this freedom they were entitled by every known principle of justice and humanity. Dear brother, could I die for a more noble cause?"

No one among Brown's band implicated anybody else. On December 2, the day of his execution, John Brown scrawled on a piece of paper which he left with his jailer, "I, John Brown, am now quite certain that the crimes of this guilty land will never be purged away but with blood. I had, as I now think vainly, flattered myself that without very much bloodshed it might be done." On a clear, cool, sun-bright morning, they rode John Brown to the scaffold in an open cart. The old man looked at the Blue Ridge Mountains in the distance and said, "This *is* a beautiful country."

Burying the dead insurgents.

Marines storming Brown's men in the engine house. In this prologue to the Civil War, Colonel Robert E. Lee commanded the troops and Lieutenant J. E. B. Stuart carried out his orders.

John Brown, one son lying dead beside him, holds a rifle in one hand and feels the pulse of a second dying son with the other.

Governor Henry Wise of Virginia and reporters interrogate the wounded John Brown.

John Brown ascending the scaffold at Charlestown, West Virginia.

Lewis Sheridan Leary, whose widow married H. Langston, of the Oberlin-Wellington rescue.

Dangerfield Newby, whose father was his white master and whose mother was a slave.

The prisoners in the Charlestown jail.

"High Noon"

"In firing his gun, John Brown has merely told us what time of day it is. It is high noon, thank God!"

— William Lloyd Garrison

"The day of a new revolution, quite as much needed as the old one."

— Henry Wadsworth Longfellow

"Already from your prison has come a shout of triumph against the giant sin of our country."

— Frances E. W. Harper

"The Commonwealth of Virginia . . . is a pirate ship, and John Brown sails the sea as a Lord High Admiral of the Almighty, with his commission to sink every pirate he meets on God's ocean of the nineteenth century . . . John Brown has twice as much right to hang Governor Wise as Governor Wise has to hang him."

— Wendell Phillips

"Brown is a bundle of the best nerves I ever saw, cut and thrust, bleeding and in bonds. He is a man of clear head, of courage, fortitude. He is a fanatic, vain and garrulous, but firm and truthful and intelligent."

— Governor Henry Wise

"To his own soul he was right, and neither 'principalities nor powers, life nor death, things present nor things to come,' could shake his dauntless spirit or move him from his ground. . . . Those who looked for confession heard only the voice of rebuke and warning."

— Frederick Douglass

"New saint who will make the gallows glorious like the cross."

— Ralph Waldo Emerson

"Old John Brown is dead—John Brown the immortal lives."

— Henry Thoreau

Osborn Perry Anderson, who escaped to write *A Voice from Harper's Ferry* and fight in the Civil War.

JOHN BROWN'S SONG.

John Brown's body lies a mouldering in the grave,
John Brown's body lies a mouldering in the grave,
John Brown's body lies a mouldering in the grave.
His soul's marching on!
Chorus: Glory Hally, Hallelujah! Glory Hally, Hallelujah!
Glory Hally, Hallelujah!
His soul's marching on

He's gone to be a soldier in the army of our Lord,
He's gone to be a soldier in the army of our Lord,
He's gone to be a soldier in the army of our Lord,
His soul's marching on.
Chorus: Glory Hally, Hallelujah, Glory Hally, Hallelujah!
Glory Hally, Hallelujah!
His soul's marching on.

John Brown's knapsack is strapped upon his back,
John Brown's knapsack is strapped upon his back,
John Brown's knapsack is strapped upon his back.
His soul's marching on!
Chorus: Glory Hally, Hallelujah! Glory hally, Hallelujah!
Glory hally, Hallelujah!
His soul's marching on.

His pet lambs will meet him on the way,—
His pet lambs will meet him on the way,—
His pet lambs will meet him on the way,—
They go marching on.
Chorus: Glory Hally Hallelujah! Glory Hally, Hallelujah!
Glory hally, Hallelujah!
They go marching on!

They will hang Jeff Davis to a tree!
They will hang Jeff Davis to a tree!
They will hang Jeff Davis to a tree!
As they march along!
Chorus: Glory Hally, Hallelujah! Glory Hally, Hallelujah!
Glory Hally, Hallelujah
As they march along!

Now, three rousing cheers for the Union!
Now, three rousing cheers for the Union!
Now, three rousing cheers for the Union!
As we are marching on!
Chorus: Glory Hally, Hallelujah! Glory Hally, Hallelujah!
Glory Hally, Hallelujah!
Hip, hip, hip, hip, Hurrah!

A political cartoon of 1860, showing a Negro in Lincoln's corner, a Southern planter seconding Douglas.

Lincoln Runs
for President

"A house divided against itself cannot stand," declared Abraham Lincoln in accepting the Republican nomination for Senator from Illinois in the spring of 1858. "I believe this government cannot endure permanently half-slave and half-free. I do not expect the Union to be dissolved—I do not expect the house to fall—but I do expect it will cease to be divided. It will become all one thing, or all the other."

In his series of seven celebrated debates in the fall of 1858 with his Democratic opponent, Stephen A. Douglas, author of the Kansas-Nebraska bill, Lincoln said, "You say slavery is wrong; but don't you constantly argue that this is not the right place to oppose it? . . . It must not be opposed in politics, because that will make a fuss; it must not be opposed in the pulpit, because it is not religion. Then where is the place to oppose it?"

Lincoln lost this election to Douglas but won wide support in the West and North for his resistance to the spread of slavery. Early in 1860, politicians in the deep South openly threatened that the election of a "Black Republican" would be grounds for secession. As the presidential campaign began, the Democratic Party split into two factions at Charleston.

The extreme pro-slavery elements later nominated for President John Breckenridge of Kentucky, while the regular Democratic nomination went to Stephen A. Douglas. In Chicago, the Republicans nominated Abraham Lincoln on a platform which, though it did not call for the end of slavery, stood resolutely for no further extension of the slave system.

Abraham Lincoln riding through the streets of Springfield, after his nomination.

As I would not be a slave, so I would not be a master. This ex:presses my idea of democracy.— Whatever differs from this, to the extent of the difference, is no democracy.—

A. Lincoln.—

E UNION MUST AND

SHALL BE PRESERVED

FREE SPEECH,
FREE HOMES,
FREE TERRITORY.

PROTECTION
TO
AMERICAN
INDUSTRY

FOR PRESIDENT
ABRAHAM LINCOLN
OF ILLINOIS

FOR VICE PRESIDENT
HANNIBAL HAMLIN
OF MAINE

Y W.H.REASE

COR 4TH & CHESTNUT STs. PHILADA.

A Republican poster of the 1860 campaign.

A cartoon picturing Lincoln as a stableboy attempting to please jockey William Yancey, the Alabama secessionist. Lincoln had stated to the South that the Republicans would not "directly or indirectly interfere with their slaves."

"House Divided"

Southerners called the Republican Party a "party of destruction and rebellion," while Democratic cartoonists pictured Lincoln as one of the ugliest men on earth. Republicans countered by saying that if all the ugly men of the country voted for Lincoln, he would certainly become President. The campaign was a bitter one. But on November 6, 1860, Lincoln was elected President. He had won a majority of the electoral vote but only about 40 per cent of the popular vote. Six weeks after the Lincoln victory, South Carolina, at a popular convention called by the state legislature, voted unanimously to sever all connections with the Union, to adopt a flag of its own and to take over all federal buildings. There was dancing in the streets of Charleston, and within a few weeks Mississippi, Florida, Alabama, Georgia, Louisiana and Texas had all declared themselves no longer a part of the United States. Under the doctrine of states' rights, long preached by John

C. Calhoun and other Southern leaders, they felt they had the right to withdraw from the Union.

In February, 1861, at Montgomery, Alabama, a provisional government was established, called the "Confederate States of America," and Jefferson Davis of Mississippi was elected President. In Washington, James Buchanan began to think of himself as "the last President of the United States," as many Southern residents of the capital packed their bags and left for the Confederacy. Garrisonian abolitionists, who had long felt the slave-holding South had no right in the Union, agreed with Wendell Phillips when he said, "Let the South march off with flags and trumpets, and we will speed the parting guest . . . and rejoice that she has departed."

In such a climate of defiance and disunity, on March 4, 1861, Lincoln took the oath of office. On April 12 Confederate forces bombarded Fort Sumter. The Civil War had begun.

In December, 1860, a mob broke up a meeting commemorating the anniversary of John Brown's execution. Frederick Douglass was flung down the staircase of Tremont Temple in Boston. "Liberty is meaningless," Douglass said, "where the right to utter one's thoughts and opinions has ceased to exist."

A newspaper cartoon showing the Negro supporting the cotton economy of the Confederacy.

Secessionists unfurl the first states' rights flag before the South Carolina capital.

Nicholas Biddle was sixty-five when he became an unofficial member of the Washington artillerists.

Work, Yes—Fight, No

During the first year of the Civil War participation by Negroes was limited almost entirely to non-military service. The government feared that the border states might join the rebels if Negroes were enlisted and also that white troops might refuse to fight alongside colored troops. The Negroes, for whom, to a large degree, the war was being fought, could not themselves engage in the fighting.

From the beginning, men of color stood ready to enlist and in Boston, Providence, New York and other cities, Negroes, at their own expense, organized and equipped drill units. But in response to the offers to volunteer, the War Department replied that it had "no intention to call into the service of the Government any colored soldiers."

Negro activities were limited to labor behind the lines as teamsters, camp attendants, waiters and cooks. However, the first man to be honorably discharged from the Union Army shortly after the war started was a Negro. Without mentioning his col-ored blood, this man, who had a very light complexion, enlisted in New York City. But, after a few days, his race was discovered and he was handed his walking papers.

The first Negro in uniform to be wounded in the Civil War was Nicholas Biddle, an escaped slave who settled in Pottsville, Pennsylvania. Two days after the call for volunteers Biddle attached himself to a troop unit heading for the defense of Washington, and the white soldiers gave him a uniform. As the company marched through the slave-holding city of Baltimore on April 18, 1861, taunted by white onlookers in the streets, the one Negro among them was singled out for abuse. The rabble turned into a jeering, stone-throwing mob and Biddle was felled by a rock which cut his scalp to the bone, leaving blood on the cobblestones as his white comrades supported him. The next day thousands of Balti-moreans mobbed a Massachusetts regiment in transit and four white soldiers were killed.

Negro hostlers attached to General Pleaston's cavalry brigade.

Workers at a government blacksmith shop.

Dock workers unloading Army supplies.

Negroes converting cotton to Union use at Port Royal, South Carolina.

Freedom

Negro hucksters trade with soldiers at Beaufort.

At Bull Run, on Virginia soil about thirty miles outside of Washington, in the first great conflict of the Civil War the Union troops were routed and the Confederates headed into Maryland. A blockade of the entire Eastern seaboard had proved successful, and by the end of 1861 the Northern Armies had invaded portions of the coast as far as the Sea Islands of South Carolina. These islands were used as supply stations for the blockading fleet. On the island of Hilton Head military headquarters were set up. To these islands, especially to Hilton Head and Port Royal, on which the town of Beaufort was located, flocked thousands of runaway slaves to cast their lot with the Yankees.

By September an alarmed Confederacy estimated that as many as 20,000 slaves, to the value of $15,000,000, had absconded to the enemy in that region. Sometimes the refugees brought useful information to the Union lines. Familiar with the countryside, many became foragers for the troops, bringing in fruits, vegetables, chickens and pigs, which they sold to the soldiers. When Army hospitals and barracks had to be built, Negroes went into the

PACKING COTTON

Runaway slaves became a valuable labor reserve for the government.

through Invasion

forests and felled trees for lumber. By night, from neighboring Confederate plantations, they stole horses, mules and cows, which they turned over to the Yankees.

One ex-slave, who knew where a large number of bales of cotton had been hidden up the river, was provided with a boat and some soldiers to secure it. The cache turned out to be worth several thousand dollars. The federal government's naval blockade had made it more and more difficult for the South to ship its cotton to England. By 1862 its export was cut from $100,000,000 down to about $4,000,000.

Meanwhile, Union troops continued southward to the mouth of the Savannah River and into Florida as far as St. Augustine. The Department of the South was created. During the second year of the war, Lee's attempt to invade the North was checked at Antietam; Nashville fell and General Grant captured Fort Donelson on the Cumberland River, forcing the Confederates out of Kentucky and western Tennessee; and General Butler entered New Orleans. In these areas, too, in ever-increasing numbers, bondsmen flocked to the Union camps.

Male "washerwomen" with the Army of the Shenandoah.

Education behind the Lines

Meanwhile in the East, as Douglass and others were trying to get the government to enlist Negro troops, the old abolitionist societies had begun to support the war effort with vigor. From their groups and from the American Missionary Association, with Lewis Tappan as treasurer, grew various movements to aid the Negroes who found themselves within the Union lines in the liberated areas. Churches and clubs were persuaded to send clothing, medicine, seed, farming tools and other necessary items to the Negroes.

And, of far greater import, teachers were sent to the South. A free Negro woman, Mary S. Peake, with the help of Lewis C. Lockwood, set up a school at Hampton, Virginia, in the fall of 1861. The following spring some fifty men and women sailed from New York to teach in the Port Royal area and set up thirty schools in the Sea Islands for the black followers of the Union Armies, the workers and their families. When Vincent Colyer opened a school in two small Negro churches in New Bern, North Carolina, more than 600 Negroes appeared the first night. During the day Colyer taught poor whites. In Lawrence, Kansas, a night school was started with volunteer white teachers.

Freedmen's relief societies came into being in many Northern cities to raise funds for books and teachers' salaries, as well as to help supply the physical needs of the former slaves, many of whom reached federal territory in rags and weak with hunger. These latter needs were temporary, but the need for educational opportunities grew. The foundation laid by the abolitionists in this field marked the beginnings of free education in many Southern communities. And the specialized training given some of the escaped slaves as mechanics, gunsmiths and hospital orderlies gave them skills for earning a decent living the rest of their lives.

Teamsters with General Butler at Bermuda Hundred.

Negroes mounting a Confederate cannon at Fort Sumter. Slave labor made a vast contribution to the Southern cause in the field, at fortifications and in factories.

Dock laborers at a Southern port in Union hands.

Negro cooks were highly valued by Union soldiers, as many were skilled in the arts of seasoning.

When James Hopkinson, owner of an Edisto Island plantation, fled South Carolina in 1862, he left some fifty slaves behind.

Contrabands *(right)*, heading for a federal encampment in Virginia.

Come back here, you black rascal.

Can't come back nohow, massa; Dis chile's CONTRABAN.

FORT MONROE

A cartoon *(left)*, showing slaves fleeing toward the "freedom fort," as Fortress Monroe became known among them.

Contraband

Those Negroes who were liberated as their masters fled before the advancing Union troops or who, of their own free will, escaped to the government lines were referred to by a single word whose first usage was ascribed to General Benjamin Butler, commander of Fortress Monroe, Virginia. When a Confederate officer came under a flag of truce demanding the return of three slaves, General Butler told him that since Virginia had withdrawn from the Union and had therefore become a foreign country, "I shall detain the Negroes as contraband of war."

Butler argued that since the rebels were using slaves to erect fortifications and mount batteries, it was a question of whether these three Negroes should be used for or against the government. Butler ruled they should not be used against his forces, and he kept the runaway slaves at Fortress Monroe as confiscated articles of war.

Within a week almost a hundred runaways sought sanctuary with General Butler—as contraband. They stole skiffs and sailed down the James River in the dark to Hampton Roads. All up and down the coast in the months that followed, Union warships were busy picking up at sea boatloads of runaway Negroes.

Since there was no government ruling on what to do with such Negroes, each commander did as he wished. Some protected them, others ignored them and some returned them to slavery even though recognizing their value to the Confederate war effort. But gradually the official opinion in Washington grew that since slaves were military assets to the enemy, those escaping should not be turned back. Finally, it was prohibited to return them.

The Union welcomed "contraband" as military laborers. Negroes became scouts, guides, spies, cooks and hospital workers, as well as blacksmiths and mule-drivers for government troops. Walking great distances and swimming rivers, braving dangers to escape, they brought with them many qualities useful to advancing armies. On the other hand, they brought problems which were often most difficult to cope with—for women and children came, too, as well as the ill, the aged and infirm. Besides, officially, the war was not a war to free the slaves but simply to preserve the Union. Yet hardly had the war begun than Union troops found themselves also liberators.

A prayer meeting in a contraband camp.

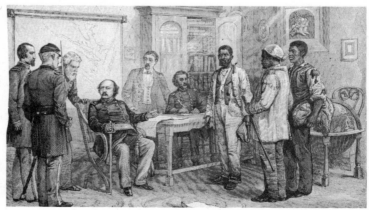

General Ben Butler (right) receiving slaves as "contraband of war."

Negro crewmen of the Confederate gunboat *Planter*: Robert Smalls (*rear*), William Morrison (*left*), A. Gradine (*right*) and John Smalls.

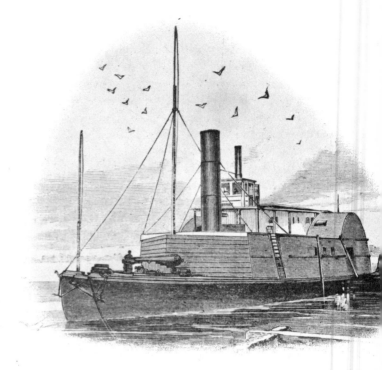

Federal distribution of captured clothing to needy contrabands.

Jefferson Davis' slaves arriving within the Union lines.

Slaves Deliver

One of the most amazing escapes from Confederate to Union jurisdiction was led by the young South Carolina slave Robert Smalls. Smalls was a seaman on the *Planter*, a former cotton steamer which the Confederates had converted into a gunboat. Its crew was colored, its captain and mates white.

One spring night in 1862, when the white officers were sleeping ashore at their homes in Charleston, Smalls smuggled his wife, his children, his sister-in-law and his brother's wife and child aboard at midnight. He fired the boiler, hoisted the Confederate flag and just before dawn steamed out to the open sea. There he hauled down the Confederate colors and hoisted a white flag of truce as he came within sight of the block-

Negro children being fed at Hilton Head.

a Prize of War

ade vessels of the United States Navy. When Union sailors boarded the *Planter* at sunrise they found Smalls and his Negro crew, who promptly turned the ship over to the Union as their gift from the Confederacy. This daring exploit was widely publicized in the North. Congress voted Smalls a sizable sum of money for his contraband and Lincoln signed the appropriation.

That same year in Mississippi, when Jefferson Davis' plantation fell within federal lines, the President of the Confederacy lost a sizable amount of black contraband to the Union encampment at Chickasaw Bayou. By this time the government had set up camps from Washington to Memphis to care for such refugees, to feed and clothe them and to see that they were assigned work.

Contrabands in the wake of Sherman's army.

Unofficial Fighters

On Hilton Head, in the spring of 1862, a Negro minister, Abram Murchison, at the suggestion of the Union general David Hunter, called together a group of Negroes to ask how many would volunteer for fighting service. Every man stepped forward and from their enthusiasm was born the First South Carolina Volunteer Regiment under Colonel Fessenden. In the late summer of that year one of its companies was sent to an island off the Georgia coast for patrol duty. There it was learned that some former slaves, in an attempt to capture some rebel guerrilla fighters, had lost their leader in a skirmish. Named John Brown, he was the first Negro to die in combat in the Civil War. This unit, with the men ragged and still unpaid after three months of service, was disbanded without ever having been officially mustered into the Army.

Another such luckless group was the First Regiment of Kansas Colored Volunteers under General Jim Lane, formed in the fall of 1862 in defiance of the officials in Washington. They saw action twice against rebel guerrilla fighters. On the Osage River in Missouri one of their soldiers was killed and sev-

eral were wounded, battling some 600 of the enemy. They, too, had gone unpaid for months as their commander sought to persuade the Secretary of War to make their standing official, were ordered to disband.

In New Orleans, however, when General Ben Butler, without sanction from Washington and acting entirely on his own, issued a call for colored volunteers in August, 1862, the response was enthusiastic and the First Regiment Louisiana Native Guards was formed. Composed of free men of color, many of them French-speaking, this became the first Negro unit actually mustered into the Union Armies and for the duration of the war it was used to guard the approaches to New Orleans.

In November, the formerly disbanded and ill-treated contraband regiment of the First South Carolina Volunteers was mustered in. Shortly thereafter the First Kansas Colored Regiment was given official standing, becoming the initial all-colored regiment in a Northern area. But the bar to the general enlistment of Negroes remained until the proclamation of an eventful document in January, 1863. The President put his hand and seal to their freedom warrant.

South Carolina Negroes embarking for Hilton Head.

Excitement at New Bern when Negroes learn that colored troop units may be formed.

Dress parade of the first South Carolina Volunteer Regiment at Hilton Head.

A Negro regiment receiving the colors.

The Emancipation Proclamation

January 1, 1863

". . . On the first day of January, in the year of our Lord one thousand eight hundred and sixty-three, all persons held as slaves within any State, or designated part of a State, the people Whereof shall then be in rebellion against the United States, shall be then, thenceforward, and forever free; and the Executive Government of the United States, including the military and naval authority thereof, will recognize and maintain the freedom of such persons, and will do no act or acts to repress such persons, or any of them, in any efforts they may make for their actual freedom. . . . And I further declare and make known that such persons of suitable condition will be received into the armed service of the United States to garrison forts, positions, stations and other places, and to man vessels of all sorts in paid service. And upon this act, sincerely believed to be an act of justice, warranted by the Constitution upon military necessity, I invoke the considerate judgment of mankind and the gracious favor of Almighty God. In witness whereof, I have hereunto set my hand, and caused the seal of the United States to be affixed. Done at the City of Washington, this first day of January, in the year of our Lord one thousand eight hundred and sixty-three, and of the independence of the United States the eighty-seventh."

— A. Lincoln

A Union soldier in a Negro cabin in the South, reading the Emancipation Proclamation, which Lincoln had issued as a military measure against the rebel states. In Boston's Tremont Temple the audience listened to the Proclamation read aloud, then sang:

"Sound the loud timbrel
O'er Egypt's dark sea;
Jehovah hath triumphed,
His people are free."

At the Port Royal encampment of the First South Carolina Volunteers, Negro voices chorused:

"My country, 'tis of thee,
Sweet land of liberty,
Of thee I sing . . ."

Volunteers line up outside a recruiting office.

"Men of Color, to Arms!"

"From East to West, from North to South, the sky is written all over, NOW OR NEVER. *Liberty won by white men would lose half its luster. Who would be free, themselves must strike the blow. Better even die free, than to live slaves.* This is the sentiment of every brave colored man amongst us . . . Remember Denmark Vesey of Charleston; remember Nathaniel Turner of South Hampton; remember Shields Green and Copeland, who followed noble John Brown and fell as glorious martyrs for the cause of the slave. Remember that in a contest with oppression, the Almighty has no attribute which can take sides with oppressors."

— Frederick Douglass, Rochester, March 21, 1863

COME AND JO

Presentation of the colors to the 20th Colored Infantry, New York, March 5, 1864.

Company A of the First South Carolina Volunteers taking the of Allegiance at Beaufort.

MEN OF COLOR, TO ARMS! NOW OR NEVER!

This is our Golden Moment. The Government of the United States calls for every Able-Bodied Colored Man to enter the Army for the THREE YEARS' SERVICE, and join in fighting the Battles of Liberty and the Union. A new era is open to us. For generations we have suffered under the horrors of slavery, outrage and wrong; our manhood has been denied, our citizenship blotted out, our souls seared and burned, our spirits cowed and crushed, and the hopes of the future of our race involved in doubts and darkness. But now the whole aspect of our relations to the white race is changed. Now therefore is our most precious moment. Let us Rush to Arms! **Fail Now and Our Race is Doomed** on this the soil of our birth. We must now awake, arise, or be forever fallen. If we value Liberty, if we wish to be free in this land, if we love our country, if we love our families, our children, our homes, we must strike NOW while the Country calls: must rise up in the dignity of our manhood, and show by our own right arms that we are worthy to be freemen. Our enemies have made the country believe that we are craven cowards, without soul, without manhood, without the spirit of soldiers. Shall we die with this stigma resting on our graves? Shall we leave this inheritance of shame to our children? No! A thousand times No! **We WILL Rise!** The alternative is upon us; let us rather die freemen than live to be slaves. What is life without liberty? We say that we have manhood—now is the time to prove it. A nation or a people that cannot fight may be pitied, but cannot be respected. If we would be regarded *Men*, if we would forever **SILENCE THE TONGUE OF CALUMNY,** of prejudice and hate; let us rise NOW and fly to arms! We have seen what **Valor and Heroism** our brothers displayed at **PORT HUDSON and at MILLIKEN'S BEND**; though they are just from the galling, poisoning grasp of slavery, they have startled the world by the most exalted heroism. If they have proved themselves heroes, can not we prove ourselves men? **ARE FREEMEN LESS BRAVE THAN SLAVES?** More than a Million White Men have left Comfortable Homes and joined the Armies of the Union to save their Country; cannot we leave ours, and swell the hosts of the Union, to save our liberties, vindicate our manhood, and deserve well of our Country?

MEN OF COLOR! All Races of Men—the Englishman, the Irishman, the Frenchman, the German, the American, have been called to assert their claim to freedom and a manly character, by an appeal to the sword. The day that has seen an enslaved race in arms, has, in all history, seen their last trial. We can now see that **OUR LAST OPPORTUNITY HAS COME!** If we are not lower in the scale of humanity than Englishmen, Irishmen, white Americans and other races, we can show it now.

MEN OF COLOR! BROTHERS and FATHERS! WE APPEAL TO YOU! By all your concern for yourselves and your liberties, by all your regard for God and Humanity, by all your desire for Citizenship and Equality before the law, by all your love for the Country, to stop at no subterfuges, listen to nothing that shall deter you from rallying for the Army. Come forward, and at once Enroll your Names for the **Three Years' Service. STRIKE NOW,** and you are henceforth and forever **FREEMEN!**

E. D. Bassett,	John W. Price,	Rev. J. Boulden
Wm. D. Forten,	Augustus Dorsey,	Rev. J. Asher,
Frederick Douglass,	Rev. Stephen Smith,	Rev. J. C. Gibb
Wm. Whipper,	N. W. Depee,	Daniel George,
D. D. Turner,	Dr. J. H. Wilson,	Robert M. Adg
Jas. McCrummell,	J. W. Cassey,	Henry M. Crop
A. S. Cassey,	P. J. Armstrong,	Rev. J. B. Ree
A. M. Green,	J. W. Simpson,	Rev. J. A. Will
J. W. Page,	Rev. J B. Trusty,	Rev. A. L. Stan
L. R. Seymour,	S. Morgan Smith,	Thomas J. Bow
Rev. J. Underdue,	Wm. E. Gipson,	Elijah J. Davis

A Negro recruiting poster.

A Negro soldier on picket duty.

Negro Recruits

A rifle company in front of an Army barracks.

A federal military band.

here were Negroes among the crewmen of the Union warship *Monitor*.
ne-fourth of the Union Navy's sailors were Negroes. Four won the Navy's
ledal of Honor.

legro and white sailors on the deck of the U. S. gunboat *Mendota*.
he mess and quarters were shared by all, regardless of color.

Captain P. B. S. Pinch-
back, Second Louisiana
Volunteers.

Major A. T. Augusta,
senior surgeon at Camp
Stanton, Maryland.

Lieutenant W. H. Du-
pree, 55th Massachusetts
Volunteers.

Lieutenant James Mon-
roe Trotter, 55th Massa-
chusetts Volunteers.

Harriet Tubman acted as a nurse, scout and intelligence agent for the Union Armies in the South. General Saxton reported she "made many a raid inside
the enemy lines, displaying remarkable courage, zeal
and fidelity."

Major Martin R. Delany, 104th Regiment at
Charleston, a graduate of the Harvard Medical School and the first Negro field officer
to serve in the Civil War.

Colonel Robert Gould Shaw commanded the 54th Massachusetts Regiment.

Sergeant William H. Carney declared, "The old flag never touched the ground, boys."

54th Massachusetts Colored Regiment charging Fort Wagner, South Carolina, July 18, 1863. Charles and Lewis Douglass, sons of Frederick Douglass, served with this group.

Negro Troops in the

A Negro guard asks General Grant to throw away his cigar before entering an Army storehouse.

The First South Carolina Volunteers repelling a Confederate attack near the Doby River in Georgia.

Assault of the Louisiana Colored Volunteers on the Confederate breastworks at Port Hudson. Louisiana, May 27, 1863. This was the first major battle in which Negro troops took part.

Union Army

Bringing in a captured Confederate battery.

The Battle of Milliken's Bend on the Mississippi River, June 6, 1863, in which a Negro soldier took his former master prisoner.

Cavalrymen bringing in Confederate prisoners.

Dark Days for Dark Men

At the assault on Port Hudson the Negro troops s[...] fered thirty-seven dead, 116 missing, 155 wounded. [...] the battle of Milliken's Bend "dead Negroes lined t[...] ditch inside of the parapet, or levee," and almost h[...] the colored unit was killed or wounded. There we[...] 247 Negro casualties at Fort Wagner and, accordi[...] to the New York *Tribune*, "the ocean beach was crow[...] ed with the dead, the dying and the wounded." At F[...] Pillow 300 Negroes were massacred, five buried ali[...]

"Then we saw the lightning, and that was the gu[...] and then we heard the rain falling, and that was t[...] drops of blood falling; and when we came to get in t[...] crops, it was dead men that we reaped," so Harr[...] Tubman described a Civil War battle. As a nurse [...] dark men in those dark days, Harriet Tubman tend[...] hundreds of wounded and comforted the dying fr[...] the Carolinas to Florida.

In the North, on the civilian front, there were som[...] times dark days, too. In July, 1863, in New York, wh[...] mobs, resenting a conscription law that favored the ri[...] and believing they were being ordered to fight on beh[...] of Negroes, whose liberation might threaten their jo[...] destroyed Manhattan's draft headquarters; set up[...] every colored person who crossed their paths, beat a[...] killed hundreds of them, destroyed the Colored O[...] phan Asylum and burned Negro homes and shops. T[...] furor lasted four days. Similar rioting took place [...] Boston, Albany and Chicago. In Cleveland almost [...] hundred Negroes were killed and in Detroit a large p[...] of the colored section was burned.

Meanwhile, the Confederacy had stated that it wou[...] not treat captured Negro soldiers as prisoners, th[...] their white officers would be put to death and "all Neg[...] slaves captured in arms" would be returned to bondag[...] But Negroes, runaway and free, continued to enlist [...] the Union forces once they were permitted to do s[...] even though their monthly pay was only a little mo[...] than half that of white soldiers. As a protest against t[...] discrimination, the 54th Massachusetts Regime[...] served for a year without drawing any pay whatsoev[...] Nevertheless it fought so gallantly at Fort Wagner th[...] it was almost wiped out there—where their Comman[...] er Shaw was killed. He was buried with his Negro s[...]

ANDREWS OF VIRGINIA & OTHER RINGLEADERS

HANGING A NEGRO IN CLARKSON ST.

BURNING OF THE COLORED ORPHAN ASYLUM

Anti-Negro draft riots in New York, 1863.

180

First South Carolina Colored Regiment attacked by Confederate bloodhounds at Pocatalago Bridge, October 23, 1862.

s by a contemptuous Confederate commander, who
ght that such a burial would somehow humiliate
Boston abolitionist after death.

at white commanders like Colonel Thomas Went-
h Higginson continued to lead their troops into
e. Sometimes they marched, singing a song Julia
d Howe had written, to the tune of "John Brown's
y":

> Mine eyes have seen the glory
> Of the coming of the Lord.
> He is trampling out the vintage
> Where the grapes of wrath are stored.
> He hath loosed the fateful lightning
> Of his terrible swift sword . . . .

Confederate generals Johnson and Stewart as prisoners under a Negro guard.

ing Union prisoners being fed by slaves in their master's
behind the rebel lines.

The massacre at Fort Pillow, April 12, 1864, where Confederates killed all captured Negro soldiers.

The soldiers are mustered out and allowed to return to their homes.

The War Ends

In the fall of 1863 Sherman began his devastating march through Georgia. On April 2, 1865, the capital of the Confederacy, Richmond, was abandoned to the Union forces. The government again occupied Fort Sumter. On April 9 General Lee surrendered to General Grant at Appomattox. And on May 10 the rebel president Jefferson Davis was captured and imprisoned at Fortress Monroe, the former haven of slave contrabands. Although the war was over, the 62nd U. S. Colored Infantry engaged in a minor skirmish in Texas on May 13 with recalcitrant rebels. Sergeant Crocket, a Negro, is believed to have been the last man to shed blood in the Civil War.

When Richmond fell, President Lincoln himself went to the city by boat and entered it on foot, surrounded, as he walked through the streets, by weeping Negroes to whom his name had come to mean "Saviour." Ten days later, Lincoln was dead, assassinated by a fanatic actor who wished to avenge the cause of the South. Some 186,000 Negroes enlisted in the Union Army: 93,000 from the seceded states, 40,000 from the border states, 52,000 from the free states. At least 38,000 Negro soldiers died to save the Republic and to put an end to slavery.

s the federal Army entered Richmond, white persons fled indoors, aving only Negroes in the streets to greet the government troops.

Lincoln enters Richmond on April 4, 1865.

ncoln's funeral procession, April 19, 1865.

183

On the day the Thirteenth Amendment was passed in the House of Representatives, there was great excitement, wild cheering and applause in the spectators' galleries and the women waved their handkerchiefs. At a meeting of the American Anti-Slavery Society in New York that spring, Garrison called for the society's dissolution, declaring it to be "an absurdity to maintain an anti-slavery society after slavery is killed." But Phillips did not agree with him, feeling that, for the Negro, civil equality and equality before the law were still to be achieved.

"Set Free"

In his second inaugural address Abraham Lincoln said that at the beginning of the Civil War, "One-eighth of the whole population were colored slaves, not distributed generally over the Union, but localized in the Southern part of it. These slaves constituted a peculiar and powerful interest. All knew that this interest was, somehow, the cause of the war. . . ." Lincoln's Emancipation Proclamation of 1863 had been issued during the war as a military edict affecting *only* the slaves in those portions of the commonwealth then in rebellion.

It was the Thirteenth Amendment to the Constitution which finally abolished slavery everywhere in the United States. Before his death Lincoln had urged Congress to take such action. On January 31, 1865, the Thirteenth Amendment passed the House of Representatives, was ratified during the year by the required number of states and on December 18 was proclaimed in effect. Slavery was now no longer legal anywhere in America. The long fight of the white abolitionists, the black runaways, the Negro and white Underground Railroad workers had at last reached its fruition. The Thirteenth Amendment declared, "Neither slavery nor involuntary servitude, except as a punishment for crime whereof the party shall have been duly convicted, shall exist within the United States, or any place subject to their jurisdiction. Congress shall have power to enforce this article by appropriate legislation."

The struggle that had begun ostensibly over states' rights, and only secondarily over slavery, had culminated in the freedom of the slave—at first partially, during the conflict at arms, then finally, through political action, thus vindicating the faith of Frederick Douglass in the American Constitution.

As for the slaves themselves, newly set free, a new world came into existence and a new way of life began. Eventually each man had to stand on his own and there were grave problems in the South for both former master and former slave. "What I likes best, to be slave or free?" said one old Negro. "Well, it's this way. In slavery I owns nothing and never owns nothing. In freedom I owns the house and raise the family. All that causes me worriation—and is slavery I has no worriation—*but I takes the freedom.*"

Part Four

UP FROM SLAVERY

1863-1900

"YOU BEEN SET FREE" "When freedom came, my mama said Old Master called all of 'em to his house, and he said, 'You all free, we ain't got nothing to do with you no more. Go on away. We don't whup you no more, go on your way.' My mama said they go on off, then they come back and stand around, just looking at him and Old Mistress. They give 'em something to eat and he say, 'Go on away, you don't belong to us no more. You been freed.' They go away and they kept coming back. They didn't have no place to go and nothing to eat. From what she said, they had a terrible time. She said it was bad times. Some took sick and had no 'tention and died. Seemed like it was four or five years before they got to places they could live. They all got scattered . . . Old Master every time they go back say, 'You all go on away. You been set free. You have to look out for yourselves now.'"

— An ex-slave's account in *Lay My Burden Down: A Folk History of Slavery*, Ben Botkin, 1945

Booker T. Washington.

The Freedmen's Bureau

"The Yankees freed you; now, let the Yankees feed you," was the dominant attitude of the former Confederacy toward the Negroes. "When the Hebrews were emancipated," said Frederick Douglass, "they were given three acres of ground upon which they could live and make a living. But not so when our slaves were emancipated. They were sent away empty-handed, without money, without friends and without a foot of land to stand upon."

Rootless Negroes roamed the Southern roads like bands of gypsies. "A laborless, landless and homeless class," Lincoln termed them. Caught "in a hazy realm between bondage and freedom," after a lifetime of slavery they received no recompense for past labor, just as the slave-holders received no recompense for their loss, through emancipation, of some two billion dollars in human property. The South was a shambles, its major cities gutted or shelled, its farms neglected, crops ungathered, banks closed, Confederate money worthless and about one-third of its male citizens killed or wounded.

For both black and white men there was a prospect of desolation and starvation, but the immediate future looked bleaker for the Negroes. To cope with this situation, in March, 1865, Congress set up the Freedmen's Bureau under the Army.

A Negro cabin.

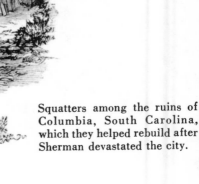

Squatters among the ruins of Columbia, South Carolina, which they helped rebuild after Sherman devastated the city.

"Slabtown," built largely of barrel staves by ex-slaves near Hampton, Virginia.

Liberated Negroes lining up for aid at the office of the Freedmen's Bureau in Memphis, Tennessee.

Major-General Oliver O. Howard was assigned to head the Freedmen's Bureau.

By 1867 almost every county in the South had at least one school for Negroes, attended by both old and young.

A New England schoolma'am holds primary classes in Vicksburg, Mississippi.

Free Schools for All

Against violent Southern opposition, the Freedmen's Bureau, supported by federal troops, distributed rations and medicine to both Negroes and poor whites. It attempted, without much success, for lack of land, to resettle Negroes in rural areas, found them jobs, supervised work contracts and sought fair wages, acted as the Negroes' friend at court or set up courts of its own. It built or aided in the creation of more than 4,000 schools, with some 9,000 teachers and almost 250,000 Negro students. This was the first widespread free public school system in the South and led to free education for whites as well as Negroes. Only one Negro in ten among the newly freed could read and write.

Encouraged by the Freedmen's Bureau, but largely through the efforts of the American Missionary Society, the Baptist Home Mission Board, the Methodists, the Quakers and the Presbyterian Synod, thousands of Northern white men and women came into the South, some into communities so hostile that they daily risked their lives, to teach the Negroes. The colored churches also sent teachers and money to their brethren there.

The Abraham Lincoln School for Freedmen in New Orleans.

Many primary schools and colleges were set up, among others—Shaw University (1865); Fisk (1866); Talladega and Morehouse College (1867); Clark College (1869). In Washington, D. C. in 1867 the government granted a charter to Howard University for the education of Negro youth. By the time the Freedmen's Bureau was abolished in 1870, 21 per cent of the newly freed Negroes were literate.

The Penn school on St. Helena Island, South Carolina, established by the Quakers. Sometimes former rebels burned Negro schools and chased the white teachers away but—with abolitionist zeal—they often returned in spite of danger.

191

Chaplain Warren of the Freedmen's Bureau at Vicksburg marries a Negro couple.

A Negro policeman in New Orleans in 1873.

A colored orator addresses a pre-election meeting on the steps of the State House in Richmond.

For the First Time

In petitioning President Andrew Johnson for the right to vote, the Negroes of North Carolina included in their appeal of 1865 this statement: "In many respects we are poor and greatly despised by our fellowmen; but we are rich in the possession of the liberty brought us, and our wives and our little ones." For it was now true that *for the first time in their lives* Negro wives belonged to husbands and the little ones, the children of these former slaves, belonged to their parents—not to some master—and parents could keep their own offspring with them. Now marriages among Negroes could be solemnized and legalized. And when Negroes worked they were due to be paid, and the money received was *theirs* to learn to budget, spend wisely or squander as they wished. They could go to town from the farm and come back with gifts for their children—*for the first time in their lives.*

Henry Ossian Flipper, who was born a slave in Georgia, was graduated from the U. S. Military Academy at West Point in 1877.

Plantation workers after a pay-day visit to the general store.

Free workers on a plantation receiving their first pay.

The first petit jury impaneled to try Jefferson Davis, May, 1867.

Walking the railroad ties westward to Louisiana and Texas in search of work.

First Mixed Jury

"We'll hang Jeff Davis to a sour apple tree," the soldier of the Union Army had sung to the tune of "John Brown's Body." This never happened but when, for the trial of the ex-President of the Confederacy in Richmond, the first mixed jury ever drawn in the South was impaneled, half of the petit jurors were Negroes. But the trial was postponed. The second process ended in disagreement. Released on bail, Jefferson Davis lived for twenty years and was not tried again. But the fact that Negroes served on juries further increased bitter resentment against them in the South. Such resentment caused many colored people to migrate to the North and West in search of a less hostile environment.

Meeting of freedmen on Dr. Fuller's plantation on St. Helena Island, 1866.

Colored immigrant workers embark from Richmond.

Soldiers distributing rations to needy whites and Negroes.

Reconstruction

It was Lincoln's opinion that the states of the South should be considered as never having left the Union since they had no Constitutional right to secede. But with this lenient concept a strong Republican group in Congress, headed by Thaddeus Stevens and Charles Sumner, did not agree. They held that the Southern slave-holders had repudiated the Union and its Constitution, had been acknowledged as belligerents and that under the laws of war they should be made to pay for their dereliction. Complicating the political picture of a devastated South, with some 4,000,000 Negroes suddenly torn from generations of slavery, was the wartime birth of a powerful industrialism in the North. How could a South, long used to slavery's ways, be rebuilt upon an economy of free labor? How could the seceded states be brought back into the Union without handing over political power to the ex-Confederates, who conceivably might turn history's clock back again? What was the best way to help the new freedmen?

A conflict developed rapidly between President Johnson and Congress over Reconstruction policy. Johnson granted pardons to ex-Confederates so liberally and restored home rule in the South so rapidly that Republicans feared the revival of a slave-minded Democratic Party. Meeting in December, 1865, Congress moved to take over the

Frederick Douglass petitioned President Johnson and Congress for protection of freedmen's rights.

Freedmen discussing their political rights.

Charles Sumner of Massachusetts, the foremost champion of the Negro in the Senate.

and Dissension

Reconstruction program through a Joint Committee of Fifteen, dominated by Thaddeus Stevens. Johnson vetoed the bills which would make the Freedmen's Bureau permanent and would guarantee civil rights to Negroes. When Congress overrode his vetoes Johnson took his case to the country, but in the 1866 Congressional elections overwhelming Republican majorities were elected to both houses.

Aroused by the refusal of most Southern states to ratify the Fourteenth Amendment protecting Negro citizenship, by the revival of the Black Codes of slavery days and by growing violence against the Negro, the Stevens Committee won Congressional approval for its Reconstruction Act of 1867. It divided the South into five military districts controlled by martial law, proclaimed universal manhood suffrage, required that new state constitutions be drawn up and that the Fourteenth Amendment be ratified by all states seeking admission to the Union. Whenever possible, abandoned lands were to be sold or leased to freedmen, but in the end little came of this.

The freed Negroes found themselves in possession of the ballot, counted as *whole* men now rather than three-fifths of a population. Now, they were—on paper at least—entitled as citizens to the equal protection of the country's laws.

Representative Thaddeus Stevens of Pennsylvania, a Republican leader.

vens discussing plans for Reconstruction with his committee.

Thaddeus Stevens being assisted to the Senate Chamber.

The Black Codes

To fight the postwar carpetbaggers and to block the Freedmen's Bureau's efforts to bring a measure of safety and economic security into the lives of the Southern Negroes, the white Ku Klux Klan came into being. Hooded night riders began to terrorize colored people by tarring-and-featherings, beatings and murder. To offset federal edicts, each former Confederate state had passed its own set of Black Codes.

In some localities any Negro caught without "visible means of support" could be indentured by the court to an employer whom he could not leave under pain of imprisonment. In other communities Negro orphans were bound over to white masters to work out their childhood. Curfew laws were prevalent, forcing colored citizens off the streets after sundown. Negro witnesses could not testify against whites in court as to any abuses or shortages in wages they might suffer. Negroes migrating to some states had to post bonds or be declared vagrants, subject to arrest. Other states required colored travelers to carry passes. Others prohibited assembly unless a white man were present to monitor the proceedings. Peonage was encouraged by police courts, which often sentenced Negroes to work for planters who paid their fines. And excessive fines were levied with impunity for minor offenses.

Negroes generally were prohibited from jury service and took no part in the machinery of the courts —until such flagrant infringements of freedmen's rights brought about the passage in Congress of the first civil rights bill, followed by instructions to the commanders of military districts in the South to do all possible to prevent such abuses. Such federal intervention infuriated the South. Race riots broke out. The *New York Times* reported that in Memphis in 1866 large numbers of armed citizens "commenced firing upon every Negro who made himself visible. One Negro on South Street, a quiet, inoffensive laborer, was shot down almost in front of his own cabin, and after life was extinct his body was fired into, cut and beat in a most horrible manner ... from fifteen to twenty were killed. So far as I have been able to learn, not a white man was fired upon by a Negro."

Meanwhile, everything possible was done to keep the freedmen in the South from exercising the right of suffrage. Before any election the Klan was sure to ride and the White League was organized to guard ballot boxes against black ballots.

White Leaguers keeping Negroes from the polls.

Masked Ku Kluxers in Mississippi. The Klan was formed in 186 its first Grand Wizard Confederate general Nathan Bedford Forre

The burning of a freedmen's school (*above*) during a riot in Memphis in 1866. In similar riot in New Orleans, (*left*) forty Negroes and twenty whites were killed.

Julia Hayden, a seventeen-year-old Negro schoolteacher, was murdered by the White League for being in charge of a freedmen's school in Tennessee.

Albion W. Tourgee, a North Carolina judge, wrote *A Fool's Errand*, containing documentary proof of Klan activities and organization.

The Reverend B. F. Randolph, an Oberlin graduate and a Methodist minister. A member of the South Carolina Senate, he was murdered in 1868 while on a lecture tour.

The Fourteenth and Fifteenth Amendments

John Mercer Langston, a Negro abolitionist and a Reconstruction leader, who became a Representative from Virginia.

The combined effects of the federal Civil Rights Act of 1866, the Reconstruction Act of 1867 and the ratification of the Fourteenth Amendment in 1868 brought some legal protection to Southern Negroes against former slave-holders and also inflamed the poor whites. The Civil Rights Act, which conferred rights of citizenship on the freedmen, was further bolstered by the Fourteenth Amendment: no state shall "deprive any person of life, liberty or property without due process of law."

The Reconstruction Act, having placed ten states of the South under military government, put teeth in federal edicts of Army backing. Soldiers and officials of the Freedmen's Bureau attempted to protect the Negro's right to the ballot, fair working conditions and an education but with no help from former Confederates or the Southern press. When, in 1870, the Fifteenth Amendment guaranteed Negroes the right to vote—and Negroes in large numbers duly exercised this right—that was the last straw. Animosities developed which have festered to this day.

A Southern newspaper cartoon depicting Negroes bayoneting the defenseless South, feeding from the government trough and escorting white women.

Ebenezer D. Bassett, a Reconstruction leader who had studied at Yale, was appointed United States Minister to Haiti.

Jonathan Jasper Wright served in the South Carolina Senate and as an associate justice of the State Supreme Court.

A cartoon questioning whether slavery was dead and quoting from news items describing the court sale of a convicted Negro into peonage in Maryland and the whipping of a Negro by court order in North Carolina.

Electioneering in the South, as Negroes sought public office.

The Negro in Politics

Under federal military occupation of the South some 700,000 Negroes were adding to the voting rolls. They flocked to the polls and many freedmen participated in municipal and state governments. There were black majorities in the states of Alabama, Louisiana, South Carolina, Florida and Mississippi and the Republicans took full advantage of this situation to break the former Democratic stranglehold. With the aid of some Southerners, derisively called "scalawags" by the Confederates, and the sometimes sincere, sometimes opportunistic help of Northerners, contemptuously termed "carpetbaggers," the Republican Party for a time controlled the vote within most Southern states.

The Union League, organized in the North during the war, stated that it believed "that the ballot in the hands of the Negro would be preferable to bullets in the muskets of a standing army" of occupation in the South. It supported the government in protecting Negro voters through the so-called "Force Bills" of 1870-71 which provided, among other things, for the use of federal troops at the polls. But after the last rebel state was admitted to the Union in 1870 and the last federal troops were withdrawn from the South in 1877, political retrogression began for Negroes and the terror of the more powerful Klan prevented the exercise of suffrage by the freedmen. Their political activity in the South was short-lived, but while it lasted many offices were for the first time filled by Negroes.

Because in 1868 in Alabama all Negroes who voted were threatened with the loss of their jobs, the new state constitution lacked ratification by 8,000 votes.

Negro and white poll watchers in New Orleans wearing the badges of U. S. deputy marshals, 1876.

The first municipal election held in Richmond after the Civil War.

Freedmen as Legislators

Radical members of the "reconstructed" South Carolina legislature of whom fifty were colored and thirteen white. Most of them were former slaves who learned to read and write while in office. A few Negro legislators were highly educated and notable leaders.

Lieutenant-Governor O. J. Dunn of Louisiana and colored members of the state legislature in 1868. Between 1868 and 1896, Louisiana elected 32 Negro state senators and 95 representatives.

A colored convention meets in Washington, D. C., in 1869 to discuss Reconstruction problems. The Negro churches, having grown by leaps and bounds under freedom, produced from their ranks many leaders. They housed numerous meetings and conventions concerned with civil rights and political problems.

Makers of Good Laws

Not all the Negroes in Southern politics were illiterate former bondsmen. Some had been born free. Some were highly educated. None of them voted for vindictive acts against their fellow white Southerners or former masters. Beverly Nash, addressing the Constitutional Convention of South Carolinia, said, "We recognize the Southern white man as the true friend of the black man.... In these public affairs we must unite with our white fellow-citizens." Together Negroes worked willingly with whites at law-making.

In spite of lack of political experience on the part of many Negro office-holders, the law-making bodies in the states in which they sat during Reconstruction made a number of social advances unknown before the war. Uneducated Negro legislators wanted education themselves, so they wrote into the new state constitutions provisions for free public schools. Colored men wanted equality be-

fore the law, so liberal measures upholding this concept were introduced by them and passed. The freedmen wished to maintain the federally-granted suffrage, so they saw to it that it was written into the official codes of their states, supported by provisions for representation based on population. Since they were poor, Negro law-makers proposed no property qualifications for voting or for holding office.

"They opened the ballot box and jury box to thousands of white men who had been debarred from them by lack of earthly possessions," wrote Albion W. Tourgee. "They introduced home rule in the South. They abolished the whipping post and branding iron." The new state constitutions drawn up by these Reconstruction assemblies were the most progressive the South had ever known, benefiting all citizens. Many of their provisions remain in effect today.

The Negro gallery at the Opera House in New Orleans. It was illegal to exclude persons of color from public places in the city, but they might be segregated from whites.

"The Promises of the Declaration of Independence Fulfilled," an allegorical drawing commemorating the passage of the Fifteenth Amendment to the Constitution, which guaranteed the Negro the permanent right to vote.

Negroes

The first Negro elected to the national House of Representatives was John Willis Menard of Louisiana, chosen to fill a vacancy caused by death. But his seat was challenged and he never served. The first colored Representative to be seated in Washington was Jefferson P. Long of Georgia, who served from 1869 to 1871. Between that time and 1876 thirteen other colored men were elected to the House from the Southern states.

There were two Negro Senators, both from Mississippi: Hiram Rhoades Revels, 1870-71, and Blanche Kelso Bruce, 1875-81. Revels, who was elected to fill out the uncompleted term of the rebel Jefferson Davis, served for one year. Free-born in North Carolina, he had studied at a Quaker seminary in Ohio and at Knox College. As a minister of the A. M. E. Church, Revels had been an Army chaplain in Mississippi. Bruce, following Revels in the Senate, had been a Virginia slave who escaped to the North, studied at Oberlin and later became a planter in Mississippi. In all, from the states of Mississippi, Alabama, Georgia, Florida, Louisiana, Virginia, North Carolina and South Carolina, twenty-two Negroes were elected to Con-

Senator Blanche K. Bruce, who had been a tax collector in Natchez, a sheriff and a superintendent of schools before being elected to the Senate at the age of thirty-three.

(*Left to right*) Hiram R. Revels, Mississippi; Benjamin S. Turner, Alabama; Robert C. De Large, South Carolina; Josiah T. Walls, Florida; Jefferson H. Long, Georgia; Joseph H. Rainey and Robert Brown Elliott, South Carolina. From a Currier & Ives print.

in Congress

gress before 1901, the largest number, eight, being from South Carolina, all of whose Representatives were colored at one time. J. H. Rainey and Robert Smalls of that state each completed five terms.

Most of these men had served in state legislatures or had been state or local officials before going to Congress, so were not without parliamentary experience. Their education was on a par with that of most other politicians of their day. They took their positions seriously, and their voting records show that they were not only interested in civil rights for Negroes but in all of the leading issues of the times. Few became involved in the scandals of graft and corruption which swept the country during those years. The Republican leader James G. Blaine said of them, "They were as a rule studious, earnest, ambitious men, whose public conduct . . . would be honorable to any race."

Nevertheless, these Negro legislators were often blamed for the ills which beset the defeated states in the wake of war and many biased historians of the period recorded unsubstantiated charges against them but not the good things done by legislatures in which Negroes served.

A cartoon depicting Revels occupying Jefferson Davis' former seat in the Senate, surrounded by (*left to right*) Henry Wilson, Oliver Morton, Carl Schurz and Charles Sumner. Revels advocated desegregation in schools and on railroads.

John W. Menard of Louisiana.

John R. Lynch of Mississippi.

Richard Cain of South Carolina.

Robert Smalls of South Carolina.

Fruits of the Ballot

Frederick Douglass, active in the Republican Party, was appointed U. S. marshal of the District of Columbia by President Hayes. Douglass is depicted here officiating as marshal at Garfield's inauguration.

During the Reconstruction era, Negroes were elected to a number of high offices in the South. In Little Rock, Arkansas, Mifflin W. Gibbs became the first Negro municipal judge in the United States, the electorate being largely white. Louisiana had three colored lieutenant-governors, C. C. Antoine, Oscar J. Dunn and P. B. S. Pinchback. The latter, in 1873, become acting governor of the state after the removal of the white incumbent. Later, Pinchback was elected to the United States Senate but was never seated.

Jonathan Gibbs, a graduate of Dartmouth, was Secretary of State in Florida and later Superintendent of Public Instruction. In South Carolina, Glasgow- and London-educated Francis L. Cardozo was, from 1872 to 1876, State Treasurer. In Mississippi, in 1872, John R. Lynch became the Speaker of the House and, in 1873, A. K. Davis was Lieutenant-Governor, James Hill was Secretary of State, J. J. Evans a tax collector and William Carey a postmaster. South Carolina had two Negro lieutenant-governors: Alonzo J. Ransier and Richard H. Cleaves.

Many colored conventions were held in the North and South in which Negro citizens were urged to political action. In the North, two days after the passage of the Thirteenth Amendment, abolishing slavery, John H. Rock was the first Negro lawyer to be admitted before the U. S. Supreme Court.

Mifflin W. Gibbs.

Pinckney B. S. Pinchback.

Oscar J. Dunn.

John H. Rock.

The Colored National Convention, held April 5-7, 1876, in Nashville, Tennessee, studied the civic and political problems of the Negro.

NEW NATIONAL ERA.

OL. V.—NO. 9.]   WASHINGTON, D. C., THURSDAY, MARCH 19, 1874.   { $2.50 a year in advance.
                                                                                 5 Copies for $10.

Douglass purchased the *New National Era* in 1870 and edited it with the help of his two sons. When Douglass was elected president of the National Colored Labor Union, this paper became ts official organ.

Reaction Sets In

"ONE VOTE LESS." —*Richmond Whig.*

A Nast cartoon of a murdered Negro in Richmond, with the letters "K.K.K." scratched on the wall.

Statue of the "Freed Slave" at the Centennial Exposition.

The Republicans utilized the interest of the freedmen in politics to strengthen their party in the South to the anger of the Democrats, who berated both carpetbaggers and Negroes to intimidate Negroes who dared to vote, other secret orders were organized in addition to the Klu Klux Klan such as the White Brotherhood, the Rifle Clubs, the Council of Safety, the Pale Faces and the powerful Knights of the White Camellia. The whip, the gun, the rope and fire were their instruments and lynching their common method.

In South Carolina in 1871 various legally elected Negro office-holders were ordered to resign immediately on pain of "retributive justice." Night raids on the homes of Negroes active in politics were frequent, with women and children as well as men tortured and whipped. A petition to Congress signed by the colored citizens of Frankfort, Kentucky, in 1871 asking for relief from "the Klu Klux Klans riding nightly over the country" listed by name, place and date more than a hundred outrages.

In the summer of 1876 in Hamburg, South Carolina, the "disgraceful and brutal slaughter of unoffending men . . . for opinion's sake or on account of color" so shocked President Grant that in a letter to the South Carolina governor he continued to describe the scene at Hamburg as "cruel, bloodthirsty, wanton, unprovoked . . . a repetition of the course that has been pursued in other states within the last few years, notably in Mississippi and Louisiana." A few weeks later, in Aiken County, another riot occurred in which from eighty to 125 Negroes were beaten and shot to death. When violence still failed to keep Negroes from going to the polls, white men at Edgefield, South Carolina, blocked the courthouse steps so that Negroes voting the Republican ticket could not reach the ballot boxes. The Democrats won the election.

The Massachusetts Senator Charles Sumner had tried for several years to get a new civil rights bill through Congress but without success. Finally, the year after his death, a watered-down version of his bill passed both Houses of Congress to become the Civil Rights Act of 1875. Little attention was paid, however, to its provisions for the protection of Negro rights and in 1883 it was declared unconstitutional by the Supreme Court.

A cartoon from *Harper's Weekly* after the Hamburg riot picturing a reformer dripping red tape from his hat as Negroes lie dead.

Robert B. Elliott of South Carolina, delivering his great speech on civil rights in the House of Representatives January 6, 1874. Elliott was educated at Eton College in England and served two terms in Congress.

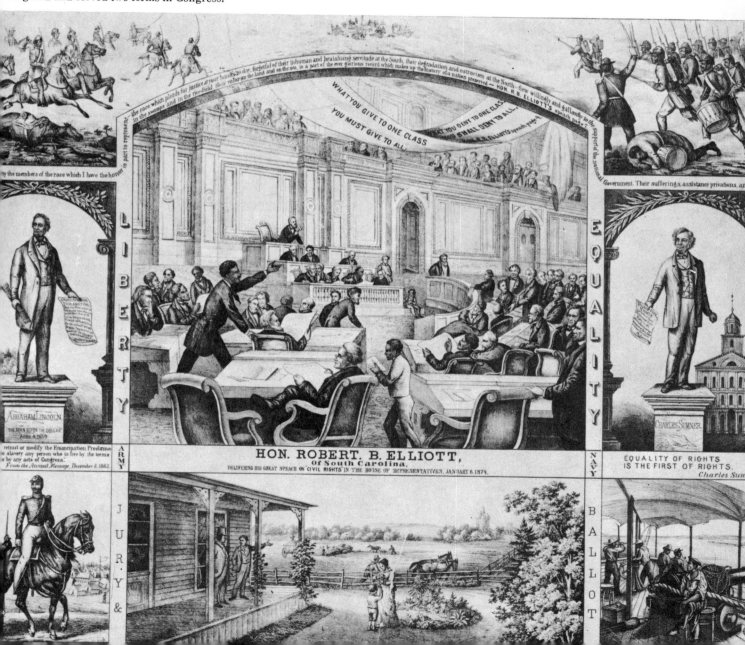

HON. ROBERT. B. ELLIOTT,
of South Carolina,
DELIVERING HIS GREAT SPEECH ON CIVIL RIGHTS IN THE HOUSE OF REPRESENTATIVES, JANUARY 6, 1874.

EQUALITY OF RIGHTS
IS THE FIRST OF RIGHTS.
Charles Sum

Frederick Douglass filled the position of U. S. marshal for the District of Columbia with credit, having previously served as secretary of the Santo Domingo Commission and as a member of the Territorial Council of the Federal District. Although Democratic newspapers raised a hue and cry concerning his appointment, the Senate nevertheless confirmed it.

Representative Thaddeus Stevens, the "Great Commoner," died in 1868. Senator Charles Sumner, author of the famed civil rights bill, died in 1874. With these two champions of the rights of freedmen gone, there was no voice of power left in Congress to defend Negro rights. In March, 1877, Rutherford B. Hayes of Ohio became the nineteenth President of the United States. A month after his inauguration he began the removal of federal troops from the South.

Behind the disputed Presidential election of 1876 were economic and political issues of far more importance than the question of who would sit in the White House. Hayes' opponent, the Democrat Samuel J. Tilden of New York, received the larger popular vote, but there were conflicting returns concerning twenty electoral votes from South Carolina, Florida, Louisiana and Oregon. The Republican Party no longer cherished the idealistic war aims of freeing

Frederick Douglass being congratulated on his appointment as U.S. marshal of Washington, D. C.

Federal troops leaving New Orleans, April 24, 1877.

Reconstruction

and protecting the Negro. It was now the party of the new industrialists and businessmen, open to urgings from compromisers that the Negro be abandoned to his former masters and that the South be given a share of the economic future so that the tariffs, subsidies and other special privileges enacted while the Republican Party was unchallenged in Congress would not be threatened.

A behind-the-scenes caucus between Hayes partisans and Southern Democrats eventually came to an agreement that if the vote swung to Hayes, federal troops would be withdrawn from the South, substantial subsidies for Southern internal improvements such as railroads would be appropriated and more federal jobs would go to Southerners. By a vote of eight to seven, the Commission awarded the election to Hayes. He promptly appointed a former Confederate general to his Cabinet as Postmaster General and moved to end military protection of Negro suffrage. On April 10, 1877, federal troops were withdrawn from South Carolina; on April 24 those stationed in New Orleans left and in 1878 an order was issued forbidding the use of government troops in elections.

By a combination of illegal terror and state laws limiting Negro suffrage, the Democratic Party returned to power below the Mason-Dixon line and the South again became the "solid South."

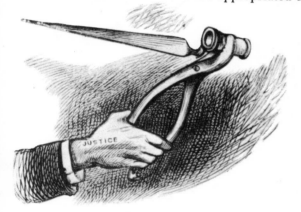

A federal bayonet depicted as the "Aching Tooth of the South" being removed by President Hayes in this cartoon of 1877.

President Rutherford B. Hayes.

A Negro chain gang cleaning Richmond streets in preparation for a reception for President Hayes.

The Negro exodus: old-style and the new, the slave and the freedman.

The Vicksburg wharf, from which many Negroes departed for the "freedom lands."

Exodus to Kansas

With the former Confederate leaguers again in the saddle, thousands of Negroes from the Deep South fled to the North and West, seeking a livelihood without the chicaneries of the sharecropping system and personal safety away from the terror of mobs by day or the Klan by night. But the South did not want to let its Negro laborers go. Transportation companies were forbidden to sell them tickets, vagrancy laws were invoked to arrest travelers, and Negro "agitators" who preached migration were horsewhipped and driven away.

But two colored men succeeded in organizing large mass migrations. One was Henry Adams of Louisiana and the other was "Pap" Singleton of Tennessee. Both set Kansas as a goal—the Kansas of old John Brown. About this time Southern Democrats accused Northern Republicans of enticing Negroes away from the South in order to add their names to Republican voting rolls in the North. Democratic Senator Voorhees of Indiana in 1878 asked Congress to appoint a committee to investigate the matter.

Both "Pap" Singleton and Henry Adams were called to Washington to testify. Each gave evidence of the ill treatment of the colored race: how schools were burned, children were forced to work in the cotton fields and black tenants were kept in debt by plantation trickery and high commissary prices—two dollars for a gallon of molasses worth only a quarter, for example. Despite 1,700 pages of such testimony, the Democrats still contended that Republicans had instigated the Negro mass migration. Certainly freedmen continued to leave the South by the thousands.

Some of them settled on the public lands that the government had opened up to squatters. Some went into the Indian territories where, until they came in large numbers, they were welcomed and prospered. But the largest number went to Kansas. Soon messengers were sent South from Kansas to advise that no more Negroes should come there, for most of them arrived ragged, hungry and penniless. Under the Homestead Law some of the migrants acquired land, but most had no funds for livestock or farming tools. The Freedmen's Relief Association and Eastern philanthropists aided the new settlers to some extent and some cash and clothing reached them from England. But although schools were built, neither the state of Kansas nor the federal government gave the Negroes any direct help. Western winters were cold and the snow deep and some of the Negroes arrived barefooted. But few returned to the South.

Benjamin "Pap" Singleton, the Moses of the exodus, was born a slave.

All Colored People
THAT WANT TO
GO TO KANSAS,
On September 5th, 1877,
Can do so for $5.00

A Lexington, Kentucky, handbill of 1877.

Louisiana freedmen enroute to Kansas after the great yellow fever epidemic.

1809. 1882.

GRAND COMPLIMENTARY

ANNIVERSARY

CELEBRATION!

TENDERED TO

"Pap" Singleton,

The originator of the Colored Emigration from the south to the west, and father of the late great "EXODUS," in the seventy-third year of his age, by the citizens of Kansas, for his untiring efforts to ameliorate human suffering,

TUESDAY, AUG. 15th,

To be held at HARTZELL PARK,

— NEAR THE CITY LIMITS OF —

TOPEKA, - KANSAS.

(Street cars run to and from the Park.)

BENJAMIN SINGLETON, better known as "Old Pap," was born in August, 1809, and therefore will be seventy-three years old that day. And on that day let every loyal citizen, be he speaker, statesman or minister of the Gospel, come forward and extend the right hand of fellowship.

Invitations have been extended to leading citizens in different cities of the State, and excursions are expected from each city.

-PROGRAMME FOR THE DAY:-

OPENING CHORUS..Song, JOHN BROWN.

PRAYER.

" WHY WE CELEBRATE TO-DAY ".......JUDGE W. I. JAMISON, of North Topeka.

After which addresses will be delivered by the following prominent speakers and divines:

Gov. John P. St. John,	Rev. Jno. M. Wilkerson,	Mayor Joseph Wilson,
Rev. John F. Thomas,	James Troutman, Att'y,	D. B. Garrett,
" Peter Rucker,	Rev. R. F. Markham,	Rev. S. C. Pierce,
" L. S. Cooper,	" W. W. Williams,	" Sanford Griffin,
" Layer,	Hon. Thomas Ryan,	" J. Turner, Kan.City.

—*MUSIC WILL BE INTERSPERSED BETWEEN EACH SPEECH.*—

COMMITTEE OF INVITATION:

J. Wiley, J. Johnson, H. Etherly, D. Ware, Wm. Cole, B. Perkins, Dr. J. M. Jamison, J. Brashears, G. White, Wm. Love, G. W. Smith,

COMMITTEE OF RECEPTION:

G. W. Ware, Wm. Love, A. Scales, C. McNairy, D. Ware. Louis Morgan, Chas. Williams, B. Jones, B. Duncan, J. H. Slaughter, F. M. Stonestreet.

COMMITTEE OF ARRANGEMENTS:

A. Scales, Joseph Jones, H. Roling, T. Bird, Rev. Jas. Bradshaw, C. H. Brown, A. D. Defrantz.

A. D. DEFRANTZ, President of the Day!

☞ 100 salutes will be fired at early sunrise, and at 7 o'clock, P. M., by Officer James Mason. Stands can be had on the grounds by referring to the Committee of Arrangements.

Admission to Park, Five Cents.

All Sabbath School Scholars and their Teachers will be admitted FREE!

Topeka Daily Capital Publishing Company.

A cartoon showing Negroes going West and California Chinese fleeing East to escape racial persecution.

218

Topeka, Kansas, fairgrounds, (*above*) the buildings of which were used as a terminus of the colored exodus.

Migration or Protection?

The early colored settlers in Kansas were not unwelcome, but when they began to arrive in great numbers a steamboatload of black migrants was forbidden to dock at Leavenworth and forced to continue down the Missouri River. At Topeka a mob destroyed newly built shacks of Negro newcomers and threw their lumber into the Kaw River. At Atchison, the City Council passed an ordinance prohibiting the entrance of paupers into the town. But still the Negroes came to Kansas in droves and in lesser numbers to Iowa and Nebraska.

What did the Negroes give as their reason for migrating? *Senate Report 693* of the Forty-Sixth Congress recorded: "They stated that they had no security for life, limb or property; that they worked year in and year out and, notwithstanding they raised good crops, they were at the end of the year in debt; that they were charged exorbitant prices for provisions. . . . Men were shot down for political purposes. . . . They said they would rather go into the open prairie and starve."

Frederick Douglass declared that in protest the Negro had "adopted a simple, lawful and peaceable measure—emigration—the quiet withdrawal of his valuable bones and muscles from a condition of things which he considers no longer tolerable." Yet Douglass opposed this mass movement on the grounds that "it would make freedom and free institutions depend upon migration rather than protection; by flight, rather than right. . . . It leaves the whole question of equal rights on the soil of the South open and still to be settled." In answer to this, Richard T. Greener, the first Negro graduate of Harvard College, argued, "No favorer of migration claims it as the sole, proper or only permanent remedy. . . . It is approved as *one* remedy, thus far the most salutary, in stopping lawlessness and exactions."

Richard T. Greener.

Frederick Douglass.

An allegorical poster heralding George Foster Peabody's gift to Southern education.

The Fisk Jubilee Singers.

Lumpkin's Jail in Richmond where slaves had been imprisoned, became a Negro college.

Students on the campus of Howard University in its early days.

"Keep Inchin' Along"

But for every hundred Negroes that left the South, 10,000 stayed, as the old spiritual said, to "keep inchin' along." From the old slave songs and spirituals grew a great Negro university. Established by the American Missionary Association at Nashville in 1866 in the abandoned barracks of the Union Army and overcrowded from the beginning, the Fisk School, for lack of money, feared it would have to close its doors. But its young treasurer had an idea; George L. White loved the old songs his students sang and he thought if he took a group of them on a tour of the North they might raise some money for the school.

On a cold autumn day in 1875 nine young men and women dressed in hand-me-downs started out on a tour. At first it went badly, so badly that they thought they would have to turn back. But at Oberlin their spirituals drew tears and the waving of handkerchiefs from a crowd that could not applaud in church. From then on, the Fisk Jubilee Singers sang their way from Henry Ward Beecher's church in Brooklyn to the White House and even to Europe on a tour that lasted seven years. When they finally came back to Nashville to stay they brought their school $150,000 for the land and buildings that became Fisk University. These student singers were the first group of Negro musicians to win international acclaim.

The thirst for knowledge was great among the freedmen and their children; cabins, churches and even jails were utilized as schoolrooms. Virginia University in Richmond began in 1867 in Lumpkin's Jail, started by the Reverend Nathaniel Colver of Tremont Temple, Boston. Out of a prayer meeting at the First Congregational Church in Washington, Howard University developed and was granted a charter by the government in 1867. That same year the wealthy Northern merchant George Foster Peabody established an education fund of more than $2,000,000 to aid in training "the young people of the more destitute portions of the Southern and Southwestern states," both white and colored.

Francis L. Cardozo, of Negro, Indian and Jewish ancestry, a free-born Negro who became the principal of Avery Institute in Charleston.

General Samuel Chapman Armstrong, first president of Hampton Institute, which opened in 1868.

In the years that followed, the gifts from Northern philanthropists helped greatly in the building of Southern Negro colleges and in giving Negro aspirations an outlet through study. Once, when General O. O. Howard of the Freedmen's Bureau asked a group of colored children in a freedmen's school in Atlanta what message he might carry back to the people of the North, a little boy in the front row jumped up and cried, "Tell 'em, Massa, we's rising."

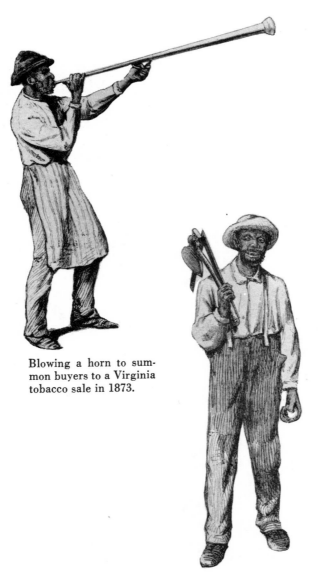

Blowing a horn to summon buyers to a Virginia tobacco sale in 1873.

A carpenter carrying his tools.

Child workers in a tobacco factory.

A phosphate company works.

Chickens crated for shipping on the levee at Cairo, Illinois, 1873.

A South Carolina turpentine camp.

A NEW SYSTEM

OF

CHAIN-GANG SLAVERY

IN GEORGIA.

Little girls and boys under ten years of age are sent to chain-gangs for three potatoes or singing Shoo-fly, with great locks and chains around their necks; colored bogusly-convicted women and men are let out for ten cents per day to do out-doors work that

A handbill announcing a protest meeting in Georgia signed by Senator Alepeora Bradley, 1870.

Hard Work–Low Wages

That employers took advantage of the penniless freedmen is shown in one instance by a statement of the tobacco workers of Richmond: "In 1858 and 1859 our master hired us to the tobacconist at prices ranging from $150 to $180. The tobacconist furnished us lodging, food and clothing." But after the war, they said, they were "compelled to work at low wages, $5 per week and sometimes less, and paying $18 or $20 per month Rent. It is impossible to feed ourselves and family—starvation is Cirten unless a change is brought about."

Further misuse of Negro labor was fostered by a system of arrests and fines, with black prisoners hired out sometimes for as little as ten cents a day. A wage differential based on race developed in the trades. Former slaves who were skilled as brickmasons and carpenters were paid less than white workers for the same labor, and generally the hardest, dirtiest and least attractive work was allotted to the Negroes. In the foundries they shoveled coal, loaded flatcars and cleaned the furnaces.

White workers considered cheap Negro labor a threat, in both the North and the South, but would not, in most trades, allow the Negro the protection of unionization. Negroes, if they worked at all in some industries, had no choice but to work as strike-breakers, when employers chose to use black labor to impede the progress of whites. Bitter antagonisms developed and racial factors confused the basic economic issues in the minds of both groups.

The labor unions inevitably were faced with the problem of whether to organize black workers or not, and if they were organized, whether it should be on a mixed or a segregated basis. At its first meeting in 1866 the National Labor Union voted to organize Negroes. But at its third annual convention in 1869 it decided instead to urge Negroes to form their own separate unions. At the convention a representative of the Colored Caulkers' Trade Union Society of Baltimore, Isaac Myers, warned that "American citizenship for the black man is a complete failure if he is proscribed from the workshops of the country."

NEW ERA.

WASHINGTON, D. C., THURSDAY, JANUARY 13, 1870.

VOL. I.—NO. 1.}   { $2.50 a year in ad
                                                          { 5 Copies for $

Convention, and it was read; after which   Rapier, and others; after which it adjourned   sugar-cane; the seasons and their usual and   still the mutual and dependent relations of labor   vada, Robert H. Small ; Ohio, J.
convention adjourned to 7½ P. M.   to reassemble at 10 o'clock A. M. on Wednes-   abnormal effects upon crops; the agricultural   and wealth we would neither ignore nor rudely   Pennsylvania, Robert Adger ; R
ereas labor has its privileges no less than day, December 8.   implements and their proper regulation for use,   disturb. The laborer needs and must have the   John T. Waugh ; South Carolina,
ties, one of which is to organize, and, if   as to make him   for the time   compen   ings. Without it   Te   Somerville; Te
se, to furnish reasons for its organization ;   THIRD DAY'S PROCEEDINGS.   of life   larke : Virginia, William H.
ore,   Con
olved, That labor was instituted by Al-
y God, as a means of revealing the
rments of inanimate creation to be
and used by man, and that labor i
on to, and the natural heritag
n family; each person havi
to labor in any field of
she is capacitated, th
d restricted only by
any.
olved, That capit
by l

Freedmen and the New Unions

Since they were generally barred from white labor organizations, a colored labor convention of more than 200 delegates met at the Union League Hall in Washington on December 6, 1869, to form the Colored National Labor Union to co-operate with white workingmen "until the necessity for separate organization shall be deemed unnecessary." John Mercer Langston drew up a statement adopted by the delegates which began: "In our organization we make no discrimination as to nationality, sex or color."

But white workers rioted against Negroes in many cities and called strikes a number of times rather than work with them or, on the West Coast, with the Chinese. However, the new Knights of Labor in 1875 appointed Negro organizers and announced as its hope the organization of all workers, white and Negro, skilled and unskilled. Older craft unions opposed this plan and when, in 1886, under the leadership of Samuel Gompers, the American Federation of Labor came into being, each affiliated union was allowed to make its own racial rules. Needless to say, most locals excluded colored workers. Meanwhile, denounced as radical, the Knights of Labor declined but at their peak had 60,000 Negro members.

A waiter at the Galt House, Louisville, 1873.

Boiling down the juice in sugar manufacture.

Isaac Myers, a labor leader.

Frank J. Farrell, a machinist and a Knights of Labor delegate.

Sewer diggers in Savannah, Georgia.

Stokers on a Mississippi River steamboat.

Negro Inventors

Early in the 1870's Jan Matzeliger came to the United States from Dutch Guiana and worked as a shoemaker's apprentice in Philadelphia and New York. When he was twenty-five he went to Lynn, Massachusetts, to work in a shoe factory. Disturbed by the amount of time it took to last shoes by hand, he began to work at night on a machine to do this exacting labor. After five years he had made a model for pleating leather at the toe of a shoe for which he was offered $1,500. But he refused to sell. Instead, he kept on working at his model for another five years until he had perfected a method of attaching the uppers of a shoe to the sole by machine as smoothly as hand-lasters could do it.

In 1883 Jan Matzeliger patented his lasting machine, which revolutionized the shoe industry and enabled the United Shoe Manufacturing Company, which bought the invention, to control within a few years, 98 per cent of the shoe machinery trade, with a capital stock of $20,000,000 and forty subsidiary companies. The income from shoe manufacturing in New England increased 350 per cent, exports rose to $16,000,000 and Matzeliger's American method of manufacturing shoes was adopted in factories around the world. Matzeliger's lasting machine was termed the first of its kind "capable of performing all the steps required to hold a shoe on its last, grip and pull the leather down around the heel,

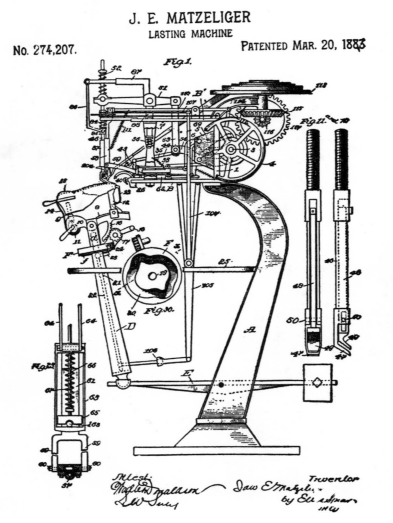

Jan Matzeliger.

Jan Matzeliger's own drawings of his lasting machine, 1883.

guide and drive the nails into place and then discharge the shoe from the machine.''

During slavery a bondsman could not take out a patent nor make a contract. But free men of color were not so restricted. The first patent granted a Negro was for a corn harvester invented in 1834 by free-born Henry Blair of Maryland. In 1846 Norbert Rillieux of Louisiana patented a vacuum pan that revolutionized the sugar-refining process. In 1852 Elijah McCoy of Detroit began work on various appliances related to the lubrication of engines and perfected a cup, now generally used on railroads and ocean steamers, which makes it unnecessary to stop machines in order to oil them. McCoy was eventually granted some fifty-seven patents. In 1884 John J. Parker set up his own foundry and machine company to manufacture a screw for tobacco presses which he had invented. And about 1885 in Cincinnati, Granville T. Woods began work on a series of inventions in several fields, ranging from electronics to steam-boilers and automatic air brakes. His patents included several in telegraphy, one a system of sending telegrams from a train in motion. Various of his inventions were sold to the American Bell Telephone Company, the General Electric Company and the Westinghouse Air Brake Company before his death in 1910.

So Negroes, who were generally not allowed to work in skilled capacities in factories, contributed to the increased mechanization of American manufacturing through a number of important inventions.

Granville T. Woods.

Norbert Rillieux.

Elijah J. McCoy.

PORTIA.—"*Which is the Merchant here, and which the Jew?*"—SHAKSPEARE.

"The Great Labor Question from a Southern Point of View."

"A Hard Row to Hoe"

"After the Proclamation was issued, the government had agents who went all through the country to see if the slaves had been freed. They would see how the Proclamation was being carried out. They would ask them, 'How are you working?' 'You are free?' 'What are you getting?' Some of them would say, 'I ain't getting nothing now.' Well, the agent would take that up, and they would have that owner up before the government. Maybe he would be working people for a year and giving them nothing before they found him out. There are some places where they have them cases yet, where they have people on the place and ain't paying them nothing."

—An ex-slave's account in *Lay My Burden Down: A Folk History of Slavery* by Ben Botkin, 1945.

Women and children at work in a cotton field.

Women, as well as men, worked in the rice fields.

A man pulls a plow as a woman guides it.

By the end of the Civil War most Southern planters had little or no money left. With their slaves freed, their problem was how to secure labor for the great plantations. But the freedmen had no money and barely a change of clothing, so they were driven by hunger to work for little or nothing. The planters took advantage of the former slaves' destitution. Since some form of agreement between the planter and worker had to be reached, the tenant sharecropping system developed under which, in return for housing, seed and credit at the commissary store a family would work a crop.

Theroetically, when the crop was sold they would share in the profits. But usually debt, sometimes combined with dishonest bookkeeping, left the worker at the end of each year owing the planter. So the black peasant became bound to the soil. Under pain of arrest for debt, he could not leave and thus peonage developed in the South. The courts added to the misery of the landless Negro by leasing convicts to work on many plantations, turpentine flats and mines and in building railroads. The brutality of the convict-lease system, recorded in official sources, was a bitter contradiction of the South's vaunted paternalism.

Three-quarters of the Negroes lived in the South and the majority of these had been rural workers, mostly accustomed to the cultivation of cotton. But cotton was no longer as profitable as it had once been, and Southern fields received no crop rotation or fertilization to revitalize the soil. Agricultural workers, black and white, "had a hard row to hoe."

During the Reconstruction period many discouraged planters sold their acreage and moved to the cities. Whatever graciousness there had been in plantation life began to disappear. Freedmen able to buy land were few. After ten years of freedom only about 5 per cent of the Negroes in the South had acquired farms and none were large plantation-owners.

In 1871 and 1873 financial panics left depression in their wake. Cotton prices slumped until 1878, when it was worth only ten cents a pound, and continued to decline. Poor white farmers suffered even more than the Negroes, who were used to abject poverty. Out of the small farmers' discontent grew the Southern Farmers' Alliance, which by the 1890's had acquired considerable political influence in attempting to force agricultural reforms in Washington and in voting out of office many local officials thought to favor the big planters and the rich "Bourbons." In South Carolina, the poor whites elected to the governorship a one-eyed farmer, Benjamin R. Tillman, and later sent him to the Senate. In Georgia, the Farmers' Alliance elected the governor, gained control of the state legislature and sent Thomas E. Watson to represent them in Congress.

As the white Alliance spread rapidly through the South the Colored Farmers' National Alliance moved with it. The agrarian radicalism of the whites was shared by the Negroes, but Jim Crow kept their organizations separate. Each at its peak was reported to have more than 1,250,000 members. At first, through the Colored Alliance, Tillman and Watson made overtures for the Negro vote, but later became violently anti-Catholic, anti-Jewish and anti-Negro.

229

Battle over

During the 1890's, a period of falling prices for the small white farmer, a new political party called the People's, or Populist, Party developed out of the Farmers' Alliances. It demanded relief for the farmers, government ownership of railroads and communications and graduated income taxes. In 1892 this new party, born of agrarian revolt, polled more than a million votes for the presidency, sent fourteen men to Congress and elected four governors, a record for a third political party up to that time. In North Carolina the Populists and the Republicans combined forces and in 1894, with Negroes voting, they gained control of the legislature and large numbers of local offices went to colored men. In various cities Negroes became policemen, sheriffs and aldermen and John C. Dancy was made Collector of the Port of Wilmington.

This in turn aroused the Southern Democrats to allow Negroes more access to the polls, provided they voted for Democrats, not Populists or Republicans. There was a temporary upsurge of Negro political influence in some parts of the South. Tom Watson of Georgia told poor whites and Negroes they were being kept apart that they might more easily be robbed by the big land-owners and urged them to vote together on a platform of democratic reform.

Tillman addressing some South Carolina farmers.

Ballots

But the time when all three parties bid for the Negro vote was brief. Whites of all parties decided to keep the franchise lily-white and to fight their political battles among themselves, with the Negro again left out at the ballot box. The Mississippi politician J. K. Vardaman declared he was against any Negro voting, whether he was educated or not, and even before the rise of the Populists his state had disfranchised Negroes through a constitutional convention. Cole Blease, Hoke Smith, Ben Tillman and Tom Watson, among other political demagogues, worked with those seeking to disfranchise the Negro through property, poll tax and literacy requirements incorporated eventually into state constitutions.

In 1898 Louisiana invented a new legal device destined to spread in the South—the "Grandfather Clause," which declared eligible for the ballot only those men whose grandfathers or fathers had voted prior to 1867. Of course this meant that freedmen or sons of former slaves—in other words, Negroes—were kept off the registration books. The more than 130,000 registered colored voters in Louisiana were reduced within two years to about 5,000. In Alabama, by 1900, only 3,000 Negroes remained on the voting lists. Riots broke out and in Georgia and Virginia elections a number of Negroes were killed. In 1898 in Wilmington, North Carolina, eleven Negroes died and twenty-five were wounded.

When the Democratic Party in the South instituted the all-white primaries—the solid South having become solidly Democratic after the decline of the Populists—Negroes were almost totally disfranchised. Because of a fear of the potential of the Negro vote, the Democrats forestalled the development of a two-party system in the South, lest Negroes gain the balance of power and perhaps benefit from some of the political jobs. At the turn of the century white supremacy had won its political battle, the high hopes of the Negroes which had been born during the Reconstruction era were dashed and the Negroes of the South were no better than slaves again insofar as their right to the ballot was concerned.

Benjamin R. Tillman.

Thomas E. Watson.

"A Pitiful Spectacle," an anti-Populist cartoon of 1896, the year of the St. Louis Populist convention, showing "Democracy" pleading for her virtue.

Congressman Robert Smalls.

Congressman Henry P. Cheatham.

Congressman George H. White.

Congressman John M. Langston.

As the Century Ends

Negro leaders throughout the South attempted to stem and turn back the rising tide of disfranchisement. At the South Carolina Constitutional Convention of 1895 former Congressman Thomas E. Miller proposed that the new state constitution be submitted to the people for ratification. But no popular vote was ever taken on the constitution. Five other Negroes, including former Congressman Robert Smalls, presented to the same convention proposals guaranteeing *every citizen*, women as well as men, white and black, the right to register and vote, but their proposals were rejected by a vote of 130 to 6, the minority votes being those of the Negro delegates.

Before complete disfranchisement set in, the last six Negroes to represent Southern states in Congress were the Representatives Henry P. Cheatham of North Carolina, 1889-93; John Mercer Langston of Virginia, 1890-91; Thomas E. Miller of South Carolina, 1890-91; George W. Murray of South Carolina, 1893-97; and George H. White of North Carolina, 1897-1901. George White was the last colored Representative from the South. All of these men continued active in civic and political affairs after leaving Congress. President McKinley appointed Henry P. Cheatham as Registrar of Deeds for the District of Columbia. John Mercer Langston, an Oberlin graduate and lawyer, was a member of the Oberlin City Council and the Board of Education, then an inspector for the Freedmen's Bureau under General Howard. He organized the law department of Howard University at Washington, served on the Board of Health under President Grant and was appointed Minister to Haiti by President Hayes. In 1894 his book, *From the Virginia Plantation to the National Capitol*, was published.

On January 20, 1900, George H. White introduced into the House of Representatives the first bill designed to make lynching a federal offense. The year before White introduced his bill, 87 Negroes and twelve white men had been lynched. During the decade from 1890 to 1900 1,217 mob murders by hanging, burning, shooting or beating were recorded. Newspapers from January to October, 1900, reported 114 lynchings, all but two in the South. "It is evident that the white people of the South have no further use for the Negro," wrote an Arkansas minister, E. M. Argyle, to the *Christian Re-*

corder in 1892. "He is being treated worse now than at any other time since the surrender."

But that same year Frederick Douglass said, "Nor is the South alone responsible for this burning shame. . . . The sin against the Negro is both sectional and national; and until the voice of the North shall be heard in emphatic condemnation and withering reproach against these continued ruthless mob law murders, it will remain equally involved with the South in this common crime." The Cleveland *Gazette* reported in 1898 violence against two Negro postmasters: the shooting of Isaac H. Loftin in Georgia and the burning of the post-office and lynching of a Postmaster Baker in Lake City, South Carolina. His wife, three daughters and a son were wounded and a baby in arms was killed. In both of these cases, the paper stated, concerning the mob, "No effort to arrest and punish them has ever been made."

A demand for the arrest and punishment of lynchers became a major Negro crusade at the turn of the century. The outstanding figure in this movement was a Negro woman, Ida B. Wells, who compiled in 1895 the first statistical pamphlet on lynching, *The Red Record*. Miss Wells, born in Mississippi in 1869, taught school in Memphis, Tennessee, until she became the editor and part-owner of a newspaper, the Memphis *Free Speech*, which circulated throughout the Mississippi Delta. When in May, 1892, her paper exposed some of the forces involved in the lynching of three young Negro businessmen in Memphis, her offices were demolished by white hoodlums and she was driven from the city.

In Chicago, Ida B. Wells married the militant race leader Ferdinand Barnett and both became active in the National Equal Rights League. Mrs. Wells-Barnett became chairman of the Anti-Lynching Bureau of the National Afro-American Council and a famous speaker at home and abroad on Negro rights. Statistically, she proved that the "protection of white womanhood," as the South claimed, was not the basis for lynchings, since in no given year had even half of the Negroes who were lynched been charged with rape or attempted rape and that in 1900 less than 15 per cent of those lynched had been so suspected. Lynching, she contended, was a form of intimidation to preserve the plantation economy and the white ballot box of the South.

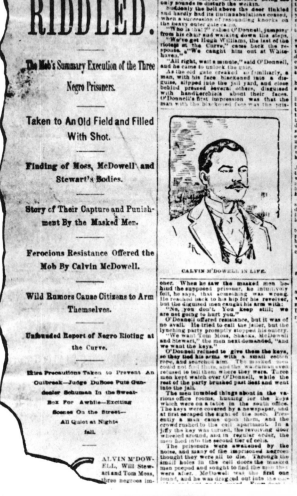

Ida B. Wells, author of a three-year statistical record of lynchings, *A Red Record*.

Joel Chandler Harris of Georgia
(1884-1908)

Words Cast

While accounts of race riots and lynching parties filled many a newspaper column and the flaming crosses of the Klan luridly lighted the Southern night, many leading writers were putting words on paper that cast a golden glow over such unpleasant realities. In much of the literature Negroes were made to appear either as happy children or else as vicious brutes, threatening a charming land of magnolias and gentility. Prewar times were pictured as the "good ol' days" and Reconstruction as an unmitigated evil.

Even that "kindly amanuensis for the illiterate Negro peasant," Joel Chandler Harris, used his Uncle Remus stories to present a picture of a childlike old colored man, who declares that education would ruin his race and that, for a Negro, beatings are better than books. Says Uncle Remus in plantation dialect, "Wid one bar'l stave I kin fa'rly lif' de vail er ignunce." Harris was a Georgia newspaperman whose enormously popular transcriptions of Negro animal fables concerning the cunning Brer Fox, Brer Rabbit, Brer Terrapin and other talking beasts began to appear in 1881. The genuine folklore of the animal tales were combined with the fictional character of an illiterate Negro narrator whose comments on social conditions upheld the nostalgic myth of the "Old South."

Thomas Nelson Page of Virginia
(1853-1922)

George Washington Cable of Louisiana
(1884-1925)

Mark Twain of Missouri
(1835-1910)

a Golden Glow

Thomas Nelson Page, lawyer turned writer, glorified the "Old South" in romantic style. One of his most popular books was *In Ole Virginia*, a collection of stories mostly in Negro dialect, which was published in 1887. In Page's fiction Negroes were pictured as superstitious and amusing liars, chicken stealers and nostalgic fellows sighing for the return of "de good ole times" of slavery or else as bestial and dangerous animals, such as Moses in *Red Rock*, whom Page termed "a hyena."

But the most venomous portraits of Negroes in Southern fiction appeared in *The Leopard's Spots* and other novels of the Reverend Thomas Dixon, whose *The Clansman* was dedicated "to the memory of . . . Colonel Leroy McAfee, Grand Titan of the Invisible Empire, Ku Klux Klan." Dixon pictured the Reconstruction era as a Negro-Yankee reign of terror, with the Klansmen as the nightly protectors of "the Southern way of life." The character of Stoneman was a thinly veiled portrait of Thaddeus Stevens as an evil spirit of villainy. This sensational novel eventually became one of Hollywood's most profitable motion pictures, "The Birth of a Nation."

A more objective report of the Reconstruction period appeared in *A Fool's Errand* by "One of the Fools," who was in reality Albion W. Tourgee, a former Union Army officer who remained in North Carolina after the war as a judge and who put into his book the facts of mob violence, klanism and the intimidation of Northern teachers he had observed. His largely autobiographical volume has been termed the *Uncle Tom's Cabin* of the Reconstruction.

The first Southern writer of importance to portray the Negro sympathetically was George Washington Cable, a former Confederate cavalry officer of New Orleans, whose sketches, later expanded into *Old Creole Days*, first appeared in *Scribner's Monthly*. His frank treatment of Negro problems in *The Silent South*, 1885, so angered Southern readers that Cable moved to Massachusetts. Cable sometimes accompanied Mark Twain on lecture tours. Twain's books punctured some of the pretenses of the romantic Old South. The character Jim in *Huckleberry Finn*, which was published in 1884, is considered one of the best portraits in American fiction of an unlettered slave clinging to the hope of freedom.

THE CLANSMAN

AN HISTORICAL ROMANCE
OF THE KU KLUX KLAN

BY

THOMAS DIXON, Jr.

ILLUSTRATED BY

ARTHUR I. KELLER

NEW YORK
DOUBLEDAY, PAGE & COMPANY
1905

A

FOOL'S ERRAND.

BY

ONE OF THE FOOLS.

VARR. SERV. Thou art not altogether a fool.
FOOL. Nor thou altogether a wise man: as much foolery
As I have, so much wit thou lackest.
Timon of Athens.

NEW YORK:
FORDS, HOWARD, & HULBERT.
1880.

Industry and the Negro

As Northern capital moved into the South after the Civil War, taking advantage of the large supply there of cheap non-unionized labor, water-power and rich coal, iron and oil resources, new mills, plants and foundries were constructed in many Southern communities. By 1880 this region had a fourth of the nation's cotton mills. New railroads were built and mining, smelting and lumber industries developed rapidly. Local management was largely in the hands of Southerners and white workers were given preference. The new industries welcomed Negroes, if at all, only as heavy laborers at the lowest wage scales. Except for porters, the textile mills were almost 100 per cent white. On railroad engines, Negro firemen were often used to shovel coal but were never promoted to positions as engineers. By 1900 only 4 per cent of the Negroes in the South were employed in skilled industries; the rest were unskilled laborers.

Road - building, sewer - digging, street - cleaning, brick - making, rock - quarrying, furnace - stoking and mining were jobs allotted Negroes. By 1890 one-third of all black workers were female domestic servants, the lowest paid in America. The old skilled Negro artisans of ante-bellum days—brickmasons, carpenters, cabinetmakers and painters—found their places increasingly filled by white workers, who formed guilds barring Negroes and who would strike rather than work alongside black men. In or out of industry racial barriers were erected which left Negroes on "the mudsill of Southern economic life." Prior to the Civil War most of the construction workers in the South were colored, but by 1890 these constituted less than a third of the plasterers and less than a fifth of the carpenters. Contractors employed increasingly fewer Negroes in the building trades. In the heavy industries in 1890 there were less than 8,000 Negro steelworkers, about 800 machinists and only 200 boilermakers. The Iron, Steel and Tin Workers of the A. F. of L. barred Negroes.

Union barriers to colored membership, North and South, reacted to the detriment of white labor in that, in the case of strikes, employers did not hesitate to use Negroes as strike-breakers. On the other hand, Negroes often had no qualms about strike-breaking in a situation in which their color would permit them no chance to work otherwise. But when the steel mills began to use Negroes as strike-breakers, the A. F. of L., in self-protection, formed separate Negro locals.

As early as 1867 Negro shipyard workers were brought from Virginia to Boston to break the strike of white workers seeking an eight-hour day. In the first great Chicago Pullman strike of 1894, when white stockyard workers struck in support of the American Railway Union, Negroes took their places and thus gained a foothold in the meat-packing industry. Since the Railway Union had in its charter an anti-Negro clause, the colored workers formed what they called an Anti-Strikers Railroad Union.

Separate groups or no unionization at all was often the dilemma of the black worker. In both the North and South colored painters had separate locals. Negroes in Pittsburgh created the National Association of Afro-American Steam and Gas Engineers and in Philadelphia, the United Laborers and Hod Carriers Association. There was a strong organization of dock workers in Charleston.

White organized labor both South and North often refused to recognize Negro labor organizations or to work with black workers, organized or not. Having thus little or no protection in the field of labor, black workers could not help but accept lower wages in order to live. Many employers were not averse to paying a worker as little as possible or to securing labor for free. In some parts of the South a system of almost free labor was worked out by the courts in relation mostly to Negro prisoners. In the convict-lease system those incarcerated were hired out to companies or individuals and put to work in lumber mills, quarries, mines, brickyards or factories to the profit of the state or county, but not to the gain of the workers. In South Carolina, Governor Ben Tillman made flagrant use of this penal system. From the Carolinas to Florida convicts in striped garb helped to build the chains of new roads needed for the increased transport requirements of the growing industries of the South. Farther West, along the Mississippi, chain gangs kept the flood levees in repair. For petty crimes, men were given long sentences or heavy fines, then used as free labor, molding a system which decreased the number of jobs available for poor whites and needy Negroes.

The Rockwood iron furnaces in eastern Tennessee.

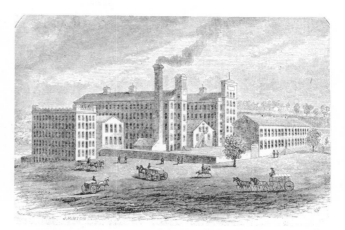

The Eagle and Phoenix cotton mills in Columbus, Georgia.

A chain gang on a Mississippi levee.

Henry W. Grady, whose speeches and editorials urged the continued industrialization of the South.

"The Queen of Industry, or the New South," showing the merger of agriculture and industry.

A Precedent Is Set

Henry W. Grady, part-owner and editor of the Atlanta *Constitution*, became the South's most famous voice through a speech called "The New South" which he made before the New England Society of New York in 1886 and repeated on many platforms until his death. His objective was to encourage Northern investments in the South and to pacify the Northern conscience concerning the Negro. Grady claimed that black workers prospered in the South, that Negroes shared equitably in school funds and that they had the "fullest protection" of the laws. Therefore, he argued, the problem of the Negro should be left in the hands of the South, "to those among whom his lot is cast, with whom he is indissolubly connected and whose prosperity depends

upon their possessing his intelligent sympathy and confidence." As to relations between the North and South, Grady declared that he stood upon "the indissoluble union of American states and the imperishable brotherhood of the American people."

When Grady sat down, the band played "Dixie." Among the 240 guests who lustily applauded his speech were such leaders of American industry and opinion as J. Pierpont Morgan, Charles L. Tiffany, Elihu Root, Russell Sage and the editor of the *New York Times*, Charles R. Miller. The *Times*, like most of the country's leading papers, extolled the speech to the highest but neglected to comment upon its gross untruths regarding the Negro. The Boston *Transcript* approvingly quoted the Springfield *Republican,* "New England rejoices in the New South most heartily." The Negro press, however, did not think so highly of Grady's nationally acclaimed oration. As he continued to deliver the same speech before various prominent groups, the *Christian Recorder* commented, "In that address, beneath the glamour of eloquence, the old rebel spirit and the Old South are seen throughout."

The Supreme Court, made up mostly of Northerners and Republicans, strongly supported the growing national opinion that the Negro was not entitled to the same civil rights as white men. The 1883 Supreme Court decision on civil rights written by Justice Joseph Bradley, a New Jersey Republican, sanctioned the segregation of Negroes by individuals in all states. In the Plessy v. Ferguson decision of 1896, which upheld the constitutionality of state laws providing "separate but equal" accommodations for Negroes, a precedent was set which greatly aided the spread of segregation on public carriers and in public places throughout the nation. Lower federal courts and the Interstate Commerce Commission had already approved such segregation, although Negroes correctly contended that separate accommodations were rarely, if ever, equal. One federal court decided, "Equality of right does not mean identity of right."

When Homer Plessy was forced from a "white" railway coach in Louisiana, the Supreme Court in its majority opinion, written by Justice Henry B. Brown, a Michigan Republican, upheld the state segregation statute, declaring that the Fourteenth Amendment "could not have been intended to abolish distinctions based on color, or to enforce . . . a co-mingling of the two races upon terms unsatisfactory to either."

But in a strong dissenting opinion Justice John Marshall Harlan declared, "In view of the Constitution, in the eye of the law there is in this country no superior, dominant, ruling class of citizens. There is no caste here. Our Constitution is color-blind and neither knows nor tolerates classes among citizens . . . It is therefore to be regretted that this high tribunal . . . has reached the conclusion that it is competent for a State to regulate the enjoyment by citizens of their civil rights solely upon the basis of race. In my opinion, the judgment this day rendered will, in time, prove to be quite as pernicious as the decision made by this tribunal in the Dred Scott case. The thin disguise of equal accommodations for passengers in railroad coaches will not mislead anyone nor atone for the wrong this day done."

Justice John Marshall Harlan.

Justice Henry B. Brown.

Justice Joseph Bradley.

Southern Senators confer in a cloakroom.

A School Is Born

As a child, the Negro destined to become one of the most famous Americans of his time worked in the salt mines of West Virginia. Booker T. Washington was his name. He was born in bondage on April 5, 1856. Like Frederick Douglass, his father had been a white slave-owner, his mother a colored slave. As a small boy he was called one day to the "big house" of the Virginia plantation and there, crowded in among other slaves, he heard his master read to them the Emancipation Proclamation and watched the tears stream down his mother's face at the news that they were free.

After rising at four and working all day in the mines, Booker and his mother tried to learn their A-B-C's at night by the light of the fire. One day in the dark mine Booker heard the men talking about a Virginia school called Hampton where Negroes were taught trades, and he made up his mind to go there. The old people of the town helped him with nickels, dimes and quarters. When he was fifteen, he started out, riding a stagecoach until his money ran out, then walking, working and begging rides until he reached Hampton. He worked his way through as a painter.

Young Washington was deeply impressed by General Samuel C. Armstrong, the founder of Hampton, and by the dedicated New Englanders who taught there. "What a rare set of human beings," he later wrote, declaring that their role in the education of Negroes in the hard days after the Civil War would "make one of the most thrilling parts of the history of this country." Like them, he wanted to become a teacher. Booker went back to West Virginia where, the only teacher among many eager learners, he taught children all day and grown-ups at night. Then Hampton asked him to return there to supervise a dormitory for sixty Indians arriving there to study.

When Booker was in his mid-twenties, a white banker and a Negro mechanic in an Alabama village wrote to Hampton, asking for a teacher to open a normal school for rural Negroes. General Armstrong sent Booker. A leaky old church was his school and he was the sole teacher, with an umbrella opened over his desk when it rained. There was a little money for his salary, but none for books, land or a building. The young teacher and his students decided to raise funds for land and to build a school. Between sessions in reading, writing and figuring they laid the foundations and raised the walls. In this way, in 1881, Tuskegee Institute came into being.

Freedmen processing salt in Saltville, Virginia. Booker began work in the salt mines when he was nine.

An algebra class at Tuskegee Institute. In the early days most of the students were older than the average high school and college students of today.

Tuskegee students plowing according to Tuskegee's "learning-by-doing" methods which they, in turn, carried to the backwoods.

Children's garden at Tuskegee, where a movable classroom-on-wheels brought instruction to rural areas.

George Washington Carver, an agricultural chemist and Tuskegee's most famous teacher, conducting a chemistry class about 1900.

The Spiri

Tuskegee was destined to become a pioneer examp of an independent industrial school. To learn how " do a common thing in an uncommon manner," Book T. Washington wanted his first students to build the own school with their own hands so that they wou learn how to build and how to be independent. The bought enough land for a small farm and learned cultivate the soil around their school, raise their ov food and take care of livestock. To educate the hea the heart *and the hand* was his aim, after which wanted to transmit the learning to the community.

The idea caught on well with both Negroes ar whites in the county, then throughout the state. He came in the form of small gifts of money, food, clothir quilts. One old ex-slave woman even brought six eg

Former President Theodore Roosevelt addressing the N Negro Business League at Washington, D. C. in 1910.

# of Tuskegee

er hen had laid for "de eddication of dese boys and
als," since she had nothing else. Eventually large sums
money came to the school from some of the great
hilanthropic foundations. The campus and its farms
rew and U. S. presidents and famous people came to
sit. The Tuskegee spirit of practical education for
ommunity usefulness spread. Similar institutions were
tablished in the South, and Tuskegee became a model
r other schools in far-off lands.

Booker T. Washington's agricultural and industrial
ojects, his part in establishing small businesses by and
r Negroes and in the practical rehabilitation of the
ral South and his efforts toward Negro-white coopera-
n under existing conditions made his name almost a
usehold word by the early twentieth century.

Booker T. Washington in the principal's office
at Tuskegee, with his secretary Emmett J.
Scott, who became a special assistant to the
Secretary of War during World War I.

A Negro bank in New York City. Booker T.
Washington believed that successful economic competition with whites in business
would help to break down prejudice.

Tuskegee backers at the twenty-fifth anniver-
sary of the school in 1906. (*First row, left to
right*) George T. MacAnany, Robert C. Ogden,
Booker T. Washington, Andrew Carnegie,
President Eliot of Harvard. (*Second row*) J.
G. Phelps Stokes, the Reverend Lyman Abbott,
President Frissell of Hampton.

An Atlanta Speech

Booker T. Washington put forward in his most famous speech a concept which many Negroes did not endorse but condoned: "When your head is in the lion's mouth, use your hand to pet him." Misery sat on the Negro doorsteps of the South in the 1890's and the Klan rode its back roads. "In all things that are purely social," he said, "we can be as separate as the fingers, yet one as the hand in all things essential to mutual progress. . . . The wisest among my race understand that the agitation of questions of social equality is the extremest folly. . . . The opportunity to earn a dollar in a factory just now is worth infinitely more than the opportunity to spend a dollar in an opera house."

Delivered at the Cotton States' Exposition in Atlanta in 1895, this speech was termed by Negro critics "The Great Booker T. Washington Compromise," a diplomatic statement in a time of racial stress but hardly a workable formula for the future of a land in which the two races were already greatly intermingled. The speech put Booker T. Washington on the front pages of papers across the nation and in the eyes of white America made him the "official" leader of the Negro race. The "Negro Moses," as the New York *World* called him, became the head of a machine which wielded great power nationally in all racial matters, from educational and editorial policy-making to job appointments, high and low. From that time on, Washington was supported by governmental, industrial and educational leaders throughout the nation.

The slave-born editor of the New York *Age*, T. Thomas Fortune, said "It is impossible to estimate the value of such a man as Booker T. Washington." But the violent objections of the editor of the Boston *Guardian* to his speaking in New England resulted in William Monroe Trotter's spending some time in jail. In the judgment of the scholarly W. E. B. Du Bois, Washington was "leading the way backward." A philosophical breach soon widened over the years. It was the Washington school's contention that the Negro must crawl before he could walk, that industrial education was more necessary than academic learning and that compromise on suffrage and equal rights might preserve half a loaf. His opponents claimed such a sacrifice of democratic rights and loss of pride was useless when Southerners like "Pitch-

T. Thomas Fortune, a Negro journalist and supporter of Booker T. Washington.

William Monroe Trotter, a Harvard graduate, was a fiery speaker and newspaperman.

fork" Ben Tillman declared they wanted no Negroes to vote—not even men like Booker T. Washington—and Governor Vardaman of Mississippi said, "God Almighty created the Negro for a menial."

While controversy raged among his own people, Booker T. Washington dined at the White House with President Theodore Roosevelt, received an honorary degree from Harvard, money from Carnegie and was a guest of Queen Victoria at Windsor Castle. He was not indifferent to the barbs of other Negro leaders. He knew that to "walk the razor's edge between Negro pride and white prejudice" was not always a grateful task. But, of all outstanding Negroes, at this Booker T. Washington proved to be most adept.

President Cleveland visits the Negro Building at the Atlanta Exposition, October 23, 1895.

New Orleans Tribune,

21 Conti Street.   Published Daily, Mondays Excepted.   21 Conti Street.

FIRST YEAR.   NEW ORLEANS, TUESDAY, OCTOBER 18, 1864.   VOL. I.—No. 45.

The Weekly Louisianian.

TERMS—$2 00 PER ANNUM. | "REPUBLICAN AT ALL TIMES, AND UNDER ALL CIRCUMSTANCES."   [SINGLE COPIES—5 CTS.

THE ADVOCATE OF THE RIGHTS OF MAN.

VOLUME 10.   NEW ORLEANS, LOUISIANA, SATURDAY, JUNE 5, 1886.   NUMBER 23.

The Conservator.

VOLUME V.   CHICAGO, SATURDAY MORNING, DECEMBER 23, 1882.   NUMBER 47.

THE NEW YORK GLOBE.

NEW YORK, SATURDAY, FEBRUARY 23, 1884.

Richmond Planet.

VOL. II.   RICHMOND VIRGINIA, SATURDAY, FEBRUARY 21 1885.   NO. 10

THE ELEVATOR,

A Weekly Journal of Progress.

"EQUALITY BEFORE THE LAW."

Vol. 1.   San Francisco, California, Friday, October 13, 1865.   No. 28.

PROSPECTUS.   The Dying Soldier.   The Last Visit of Gen. Lafayette. Description of a Negro Contra-   Extraordinary Decision of a Negro band School   Meeting.

THE COLORED AMERICAN.

BY JOHN T. SHUFTEN.   Augusta, Ga., Saturday, December 30, 1865.   VOL. I.—NO. 3.

The first Negro daily newspaper in the U. S. was the New Orleans *Tribune*, print- ed in both French and English, which began as a weekly in 1864, ran as a daily in 1865, then reverted to a weekly. In 1865 in New Orleans the first convention of Negro newspapermen met and out of it eventually grew the Associated Negro Press. Former Lieutenant-Governor P. B. S. Pinchback, the convention chairman, founded the New Orleans *Louisianian*. The earliest colored journal in Illinois, the *Conservator*, was founded in Chicago in 1878 by Ferdinand L. Barnett. The most widely read Negro paper in the late nineteenth century was the New York *Globe*, edited by T. Thomas Fortune.

New Wards
Of Color

During the year 1900, when Booker T. Washington's autobiography *Up from Slavery* was published, Robert S. Abbott, also a Hampton graduate, founded the Chicago *Defender,* an outspoken newspaper which was to preach a racial doctrine quite the opposite of Booker T. Washington's and to demand in no uncertain terms the ballot, equal rights and an end to lynchings and Klan terror. Five years earlier, shortly before Washington made his famous Atlanta speech the greatest of the ante-bellum and Reconstruction leaders—Frederick Douglass—died.

But in 1895 a new leader was destined to gain wide influence in the sphere of race relations. William Edward Burghardt Du Bois received his doctorate from Harvard and went to Europe for further study. That year, too, Charles Young was a freshman at West Point. He was graduated from the U. S. Military Academy in 1889 and commissioned a second lieutenant in the Negro Tenth Cavalry at a time when American interests were spreading to islands in the Pacific and the Caribbean—Hawaii, the Philippines, Cuba, Puerto Rico.

In 1898, the year of the Spanish-American War, the "Grandfather Clause" depriving Negroes of the vote was adopted in Louisiana. That spring Roosevelt's Rough Riders rode up Santiago Ridge to meet the enemy. Negro troops of the Ninth and Tenth Cavalry battered down a Spanish fort, cut the barbed wire and made an opening for the Rough Riders. A Southern officer said, "The Negroes saved that fight." And concerning their gallantry at San Juan Hill, Theodore Roosevelt said, "Well, the Ninth and Tenth men are all right. They can drink out of our canteens."

Charles Young served as a major. He later saw service in the Philippines, Mexico and Haiti and was made a lieutenant-colonel in 1916. During Young's military career the United States acquired guardianship of two Pacific Islands with a preponderantly colored population, two West Indian islands with almost a million citizens of Negro blood and the Canal Zone in which many blacks lived. When the United States took up, at the turn of the century, the "white man's burden," black soldiers helped bear it.

Charles Young, the third Negro to be admitted to the U. S. Military Academy at West Point, was graduated in 1889.

The Negro cavalry supporting the Rough Riders near Santiago, Cuba, 1898.

A cartoon from *Puck,* "School Begins," satirizing the American "civilization" argument in support of imperialism. Uncle Sam is saying to his new class in Civilization, "Now, children, you've got to learn these lessons whether you want to or not! But just take a look at the class ahead of you and remember that, in a little while, you will feel as glad to be here as they are!"

Part Five

THE SOULS OF BLACK FOLK

1900-1920

"THE PROBLEM OF THE TWENTIETH CENTURY is the problem of the color line—the relation of the darker to the lighter races of men in Asia and Africa, in America and the islands of the sea." So wrote W. E. B. Du Bois in *The Souls of Black Folk* as the new century began. The Negro population of the United States was then 8,833,994. On July 4, 1900, the New Orleans population had been increased by the birth of Louis Armstrong, destined to become America's greatest hornblower. On August 15 of that year New York City's fourth great race riot occurred, and the comedian Ernest Hogan, who was performing at the Winter Garden, dared not leave the theater all night, while Bert Williams and George Walker, who were playing near Times Square, narrowly escaped injury. That year, too, the first meeting of the National Negro Business League, founded by Booker T. Washington, was held in Boston. And at Atlanta University a survey of Negro college graduates was made which indicated that there were some 2,500 in the country, 400 of whom were graduates of leading institutions such as Oberlin, Harvard and Yale.

It was partly due to Booker T. Washington's stress on industrial rather than liberal arts education that the controversy developed between his followers and those of W. E. B. Du Bois. "Education," said Washington at Tuskegee, "is meant to make us give satisfaction, and to get satisfaction out of giving it. It is meant to make us get happiness out of service for our fellows. . . . No man who has the privilege of rendering service to his fellows ever makes a sacrifice. . . . There is as much dignity in tilling a field as in writing a poem." Du Bois, on the other hand, felt, "We shall hardly induce black men to believe that if their stomachs be full, it matters little about their brains." Without disputing the values of industrial education, he continued, "So far as Mr. Washington preaches thrift, patience and industrial training for the masses, we must hold up his hands and strive with

him. . . . But so far as Mr. Washington apologizes for injustice, North or South, does not rightly value the privilege and duty of voting, belittles the emasculating effects of caste distinctions and opposes the higher training and ambition of our brighter minds —so far as he, the South, or the Nation, does this— we must unceasingly and firmly oppose them. By every civilized and peaceful method we must strive for the rights which the world accords man."

William Edward Burghardt Du Bois was born of African, French and Dutch ancestry in Great Barrington, Massachusetts, in 1868, the year of the enfranchisement of the freedmen by the Fifteenth Amendment. At sixteen he was graduated from high school and for the first time went into the South as a scholarship student at Fisk University, where he edited the Fisk *Herald* and wrote his first articles. During the summers he taught in log-cabin schools in sharecropping districts. In 1888 Du Bois entered Harvard, where he won the Boylston oratorical contest. He was one of six commencement speakers, his subject being "Jefferson Davis." Santayana, William James and Albert Bushnell Hart were among his teachers and he knew Oliver Wendell Holmes and James Russell Lowell. Then followed two years of study in Germany and a return to Harvard to receive his doctorate in 1895, the first Ph. D. conferred on a Negro by that institution. Du Bois then served briefly as an instructor at Wilberforce and at the University of Pennsylvania, then for thirteen years headed the department of history and economics at Atlanta University. There he conducted the annual Atlanta conference on Negro problems, which published thirteen documented studies of Negro life.

Meanwhile the young professor wrote articles for the *Atlantic Monthly, World's Work* and other leading publications and compiled them into his poetic sociological study of the Negro people, *The Souls of Black Folk*, which went into twenty-eight editions and was translated abroad.

William Edward Burghardt Du Bois.

The New Liberation Movement

Shortly after Dr. Du Bois joined the faculty at Atlanta University, there came to nearby Atlanta Baptist College (now Morehouse) as professor of Latin and Greek the young Georgia-born John Hope. He and Du Bois, both the same age, became lifelong friends and colleagues in many movements for Negro advancement. John Hope attended Worcester Academy in Massachusetts, was graduated from Brown University in 1894, then entered the service of the American Baptist Home Mission Society as a teacher. Both Du Bois and Hope had grave doubts concerning the Booker T. Washington program. Eventually, Du Bois contended, "Things came to such a pass that when any Negro complained or advocated a course of action, he was silenced with the remark that Mr. Washington did not agree."

Washington's power over the Negro press became so great that only a few colored newspapers dared oppose him editorially. Among these was Monroe Trotter's Boston *Guardian*, to which John Hope contributed. Many Negro intellectuals felt, with Du Bois, that "Washington arose as essentially the leader not of one race but of two—a compromiser between the South, the North and the Negro." It was this element

of compromise in Washington's program that brought about a meeting in July, 1905, at Fort Erie, of a group of twenty-nine Negro teachers, editors and professional men from fourteen states. They gathered in answer to a call from Dr. Du Bois for "organized, determined and aggressive action . . . for the following purposes: 1, To oppose firmly the present methods of strangling honest criticism, manipulating public opinion and centralizing political power by means of the improper and corrupt use of money and influence. 2, To organize thoroughly the intelligent and honest Negroes throughout the United States for the purpose of insisting on manhood rights, industrial opportunity and spiritual freedom. 3, To establish and support major proper organs of news and public opinion."

Among the Negro leaders who initiated the Niagara Movement were the editors Monroe Trotter and J. Max Barber, joined later by John Hope and a number of others. But Hope, who had meanwhile become president of Atlanta Baptist College, was the only high-ranking Negro educator who dared align himself openly with this "radical" group of men who were critical of the Man of Tuskegee.

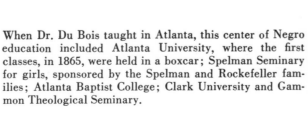

When Dr. Du Bois taught in Atlanta, this center of Negro education included Atlanta University, where the first classes, in 1865, were held in a boxcar; Spelman Seminary for girls, sponsored by the Spelman and Rockefeller families; Atlanta Baptist College; Clark University and Gammon Theological Seminary.

THE GUARDIAN.

VOL. I. NO. 44. BOSTON, MASS., SATURDAY, SEPTEMBER 6, 1902. PRICE 5 CENTS

THEY SLIPPED ROGERS AWAY.

Brockton Officers Took the Prisoner Off While
Under a Habeas Corpus.

The *Guardian* was founded by Monroe Trotter in 1901.

"The Most Celebrated Buck and Wing Dance of Modern Times," a *Guardian* cartoon showing Booker T. Washington dancing to the tune of white Southerners. Other *Guardian* cartoons pictured Washington as a gravedigger burying Negro rights and as a cheerful observer of whites tearing bricks from the temple of racial liberty to erect buildings for Tuskegee.

John Hope, blond and blue-eyed, was the son of a Scottish immigrant, James Hope, who became a wealthy importer of wines and liquors. His mother was a beautiful colored woman who had attended high school in Charleston. There were a number of brothers and sisters in a happy childhood home shared by both parents in Augusta, Georgia, and ample money for the children's education. Among John Hope's few unpleasant childhood memories was that of the Hamburg race riots across the river from Augusta. He was a man of cultivated tastes, witty and warm-natured, with an interest in youth.

251

"Lift Every Voice and Sing"

"Lift every voice and sing
Till earth and heaven ring . . .
Sing a song full of the faith

That the dark past has taught us . . .
Facing the rising sun
Of our new day begun . . . "

So wrote James Weldon Johnson in Jacksonville, Florida, in 1900 to music composed by his brother, J. Rosamond Johnson. The following year the two went to New York, where Rosamond became famous as a popular composer—"Under the Bamboo Tree," "Oh, Didn't He Ramble," "Lazy Moon"—and James became a distinguished writer, diplomat and race leader, while he continued to create lyrics for songs and shows.

Negro participation in the professional musical theater began as early as 1865, when Charles Hicks organized the Georgia Minstrels, which later went to Europe as Haverly's European Minstrels. In 1882 Callender's Consolidated Spectacular Colored Minstrels toured America, and in 1893 the first mixed troupe, The Forty Whites and Thirty Blacks, performed. Songs derived from Negro folk sources were featured in the minstrels, and as early as 1855 the name of a colored barber in Philadelphia, Richard Milburn, appeared as composer on the title page of "Listen to the Mocking Bird." A popular minstrel song of the 1870's was "Carve Dat Possum" by Sam Lucas.

In the nineties, songs by Alex Rogers and Tim Bryan achieved popularity and Tom Lemonier's "Just One Word of Consolation" and several ballads by Gussie L. Davis such as "In a Lighthouse by the Sea" were hits.

James A. Bland, who composed "Carry Me Back to Old Virginny," "In the Evening by the Moonlight," and "Oh, Dem Golden Slippers," was one of America's most prolific songwriters. His songs were sung by the leading minstrels, white and Negro, and Bland himself became a famous minstrel performer. In 1881, with Haverly's European Minstrels, he went to London and remained there most of the time for the next twenty years, a famous star. From the 1870's to his death, Bland is said to have written almost 700 songs, but, careless of copyrights, only thirty-eight of his compositions were registered in Washington.

However, some of his songs have become American classics, and in 1940 the House of Delegates of the Commonwealth of Virginia officially adopted Bland's "Carry Me Back to Old Virginny" as the state song.

Another composer of sweet melodies, Will Marion Cook, who, unlike Bland, had had excellent formal musical training in Europe, composed in 1898 a one-act musical which became the talk of New York. "Clorindy—The Origin of the Cakewalk," with lyrics by the poet Paul Laurence Dunbar, ran for an entire summer, with a large cast of Negro singers and comedians at the Casino Roof Garden. This musical demonstrated for the first time the happy possibilities of syncopated music in sustained form. The following year the Winter Garden presented another of Cook's musical sketches and from that time on, he wrote a great deal for the Broadway theaters, including several scores for Williams and Walker shows.

During the World's Fair in Chicago in 1893 "The Creole Show," featuring a chorus of sixteen beautiful Negro singing and dancing girls, ran for the entire season, then toured for several years. In 1895 the colored producer John W. Isham staged a musical melange, "The Octoroons," and later "Oriental America," which closed with an operatic medley. Meanwhile Sissieretta Jones, known as Black Patti, toured with her musical, "Troubadours," a revue written by Bob Cole, a talented young man who was shortly to produce the first complete Negro musical comedy, with book, lyrics and music by himself. With J. Rosamond Johnson he later wrote the operettas "The Shoofly Regiment" and "Red Moon."

But the most successful Negro musicals at the turn of the century were those featuring the popular singing and dancing comedians Williams and Walker. This team came East from California in 1896, doing the cakewalk with two beautiful girls. They were an immediate success in the music halls. In 1900 they appeared in "The Song of Ham," a musical farce which ran for two years, with Williams as a burnt-

James A. Bland (1854-1911) (*left*) was born on Long Island of free Negro parentage. He studied at Howard University and wrote his first songs while still in college.

Will Marion Cook (1869-1944) (*right*) was born in Washington, D. C. He studied composition with Anton Dvorak, trained choruses for Broadway shows and toured Europe with his own syncopated orchestra.

cork comic and Walker as a well-dressed dandy. Then came their great success, "In Dahomey," with music by Will Marion Cook, lyrics by Paul Laurence Dunbar and book by Jess A. Shipp, which opened in 1902. The following year "In Dahomey" went to London, where it was so popular that the royal family heard of it and ordered a command performance at Buckingham Palace. Its hilarious comedy, melodic singing and lively dancing set a vogue in Negro entertainment for a decade.

George Walker was from Kansas and Bert Williams had been born on the island of Antigua in the British West Indies. With Walker, he had clowned for tips in the cabarets of the Barbary Coast in San Francisco before they had sung and danced their way to New York. With the sad funny songs of his own composition, like "I May Be Crazy But I Ain't No Fool" and "You're in the Right Church but the Wrong Pew," Williams delighted audiences, while Walker entertained them with sparkling repartee and lively syncopated steps. After ten years of joint stardom, George Walker died. Bert Williams continued as a featured performer in otherwise all-white Broadway musicals. In 1910 he signed a long-term contract with the Ziegfeld Follies, touring America for ten years in various editions of that famous revue, singing and recording such lugubriously comical songs as his own "Nobody" and Irving Berlin's "Woodman, Spare that Tree" and Cook's "Oh, Death, Where Is Thy Sting?"

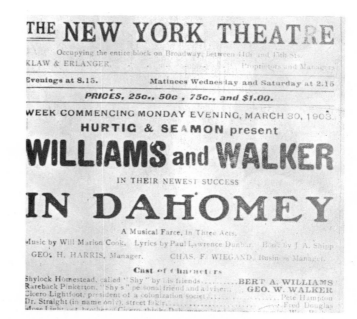

A Williams and Walker playbill, New York, 1903.

Bert Williams (*left*) and George Walker.

253

John W. Cromwell, historian and secretary of the American Negro Academy for "the promotion of literature, science and art," founded in 1897.

George W. Williams, a lawyer, historian and a Civil War veteran, wrote *A History of Negro Troops in the War of the Rebellion*, published in 1887.

Archibald H. Grimké, a graduate of Harvard Law School, was the author of biographies of Charles Sumner and William Lloyd Garrison.

Carter G. Woodson founde 1915 the Association for Study of Negro Life and tory. He was the publishe the *Journal of Negro His*

History and the Arts

Dissatisfied with the often biased and scanty attention given Negroes by historians, colored men early began to record their own findings. From the slave narratives through the personal stories of the postwar period, such as Henry O. Flipper's *The Colored Cadet at West Point* (1889) and Booker T. Washington's best-selling *Up from Slavery* (1900), there were many pictures of the times set down by Negroes. Joseph T. Wilson in 1882 published *Emancipation: Its Course and Progress* and in 1888, *The Black Phalanx*.

But the first comprehensive historical study by a Negro to receive scholarly approbation was the *History of the Negro Race in America*, by George Washington Williams in two volumes in 1882. And in 1887 his highly regarded *History of the Negro Troops in the War of the Rebellion* appeared. In 1891 Luis F. Emilio published *A Brave Black Regiment*, the record of men of the 54th Massachusetts in the Civil War. During the post-Reconstruction period, John Wallace wrote *Carpetbag Rule in Florida*, E. A. Johnson published *A School History of the Negro Race in America*, and John W. Cromwell produced *The Negro in American History*. The appearance in 1896 of the initial volume in the Harvard Historical Series, *The Suppression of the African Slave Trade* by twenty-four-year-old W. E. B. Du Bois, marked the publication of the first scientific historical mono-

graph by a Negro in the United States. In 1900 came his *The Philadelphia Negro*.

Carter G. Woodson became the great popularizer of the study of Negro history in the colored schools and colleges, and Negro History Week, which he established, has come to be celebrated at numerous non-Negro institutions as well. In 1896 Woodson entered the South's one interracial institution of higher learning, Berea College, in Kentucky, and from there went to the University of Chicago. Woodson received his doctorate at Harvard in 1912, his thesis being "The Disruption of Virginia." Among his numerous books are *The Education of the Negro to 1861, A Century of Negro Migration, History of the Negro Church, African Heroes and Heroines* and his widely consulted *The Negro in Our History*.

Dr. Woodson edited the letters, sermons and papers of Francis J. Grimké. The Grimké brothers, Francis and Archibald, were prominent in Negro intellectual life for a half-century following their graduation from Lincoln University in 1870. They were nephews, on their father's side, of the Southern abolitionist sisters Angelina and Sarah Grimké, who acknowledged the relationship and helped the boys through college. Archibald became the first Negro librarian of Lincoln University, whose faculty was then all-white. Later he went into law and in 1883 became part-owner and editor of the Boston *Hub*. He contributed articles to numerous national publications, including the *Atlantic Monthly*. His brother, Francis James Grimké, was graduated from Princeton Theological Seminary in 1878 and served as the distinguished minister of the Fifteenth Street Presbyterian Church in Washington for nearly fifty years.

The first nationally known Negro poet in the United States was Paul Laurence Dunbar, born in 1872 of ex-slave parentage in Dayton, Ohio, where he was the only colored student in his high-school graduating class. Dunbar was sixteen when his earliest poems appeared in the Dayton *Herald* and twenty-one when his first book, *Oak and Ivy*, was published locally. At the Negro Pavilion of the World's Fair in Chicago he worked as an assistant to Frederick Douglass and read his poems. William Dean Howells wrote the introduction for young Dunbar's *Lyrics of Lowly Life*, published in New York in 1896. During Queen Victoria's Diamond Jubilee, Dunbar went to London to recite his work. In that era when the poems of Robert Burns, Eugene Field and James Whitcomb Riley were popular, the simple musical dialect verses of Dunbar also achieved a wide audience, especially his humorous poems in the quaint broken English of the newly freed Negroes. Dunbar wrote many short stories which were printed in leading magazines, but it is his poetry that still lives.

In Boston, William Stanley Braithwaite's quiet lyrics did not treat of Negro life at all but were personal and non-racial in content. Like Braithwaite, the painter Henry O. Tanner, who was born in Pittsburgh in 1859, seldom if ever portrayed racial subject matter in his work, devoting himself largely to Biblical canvases. Tanner passed most of his creative years in Paris and died there at the age of seventy-eight. In the arts, racial problems, the turbulence of the Reconstruction and the tensions of the years that followed were reflected most forcefully in the work of the novelist and short-story writer Charles Waddell Chesnutt, of Cleveland. Light enough himself to pass for white, Chesnutt wrote dramatically about the families of mixed blood in *The Marrow of Tradition*. This novel had as a background the Wilmington, North Carolina, race riots of 1898. Chesnutt's *The Conjure Woman*, a collection of short stories, appeared in 1899, and in 1900 his first novel, *The House Behind the Cedars*, was published, establishing the author as the outstanding Negro fiction writer of his time.

William Stanley Braithwaite, author of *Lyrics of Life and Love*, was an editor of the *Boston Transcript* and editor of the *Anthology of Magazine Verse*.

Charles W. Chesnutt's "The Goophered Grapevine," published in the *Atlantic*, marked the first use by a Negro of the short story for literary expression.

Paul Laurence Dunbar's lyrics were set to music by Will Marion Cook, J. Rosamond Johnson and other composers.

Henry Ossawa Tanner, a graduate of the Pennsylvania Academy of Fine Arts, received a medal of honor from the Paris Exposition of 1900.

Lynchings and Race Riots

One of the worst of American race riots began on a September Saturday in 1906 when Atlanta was full of country people, who joined the mobs in chasing Negroes through the streets, beating and killing them and putting the torch to Negro property, aided and abetted by officers of the law, who gave the Negroes no protection. The president of Gammon Theological Seminary was pistol-whipped by a police officer when he asked for help. Seventy persons were injured, some for life, and twelve were killed. That same year in Brownsville, Texas, a portion of the colored 25th Regiment was involved in a race riot. While whites went unpunished, President Roosevelt, under whom Negroes had served in the Spanish-American War, dishonorably discharged the entire battalion.

While Booker T. Washington was preaching the virtues of industry and thrift, mobs in both the North and the South were burning the homes of Negro workers and t[erro?]rorizing black citizens. There were two race riots in Spri[ng]field, Ohio, within a few years, and in 1904 a Negro w[as] hanged there on a telegraph pole and riddled with bulle[ts.] The same year in Statesboro, Georgia, two men we[re] lynched, two colored women whipped, a young mot[her] beaten and kicked, her husband killed and many Neg[ro] homes wrecked. In the Greensburg, Indiana, riot of 19[—] Negroes were beaten and driven out of town. In Spri[ng]field, Illinois, that year, in spite of the state militia, a m[ob] destroyed Negro homes and businesses, lynched an eigh[ty-]four-year-old man within sight of the state capitol a[nd] strung up an innocent barber after burning his shop. [For] these public crimes, no one was ever punished. In ma[ny] communities Negroes felt that they had no legal prot[ec]tion against violence.

RECORD KEPT BY TUSKEGEE OF LYNCHINGS IN THE FIRST QUARTER OF THE TWENTIETH CENTURY

1900 — 115	1913 — 52
1901 — 130	1914 — 55
1902 — 92	1915 — 69
1903 — 99	1916 — 54
1904 — 83	1917 — 38
1905 — 62	1918 — 64
1906 — 65	1919 — 83
1907 — 60	1920 — 61
1908 — 97	1921 — 64
1909 — 82	1922 — 57
1910 — 76	1923 — 33
1911 — 67	1924 — 16
1912 — 63	1925 — 17

LYNCHINGS BY NAME AND PLACE FOR THE FIRST PART OF THE YEAR 1900

Jan. 9 — Henry Gingery, Ripley, Tenn.
Jan. 9 — Roger Gingery, Ripley, Tenn.
Jan. 11 — Rufus Salter, West Springs, S. C.
Jan. 16 — Anderson Gause, Henning, Tenn.
Feb. 17 — William Burts, Basket Mills, S. C.
Mar. 4 — James Crosby, Selo Hatchel, Ala.
Mar. 4 — George Ratcliffe, Clyde, N. C.
Mar. 10 — Thomas Clayton, Hernando, Miss.
Mar. 11 — Unknown Negro, Jannings, Neb.
Mar. 18 — Charles Humphries, Lee County, Ala.
Mar. 18 — John Bailey, Manetta, Ga.
Mar. 22 — George Ritter, Canhaft, N. C.
Mar. 24 — Walter Cotton, Emporia, Va.
Mar. 26 — Lewis Harris, Belair, Md.
Mar. 27 — William Edward, Deer Creek, Miss.
Apr. 3 — Allen Brooks, Berryville, Ga.
Apr. 5 — Unknown Negro, Southampton Co., Va.
Apr. 16 — Moses York, Tunica, Miss.
Apr. 19 — Henry McAfee, Brownsville, Miss.
Apr. 20 — John Peters, Tazewell, W. Va.
Apr. 22 — John Hughley, Allentown, Fla.
Apr. 28 — Mindee Chowgee, Marshall, Mo.

The inflammatory headlines in the Atlanta papers the afternoon of the race riots proved to be unverifiable upon investigation.

A Detroit *Free Press* cartoon of 1907 showing "Pitchfork" Ben Tillman throwing fertilizer on racial strife.

Cartoon showing resistance to Jim Crow on Nashville's streetcars. Negroes pooled their money to purchase cars.

"Buster Brown in a New Role," a cartoon of Theodore Roosevelt after his dismissal of the Negro soldiers at Brownsville.

Meeting at

"The men of the Niagara Movement . . . turn toward the nation and ask in the name of ten million the privilege of a hearing. In the past year the work of the Negro-hater has flourished in the land. Step by step, the defenders of the rights of American citizens have retreated. The work of stealing the black man's ballot has progressed and the fifty and more representatives of stolen votes still sit in the nation's capital. . . .

"Against this the Niagara Movement eternally protests. We will not be satisfied to take one jot or tittle less than our full manhood rights. We claim for ourselves every single right that belongs to a freeborn American, political, civil and social; and until we get these rights we will never cease to protest and assail the ears of America. The battle we wage is not for ourselves alone but for all true Americans."

The original leaders of the Niagara Movement in 1905, in a photograph (*below*) taken on the Canadian side of the Falls, with Du Bois the second from the right in the second row.

— From an "Address to the Country" issued by the second annual Niagara meeting, held August 16-19, 1906, at Harper's Ferry, West Virginia.

Jesse Max Barber, the Atlanta editor of the *Voice of the Negro*, where the first Du Bois account of the Niagara Movement appeared. Barber's life was threatened during the 1906 riot and he was forced by whites to get out of town. His publication ceased shortly thereafter.

Harper's Ferry

With the shadows of race war and lynching menacing the land, the second Niagara conference, with Du Bois, Hope and 100 others in attendance, met at Harper's Ferry in 1906 and, before beginning its sessions, paid tribute to the martyred John Brown. They all marched at dawn to the engine house where John Brown had made his last stand and sang "The Battle Hymn of the Republic." Among those who addressed the conference were the ex-Congressman Richard T. Greener, formerly American consul at Vladivostok, the A. M. E. bishop Reverdy C. Ransom, who had been dragged from a Pullman car and beaten by whites, and Lewis Douglass, son of Frederick Douglass and a Civil War veteran. Mary White Ovington covered the meeting for the New York *Evening Post* and became deeply interested in its objectives. These annual meetings were an impetus to the organization of the National Association for the Advancement of Colored People. On its Board of Directors were eight members of the Niagara Movement.

Incorporated in the resolution passed at Harper's Ferry were the following demands: "First, we want full manhood suffrage and we want it now. Second, we want discrimination in public accommodations to cease. Third, we claim the right of freemen to walk, talk and be with them that wish to be with us. Fourth, we want the laws enforced against rich as well as poor, against capitalist as well as laborer, against white as well as black. Fifth, we want our children educated. They have a right to know, to think, to aspire. We do not believe in violence. Our enemies, triumphant for the present, are fighting the stars in their courses. Justice and humanity must prevail. We are men, we will be treated as men. And we shall win."

Robert S. Abbott, whose Chicago *Defender*, founded in 1905, became the most influential and militant Negro newspaper, supporting in full the demands of the Niagara Movement.

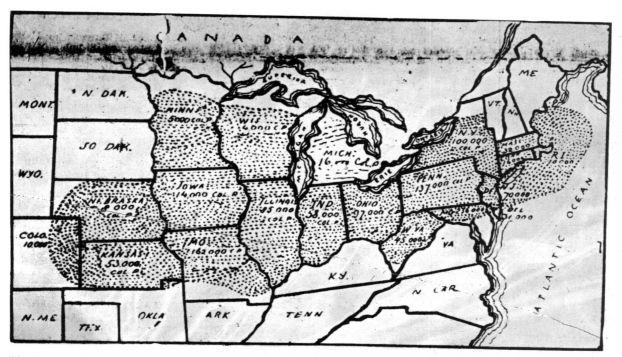

"A Glance at the Power of the Colored Ballot," from the *Guardian*, showing the Negro's political strength.

Arthur B. Spingarn, a lawyer, became president of the N.A.A.C.P. in 1940.

W. E. B. Du Bois in the editorial offices of the *Crisis* at New York headquarters of the N.A.A.C.P. Jessie Fauset was his editorial assistant and Augustus Granville Dill, his business manager.

Interracial

The National Association for the Advancement of Colored People developed from a conference of white liberals in protest against a savage Springfield, Illinois, lynching. The meeting, held in New York City on Lincoln's birthday in 1909, was called "for the discussion of present evils, the voicing of protests and the renewal of the struggle for civil and political liberty" at the instigation of Mary White Ovington, William English Walling, Dr. Henry Moskowitz and Oswald Garrison Villard. Monroe Trotter was absent, he said he did not "trust white folks." But present were Dr. Du Bois, Jane Addams, Francis J. Grimké, John Dewey, Ida Wells Barnett, John Haynes Holmes, Bishop Alexander Walters and William Dean Howells.

In 1910, offices were set up in New York with Moorfield Storey, a white Boston lawyer who had been Charles Sumner's former secretary, as president and Dr. Du Bois (who

resigned his position in Atlanta) as director of publicity and research and editor of the *Crisis*. This official organ of the N.A.A.C.P. presented in its first editorial the organization's "stand for the rights of men, irrespective of color or race, for the highest ideals of American democracy, and for reasonable but earnest and persistent attempts to gain these rights and realize these ideals." A legal redress committee was established, headed by Arthur B. Spingarn who, with his brother, Joel E. Spingarn, had become a member of the interracial board of directors.

Moorfield Storey and other distinguished attorneys such as Clarence Darrow, Louis Marshall and Felix Frankfurter gave their services free to this committee, whose first important victory was won in 1915 when the Supreme Court declared the "grandfather clauses" in the Oklahoma and Maryland State Constitutions violated the Fifteenth

Amendment and were, therefore, null and void. In 1917 a Louisville city ordinance upholding segregated residential areas was declared unconstitutional. And in 1923, concerning an Arkansas case the Supreme Court held that if Negroes were excluded from juries, a fair trial for a colored defendant was impossible. By 1921 the National Association for the Advancement of Colored People had more than 400 branches.

The Rosenwald Fund was established by the Chicago philanthropist Julius Rosenwald, who became a member of the Board of Trustees of Tuskegee in 1912. This Fund helped to build more than 5,000 public schools for Negroes in the South by offering to match community and state contributions with its own funds, thus stimulating local initiative. In 1900 the South was spending twice as much for the education of white children as it was for Negro

Julius Rosenwald of Sears, Roebuck, whose gifts helped to build schools for Negroes.

The seal of the National Urban League, whose slogans are "Jobs at All Levels," "Vocational Guidance," "Better Housing," "Better Health," "Education and Good Citizenship."

Eugene Kinkle Jones, who as field secretary and as executive secretary of the National Urban League helped to integrate Negroes in industry.

Organizations

children, and many rural counties had no schools at all for Negroes. The Fund also aided in the training of colored teachers and, under the direction of Edwin R. Embree, established fellowships for Negro leaders in various educational fields. Other Northern philanthropic organizations assisting Negro learning were the Peabody Education Fund, established in 1867; the Slater Fund, started in 1882; the Jeanes Fund, in 1905; the General Education Board, founded in 1903 by John D. Rockefeller and the Phelps-Stokes Fund, set up in 1911. The Carnegie and Duke Foundations also aided Negro academic progress.

The National Urban League grew out of the Committee on Urban Conditions among Negroes, which was formed in 1910 by a young Negro graduate student in social work at Columbia University, George Edmund Haynes, and Mrs. William H. Baldwin, Jr., a white woman who

had been active in the League for the Protection of Colored Women. The League's objectives were the improvement of the industrial and living conditions of city Negroes, with special reference to the broadening of occupational opportunities. Interracial in composition, its sponsors included Julius Rosenwald, Roger Baldwin, Booker T. Washington, L. Hollingsworth Wood, Kelly Miller and the Negro journalist Fred R. Moore. The first chairman of its board was Edwin R. A. Seligman of Columbia University, and its executive officers were Haynes and Eugene Kinkle Jones, a Cornell graduate who had specialized in economics and sociology. He became its executive secretary in 1914.

With headquarters in New York, the Urban League soon had branches in major cities across the country. The sociologist Charles S. Johnson became in 1921 its director of research and investigation. In 1923 he

founded the League's magazine *Opportunity, A Journal of Negro Life*, whose motto was "Not Alms, but Opportunity." The Urban League sought to overcome discrimination in employment and, by counsel and persuasion, to induce industries employing no Negroes to give them opportunities for work and industrial training. It sought to have those plants and foundries which used Negroes only in jobs of unskilled labor to upgrade them according to ability. It sought to ease the difficulties of adjustment between white employers and black employees. It developed a program and set up fellowships for the training of young social workers. Some of the most distinguished personalities in that field gained their training and early experience through the Urban League. The annual conferences of the National Urban League became significant gatherings for social workers of both races from all over America.

The 369th Infantry of the 93rd Division were in the trenches 191 days, never lost a foot of ground and were the first unit of the Allied Armies to reach the Rhine. The Germans called them the "Hell Fighters." They suffered casualties of 1,100 dead and wounded.

World War I

Woodrow Wilson in 1913 became the first Southern Democrat in the White House since the Civil War. Half of his Cabinet appointees were Southerners. His first Congress was flooded with anti-Negro bills, more than ever before introduced at a single session, and Wilson himself issued orders segregating most Negro federal employees in Washington. In 1915, the year that Booker T. Washington died, there were sixty-nine lynchings. In 1917 the United States entered World War I under the slogan "Make the World Safe for Democracy." To clarify confusion among Negroes concerning such an objective and such a war, Dr. Du Bois in the *Crisis* wrote his famous editorial, "Close Ranks," in which he argued that Negroes had more to gain from a society in which democracy was *at least an ideal* than they would have under German autocracy. He urged colored citizens to participate in America's war effort.

The court-martial of sixty-four members of the 24th Infantry, November 1, 1917, before an all-white military tribunal on charges of mutiny and murder. The trial was held in Gift Chapel, Fort Sam Houston, Texas.

Within a week after the United States entered the war the War Department stopped accepting Negro volunteers; colored army quotas were filled. No black men were allowed in the Marines, Coast Guard or Air Force and in the Navy only as messmen. However, when drafting began, of the more than 2,000,-000 Negroes registered 31 per cent were accepted, to 26 per cent of the white men. Negroes, then comprising 10 per cent of the population, furnished 13 per cent of the inductees. During the war the labor and stevedore battalions, except for commanding officers, were made up almost entirely of Negroes. Some 200,000 colored troops served overseas and 50,000 Negroes were engaged in combat duty. The entire 1st Battalion of the 367th Infantry was cited for bravery; fifty-seven of its men were awarded the Distinguished Service Cross. General Pershing said of the Negro soldiers of the 92nd Division, "You have measured up to every expectation of the Commander-in-Chief."

In 1917 Emmett J. Scott, former secretary to Booker T. Washington, was appointed special assistant to the Secretary of War, as an adviser in matters affecting the Negro. Scott was assigned the task of dealing with problems of segregation in Army camps at home and abroad. No provisions had been made for the training of Negro officers. Major Joel E. Spingarn, N.A.A.C.P. board member, took up this situation with the War Department. A committee of Negro college men also brought pressure to bear, and a camp for such training was set up at Fort Des Moines, Iowa, from which were commissioned 106 Negro captains and 533 first and second lieutenants. However, the highest-ranking Negro officer in the U. S. Army, West Pointer Colonel Charles Young, was retired on the grounds of health. To prove he was not unfit, Young rode a horse alone from Ohio to Washington. He was then assigned to non-combatant service as a military attaché but was not permitted to serve in Europe.

The South objected to Negro soldiers—particularly those from the North—being trained there, and black men in uniform were subjected to even more than the customary Jim Crowisms shown colored civilians. At Camp Greene, North Carolina, for example, all the Y.M.C.A. canteens were marked for the exclusive use of white troops. At Spartanburg, South Carolina, whites who objected to the 15th New York Infantry's training nearby beat and kicked drum major Noble Sissle. An impending race riot was averted by removing the Negro troops and sending them to Europe to face the German armies. But disorder broke out in Houston, Texas, where, after numbers of them had been ganged and beaten, Negro soldiers had been disarmed. Seventeen whites were killed and sixty-four members of the 24th Infantry were court-martialed. At the largest mass murder trial in the history of the United States, thirteen Negro soldiers were sentenced to death by hanging, forty-one were imprisoned for life and a number of others were held in custody pending further investigations. Brigadier-General G. K. Hunter presided.

Medals and Music

The 369th Infantry reached France early in 1918, where they attended a French divisional training school under French command. They went into action at Bois d'Hauza in April, holding for two months an entire sector against German fire. They also fought at Minaucourt and took part in the great attack at Maison-en-Champagne, which carried them to the Rhine. No man of their number was ever captured and the unit never retreated. Eleven times the 369th Infantry was cited for bravery and the entire regiment received the French Croix de Guerre for gallantry under fire. Individually, 171 of its officers and enlisted men were decorated with the Croix de Guerre or the Legion of Honor.

The 371st Infantry Regiment, which received its training at Camp Jackson, South Carolina, served as part of the 157th French Division under General Goybet, remaining in the front lines for more than three months. Montfauxelles, a strategically vital point which the Germans had held for almost a year, was captured by

Returning soldiers of the 369th Infantry Regiment wearing the Croix de Guerre, aboard the S.S. *Stockholm*, February, 1919. This regiment was the first of the returning American troops to march under the Arch on Fifth Avenue at Washington Square.

this regiment. It also took a number of prisoners, captured a munitions depot and several railroad cars full of supplies. It lost almost half of its 2,384 men. It was praised by General Goybet as having "a most complete contempt for danger." Other Negro units to serve with distinction in World War I were the 8th Illinois (renamed the 370th) and the 372nd Infantry, many of whose men were decorated for bravery.

Credited with being the first group of musicians to introduce jazz to Europe, the 369th Regimental Band, led by Lieutenant James Reese Europe, became famous on the battlefronts. Its drum major was Sergeant Noble Sissle, later to become well known on Broadway as a singer, conductor and composer. Europe, who "had enough jazz in stock to last until the war was over," played for both American and French troops in camps, in hospitals, for civilians behind the lines and in Paris. Once the members of a French military band, unable to believe such strange jazz sounds could be produced by ordinary instruments, offered to exchange brasses and woodwinds with the Negro band. The Negroes played just as well on the French instruments, but the puzzled French soldiers could not produce jazz on the American ones. Another popular Negro military musical unit in France was the 350th Field Artillery Band, directed by J. T. Bynum.

The first American soldier in World War I to receive the French Croix de Guerre with star and palm was Sergeant Henry Johnson, a red-cap of Albany, New York. The battle in which he fought became known as "The Battle of Henry Johnson." With a fellow soldier of the 369th Infantry, Needham Roberts of Trenton, New Jersey, Johnson was on outpost guard duty before dawn on May 14, 1918, when a raiding party of twenty Germans swooped down upon them and wounded them both with surprise grenades. After Johnson had fired his last bullets the Germans began to drag Roberts away as a prisoner. Using the butt end of his rifle and a bolo knife, Johnson freed Roberts. Both Negroes then killed four Germans, wounded several others and held their post as the rest fled. Johnson and Roberts were decorated by the French government and their exploit was headlined in the newspapers back home.

Sergeant Henry Johnson.   Needham Roberts.

Lieutenant James Reese Europe conducting the 369th Regimental Band before the American Red Cross Hospital No. 9 in Paris. Before entering the service, Europe had conducted syncopated orchestras in New York, had served as a musical director for Broadway shows and had given concerts in Carnegie Hall.

A full-page N.A.A.C.P. advertisement published in the *New York Times* and other leading dailies in November, 1922, as part of an effort to secure passage of the Dyer Anti-Lynching Bill and to call attention to America's racial plight.

"If We Must Die"

If we must die, let it not be like hogs
Hunted and penned in an inglorious spot,
While round us bark the mad and hungry dogs,
Making their mock at our accursed lot.
If we must die, O let us nobly die
So that our precious blood may not be shed
In vain; then even the monsters we defy
Shall be constrained to honor us though dead!
O kinsmen! We must meet the common foe!
Though far outnumbered let us show us brave,
And for their thousand blows deal one death blow!
What though before us lies the open grave?
Like men we'll face the murderous, cowardly pack,
Pressed to the wall, dying, but fighting back!

—from *Harlem Shadows* by Claude McKay

During the war, stories of race riots and lynchings filled the front pages, rivaling only the war news in death and violence. In July, 1917, a massacre occurred in East St. Louis, Illinois, in which many Negroes were burned alive in their homes, 6,000 driven from the city and $400,000 worth of property destroyed. In Elaine, Arkansas, in 1919, ten white persons and eleven Negroes were killed and dozens were injured. In Chicago that year the home of the actor Richard B. Harrison was dynamited, and during the next four years under lackadaisical police protection there were fifty-eight bombings of Negro homes in that city.

Prisoners Given to Bloodthirsty Whites by Sheriff, Who Sees Them Lynched

TORCH LAW SANCTIONED

The Chicago Defender

SATURDAY, MAY 24, 1919

WANTED TO LEAVE FARM; IS LYNCHED

Dublin, Ga., May 23.—James Water who was accused of assaulting a white girl in Johnson county two weeks ago was turned over by Sheriff O. L. Smith to a mob while on his way to the county jail. It appeared that the re...

ANTI-NEGRO RIOTERS AGAIN PLY THE TORCH

Three More Bodies Found To-Day at East St. Louis, Making Total 27—Additional Troops May Be Sent There.

EAST ST. LOUIS, Ill., July 3.—Fires which were started by rioters in three Negro quarters at noon to-day were fanned by a high wind and spread rapidly, getting beyond control...

Thousands Are Driven From South at Point of Gun; Troops Aid Possemen

(By Century News Service)

Elaine, Ark., Oct. 10.—It was necessary to call federal troops, statione...

"We return. We return from fighting. We return fighting. Make way for Democracy! We saved it in France, and by the Great Jehovah, we will save it in the U. S. A., or know the reason why!" In the name of the returning Negro soldiers, so spoke Du Bois in the *Crisis* in the spring of 1919. That summer race riots became race wars; Negroes fought back. After having fought "to make the world safe for democracy," some were at least determined to protect their own lives on home soil.

There were, in 1919, eighty-three lynchings, several of Negro veterans in uniform, some of whom were burned alive. The Ku Klux Klan held more than 200 public meetings from Indiana and New England to Florida. There were twenty-five major race riots within seven months. In Long View, Texas, a mob searching for a teacher accused of writing for the *Chicago Defender* burned homes, flogged a school principal and ran many Negroes out of town.

In Washington mobs roamed the city for three days. A number of Negroes and whites were killed and scores were injured. That same month in Chicago, with a population of 100,000 colored people, fifteen whites and twenty-three Negroes were killed, almost 600 wounded and 1,000 families burned out. Similar riots occurred in Knoxville, Tennessee, and Omaha, Nebraska, where a Negro was dragged through the streets, shot more than a thousand times and hanged on the main street.

That summer in New York City, under the auspices of the N.A.A.C.P., 10,000 Negroes silently marched down Fifth Avenue bearing banners protesting such violence, and radical Negro magazines like *Messenger*, edited by A. Philip Randolph and Chandler Owen, published such strong editorials that the Department of Justice felt a government investigation into their sponsors was required.

The Silent Protest Parade, July 28, 1917, in which thousands of New Yorkers marched, bearing banners asking, "Mr. President, Why Not Make America Safe for Democracy?", "Give Me a Chance to Live" and "Thou Shalt Not Kill."

Senator J. Thomas Heflin of Alabama, "Champion of White Protestantism."

Senator James Vardaman of Mississippi, where Negroes were disfranchised.

Theodore G. Bilbo, twice governor of Mississippi and later a U. S. Senator

The Headless Worker

When the Ku Klux Klan was reactivated in 1915 beneath a fiery cross on Stone Mountain near Atlanta, its Imperial Wizard William Joseph Simmons declared that to the Anglo-Saxon "must yield the self-centered Hebrew, the cultured Greek, the virile Roman and the mystic Oriental," for the Klan was not only anti-Negro, but also anti-Jewish, anti-foreign-born, anti-Roman Catholic and anti-Oriental. Many Southern politicians mouthed Klan precepts and supported its objectives in the legislative halls. Among such bigots were Heflin, Vardaman and Bilbo. In the Senate, Theodore G. Bilbo, "The Man" from Mississippi, became a leader of the filibusters against anti-lynching and anti-poll tax bills, introduced a measure to resettle Negroes in Africa and attacked all steps designed to ameliorate the condition of the Negro. Said "pious" Bilbo, "We, the people of the South, must draw the color line tighter and tighter. . . . The white race is the custodian of the Gospel of Jesus Christ."

Meanwhile, the decline in cotton prices in the South, floods and the boll-weevil in the fields were conditions which, added to racial pressures, caused whole families of Negroes to migrate to Harlem in New York and Negro areas of Philadelphia, Cleveland, Detroit, Chicago, Pittsburgh and St. Louis, where there were higher wages, less racial prejudice and superior educational opportunities for their children. The Chicago *Defender* declared that it was better to die of frostbite in the North than at the hands of a mob in the South. In some Southern cities the sale of Negro papers was made illegal, and deputy sheriffs hauled Negroes off northbound trains to prevent the loss of cheap labor. Nevertheless, the northward trek continued.

When the war cut off the supply of

"The South's Conception of the Ideal Colored Worker,"—strong, but headless, therefore brainless. A New York *World* cartoon.

European immigrant labor, conditions for Negro workers improved in Northern plants and foundries. Steel mills, stockyards, ammunition depots and the automotive industries employed increasing numbers of Negroes. The Pennsylvania Railroad brought 12,000 colored men from the South to work on its tracks and in its yards. Many Negro women found employment in factories. The National Urban League helped in the placement of black workers and studied their problems of adjustment. At the end of the first quarter of the twentieth century in America the Negro had become—even though largely at the lower economic levels—a fixture in Northern industrial life.

Southern white workers also came North in large numbers, bringing their racial bias with them. Klan cells sprang up, not only in the industrial Midwest, but in the East as well. A number of Negro leaders and Negro publications protesting the spread of prejudice were labeled subversive by Attorney General Palmer in 1919. A. Philip Randolph, the Socialist editor of the *Messenger*, was arrested, and Department of Justice agents visited Dr. Du Bois at the *Crisis* offices to inquire just what the N.A.A.C.P. was fighting for. Du Bois' reply was: "For the enforcement of the Constitution of the United States."

NEGROES HAVE COME NORTH TO STAY; FIND CHANCE FOR INDEPENDENCE HERE

In spite of attempts to halt the migration, more than 2,000,000 Negroes left the South within five years after World War I, headed for the industrial cities of the North.

FILIBUSTER BLOCKS ANTI-LYNCHING BILL

House Democrats Succeed in Preventing Debate on Measure Until After Holidays.

WIN BY BREAKING QUORUM

NORFOLK, VIRGINIA, SATURDAY DECEMBER 17, 1921

Lynchings Continue As Congress Debates Anti-Lynch Bill

New York.—The National Association for the Advancement of Colored People, today made public a statement to the effect that since the introduction of the Dyer Anti-Lynching Bill in Congress on April 11, 192_ there had been 28 persons murd____ _____ in the United Sta___

ha_e been seven lynchings, one bod_ be ng publicl_ k_nsas.
Among these lync_ _olored m_ _hite girl_ a note h_ l_nche_ _ as _ _c_

From the time of the introduction of the Dyer Anti-Lynching Bill in April, 1921, to the end of the year, there were twenty-eight lynchings in the United States.

The Ku Klux Klan paraded in full regalia in 1925 down Pennsylvania Avenue past the White House.

269

Marcus Garvey

Discouraged by the slowness with which organizations like the N.A.A.C.P. were making headway and disappointed with national laxity in the enforcing of constitutional and even local provisions for civil rights, thousands of colored citizens in the early 1920's were attracted by the rising tide of Negro nationalism expressed in Marcus Garvey's "Back-to-Africa" movement. Feeling that black men could not prosper in a "white land" where "poverty is no virtue; it is a crime," Garvey urged Negroes to build a civilization of their own in Africa and make it a homeland for 400,000,000 black people. For a few years the most famous Negro leader in the world, Garvey held a position of leadership less than a decade.

Born, as he liked to boast, "a full-blooded black man" in 1887 in Jamaica, Marcus Manasseh Garvey was the son of a carpenter. At sixteen he was apprenticed to a printer in Kingston and became a foreman at twenty-two. But after joining journeymen printers in a strike which was defeated, he was barred by white printers from further employment in Jamaica. Garvey then went to England, where he worked for the African-Egyptian publisher Mohammed Effendi and studied nights at the University of London. There he met many Africans and learned of the problems and oppressions of colonialism. In 1914, when Garvey returned to Jamaica, he organized the Universal Negro Improvement Association, with the objective of taking Africa from the imperialists, organizing it and making it "the defender of Negroes the world over."

Meanwhile, the young man dreamed of establishing in Jamaica a school like Tuskegee. Toward this end, Garvey began a correspondence with Booker T. Washington, who invited him to come to the United States. But when Garvey arrived Washington was dead and his successor as president of Tuskegee, Robert Russa Morton, did not approve of Garvey's African nationalism.

Harlem, where there were many West Indians from the Caribbean, attracted Garvey. There, in 1917, Garvey reorganized his Universal Negro Improvement Association and announced as its objective the creation of a strong Negro nation in Africa, the co-fraternity of Negroes the world over and the setting up of branches and schools in all lands having black populations. He founded a newspaper, the *Negro World,* with "Africa for the Africans" as its slogan. As with previous colonization movements in the United States, those whites who wanted to get rid of the Negro and his problems hailed the Garvey movement, and even the Ku Klux Klan approved of it. But no whites were admitted to membership, no funds were solicited from them, nor could they buy stock in the various business enterprises the movement proposed to set up. Garvey denounced white philanthropy, excoriated the interracial N.A.A.C.P. and directed his appeal to the ordinary black man and woman, urging them, much as Booker T. Washington had done, to do something for themselves. "Up, you mighty race!" Garvey cried in thirty-eight states in hundreds of speeches. "You can accomplish what you will. . . . No one knows when the hour of Africa's redemption cometh. . . . One day, like a storm, it will be here!"

Negro workers within a few years poured some $10,000,000 into the Garvey movement, in the face of almost unanimous denunciation by Negro intellectuals, who termed him a visionary, a demogogue and even a charlatan. But attending the second U. N. I. A. convention in New York in 1921 were 25,000 Negroes from all over the United States, the West Indies, Africa and South America, who confirmed Garvey as the Provisional President-General of Africa and who listened to the prayers of the black archbishop of the African Orthodox Church which Garvey had created, complete with a black Holy Trinity, a black Christ of Sorrow and a black Madonna. Joined by Harlemites, the Garveyites, some 50,000 strong, paraded down Lenox Avenue to trumpets and drums, held a mammoth mass meeting in Madison Square Garden and sent a resolution to the League of Nations affirming "the right of Europe for the Europeans, Asia for the Asiatics and Africa for the Africans . . . at this time when . . . 400,000,000 Negroes demand a place in the sun of the world."

Garvey wore a uniform of purple and gold with a helmet of feathers as "tall as Guinea grass," and he walked into his crowded meetings at Liberty Hall in Harlem surrounded by his African Legion. The Black Cross nurses were all in white, while the African Motor Corps, the African Legion and

Marcus Garvey (1887-1940). "I asked 'Where is the black man's government? Where is his king and his kingdom? Where is his president, his country and his ambassador, his army, his navy, his men of big affairs? I could not find them. I declared 'I will help to make them'."

the Black Eagle Flying Corps wore uniforms of green, black and red, like their banner. "Black for our race, red for our blood and green for our hope," said Garvey. But hope, at least in its material form, soon went on the rocks, along with the unseaworthy ships of the Black Star Line, which Garvey had founded to transport Negroes from the United States and the West Indies to Africa.

In 1923 Garvey was tried in federal court for using the mails to defraud and was sentenced to five years in prison, with a $1,000 fine. He appealed, lost and was sent to the Alabama Penitentiary. His paper, the *Negro World*, was termed by the Lusk Legislative Committee as "dangerous to the comfort and security" of whites. In 1927 Garvey was deported to Jamaica. He died in 1940 in London. But the Negro attorney Henry Lincoln Johnson remarked at Garvey's trial, "If every Negro could have put every dime, every penny, into the sea and if he might get in exchange the knowledge that he was somebody, that he meant something in the world, he would gladly do it. . . . The Black Star Line was a loss in money, but it was a gain in soul."

Part Six

THE NEGRO

1920-1941

BY THE END OF WORLD WAR I, Harlem in New York City had become the largest Negro urban community in the world. By 1924 its colored population exceeded that of any Southern city. It had become the Negro cultural center of the Americas. British West Indians, Cubans, Puerto Ricans and Haitians contributed colorful elements and its crowded streets were alive with a variety of accents and languages. Its music ranged from jazz to rhumbas, hymns to parlor ragtime, spirituals to chamber quartets. Marcus Garvey thundered and Claude McKay, also from Jamaica, read his poems. Arna Bontemps, from Louisiana by way of California, wrote poetry, and Wallace Thurman, from Salt Lake City, wrote stories. Magazine editors and book publishers were more aware of Negro writers.

Encouraged by the publication in 1925 of Alain Locke's anthology, *The New Negro*—a collection of poems, stories, essays and pictures—a vogue for things Negro in the arts developed among white New Yorkers and spread across the country. The twenties were, in a way, a Negro Renaissance. Dr. Alain Locke had been a Phi Beta Kappa at Harvard, a Rhodes Scholar at Oxford and had studied at the University of Berlin before becoming a professor of philosophy at Howard University in Washington. An influential lecturer, essayist and critic, he imbued many Negroes with the idea that art might provide a new approach to the race problem. "The fiction is that the life of the races is separate, and increasingly so," he wrote. "The fact is that they touch too closely at the unfavorable and too lightly at the favorable levels."

At the Provincetown Theater in Greenwich Village Eugene O'Neill's "The Emperor Jones" opened, with a Negro actor—Charles Gilpin—in the leading role.

Gilpin was voted by the Drama League as one of the ten persons of 1920 who had most greatly advanced the American theater. In 1921 a musical, "Shuffle Along," filled a theater for almost two years. Written, directed, performed and originally produced by Negroes—Noble Sissle, Eubie Blake, Flournoy Miller and Aubrey Lyles—it brought to fame a new singing and dancing star, Florence Mills.

The work of colored painters and sculptors also began to attract wide attention. Alain Locke brought from Europe a priceless collection of ancient African art for exhibition in America. The Hall Johnson Choir became popular for its powerful spirituals. Fletcher Henderson and Louis Armstrong brought jazz to Broadway. A Negro-originated dance called the Charleston swept the nation, followed in popularity in 1927 by a dance that had begun at the Savoy Ballroom in Harlem, the Lindy Hop. During the Prohibition era Negro entertainers and performers were popular—the tap dancer "Bojangles" Bill Robinson, the Mills Brothers and Ethel Waters. George Gershwin's "Rhapsody in Blue" had deep roots in Negro blues and Paul Green's dramas of race conflict, with excellent colored actors in the casts, came to Broadway. Critics called Rose McClendon the "Negro Duse." In 1927 "Porgy" opened. in 1928 the sparkling hit revue "Blackbirds" came to Broadway. And in 1930 "The Green Pastures," with De Lawd surrounded by colored angels, opened its lengthy run.

By this time the stock market had crashed and the depression was on its way. But as Alain Locke put it, the Negro, as a "collaborator and participant in American civilization," during the twenties had finally reached his "spiritual coming of age."

Alain Locke (1886-1954) brought to his analyses of the young writers and artists of the twenties a wealth of erudition and appreciation of the arts. His *The New Negro* is a representative anthology of the first half of this period.

"Literature by Negro authors about Negro experience," wrote Sterling Brown, a poet, critic and anthologist, "is a literature *in process* and like all such literature must be considered significant . . . because of the illumination it sheds upon a social reality." More books were published by Negro authors during the twenties than during any previous decade in American history. Although most of them were by younger writers living in Harlem, the older Negro writers also continued their literary output. W. E. B. Du Bois published *Darkwater*, a collection of essays, in 1920 and in 1921 Benjamin Brawley's *A Social History of the American Negro* appeared.

The Negro Renaissance really began with the publication of a book of poems, *Harlem Shadows*, by Claude McKay in 1922, containing his sonnets "If We Must Die," "White Houses" and "To the Lynchers." And in the same year Georgia Douglass Johnson's *Bronze* and James Weldon Johnson's *Book of American Negro Poetry* appeared. In 1923 Jean Toomer's *Cane*, a collection of stories and lyrics, came out. Walter White's novel about a lynching, *The Fire in the Flint*, Jessie Fauset's novel of intellectual middle-class life, *There Is Confusion*, and another collection of essays by Du Bois, *The Gift of Black Folk*, were published in 1924. In 1925 Countee Cullen's volume of poems, *Color*, and Alain Locke's anthology, *The New Negro*, appeared. In 1926 came the first book of poems by Langston Hughes, *The Weary Blues*, with an introduction by Carl Van Vechten; a collection of West Indian short stories, *Tropic Death*, by Eric Waldron; *Flight*, a novel by Walter White and *The Blues*, edited by W. C. Handy.

There followed in 1928 three first novels: *Home to Harlem* by Claude McKay, *The Walls of Jericho* by Rudolph Fisher and *Quicksand* by Nella Larsen. Also published was another book of verses by Georgia Douglass Johnson, *An Autumn Love Cycle*. In 1929 the singer Taylor Gordon published an amusing autobiography, *Born to Be*, and there appeared *Rope and Faggot—A Biography of Judge Lynch* by Walter White. There were four

Claude McKay (1889-1948) left the West Indies to study agriculture at Tuskegee and at Kansas State University before coming to Harlem.

Arna Bontemps has written verse, novels and books for young people. Now librarian of Fisk University, he is well known as an anthologist.

Rudolph Fisher, (1897-1934), a graduate of Howard Medical School and a writer, practiced roentgenology in New York.

Literary Mecca

novels by Negroes that year: *The Blacker The Berry* by Wallace Thurman; *Plum Bun* by Jessie Fauset; *Passing* by Nella Larsen and *Banjo* by Claude McKay, as well as a volume of poems by Countee Cullen, *The Black Christ*. Abroad, there appeared in Vienna and Leipzig a beautifully bound anthology of poems by contemporary American Negroes translated into German, *Afrika Singt*. *God Sends Sunday* by Arna Bontemps published in 1931, ended this flowering.

Opportunity and the *Crisis* conducted literary contests during the twenties and among those who received awards from these magazines were Arna Bontemps, Waring Cuney, Lucy Ariel Williams, Frank Horne, Cecil Blue and Zora Neale Hurston. In 1926 the Carnegie Foundation purchased from the Negro bibliophile Arthur Schomburg his rich accumulation of Negro books in all languages and presented them to the New York Public Library. Now housed in Harlem, the Schomburg Collection is an important research center, open to students of Negro life and letters.

Langston Hughes is shown here, a year after his first book was published, at Tuskegee with Jessie Fauset and Zora Neale Hurston.

Countee Cullen won the Witter Bynner Undergraduate Poetry Prize at New York University.

Jean Toomer of Washington, D. C. published stories and poetry in magazines such as *Broom*, *S4N*, the *Dial*.

Early in the 1920's Hall Johnson, who had been a violinist in the "Shuffle Along" orchestra, formed a group of young Harlem singers to present Negro folk songs simply, unencumbered by over-elaborate arrangements. The Hall Johnson Choir became famous in concerts and films and furnished the "singing orchestra" for "The Green Pastures."

J. Rosamond Johnson, Taylor Gordon and the young bass soloist Paul Robeson sang the spirituals simply and naturally to crowded auditoriums, too. But Roland Hayes and later Marian Anderson, who sought careers as concert singers, did not limit their repertoire to folk songs but included music by Mozart, Bach and Beethoven as well as great operatic arias. Other distinguished singers of the period were the actress Abbie Mitchell, Harry T. Burleigh, who was for many years a soloist at St. George's Episcopal Church in New York, and Jules Bledsoe, who later originated the role of Joe in "Show Boat."

It was Georgia-born Roland Hayes who broke the color bar in the concert halls for Negro singers of lieder and classical selections. After a command performance before King George V at Buckingham Palace, Hayes returned to America in 1923 to become one of the most popular concert artists. Marian Anderson went to Europe on a Rosenwald Fellowship in 1930. She returned with medals from the King of Denmark and the King of Sweden.

Meanwhile, at Hampton, the composer R. Nathaniel Dett was writing, arranging and training young singers, among whom was Dorothy Maynor. Dett's

piano suites such as "Juba Dance" are frequently performed. Other serious young composers of color who emerged in the twenties were William Grant Still, whose "Afro-American Symphony" and other works received performances by major symphony orchestras, William L. Dawson, who became director of the Tuskegee Choir, and John W. Work II.

In the field of popular music the pianist Jelly Roll Morton, W. C. Handy, called the "Father of the Blues," J. P. Johnson, famous for the Charleston, Thomas "Fats" Waller, Clarence Williams and Spencer Williams all added to America's rich music. In 1922 Duke Ellington brought his first orchestra, the Washingtonians, and his great talent for popular composition to Harlem and Broadway, and from that time on jazz has been on the upswing. Fletcher Henderson for many years had his own band and also did arrangements for other famous bands such as Benny Goodman's. John Kirby's little band, with Maxine Sullivan swinging the old folk songs, Chick Webb with Ella Fitzgerald, Teddy Wilson and Benny Carter came forward during the thirties.

Then Charlie Christian, Dizzy Gillespie and Charlie Parker brought the bop influence to bear on what became modern jazz, including such exponents as Thelonius Monk, Bud Powell, Lester Young, Chico Hamilton, Buddy Collette and Charlie Mingus. Touring around the world with America's basic music, jazz, and making friends for democracy have been such bands as those of Louis Armstrong, Lionel Hampton and Dizzy Gillespie. Air waves and records

As a child Marian Anderson sang in the choir of a Philadelphia church, which raised funds for her musical education.

R. Nathaniel Dett was graduated from Oberlin, where he won prizes in composition, conducted the Hampton choir.

Aaron Douglas, who was born in Topeka, Kansas, painted in Philadelphia on a Barnes Foundation fellowship and in Paris.

Richard B. Harrison, whose portrayal of De Lawd in "The Green Pastures," moved many play goers.

Decade

now carry the rhythms to listeners here and abroad.

The most popular Negro painter of the twenties was Aaron Douglas, who later became head of the department of fine arts at Fisk University. Utilizing African motifs, he painted murals for the Harlem Branch YMCA, the 135th Street Branch of the New York Public Library, now named for Countee Cullen, the Hotel Sherman in Chicago and the Fisk University Library. Douglas also designed book jackets for volumes of poetry by Countee Cullen and Langston Hughes, as well as decorations for James Weldon Johnson's *God's Trombones* and Paul Morand's *Black Magic*. Before migrating to Copenhagen, William H. Johnson won a Harmon Award in New York for his paintings. Other winners were Hale Woodruff and Palmer Hayden. In 1928 the Otto Kahn Prize went to Malvin Gray Johnson. The young cartoonist E. Simms Campbell came to Harlem in the twenties from St. Louis to study at the Art Students' League under George Gros. The sculptor Richmond Barthé came to Manhattan from New Orleans in 1929. The work of Augusta Savage had already attracted attention, as had that of Sargent Johnson of California.

After the production of "Shuffle Along" a series of lively all-Negro musical shows came to Broadway—in 1923 "Liza" and a few months later "Runnin' Wild," which introduced the new dance, the Charleston, and in 1924, Sissle and Blake's "Chocolate Dandies," with Johnny Hudgins and Josephine Baker, and "Dixie to Broadway," with Florence Mills. In 1926 came "Blackbirds," in 1927 "Rang Tang," also "Africana," starring Ethel Waters, then "Blackbirds of 1928," with Bill Robinson and Adelaide Hall, and in 1929 "Hot Chocolates."

In 1923 the Ethiopian Art Players presented "Salome." That same year Paul Robeson made his debut as a voodoo king in "Taboo." The following year at the Provincetown Theatre Robeson played the male lead opposite a white actress, Mary Blair, in Eugene O'Neill's "All God's Chillun Got Wings."

In 1926 Lenore Ulric played a colored role in David Belasco's production of "Lulu Belle," with a largely Negro cast. Jules Bledsoe and Rose McClendon appeared in Paul Green's "In Abraham's Bosom," which received a Pulitzer Prize. On October 10, 1927, the Theater Guild produced Du Bose Heyward's "Porgy," which had a long run in New York

and London with many fine Negro actors in its cast, including Rose McClendon, Georgette Harvey, Evelyn Ellis, Leigh Whipper and Frank Wilson. Wilson emerged as a playwright in 1928 with "Meek Mose," produced by the Negro newspaperman, Lester A. Walton. In 1929 Wallace Thurman wrote "Harlem," a melodramatic study of a Southern migrant family. This decade of almost continuous brilliant Negro entertainment closed with Marc Connelly's fantasy "The Green Pastures."

Duke Ellington, said Robert Goffin, "gradually placed intuitive music under control."

Paul Robeson, shown with Mary Blair in a scene from "All God's Chillun Got Wings."

Scholars

Carter G. Woodson founded the Association for the Study of Negro Life and History.

Less highly publicized than Negro achievements in the arts, but of no less importance, are the contribution made by colored scientists and scholars. Most of them were educated at leading Northern universities. The historians Carter Woodson and Rayford Logan received their doctorates at Harvard, the economist Abram Harris at Columbia, the biologist Ernest Just and the sociologists Charles Johnson and E. Franklin Frazier at the University of Chicago.

Many became teachers in Negro colleges. Dr. Daniel Hale Williams, upon his graduation in 1883 from the medical school of Northwestern University, became an instructor in anatomy there. At the invitation of President Grover Cleveland he headed the Freedmen's Hospital in Washington, D. C., but returned to Chicago to help found Provident Hospital there in 1891 and to set up the first training school for Negro nurses in the United States. It was in Chicago that he performed his famous pioneering operation on the human heart. He became a Fellow of the American College of Surgeons.

Dr. Charles R. Drew, who was graduated from Amherst in 1926, became chief surgeon and chief of staff at Freedmen's Hospital. As a leading authority on the preservation of blood plasma, Dr. Drew directed the medical division of the British Blood Transfusion As-

Rayford W. Logan, head of the Howard University department of history.

Abram L. Harris became professor of economics at the University of Chicago.

Ernest Just served as vice-president of the American Society of Zoologists.

and Scientists

sociation and, during World War II, aided the American Red Cross and was surgical consultant for the U. S. Army. Dr. Percy Julian, who was graduated from De Pauw University in 1920 and received his doctorate in chemistry at the University of Vienna, has made pioneer discoveries concerning uses of the soybean relative to vitamins and sex hormones.

Other distinguished Negroes in scientific fields include Dr. William A. Hinton, a clinical professor at the Harvard Medical School and originator of the Hinton test for syphilis; James A. Parsons, a metallurgical chemist; Julian H. Lewis, a pathologist; and Elmer S. Imes, a physicist. In 1921 the first Negro women to receive a doctor's degree in the United States were Georgiana Rosa Simpson, at the University of Chicago; Sadie T. Mosell, at the University of Pennsylvania; and Eva B. Dykes, at Radcliffe College.

In 1923 Charles S. Johnson founded the magazine *Opportunity* in which many young Negro writers and artists achieved first publication. Dr. Johnson has since become one of America's leading sociologists, the author of numerous books, a member of the United States National Commission to UNESCO in Paris and the recipient of six honorary degrees from leading universities at home and abroad.

A surgeon, Dr. Charles Drew became the first director of the American Red Cross blood bank.

Dr. Daniel Hale Williams first successfully operated on the human heart.

E. Franklin Frazier, head of the department of sociology at Howard University.

The first Negro president of Fisk University was Charles S. Johnson.

A Natchez child.

Children in Washington, D. C.

"Last Hired,

"Something is happening in Chicago," declared the Chicago *Defender* early in 1929, "and it should no longer go unnoticed. During the past three weeks hardly a day has ended that there has not been a report of another firm discharging its employees." Later that year the Urban League stated, "Every week we receive information regarding the discharge of additional race workers." But the ordinary Negro, who often said, "I'm the last to be hired, the first to be fired," did not need to read such statements to sense, months before the soon-to-be-concerned white workers, an impending slump in employment. In October, 1929, came the stock market crash. In its wake began the longest and most severe depression in American history.

At the height of the depression decade there were 14,000,000 unemployed, in-

Pulaski County, Arkansas, cotton pickers. They earned about 60 cents per day.

omeless men in a New York armory.

First Fired"

cluding many Negroes. Colored colleges, heavily dependent on philanthropy, fared badly. Hard-pressed Southern communities, forced to slice public school budgets, first cut the funds of the already poorly supported Negro schools. Many teachers lost their jobs and some schools closed. Cotton prices slumped and foundries shut down. By the mid-thirties almost 70 per cent of the persons on relief in Birmingham, Alabama, were colored. In Detroit the percentage was 29 and in Harlem 13. Housing became more rundown than ever. On Chicago's South Side, where almost 250,000 Negroes were crowded into eight square miles of tenement housing, health and morals suffered. Richard Wright, author of *Native Son*, wrote, "The kitchenette is our prison, our death sentence without a trial."

Father Divine

"The depression, with a devastating impact," recorded an Illinois State Commission, "reversed the trend of the twenties and turned the Negro people from a group with more than its share of gainfully employed into a population predominantly dependent upon government relief." National and local leaders, white and Negro, were at first powerless to cope with the problems. But one Negro leader would permit none of his followers to accept public relief, and none went hungry. Everyone who came to his restaurants received full meals for fifteen cents, or if one had no money, one received a free meal. He sold coal at cost from his coal yards and offered haircuts in his shops at a quarter of what other barbers charged. His name was Father Divine.

Father Divine established throughout the East and in various cities across the country a veritable chain of religious cooperatives. His followers gave of labor and income according to their abilities and received according to their needs, without any distinction as to color. Father Divine ordered any of his followers who were illiterate to attend night school, any who had been dishonest in the past to return whatever they had dishonestly acquired. He taught precepts of decency, hygiene and self-reliance. His religious meetings were combined with abundant feasting in the very midst of the depression. His Peace Missions, in spite of frequent controversy in the press regarding him, continue to be open to all today.

Early in the depression, nine Negro boys were hoboing their way on a freight train to Memphis in search of work. At Scottsboro, Alabama, they were hauled off the train by police, who also found two white women hoboes in a coal car. The police promptly accused the nine black boys of rape. One boy was only thirteen. A hasty trial was held before an all-white jury who quickly convicted the other eight boys and they were sent to the "death house" at Kilby. Defended by the Communist International Labor Defense, the Scottsboro Case became a *cause célèbre*, fought more than once all the way to the Supreme Court. None of the boys was electrocuted, but all served long years in prison.

A Father Divine shoeshine parlor; no tipping, no profanity, and no smoking allowed. Father Divine's slogan: "Peace! It's truly wonderful!"

Father Divine leads his followers ashore for a holiday at his Krum Elbow estate on the Hudson.

A Father Divine shop in Harlem which sold food to the public at cost.

Eight of the nine Scottsboro Boys, whose death sentences in Alabama aroused world-wide protest and pointed up the inequities of Southern courts and the lily-white jury system.

Votes for
Bread and Butter

Herbert Hoover, as President, had to face both depression and, in 1931, the Bonus Marchers, veterans of World War I who were routed from the capital by tanks and tear gas. During the presidential campaign of 1932, Negroes, who had been traditionally Republicans, decided to "vote for bread and butter instead of for the memory of Abraham Lincoln." Franklin D. Roosevelt was elected and the New Deal began. This liberal Democratic administration appointed many Negro advisers in various government departments, more than had ever before served in high official capacities.

The various governmental agencies which were set up to cope with the problems brought by the depression aided Negroes culturally, as well as in terms of sustenance. The Works Projects Administration, the National Youth Administration, the Civilian Conservation Corps camps, the Federal Theater and projects employing artists and writers gave hundreds of thousands of Negroes industrial training, theatrical experience and an opportunity to paint and write by opening up jobs to them from which private industry had excluded them. No wonder Negroes called F.D.R. the "Great White Father" and when he ran again for President in 1936, voted almost overwhelmingly Democratic. In 1934 Arthur W. Mitchell, the first Negro Democrat ever in Congress, was elected from Chicago.

Scene from "Turpentine," a Federal Theater production at the Lafayette Theater in Harlem, 1936.

A former South Carolina share-cropping family acquired a new house through the Farm Security Administration loan program.

The Harlem River housing project built by the Public Works Administration, which was turned over to the New York Housing Authority, June 16, 1937.

Negroes in Roosevelt's "Black Cabinet" were all highly competent specialists in various fields. In 1938 the group included (*front row, left to right*) Dr. Ambrose Caliver, Department of the Interior; Dr. Roscoe C. Brown, Public Health Service; Dr. Robert C. Weaver, Housing Authority; Joseph H. Evans, Farm Security Administration; Dr. Frank Horne (the poet), Housing Authority; Mary McLeod Bethune, National Youth Administration; Lieutenant Lawrence A. Oxley, Department of Labor; Dr. William J. Thompkins, Recorder of Deeds; Charles E. Hall, Department of Commerce; William I. Houston, Department of Justice; Ralph E. Mizelle, Post Office.

In the back row, (*left to right*) are Dewey R. Jones, Department of the Interior; Edgar Brown (tennis star), Civilian Conservation Corps; J. Parker Prescott, Housing Authority; Edward H. Lawson, Jr., Works Projects Administration; Arthur Weiseger, Department of Labor; Alfred Edgar Smith, Works Projects; Henry A. Hunt, Farm Credit Administration; John W. Whitten, Works Projects; and Joseph R. Houchins, Department of Commerce. Others included at various times William H. Hastie, attorney, Department of the Interior; Eugene Kinckle Jones, Department of Commerce; and William J. Trent, Federal Works Agency.

A workman on hydroelectric project of the Tennessee Valley Authority, established by Congress in 1933.

Federal Projects

Sterling Brown, poet and professor of English at Howard University, served as editor on Negro affairs for the Federal Writers Project. In Chicago the distinguished scholar Arna Bontemps was in charge of a unit. Writers who were given employment by the Project included Claude McKay, Richard Wright, Roi Ottley, Zora Neale Hurston, Frank Yerby, Margaret Walker, Marcus Christian, Robert Hayden, Ralph Ellison and John H. Johnson, who was to become the publisher of the leading Negro magazines *Ebony* and *Jet*. Much excellent writing and research emanated from these projects, including a number of well-documented state and regional histories.

In New York, Dean Dixon conducted the National Youth Administration Orchestra, made up of young people of all racial strains. In the Federal Theater, Negro actors in Northern cities performed in interracial units, as well as in such all-Negro companies as those in Harlem, Chicago, Birmingham, and Los Angeles, where Clarence Muse produced Hall Johnson's "Run, Little Chillun," which had the longest run of any Federal Theater group. Young colored persons interested in the technical aspects of the stage gained training and experience denied them in the commercial theater by union regulations or Broadway prejudice. At the Lafayette Theater in Harlem plays by Negro dramatists were done—Frank Wilson's "Walk Together, Children," Rudolph Fisher's "Conjure Man Dies," and "Turpentine," by J. A. Smith and Peter Morrell. Canada Lee, Edna Thomas and Jack Carter appeared in a stunning tropical "Macbeth," staged by Orson Welles and John Houseman. And in Chicago the Negro "Swing Mikado" was a jazz success.

Mary McLeod Bethune, born just after the Civil War of parents who had been slaves, worked barefooted as a child in the cotton fields of South Carolina and walked five miles a day to a mission school. She established a school in Florida—with orange crates as her first benches—which grew into Bethune-Cookman College and became director of Negro affairs in the National Youth Administration. She was a friend of the Roosevelts and a powerful figure in New Deal policies relating to the Negro.

The educational program of the National Youth Administration enrolled more than 600,000 Negroes in its classes. Many of the state and local supervisors, as well as teachers, were colored. In its student work-program

Selma Burke, WPA Federal Art Project sculptress, beside her bust of Booker T. Washington.

A WPA teacher gives a free music lesson.

more than 60,000 young colored men and women learned skilled trades. Older people were given opportunities for education through the Adult Education Projects, and jobs were provided for unemployed teachers. In the camps of the Civilian Conservation Corps some 200,000 Negro boys received practical training in reforestation and soil conservation.

By 1939 more than a million unemployed Negroes owed their livelihood to the Works Projects Administration. Other benefits accrued to the Negro through the construction by Public Works Administration subsidy of Negro college buildings, new Negro hospitals, community centers and playgrounds. Many small colleges which lacked adequate gymnasium or auditorium facilities secured such buildings through PWA. Negro artisans were gainfully employed in their construction except where white union locals prohibited them.

Jesse Owens was the top star of the 1936 Olympic Games at Berlin in which Hitler left the stands when Negro athletes came forward to receive their medals.

Ralph Metcalfe (*left*) and Eddie Tolan (*right*) at the Berlin Olympics. Tolan set world records for the 100-and 200-meter races in the 1932 Los Angeles Olympics.

In the thirties Benny Goodman began to integrate a number of Negroes into a formerly all-white band. The Benny Goodman Quartet, a unit within the band, included Lionel Hampton, vibraharp; Gene Krupa, drums; Benny Goodman, clarinet; and Teddy Wilson, piano. Later the Oklahoma guitarist Charlie Christian joined the band and by 1941 the ensemble included Negro bassist John Simmons; drummer Sid Catlett and trumpet man Cootie Williams.

A picket near the Capitol protesting congressional filibustering in 1946 of permanent FEPC legislation.

Pickets and Protest

Malcolm Ross, who was appointed chairman of the Fair Employment Practices Committee.

In many Northern cities during the depression, Negroes picketed and boycotted white-staffed businesses in Negro neighborhoods, demanding jobs. "Don't Buy Where You Can't Work" was their slogan. A number of businesses, including the Woolworth chain on the South Side of Chicago, capitulated and did hire Negro clerks. Along New York's 125th Street there were many flourishing white establishments in the heart of Harlem which depended on Negro patronage but had no colored employees. Adam Clayton Powell, Jr., later to become a Congressman but at that time the assistant pastor of the largest Baptist Church in the world, Abyssinia, sent picket lines to march in front of such shops.

When World War II broke out in Europe and the nation shifted to a war footing, many plants with government contracts refused to employ colored workers. Protests of the N.A.A.C.P., the Urban League and other groups were to no avail. A. Philip Randolph, who in 1925 had organized the Brotherhood of Sleeping Car Porters, then proposed a March-on-Washington (similar to the Bonus March) of from 50,000 to 100,000 Negroes. As large delegations from all across the nation prepared to entrain for the capital on June 1, 1941, the President called a conference of Negro leaders. On June 25, President Roosevelt issued his *Executive Order 8802* banning discrimination in industries holding government contracts and setting up a Committee on Fair Employment Practices.

A subway conductor in New York City. Such positions for Negroes were achieved as an outgrowth of agitation for jobs in the thirties and forties.

When the long-run Broadway play "The Green Pastures," with an all-Negro cast, was performing at the National Theater in Washington in 1934, no Negroes were allowed to buy tickets. Negroes could not then attend any downtown theater in the national capital. At Constitution Hall, where the Daughters of the American Revolution permitted colored patrons to buy segregated seats, no Negro could appear on the stage. In 1939 the great contralto Marian Anderson was refused permission to sing at Constitution Hall, and the ensuing protest grew to such proportions that Harold L. Ickes, Secretary of the Interior, invited Miss Anderson to sing on Easter Sunday from the steps of the Lincoln Memorial. Marian Anderson sang at the feet of the Great Emancipator, with a vast unsegregated audience stretching for blocks before her.

A decade later, by refusing to permit union actors to appear in Washington's segregated theaters, Actors' Equity broke the audience color bar in the capital. Today Negro citizens, like any other Americans, may attend theaters there. In 1955 Marian Anderson became the first Negro prima donna of the Metropolitan Opera Company in New York. A few years earlier, Janet Collins was its first colored prima ballerina.

A. Philip Randolph, executive board member of the AFL-CIO.

Strikers seeking union recognition at the Ford River Rouge plant.

Marian Anderson singing at the Lincoln Memorial on a chilly Easter Sunday, 1939, after being barred from Constitution Hall.

Dr. Ralph Bunche, as acting United Nations mediator on Palestine, conferred at Haifa in 1948 with General Lundstron. Born in Detroit in 1904, Bunche was graduated *summa cum laude* from Harvard, where he was elected to Phi Beta Kappa. He was appointed by the State Department as associate chief of the Division of Dependent Territories in 1944 and was an American adviser at the formation of the United Nations in San Francisco. He is now Under-Secretary General of the United Nations.

Part Seven

SEARCHING FOR FREEDOM

1940–1956

Patriotism and Prejudice

The first World War was fought, it was said, "to make the world safe for democracy." Millions of Blackamericans dedicated their lives, their fortunes, and their honor to achieve that goal. It has not yet been realized, even in America. World War II, President Roosevelt declared, was necessary to ensure that four basic freedoms were available to everyone. They were freedom of speech, freedom of religion, freedom from want, and freedom from fear. Again, Blackamericans rushed to offer themselves as unreserved patriots of the cause. Often they had to fight bias at home for the opportunity of fighting the enemy abroad. In consequence, they were determined that the Four Freedoms for which they offered their lives would be available to them at home, *in America*, and to their posterity. This time they did not want the nation to forget.

Even before the war, when defense preparations began and the draft act was passed, a group of black leaders, including Walter White of the NAACP, T. Arnold Hill of the Urban League, and A. Philip Randolph of the March-on-Washington Movement, presented to President Roosevelt a memorandum urging that discrimination be abolished in the Navy and the Air Force; that black recruits be given the same training as whites and accepted on the basis of ability, not race, for assignments and commissions; and that black doctors and nurses be integrated into the services. When strict segregation continued, the black press protested vigorously. The promotion of

Colonel Benjamin O. Davis, Sr., to the rank of brigadier general did little to appease the black recruits who were segregated in the Army, limited to mess service in the Navy, and denied entrance to the Air Corps or Marines. The American Red Cross even segregated the blood in its blood banks.

As a protest at the continuing racist policy in military administration, William H. Hastie, who had been appointed as a civilian aide to the Secretary of War, resigned. His place was filled by Truman Gibson, Jr., and Lester B. Granger of the Urban League was called to Washington as a naval consultant.

The Army's newly established officer candidate schools began to admit Blacks for unsegregated training in 1941. In 1942 the Navy agreed to accept Blacks for general service, as did the Marines, and the Air Force opened a "special" post for the training of black pilots at Tuskegee. Black women served as WACS and WAVES, and Harriet Pickens became the Navy's first black woman lieutenant.

Before the end of the war there were more than a million black men and women in uniform, including some six thousand officers. Integration in the ground troops of the Army began in 1945, when volunteer black infantrymen saw action alongside white soldiers in the First Army's invasion of Germany, "establishing themselves," according to a War Department communiqué, "as fighting men no less courageous or aggressive than their white comrades."

Lieutenant-Colonel Benjamin O. Davis, Jr., commanding officer of the 99th Pursuit Squadron in Europe.

Troops of the 92nd Division in Italy.

In Action in World War II

Dorie Miller, a Navy messman on the battleship *Arizona* at Pearl Harbor, shot down four Japanese planes over his ship and became one of the first heroes of World War II. Colonel Benjamin O. Davis, Jr., after taking the 99th Pursuit Squadron to Tunisia, returned to organize the 332nd Fighter Group, which flew more than three thousand missions in Europe and destroyed almost three hundred enemy planes. Eighty-eight of the group's pilots, including Colonel Davis, received the Distinguished Flying Cross.

Machine-gunners at Bougainville.

Removing Bougainville wounded.

294

Two black tank battalions participated in the ETO.

Frances Wills, black WAVE ensign.

In ground action, the 761st Tank Battalion won distinction, as did the 614th Tank Destroyer Battalion. The black soldiers of the 92nd Division saw hard fighting and lost more than three thousand men, receiving sixty-five Silver Stars, sixty-five Bronze Medals, and thirteen hundred Purple Hearts. The black soldiers of the famous Red Ball Express maintained the supply lines for the Normandy offensive under extraordinary enemy fire.

In the Pacific, the 93rd Divison saw action at Bougainville, the Dutch East Indies, and the Philippines. The 24th Infantry routed the Japanese from the New Georgia Islands. The 234th Anti-Aircraft Artillery protected Saipan. And some ten thousand black soldiers helped to build Ledo Road, while fighting the enemy at the same time. Black Coast Guardsmen were among the first to land at Okinawa. Black Marines were scattered throughout the Pacific, and black sailors served on most American battleships, bearing the brunt of the action during the war as gunners' mates, radio operators, and coxswains. In the Merchant Marine, twenty-four thousand black seamen served in mixed crews. Eighteen Liberty ships were named for Blackamericans. And some, like the S.S. *Booker T Washington*, under Captain Hugh H. Mulzac, were manned by black officers with mixed crews.

An Army Air Force paratrooper.

A helm watch aboard the submarine *Permit*. World War II brought racial integration to the Navy.

The Plaza 7-switchboard of the New York Telephone Company, whose operators are integrated.

An assembly line at the International Harvester plant in Louisville, where blacks and whites work together.

WE MUST ESTABLISH BEYOND ANY DOUBT THE EQUALITY OF MAN..

Isaac Woodward (*center*), who was blinded in 1946 by a South Carolina policeman while on his way home from military service, with Walter White (*fourth from left*), who was then the executive secretary of the N.A.A.C.P.

Jim Crow on the Home Front

America was at war and our national existence was at stake. Yet on the home front, if we were united in spirit and effort, we were separated and segregated in all else. Blacks who wanted to serve their country, whether in or out of uniform, did so at the risk of their dignity and sometimes at the risk of their lives, long before they met the "official" enemy. The enemy that dogged them most persistently and hurt them worst was Jim Crow. Jim Crow denied their manhood, ignored their citizenship, and scorned them as human beings. As the war progressed, thousands of black workers poured into Northern and Western cities. More than fifty thousand Blacks moved to Detroit alone, seeking work in the many defense industries centered there. Everywhere housing presented a problem, since white workers often resented black families moving anywhere near them and violently opposed their integration into white residential communities. Bombings, arson, and forced evictions were frequent, and serious race riots broke out in Detroit, New York, Mobile, Beaumont, Texas, and other communities.

GOV. WRIGHT BIDS NEGROES BE QUIET

Any Wanting Social Equality Had Better Quit Mississippi, He Says on Radio to Race

By JOHN N. POPHAM
Special to The New York Times.

JACKSON, Miss., May 9—In an action believed to be unprecedented in Southern history, Governor Fielding L. Wright "advised" the Negroes of this state today that if they contemplated eventual social equality and the sharing of school, hotel and restaurant facilities with white persons to "make your home in some state other than Mississippi."

Although racial ~ation has

Air Force veterans of World War II in a bombed home in Los Angeles. All black families in the block had been warned they must vacate.

Harry T. Moore, Florida secretary of the N.A.A.C.P., who, with his wife, was killed in the bombing of their home on Christmas night, 1951.

There were riots at some military centers, too, where local customs clashed with military attempts to provide decent treatment for black soldiers. German prisoners in transit could dine in railway station restaurants, while their Blackamerican guards could not! Recreational facilities for black soldiers were often lacking and USO centers were segregated, although the Stage Door Canteens were open to all.

For civilians, most CIO unions welcomed black members, and even in the South some locals were mixed. But limited transportation facilities created grave problems. It was hard for some Blacks to get to their jobs. Half-empty trains would leave black travelers standing on railway platforms if the lone Jim Crow coach was filled. Buses packed with whites often would not even stop for black passengers. Black soldiers on furlough sometimes could not get home, or if they did get there, were not able to return to camp on time.

Sharecropper Rosa Lee Ingram and her sons, Sammie, fourteen, and Wallace, sixteen, who were all sentenced to death in 1948 in Albany, Georgia, for slaying in self-defense an armed white farmer who struck Mrs. Ingram in the face while she and her sons were working in the fields.

Jim Crow Signs

The Signs of Separation

Blackamericans were never permitted to forget their assigned status for an instant, or to stray from the place America had set aside for them. Public reminders screamed the demeaning message from every likely location, and from some not so likely.

Against the Odds

A world of segregation and prejudice is not an ideal place for genius and achievement either to flower or to be recognized. Yet, in spite of the rigors of the virulent racism that conditioned the chances for a good future for black people, many made it against the odds, and some excelled before the high walls of segregation were legally breached.

In the 1950s, *Who's Who in America* listed the biographies of more than 150 Blackamericans. In sports, Jackie Robinson was signed by the Brooklyn Dodgers in 1947, and Althea Gibson broke through the color bar to become an international tennis champion. In academe a few leading colleges added Blacks to their faculties. Ira de A. Reid became head of the department of social sciences at Haverford College and John Hope Franklin, head of the department of history at Brooklyn College.

In Atlanta Dr. Rufus E. Clement was elected to the Board of Education in 1953, and in 1954 Hulan Jack became borough president of Manhattan.

Louis R. Lautier became the first black correspondent to be admitted to the Congressional press gallery, and a number of daily newspapers added Blacks to their staffs, such as Ted Poston on the New York *Post* and Carl Rowan on the Minneapolis *Tribune*.

The Columbia Broadcasting System sent William Worthy abroad as a newscaster. Louis Peterson, William Branch, Robert Lucas, and William Attaway wrote for radio and television, and Georg Olden be-

came graphic arts director of CBS.

St. Louis Woman, a musical by Countee Cullen and Arna Bontemps based on Bontemps' novel, *God Sends Sunday*, introduced Pearl Bailey to Broadway in 1946, and Louis Peterson's *Take a Giant Step* had a critical success in 1954. Earle Hyman played with otherwise all-white companies in Shakespearean productions. Juanita Hall, Frank Silvera, Lena Horne, Sidney Poitier, Dorothy Dandridge, Ethel Waters, and William Marshall earned prominent movie roles.

Frank Yerby, (whose *Foxes of Harrow* was published in 1946), was the first black writer to have a major Hollywood film based on his work. In 1950 Gwendolyn Brooks received the Pulitzer Prize in Poetry for *Annie Allen*, and Shirley Graham received the Anisfield-Wolf Award for her biography of Benjamin Banneker. In 1954 the same award went to Langston Hughes for his *Simple Takes a Wife*. In 1952 Ralph Ellison won the National Book Award for his novel *Invisible Man*, and in 1955 he was honored with an American Academy of Arts and Letters Fellowship with residency at the American Academy in Rome.

For anyone who bothered to look for it, there was a Blackamerican genius waiting to make its contribution to the mainstream of American culture if only it could be freed from the prison of prejudice and exclusion. The time for change was nearer than America ever dreamed, and when it came, America was caught unready.

Dr. Rufus E. Clement, president of Atlanta University, won his school board post by an 8,000-vote margin.

Gwendolyn Brooks, a Chicago poet and novelist, Guggenheim Fellow and Poetry Workshop Award winner.

Ralph Bunche with his wife and son after receiving the Nobel Peace Prize in 1950.

Integration in high school and collegiate athletics has increased greatly in recent years.

Reading the Bible together; Brooklyn Navy Yard chapel interracial services.

Jackie Robinson (*left*) and Roy Campanella (*right*) were the first black men to play on mixed baseball teams in the South.

William H. Hastie (*left*), the first black judge of a U.S. Circuit Court of Appeals, with Judge John Biggs.

Newspaper man Louis Lautier receiving his credentials which admitted him to the Congressional press gallery.

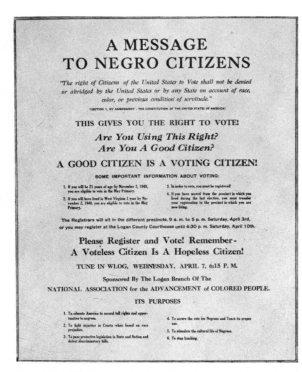

The NAACP, along with church and fraternal organizations in the South, urged Blacks to exercise their right to vote.

Charleston Blacks voted in primaries in 1948 for the first time since Reconstruction.

Despite threats of violence, Blacks voted in the Democratic primaries in Marietta, Georgia, in 1946.

Rights Reaffirmed

Of all Americans of voting age at midcentury, nearly 10 percent were black. Since Reconstruction, the ballot had generally been denied Southern black voters. But a series of court decisions in the 1940s reaffirmed their right of franchise. In the Texas primary case the U. S. Supreme Court in 1944 declared white primaries unconstitutional and delivered the opinion that "organic law grants to all citizens a right to participate in the choice of elected officials without restriction by any state because of race." Georgia refused to accept this decision, and the white killer of a black World War II veteran shot at the polls was exonerated. But in both Georgia and Alabama, federal courts upheld black voting rights. South Carolina decided to make the Democratic Party a private club, excluding Blacks. In 1947 Judge J. Waties Waring of South Carolina ruled in federal court that Blacks must be permitted to vote, regardless of the shift in state regulations, and in 1948 he issued an injunction directing the enrollment of all qualified black voters.

Many Southern state-supported universities would not admit the sons and daughters of black taxpayers. But in 1935 the NAACP won a suit against the University of Maryland law school, and Blacks were thenceforth admitted. However, it was not until 1954 that a sweeping and clearcut U. S. Supreme Court decision—vitally affecting the educational structure of the South—ruled that persons "required on the basis of race to attend separate schools were deprived of the equal protection of the laws guaranteed by the Fourteenth Amendment."

Judge and Mrs. J. Waites Waring before their Charleston home, which was stoned.

Gene Mitchell Gray in 1950 became the first black student to enter the University of Tennessee.

Roy Wilson became in 1950 the first black student to enter the University of Louisiana.

George Washington McLaurin, was the first Black to attend Oklahoma State University, where his wife *(left)* also became a student.

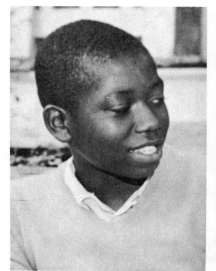

Spottswood Thomas Bolling, a Washington high school boy, was a central figure in the Supreme Court decision which caused desegregation of District of Columbia schools.

"All the News That's Fit to Print"

VOL. CIII.... No. 35,178.   Entered as Second-Post Office, New

HIGH COU

9-TO-0 DE

McCarth

Brown v. Board of Education

On May 17, 1954, the Supreme Court of the United States, in a unanimous decision, outlawed racial segregation in the public schools, setting aside the "separate but equal" doctrine that the court had upheld in 1896. "Separate educational facilities are inherently unequal. . . . Liberty under law extends to the full range of conduct which an individual is free to pursue, and it cannot be restricted except for a proper governmental objective. Segregation in public education is not reasonably related to any proper governmental objective."

Chief Justice Earl Warren read two decisions, the first of which affected seventeen states in which there was legal segregation, and the other, the District of Columbia. Implementing these decisions a year later, the court directed on May 31, 1955, that educational integration be achieved with "all deliberate speed," based on equitable principles and a "practical flexibility." And one year after that, on March 5, 1956, the Supreme Court ruled that its ban on segregation applied also to tax-supported colleges and universities.

Washington, D.C., began at once to set a positive example in prompt compliance with the court's edict. By 1956 Baltimore had integrated eleven thousand of its fifty-one thousand black pupils, but in the rest of Maryland efforts at compliance were halfhearted. In West Virginia only a few areas hung back. The formerly all-black West Virginia State College (with a black faculty), soon had more than four hundred white students, more than a third of its student body. In Kentucky some black teachers were assigned to integrated classes. The University of Louisville was opened to all races, and Berea College, which had been forbidden by Kentucky state law in 1904 to continue admittting Blacks, again accepted them. Oklahoma and Missouri officially began desegregation. Schools on federal military posts throughout the South were integrated.

New York Times.

Copyright, 1954, by The New York Times Company.

NEW YORK, TUESDAY, MAY 18, 1954.

Times Square, New York 36, N. Y.
Telephone LAckawanna 4-1000

FIVE CENTS

LATE CITY EDITION
Fair and cool today. Mostly sunny, continued cool tomorrow.
Temperature Range Today-Max., 68 ; Min., 52
Temperatures Yesterday—Max., 69 ; Min., 61
Full U. S. Weather Bureau Report, Page 51

ANS SCHOOL SEGREGATION;
ON GRANTS TIME TO COMPLY

Eisenhower Bars Report

1896 RULING UPSET

'Separate but Equal'
Doctrine Held Out of
Place in Education

N.A.A.C.P. attorneys George E. C. Hayes (*left*), Thurgood Marshall (*center*), and James Nabrit, Jr., a professor of law at Howard University. Associated with the N.A.A.C.P. for twenty years, Marshall became its chief legal counsel. Marshall commented that what the Southern Congressmen wanted must be "either a moratorium on the enforcement of the Fourteenth Amendment or local option." But concerning children's minds, he declared, "There is no place for local option in our Constitution."

Autherine Lucy, a sharecropper's daughter, was the University of Alabama's first and only black student—for three days.

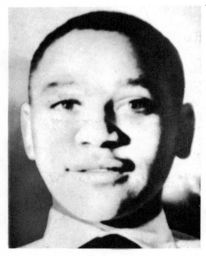

Dennis Holt of Birmingham introduced a resolution condemning mob action which was adopted by the student legislature.

Emmett Till, fourteen, whose vacation ended at the bottom of a river "to teach him a lesson."

Desegregating America: The Law Defied

But there is a darker story. In 1954 school desegregation in America became front-page news in papers throughout the world and has remained in the headlines ever since. Clinton, Nashville, Atlanta, Little Rock, and Oxford are among the places probed for their bitter opposition to the Supreme Court's ruling on desegregation. So are Boston and Chicago.

A week after the 1954 decision, a group of ten senators and twenty-seven representatives from the Southern states issued a heated declaration opposing public school integration. They termed the Supreme Court decisions "unwarranted" and a "clear abuse of judicial power," as well as an encroachment "on rights reserved to the states." "We pledge ourselves," they announced, "to use all lawful means to bring about a reversal of this decision . . . and to prevent the use of force in its implementation."

Encouraged by the stance of resistance taken by the more respectable element of Southern leadership, the perennial demagogues were soon out of hiding and wreaking terror across the South. The Ku Klux Klan turned to open intimidation, and "White Citizens' Councils" sprang up in every town and hamlet. Often the murder and maiming of black citizens had no overt relation to the desegregation issue but represented a continuing strategy of racial intimidation. In Mississippi, for example, Emmett Till, a Chicago schoolboy, was spending a summer vacation on his uncle's farm. In the middle of the night white terrorists seized him and spirited him away. Later, his body was found tied to an iron cotton-gin wheel at the bottom of the Tallahatchie River. He had been brutally beaten and shot through the head. The two white men accused of abducting him were acquitted in a brief

Mrs. Rosa Parks, a seamstress, whose arrest for refusing to move to the back of the bus started the boycott, is fingerprinted after her indictment by a grand jury under a seldom-invoked anti-boycott law.

The Reverend Ralph D. Abernathy (*left*) and the Reverend Martin Luther King, Jr., both Baptists, leave the Montgomery County courthouse after their arraignment with eighty-seven others.

An empty Montgomery bus during the boycott. Blacks normally constituted more than half of the city's bus riders. Without black patronage the company was forced to raise fares for white riders.

mockery of a trial. Till's crime? He was said to have whistled at a white woman in a country store!

Symbolic of the Deep South's defiance of the Supreme Court's desegregation decision was the outbreak in Tuscaloosa, Alabama. For three years a black woman named Autherine Lucy had been trying to enroll as a student in library science at the 125-year-old, tax-supported University of Alabama. By federal district court order she was finally admitted to the university as its first black student and attended her first class on Friday, February 3, 1956.

When she returned on Monday, February 6, riots broke out on the campus, and a mob of more than a thousand men pelted the car in which the dean of women drove Lucy between classes. Threats were made against her life, and the president's home was stoned. Lucy was suspended from the university. When she was reinstated on February 29, by order of the Birmingham federal court, university trustees met and expelled her permanently on a hastily contrived technicality. Almost a decade was to pass before a black applicant was permitted to matriculate at the university.

AN APPEAL
FOR HUMAN RIGHTS

We, the students of the six affiliated institutions forming the Atlanta University Center — Clark, Morehouse, Morris Brown, and Spelman Colleges, Atlanta University, and the Interdenominational Theological Center—have joined our hearts, minds, and bodies in the cause of gaining those rights which are inherently ours as members of the human race and as citizens of these United States.

We pledge our unqualified support to those students in this nation who have recently been engaged in the significant movement to secure certain long-awaited rights and privileges. This protest, like the bus boycott in Montgomery, has shocked many people throughout the world. Why? Because they had not quite realized the unanimity of spirit and purpose which motivates the thinking and action of the great majority of the Negro people. The students who instigate and participate in these sit-down protests are dissatisfied, not only with the existing conditions, but with the snail-like speed at which they are being ameliorated. Every normal human being wants to walk the earth with dignity and abhors any and all proscriptions placed upon him because of race or color. In essence, this is the meaning of the sit-down protests that are sweeping this nation today.

We do not intend to wait placidly for those rights which are already legally and morally ours to be meted out to us one at a time. Today's youth will not sit by submissively, while being denied all of the rights, privileges, and joys of life. We want to state clearly and unequivocally that we cannot tolerate, in a nation professing democracy and among people professing Christianity, the discriminatory conditions under which the Negro is living today in Atlanta, Georgia—supposedly one of the most progressive cities in the South.

Among the inequalities and injustices in Atlanta and in Georgia against which we protest, the following are outstanding examples:

(1) Education:

In the Public School System, facilities for Negroes and whites are separate and unequal. Double sessions continue in about half of the Negro Public Schools, and many Negro children travel ten miles a day in order to reach a school that will admit them.

On the university level, the state will pay a Negro to attend a school out of state rather than admit him to the University of Georgia, Georgia Tech, the Georgia Medical School, and other tax-supported public institutions.

According to a recent publication, in the fiscal year 1958 a total of $31,632,057.18 was spent in the State institutions of higher education for white only. In the Negro State Colleges only $2,001,177.06 was spent.

The publicly supported institutions of higher education are inter-racial now, except that they deny admission to Negro Americans.

(2) Jobs:

Negroes are denied employment in the majority of city, state, and federal governmental jobs, except in the most menial capacities.

(3) Housing:

While Negroes constitute 32% of the population of Atlanta, they are forced to live within 16% of the area of the city.

Statistics also show that the bulk of the Negro population is still:

a. locked into the more undesirable and overcrowded areas of the city;

b. paying a proportionally higher percentage of income for rental and purchase of generally lower quality property;

c. blocked by political and direct or indirect racial restrictions in its efforts to secure better housing.

(4) Voting:

Contrary to statements made in Congress recently by several Southern Senators, we know that in many counties in Georgia and other southern states, Negro college graduates are declared unqualified to vote and are not permitted to register.

(5) Hospitals:

Compared with facilities for other people in Atlanta and Georgia, those for Negroes are unequal and totally inadequate.

Reports show that Atlanta's 14 general hospitals and 9 related institutions provide some 4,000 beds. Except for some 430 beds at Grady Hospital, Negroes are limited to the 250 beds in three private Negro hospitals. Some of the hospitals barring Negroes were built with federal funds.

(6) Movies, Concerts, Restaurants:

Negroes are barred from most downtown movies and segregated in the rest.

Negroes must even sit in a segregated section of the Municipal Auditorium.

If a Negro is hungry, his hunger must wait until he comes to a "colored" restaurant, and even his thirst must await its quenching at a "colored" water fountain.

(7) Law Enforcement:

There are grave inequalities in the area of law enforcement. Too often, Negroes are maltreated by officers of the law. An insufficient number of Negroes is employed in the law-enforcing agencies. They are seldom, if ever promoted. Of 830 policemen in Atlanta only 35 are Negroes.

We have briefly mentioned only a few situations in which we are discriminated against. We have understated rather than overstated the problems. These social evils are seriously plaguing Georgia, the South, the nation, and the world.

We hold that:

(1) The practice of racial segregation is not in keeping with the ideals of Democracy and Christianity.

(2) Racial segregation is robbing not only the segregated but the segregator of his human dignity. Furthermore, the propagation of racial prejudice is unfair to the generations yet unborn.

(3) In times of war, the Negro has fought and died for his country; yet he still has not been accorded first-class citizenship.

(4) In spite of the fact that the Negro pays his share of taxes, he does not enjoy participation in city, county and state government at the level where laws are enacted.

(5) The social, economic, and political progress of Georgia is retarded by segregation and prejudices.

(6) America is fast losing the respect of other nations by the poor example which she sets in the area of race relations.

It is unfortunate that the Negro is being forced to fight, in any way, for what is due him and is freely accorded other Americans. It is unfortunate that even today some people should hold to the erroneous idea of racial superiority, despite the fact that the world is fast moving toward an integrated humanity.

The time has come for the people of Atlanta and Georgia to take a good look at what is really happening in this country, and to stop believing those who tell us that everything is fine and equal, and that the Negro is happy and satisfied.

It is to be regretted that there are those who still refuse to recognize the over-riding supremacy of the Federal Law.

Our churches which are ordained by God and claim to be the houses of all people, foster segregation of the races to the point of making Sunday the most segregated day of the week.

We, the students of the Atlanta University Center, are driven by past and present events to assert our feelings to the citizens of Atlanta and to the world.

We, therefore, call upon all people in authority—State, County, and City officials; all leaders in civic life—ministers, teachers, and business men; and all people of good will to assert themselves and abolish these injustices. We must say in all candor that we plan to use every legal and non-violent means at our disposal to secure full citizenship rights as members of this great Democracy of ours.

Willie Mays
President of Dormitory Council For the Students of Atlanta University

James Felder
President of Student Government Association
- For the Students of Clark College

Marion D. Bennett
President of Student Association For the Students of
Interdenominational Theological Center

Don Clarke
President of Student Body For the Students of Morehouse College

Mary Ann Smith
Secretary of Student Government Association For the
Students of Morris Brown College

Roslyn Pope
President of Student Government Association For the
Students of Spelman College

Part Eight

THE RANGE OF RESISTANCE

During the 1950s more than $75 million of public funds were being spent every year in Southern states on educational institutions that did not admit Blacks. Many communities having segregated schools intended to keep their white schools white and black schools black. When legal loopholes failed and federal courts became increasingly unsympathetic to judicial stalling at lower levels, members of the White Citizens' Councils and other bigoted groups urged open defiance. Elected officials backed up such groups with pronouncements, and mobs backed them with violence while, in most cases, the administrative arm of the national government found no way to back up its judiciary.

Resistance took various forms, ranging from inaction, less then "deliberate speed"; to token integration; to blatant official defiance of federal edicts, riots, and violence against Blacks. Both black and white schools were bombed in Atlanta and other cities. In Nashville, Z. Alexander Looby, venerable member of the NAACP's Legal Committee, was blown from his bed by a bomb. News- and cameramen, both white and black, covering school openings in the South, were set upon by mobs and in some cases severely injured.

In 1955 in Mississippi the Reverend George W. Lee of Belzoni and Lamar Smith of Brookhaven were slain for insisting on their right to vote, and Gus Courts of the Belzoni NAACP was ambushed. In Glendora, Clinton Melton was killed for being a "smart Nigger." For these crimes, no one was punished.

In a front-page story headed: DEFIANCE OF LAW GROWING IN SOUTH, the *New York Times* on June 15, 1959, reported "530 specific cases of violence, reprisal and intimidation" over a four-year period in Atlanta. The *Times* said: "Resistance groups, typified by the White Citizens' Council born in Mississippi in 1954, have spread across the South. . . . Gunpowder and dynamite, parades and cross burnings, anonymous calls, beatings and threats have been the marks of their trade." MISSISSIPPI SHERIFF ATE DINNER WHILE MOB HELD LYNCH PARTY was the headline in the *New York Age* following the Mack Parker lynching in 1959. The *Age* listed Parker as "the 578th human being in Mississippi who has met death at the hands of a mob since 1882."

The jubilation that millions of Blackamericans felt following a series of historic Supreme Court decisions in the 1950s, affirming their participation in the basic rights of our democracy, gradually subsided as the realization grew that noble words on paper are one thing, their application quite another. Nearly a century removed from slavery, were they still a century away from equality?

Army troops escorting black students attending Central High School in Little Rock to their homes, in the fall of 1957.

In September 1957, nine black teenagers sought to register at Little Rock's Central High School. It took not only a Supreme Court edict and a Presidential proclamation, but the 101st Airborne Division of the United States Army, plus the state militia, especially federalized to ensure that these children might safely enter Central High. Their admittance to the school was officially opposed by Governor Orval Faubus, who posted the Arkansas National Guard in front of the building to bar their way. Unrestrained by police, mobs outside the school surged around the black students and menaced everyone, black or white, including newspaper reporters, who appeared to be sympathetic to them. Reporter Alex Wilson of

Mrs. Daisy Bates, Arkansas state president of the NAACP, picketing against segregation in downtown Little Rock stores. From the schools, black leaders moved to speed the desegregation of city parks, tennis courts, golf courses, swimming pools and the city auditorium.

First of the nine black students to be graduated from integrated Central High School in Lit Rock was Ernest Green (*second from right.* Five years after the violent resistance of 195 there were 71 Blacks attending classes with white students in Little Rock.

to Ole Miss

the Chicago *Defender*, who was kicked and beaten while policemen stood by, never recovered from his injuries.

Mrs. Daisy Bates, co-owner with her husband of a black weekly, the *Arkansas State Press*, and president of the Arkansas Conference of NAACP branches, spearheaded the admission of the nine young people. The Bates' home was bombed more than once and sprayed with bullets at night; front windows were smashed by rock-throwing mobs, and flaming crosses were burned on the lawn. Newsboys selling the Bates' newspaper and its black and white advertisers were intimidated. The paper, the family's sole source of income, was forced to close. The school board's rooms and the mayor's office were bombed. Forty-four teachers who refused to side with the segregationists were ordered discharged. The superintendent of schools was removed. Anti-integrationists kept violence and disorder alive in Little Rock for three years.

By 1962 all the formerly all-white high schools in Little Rock were desegregated (although elementary schools remained separated by races). But in other, deeper South states, segregation was still supreme. Mississippi, universally considered racism's strongest bulwark, faced its test when James Meredith sought to enroll at the state university. Governor Ross Barnett, physically barring his way, said to the television cameras and the world that he would die before permitting a black student to attend "Ole Miss." It took the

armed power of the federal government to back up the Supreme Court's order that Meredith be enrolled in the university. When the governor himself failed to bar Meredith, a mob of students and others took over.

During the riots that shook the university campus and the town of Oxford, two men were killed, one of them a French correspondent. Many were wounded, including federal marshals and soldiers, and property was destroyed. White coeds shouted, "Kill the nigger," but James Meredith registered and attended classes—with fifteen thousand soldiers to escort him. "It's more for America than for me," he said.

Mobs were rarely punished even when, as a last resort, troops were used against them, as at Little Rock. Although police were on the scene and hundreds of rioters could be clearly identified from the television films, almost no arrests were made. "During the school year," Daisy Bates stated, "the FBI interviewed hundreds of persons. Many of those who had been part of the mob could easily have been identified from photographs taken in front of the school. Yet no action was taken against anyone by the U.S. Attorney or the Department of Justice." This was the pattern almost everywhere—mobsters literally (as in Mississippi) got away with murder as well as widespread property destruction. Violence spread from the schoolyard to the churchyard, to the lunchcounter, to public transportation, and to the ballot box.

James H. Meredith, a 29-year-old Army veteran, succeeded in enrolling at the University of Mississippi in 1962. He is shown flanked by NAACP attorneys Mrs. Constance Baker Motley and Jack Greenberg.

Rioters with hands over their heads at the end of a night of violence at the University of Mississippi, which resulted in two dead and many wounded. James Meredith began to attend classes that week.

Mob Violence

Nashville integration leader Z. Alexander Looby stands (*right*) before the wreckage of his home after an explosion in April, 1960.

During the 1950s more than $75,000,000 of public funds were being spent every year in Southern states on educational institutions that did not admit Blacks. Many communities having segregated schools intended to keep their white schools white and black schools black. When legal loopholes failed and Federal Courts became increasingly unsympathetic to judicial stalling at lower levels, members of the White Citizens' Councils and other bigoted groups urged open defiance. Elected officials backed up such groups with pronouncements, and mobs backed them with violence while, in most cases, the administrative arm of the national government found no way to back up its judiciary.

Mobs were rarely punished even when, as a last resort, troops were used against them as at Little Rock. Although police were on the scene and hundreds of rioters could be clearly identified from the television films, almost no arrests were made. "During the school year," Daisy Bates stated, "the FBI interviewed hundreds of persons. Many of those who had been part of the mob could easily have been identified from photographs taken in front of the school. Yet no action was taken against anyone by the U.S. Attorney or the Department of Justice." This was the pattern almost everywhere—mobsters literally (as in Mississippi) got away with murder, as well as widespread property destruction. Violence spread from the schoolyard to the churchyard, to the lunch-counter, public transportation and the ballot box.

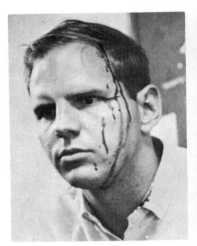

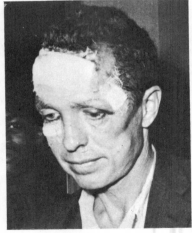

The tide of violence ran high in May, 1961. *Time-Life* writer Norm Ritter (*left*) was among several newsmen beaten by a white mob at a bus station in Montgomery, Ala. CORE leader James Peck (*right*) was attacked at a Birmingham bus station as he arrived with Freedom Riders.

A sign planted in the yards of those who advocated desegregation in Florida cities in the winter of 1959-60.

Baseball bat in hand, a segregationist assaults a black woman as black college students attempted to integrate the courthouse lunchroom in Montgomery, Ala., in 1960.

A black photographer, ordered to leave a courtroom in Jackson, Miss., where black youths were being tried in March, 1961, for "disturbing the peace," was set upon by a snarling police dog and later beaten by police officers.

A bus carrying Freedom Riders was destroyed by a fire bomb when it entered the state of Alabama.

On April 3, 1968, the day before his assassination, the Reverend Martin Luther King was photographed standing on the balcony of the Memphis motel where the shooting took place. To his left is the Reverend Jesse Jackson, and to the right is the Reverend Ralph Abernathy, who replaced Dr. King as head of the Southern Christian Leadership Conference.

Martin Luther King, Jr. and the Struggle for a Dream

The law had finally spoken, but the opposition to the letter, the spirit, and the intent of the law was formidable. On every hand there was resistance, delay, and circumvention. But the law, as expressed by the order to desegregate, rekindled a dream in the heart of Blackamerica, a dream that was perhaps best expressed for most by Martin Luther King, Jr., a young Baptist minister who grew up in Atlanta, Georgia.

Dr. King delivered his "I Have A Dream" address at the Lincoln Memorial in August 1963. It quickly became the ideological set directing the nonviolent struggle for racial desegregation—and beyond that, racial integration. As tens of thousands seated on the grass before the memorial cheered and applauded, and other millions watched via television, King declared:

> I have a dream that one day this nation will rise up, live out the true meaning of its creed: "We hold these truths to be self-evident that all men are created equal."
>
> I have a dream that one day . . . sons of former slaves and sons of former slave-owners will be able to sit down together at the table of brotherhood . . . .
>
> I have a dream that . . . little children will one day live in a nation where they will not be judged by the color of their skin but by the content of their character.
>
> I have a dream that one day . . . little black boys and black girls will be able to join hands with little white boys and white girls as brothers and sisters. . . .

Such a dream would require more than the law to make it viable. The people would have to get involved if King's dream was ever to be more than a passing fancy. They did, and Martin Luther King, Jr., became their leader and the symbol of nonviolent protest in America. It all began in 1955 in Montgomery, Alabama, citadel of the Old South, when a black woman named Rosa Parks refused to relinquish her seat on the bus to a white man. For this she was arrested. In protest, black citizens led by Dr. King, twenty-six-year-old pastor of Dexter Avenue Baptist Church, refused thereafter to ride the segregated buses. Hundreds of Blacks were arrested and otherwise intimidated. King's home was bombed. The resistance held firm, with thousands of Blacks walking to their jobs by day and gathering for prayer and spiritual reinforcement at night. After a year the buses were desegregated,

and Martin Luther King, Jr., emerged as an international hero. The stage was set for an unbelievable saga of national leadership and sacrifice that brought King the Nobel Peace Prize and, eventually, martyrdom. For twelve years, under the aegis of the Southern Christian Leadership Conference (SCLC), King preached his dream in the streets, the jails, and the churches of America. He was assassinated in Memphis, Tennessee, in 1968.

Martin Luther King, Jr., was the most prominent religious leader America has yet produced Not only did he inspire millions all over the world but, more than that, he exposed the deepseated hypocrisy that compromised our democracy. And perhaps he gave America back her conscience, if only for a fleeting interlude. The Center for Non-Violent Social Change in Atlanta is a memorial to Dr. King and his work.

An official of Lane College in Jackson, Tenn., was charged with disorderly conduct and fined for photographing this Jim Crow vending-machine.

Pickets protesting discrimination against black patrons in Southern moviehouses are bundled into police vans.

Other Dreamers, Other Dreams

There were other Blacks who shared King's dream, but only in part. Still others shared it hardly at all. They had dreams of their own, and they had their own theories as to how their dreams could best be accomplished. The common elements that linked these diverse ideologies and tendencies into a movement called The Civil Rights Movement or The Black Revolution were the rejection of racial denigration and the determination of Blacks to participate more fully in the whole range of values available to other Americans.

Student Sit-Ins

Breaking the back of segregation was the number one priority of the movement, and one of the earliest developments in this interest was the student sit-ins.

"Education without freedom is useless," said Bernard Lee, one of more than a hundred students expelled from all-black Alabama State College at the insistence of the governor. They were expelled for sitting quietly, waiting for service, at a lunch counter in the Montgomery Courthouse. It seemed that all over the South thousands of students had the same idea about education without freedom. Sit-ins, organized and unorganized, starting first with lunch counters, began in early 1960 in dozens of cities, often with support from sympathetic white students who went South to help their black counterparts. Conventional sentiments and customs were disrupted by this sudden movement on the part of black and white youth for the right to buy a hot dog or a hamburger at the

The Reverend James M. Lawson (*center*), meeting with students at Vanderbilt University Divinity School after his expulsion for leading black sit-ins in Nashville. Students and faculty protested his expulsion.

same lunch counter. Dime stores and department stores and other facilities with heavy black patronage, such as train and bus terminals, first felt the effect of student sit-ins. But soon they spread to become read-ins in public libraries, wade-ins in municipal swimming pools, kneel-ins at churches, and stand-ins at motion picture theatres that barred Blacks.

A sit-in by Blacks closed a lunch-counter in a downtown Chattanooga variety store in February, 1960.

Freedom Riders sit in the "white only" section of the waiting-room of a bus depot on Montgomery, Ala.

A new social awareness had come to the campuses of America. The students soon had the support of established civil-rights organizations such as the NAACP, CORE (Congress of Racial Equality), Dr. Martin Luther King's Southern Christian Leadership Conference (SCLC), and student groups such as the Student Nonviolent Coordinating Committee (SNCC). In Jacksonville, the *New York Times* reported, "Whites armed with ax handles, baseball bats and other weapons set upon black youth. Intermittent rioting followed. Other riots have taken place in Portsmouth, Va., and Chattanooga, Tenn. . . . There have been mass arrests in many Southern cities." In 1960, more than 40 percent of the annual budget of the NAACP went toward defending court cases involving seventeen hundred student demonstrators standing trial.

Students at the University of Chicago marched in support of the sit-in movement in the South.

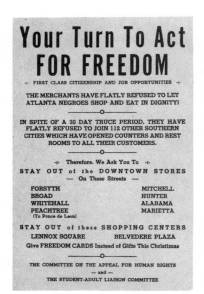

(*Left & center*) In more than 100 Southern cities leaflets were circulated and pickets marched in a campaign for equal treatment in stores and at lunch-counters. (*Right*) Upgraded job opportunities for Blacks are the goal of these demonstrators.

Boycotts and Pickets

Boycotting and picketing of restaurants and shops refusing service to Blacks followed the student sit-ins of 1960. Selective buying—trading only with establishments that did not practice segregation—was used to good effect. And in the South some shops dependent on black patronage went out of business when they refused to abolish their separate "Colored" and "White" drinking fountains or lunch counters. Northern branches of chain stores that discriminated against Blacks in the South also felt the effect of boycotts or found picket lines before their doors.

Color bars began to fall at local lunch counters, on buses, and in city parks by the summer of 1960. Boycotts combined with sit-ins speeded integration of public facilities in Atlanta,

Nashville, Dallas, and other Deep South cities—but not without violence. There were broken arms and broken heads for both men and women. Police dogs were set upon students. There were hundreds of arrests, long-drawn-out and expensive trials, exorbitant fines, and heavy prison sentences. Victory came with a Supreme Court decision in 1961 in which Justice William O. Douglas declared: "Negroes are as much a part of the public as are whites."

Most sit-in and boycott leaders followed the pattern of nonviolent action developed by the Reverend Martin Luther King, Jr., in which "the objective was not to coerce but to correct; not to break wills or bodies but to move hearts."

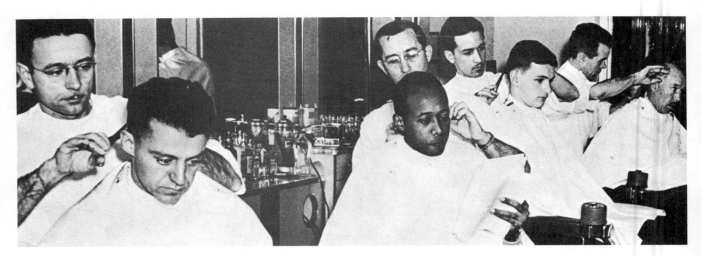

Jim Crow is chased from a barbershop in State College, Pa.

Black pickets parading before Atlanta hotels and motels, were accosted by Klansmen with anti-Negro handbills.

A Florida student leader picketing in Tallahassee, Fla.

Black boys and girls tried unsuccessfully in 1960 to use the facilities of a swimming club in Oak Park, a suburb of Detroit.

Freedom Riders

Black Freedom Riders using a white waiting room in Jackson, Miss., were jailed on "breach of the peace" charges.

The public bus has long been the chief means of transportation for Blacks and poor whites alike in the South. Seating was segregated, with Blacks required to ride the back seats. Until 1961–62, most Southern bus stations had separate waiting rooms and ticket windows for black passengers, and separate toilets (if any), although sometimes a single "Colored" toilet was required to serve both men and women. The lunch counters at rest stops did not serve Blacks, even interstate passengers, including servicemen in uniform. Protests over the years did no good. The Interstate Commerce Commission's ruling that segregation was illegal went unobserved. Finally, black students in the South got tired of waiting and began a series of "freedom rides" to test bus, rail, and air facilities. They were joined by members of the interracial Congress of Racial Equality (CORE). All were pledged to nonviolence.

The riders were met by mobs and police brutality almost everywhere along the routes between Atlanta or Nashville to Birmingham, Montgomery, Jackson, and New Orleans. This violence was unrestrained and often seemed to have the tacit approval, if not the outright support, of the National Guard units and local police. Federal agents sent by Washington to protect civil rights were actually threatened with arrest by Alabama's Governor Patterson, who said, "We do not recognize the federal marshals as law-enforcement officers in this matter." In Mississippi, Governor Ross Barnett declared: "Integration will ruin civilization." And at Jackson, officers with police dogs proceeded to arrest Freedom Riders as soon as they stepped off buses or trains. On a single day in Jackson, 150 Freedom Riders were brought to trial at the Hinds County Courthouse. Many were illegally incarcerated in Parchman Penitentiary, designed for hardened criminals. Bails were exorbitant and fines imposed to the limit.

Five Freedom Riders jailed in Montgomery, Ala., were released on bail in May, 1961.

In Albany, Georgia, four hundred hymn-singing youth were arrested for protesting the treatment of Freedom Riders, and outside Anniston, Alabama, a fire bomb was tossed into a crowded bus. The bus was destroyed and a number of its passengers badly injured. In Montgomery, a black church was surrounded by a stone-throwing mob and the congregation held captive inside all night.

The Freedom Riders won. A number of bus and railroad stations in the South integrated their facilities, and in 1962 the Interstate Commerce Commission ordered separate "White" and "Colored" signs taken down and seats anywhere in a public bus made available to everyone. But compliance was not universal; old habits die hard, and old ways of thinking survive their expressions.

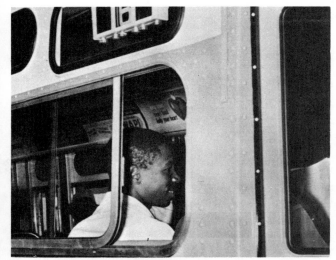

A Black sits in the front of a Birmingham bus. Thirteen Blacks were arrested for refusing to obey the driver's orders as to where they should sit.

Members of a press conference held in Montgomery, Ala., during the Freedom Rides of May, 1961, included (*from top left*) James Farmer, the Reverend Ralph Abernathy, the Reverend Martin Luther King and John Lewis, who had been beaten on his arrival in Montgomery.

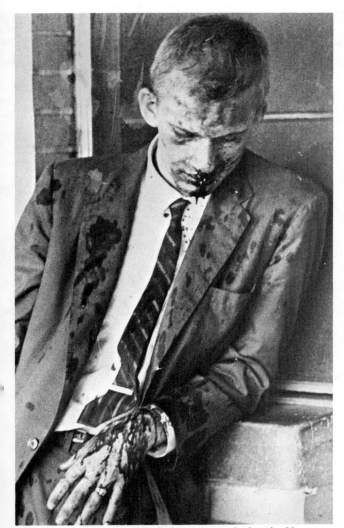

James Zerg, a white Freedom Rider, was attacked at the Montgomery, Ala., bus terminal. White ambulances refused to take him to a doctor.

Four Freedom Riders who attempted a sit-in at a diner on U.S. 40 just north of Baltimore in October, 1961, were jailed by county police.

Styles of Dissent: SNCC

The Student Nonviolent Coordinating Committee was founded in Raleigh, North Carolina, in April 1960, at the suggestion of Martin Luther King, Jr., as a student arm of the Southern Christian Leadership Conference. Its primary role was to coordinate the student sit-ins in the South. John Lewis was elected the first chairman in 1963. Under his leadership, SNCC's objective was defined as integration through nonviolent protest—sit-ins, freedom rides, and voter registration—all of which were incorporated in the famous Mississippi Freedom Summer Project launched in 1964. In

this effort the students incurred one thousand arrests, thirty-five shootings, and fifteen murders—including the lynchings of James Chaney, Andrew Goodman, and Michael Schwerner in a bizarre incident in Mississippi. However, thirty Freedom Schools were organized, and some four thousand Blacks registered in the Mississippi Freedom Democratic Party. The MFDP was organized in protest against the regular Democratic Party for seating an all-white Mississippi delegation at the national convention. In 1965 SNCC publicly opposed the war in Vietnam and the military draft. Following this, contributions fell off drastically, and Julian Bond, SNCC's director of publicity, was refused a seat in the Georgia house after being duly elected.

About the same time, SNCC also formally adopted a black-consciousness philosophy and assumed a separatist stance. John Lewis was replaced as chairman by Stokely Carmichael, who popularized the "Black Power" and "Black Is Beautiful" slogans. Northern white activists were expelled, and the group broke with Dr. King. During this period SNCC emphasized political power, third parties, self-determination, and black studies.

Carmichael was succeeded by H. Rap Brown in 1966, and two years later was voted out of the organization. The name of the organization was changed to Student National Coordinating Committee in 1969. Thereafter the organization faded from public consciousness. Its credibility was seriously eroded by its increasingly controversial policies, and it had spent its usefulness as an effective change instrument in America. Yet its contributions were substantial, and they are a provocative reminder of the potential power in coalitions of effort in a common cause.

The Black Panther chapter in Kansas City serving free breakfasts to children before school.

The Black Panthers

The Black Panthers were organized in 1966 as the Black Panther Party for Self-Defense. It was spawned in the hopelessness and anger of ghetto life. The founders were Bobby Seale and Huey P. Newton, two angry young Blacks who reasoned that their passion had a cause that must be identified and dealt with. The early days of the movement were symbolized by news pictures of tight-lipped young Blacks in leather jackets and black berets, armed with shotguns and rifles, in ominous confrontation with some element of the white establishment. Former FBI Director J. Edgar Hoover called the Black Panthers "the most dangerous group of militants in the country." Across the nation, police raids on Black Panther headquarters were frequent and bloody, and the ranks of the party were decimated by police bullets or imprisonment. Some Panthers, including Eldridge Cleaver and his wife, fled the country and took up residence in Algeria. With Cleaver in exile, Newton, as cofounder, became the dominant force within the party.

What was their dream? Said Newton, "We stand for the transformation of the decadent, reactionary, racist system that exists at this time. . . . We don't like the system. We want to negate the system." Because of their insistence on the right to arm themselves and because of frequent clashes with the police, Newton explained that the Black Panthers assumed a defense "against violence to ultimately resolve and negate violence." He made it clear that the Panthers had no faith in the American political process because "electoral politics is bankrupt and cannot solve the problems of poverty, racism, and oppression."

The Panthers ran their own community-oriented projects, including free breakfasts for ghetto children, free health clinics and testing for sickle cell anemia, and free food distribution. They also ran "liberation schools," "survival conferences," and paradoxically, voter registration drives. At the height of the movement the Panthers had a membership of about fifteen hundred in thirty-eight chapters across the United States. Bobby Seale was chairman and official spokesman for the party.

The Black Panthers were a tragic and bloody footnote to American social history. Driven by the desperate need to have their manhood affirmed in a society where the manhood of all Blacks was routinely denied, the existence of the Panthers could only be read as a final statement of the unacceptability of a social system that seemed intractable. They died in numbers for what they believed in most—themselves as persons of value. Those who survived did so only because they publicly abandoned, in time, the notions that made them so "dangerous" in the first place.

At Seattle headquarters Black Panthers organize free breakfast and free clinic programs.

Black Panther leaders Huey Newton (*left above*), a cofounder, and Dave Hilliard chief of staff. Below are cofounder Bobby Seale (*left*) and Eldridge Cleaver, who sought political asylum abroad and then broke with the cofounders.

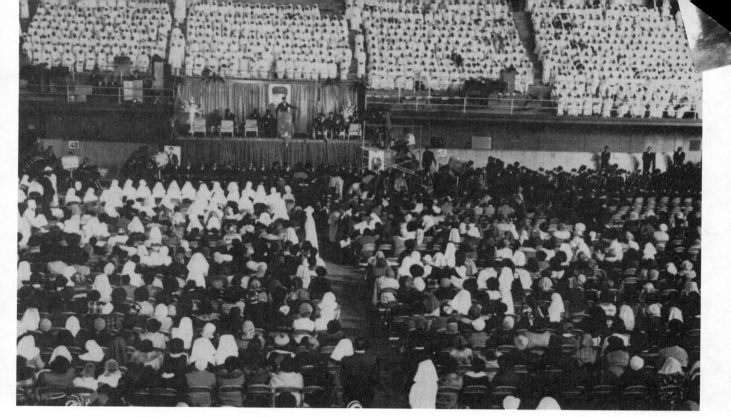

On Saviour's Day each year (Feb. 26), thousands of Black Muslims attend a convention in Chicago.

The Black Muslims

The Nation of Islam, popularly known as the Black Muslims, grew out of the poverty and frustrations of working-class black migrants living in Detroit in the early 1930s. Their dream was the restoration of Blacks in America to their rightful heritage of dignity and prominence in the world and favor in the eyes of Allah, or God. A mysterious "savior" known as Wali Fard appeared in Detroit and let it be known that he had come to rescue "the Lost-Found Nation in the West" and to deliver them from racial oppression and economic want. His program was a mixture of pride of race, self-help, and black unity woven together with a racial interpretation of Islam. Fard disappeared in 1934 and was succeeded by Elijah Poole, who took the name Elijah Muhammad and the title Messenger Of Islam. One of Muhammad's converts, Malcolm X, was instrumental in setting up mosques all across the country in the late 1950s and early 1960s. In a few years the Muslims had developed successful farming operations in Michigan, Alabama, and Mississippi. Across the country their business enterprises, ranging from bakeries and clothing stores to small factories and service industries, became standard features in the black ghettos of our large cities. The "Nation" owned a fleet of trucks, airplanes, office buildings, apartment houses, a bank, a modern printing press, and the most widely circulated black newspaper in the country. The Muslims developed their own parochial schools, and in 1972 they paid $4 million for a grand mosque in Chicago that was formerly a Greek Orthodox Church.

The Muslims demonstrated perhaps more dramatically than any other black group that hard work, efficiency, and self-sacrifice can mean a better life, on terms that stressed separation rather than integration. They made their dissent an instrument for bringing dignity, self-confidence, and material success to themselves, while postponing their dream until the Day of Armageddon, when Allah will smite their enemies and make them supreme rulers of the earth.

With the assassination of Malcolm X in 1965, the Muslim movement lost much of its glamour and excitement. With the death of Elijah Muhammad in 1975, it all but slipped from public consciousness. Wallace (Warith) Deen Muhammad, one of Elijah's six sons, gained control of the movement and changed its name, first to the World Community of Islam in the West, and then to the American Muslim Mission. Under the new leader, the teachings of Elijah Muhammad were deemphasized in favor of a more orthodox approach to Islam, and the Black Muslim dream lost its distinctiveness.

Newark in July, 1967.

Boston in June, 1967.

The Sound Is Diminished, The Fury Subsides . . . Somewhat

The riot that erupted in Harlem in the summer of 1964 suggested a pattern of racial explosions that came to be referred to as the "long, hot summers." In Watts, a black community of Los Angeles, the long, hot summer of 1965 carried a death toll of 35, with 833 injured, and 3,598 arrested. Fire damage came to $175 million and property losses exceeded $46 million. The Watts riot, like the one occurring in Harlem a year earlier, was ignited by black resentment of what was felt to be the gross mistreatment of black citizens by white policemen.

There were major riots in Chicago and Cleveland in 1966, Newark and Detroit in 1967, and in Washington, D.C., and Cleveland in 1968. A commission of distinguished Americans appointed by President Johnson investigated the causes of the riots and, in an official report to the President and the American people, placed the blame on "white racism." The document, which came to be popularly known as "The Kerner Report" (after Governor Otto Kerner of Illinois, who headed the commission), represented an official confrontation of the people of America with our most dangerous and disruptive social force.

That the problems identified by the report were not resolved became evident when the 1981 slaying of Arthur McDuffie by Miami police sparked a riot there leaving 16 dead, 300 injured and $100 million in property damage.

Since the 1970s there has been a dramatic resurgence of public Ku Klux Klan organizing in the South and the North, in schools, in colleges, and even in the military. There have been cross burnings, desecration of buildings, and demonstrations. KKK membership is estimated at seventeen thousand—nearly four times the membership of 1961. In Greensboro, North Carolina, in 1979, five people were killed in a KKK attack. Members of the Klan and Nazi party brought to trial were all acquitted, sparking a prolonged protest movement with allegations of law enforcement complicity in the assaults. In November 1982, a near-riot erupted when five thousand irate citizens sought contact with about fifty Klansmen scheduled to hold a rally in Lafayette Park, Washington, D.C.

Michael A. Donald of Mobile, Alabama, was lynched in 1981; three white men were charged but later freed. White snipers have harassed black citizens in several cities. Urban League President Vernon Jordan was shot by a mysterious gunman in Indiana.

In Wilmington, North Carolina, eight black youths, a white woman, and a United Church of Christ minister, Benjamin Chavis—the so-called "Wilmington Ten"—were arrested in 1972 for "conspiracy" in a case growing out of a protest by high school students. They were released on bond but returned to prison when the U.S. Supreme Court refused to hear the case. A national and international protest movement developed, resulting in Amnesty International declaring the Chavis group to be "political prisoners." The governor of North Carolina refused pardon but reduced their sentences in 1978, resulting in their being paroled in 1979 and 1980. A few months later the convictions were thrown out. Reverend Chavis served a total of over four years in prison.

Young people flee from looted shoe store in Boston after rioting touched off by a welfare demonstration in summer of 1967.

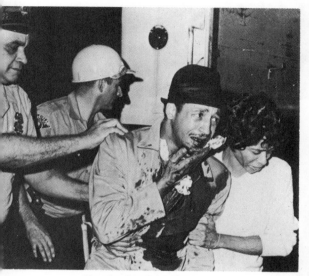

Cleveland in July, 1966.

Chicago's streets look like a battlefield after the smoke of fires clears in April, 1968.

Maggie Bozeman, age fifty-one, president of Pickens County NAACP, and Julia Wilder, age seventy, president of Pickens County Voter League, were convicted by an all-white jury of vote fraud charges and sentenced to prison in Pickens County, Alabama, in 1982. The action generated national protest and marches led by SCLC. The convictions were upheld by an all-white Alabama court of appeals.

A Solidarity Day March held in Washington, D.C., in September 1981 by civil rights and labor organizations drew over 250,000 people protesting "Reaganomics"—President Reagan's national policy of budget cuts in job training, food stamps, education loans, civil rights enforcement, and other social programs, while increasing military expenditures. Rallies and marches to make Martin Luther King, Jr.'s birthday (January 15) a national holiday have been held annually. Similar rallies and marches in support of renewal of the 1965 Voting Rights Act saw that act renewed in 1982.

Medgar W. Evers, the NAACP's field secretary in Mississippi was murdered in the driveway of his home in 1963.

In 1967 a bomb shatters the Mobile, Alabama, home of civil-rights leader J. L. LeFlore and his wife.

Dr. Martin Luther King leads thousands in 1965 protest march on state capitol in Montgomery, Alabama.

Victims of the 1963 bombing of the Sixteenth Street Baptist Church in Birmingham are removed after the explosion. Four children were killed.

A demonstration for open housing in Louisville, Kentucky.

A helicopter view of the giant "March on Washington," showing the crowd near the Lincoln Memorial on August 28, 1963.

Part Nine

SHARING THE POWER . . .

"Power corrupts," Lord Acton is reported to have said, "and absolute power corrupts absolutely." It may also be said that the deprivation of power demeans, and that total deprivation is totally demeaning. In short, where there is no power, there can be no responsibility, and responsibility without power is slavery. Black people know a lot about powerlessness. The call for black power in the 1960s was more an anguished cry for the means to be responsible than it was a summons to political revolution. Real power is the viability of decisions that affect the significant life chances of human beings, a resource few black people in America have ever shared in any meaningful way. Now the conventional picture of the Black excluded from the citadels of power has begun to change. The change is slow, uneven, and cautious, but real. Indeed, the sharing of power may well be the most significant index of progress in civil rights and racial acceptance. Sharing the power means sharing the responsibilities. That is what freedom is all about.

Civil Rights Organizations and Leaders

During the intensified period of civil rights activism in the late 1950s and the 1960s, many new organizations were spawned, most of them sharing common long-range objectives, though diverging to varying degrees in short-range strategies. With this plurality, competition was inevitable, and black leaders were sometimes critical of one another. Headlines were often devoted to the newer, more dynamic groups, while traditional organizations received less coverage. Yet much cooperation took place behind the scenes in planning protest events and in lobbying for legislation and more equitable government policies. If the established civil rights organizations sometimes received less credit, they are nevertheless among those that have endured and that continue to carry on the struggle for freedom in a more conservative time.

The NAACP

One of the most significant strategies to issue from the Black Revolution was the concept of affirmative action, wherein public and private employers and contractors were required to establish goals and timetables to ensure proportionate representation of Blacks. As the 1970s progressed and the job market tightened, this strategy met with opposition expressed in a series of lawsuits directed against the so-called reverse discrimination features of affirmative action. Important cases testing the concept included *Regents of the University of California* v. *Bakke* (1978), *United Steelworkers* v. *Weber* (1979), and *Fullilove* v. *Klutznick* (1980). As an organization that had long specialized in legal action as a means of achieving civil rights, the NAACP was uniquely equipped for its role in combating these suits through its national organization and its eighteen hundred local branches.

The effectiveness of the NAACP was threatened for a time by a $1.25 million lawsuit filed against it as a result of its promotion of selective buying from the white merchants of Port Gibson, Mississippi, in an effort to open the polls to black voters there in the 1960s. This case was favorably adjudicated in 1982, and the association was then able to divert its strategies toward the preservation of civil rights gains that seemed seriously threatened by the conservative policies of the Reagan

Benjamin Hooks, executive director, NAACP.

Administration. Particularly endangered was the Voting Rights Act of 1965, which the President did not want renewed. The act was renewed, and the NAACP could once again give leadership priority to such things as voter registration and school desegregation at all levels.

In 1977 the longtime leader of the NAACP, Roy Wilkins, who became assistant secretary in 1931, retired and was succeeded as executive director by Benjamin Hooks, a lawyer and Baptist minister. Under the leadership of Mr. Hooks and national board chairperson Margaret Bush Wilson, intensified efforts were begun to enlist corporations in black economic development through a program known as Operation Fair Share.

331

Urban League staff meet with military to discuss training programs.

The National Urban League

During the "crisis years" of the 1960s, the National Urban League director was Whitney Young, an exceedingly dynamic and charismatic professor of social work at Atlanta University. Young was drowned in a swimming accident in Africa in 1971 and was succeeded by Vernon Jordan, who had gained national acclaim as head of the Voter Registration Project in the South. Throughout the 1970s the Urban League under Jordan's leadership was the recipient of millions of dollars in federal funds to intensify job training efforts and assist corporations in implementing their affirmative action programs. However, in the wake of the Reagan administration's determination to reduce or eliminate the federal government's role in social programs, the Urban League experienced severe budget cuts, forcing drastic reductions in programs of social uplift. Early in this period of difficulty, a racially motivated assassination attempt felled Mr. Jordan in Fort Wayne, Indiana, and he resigned in 1982 after a prolonged recovery. He was replaced as executive director by John Jacobs who, as one of his first actions, renewed Whitney Young's call

for a domestic Marshall Plan to revitalize the cities. In recent years the Urban League has given increased priority to the issues of teenage pregnancy, crime, and voter participation.

Job training for youth developed by Urban League.

Southern Christian Leadership Conference

With the assassination of Dr. Martin Luther King, Jr., in 1968, leadership of the SCLC was assumed by Dr. King's lieutenant, Dr. Ralph David Abernathy. Abernathy, in turn, was succeeded as president by Dr. Joseph Lowery in 1977. While the SCLC is considerably less visible than it was at the height of the civil rights movement, it continues to be an advocate for the attainment and protection of civil rights. It regularly organizes protest marches as local and national issues dictate, and it has been particularly aggressive in opposing the Ku Klux Klan and in defending black prisoners who are the victims of racial discrimination.

Operation PUSH

Operation PUSH (People United to Save Humanity) was organized in Chicago in 1971 by a former aide to Dr. King, Jesse Jackson, who continues to serve as its president and as one of Blackamerica's more colorful leaders. A prime focus of the late 1970s was Reverend Jackson's "Push for Excellence" educational program, while attention has shifted in the 1980s to affirmative action in large corporations. Operation PUSH has employed selective buying techniques as an effective tactic for increasing corporate use of black banks, advertisers, distributors, and franchises, and for increased purchasing from black-owned businesses. Among the companies with which agreements have been reached are Seven-Up, Heublein, and Coca-Cola.

Preparing for 1984 elections, Jesse Jackson campaigns to raise registered black voters from 10 million to 15 million.

Black Leadership Forum

In an effort to avert fragmentation and to tap the full potential of social change organizations, a Black Leadership Forum, made up of the heads of sixteen major black organizations, was established in the 1970s. In the early 1980s members of the Forum—in addition to officers of the NAACP, Urban League, SCLC, and PUSH—included the Reverend Leon Sullivan, OIC; Eddie Williams, Joint Center for Political Studies, the chairperson of the National Black Caucus of Local Elected Officials; Julius Chambers, Legal Defense and Education Fund; the chairperson of the Congressional Black Caucus; and Richard Hatcher, mayor of Gary, Indiana. Also participating in the forum were Dorothy Height, National Council of Negro Women; Coretta Scott King, Martin Luther King Center for Nonviolent Social Change; Bayard Rustin, A. Philip Randolph Institute; and Theodore Hogans, National Business League.

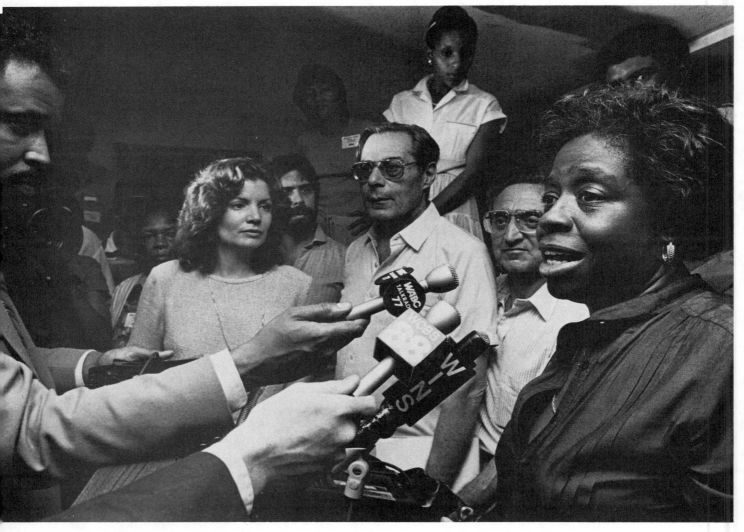

Doris Turner *(right)*, President of the National Union of Hospital and Health Care Employees, AFL-CIO.

The Economic Front

On the economic front, Blacks lost ground during the 1970s vis-à-vis whites, whereas during the 1960s the economic gap had begun to narrow. For example, in 1980 the median income for all black families ($12,674) was 58 percent of the median for all white families ($21,023), compared with 63 percent in 1969. On the other hand, in 1979 more than a fourth of all black families had incomes of $20,000 or more, compared to a fifth of all black families at that income level in 1970. This suggests that even though black income had slipped in comparison to the take-home pay of whites, a sizable segment of the black population made solid economic gains during the 1970s. These advances were made possible by growing opportunities for better prepared workers in skilled trades and office jobs, and by the increased earning power that came with upward mobility.

Still, many were left out. In 1980, 29 percent of black families were below the poverty line ($8,414), compared to 8 percent of white families. The number of poor black families increased by 12 percent during the 1970s, while poor white families decreased by 6 percent. A growing proportion of black families are headed by women. Such units—often among the poorest Blacks—represented over 40 percent of black families in 1980, compared to 28 percent in 1970. During the same period, white families headed by women grew from 9 percent to 12 percent. The increase in black families with no adult male earner—and particularly the alarming increase in the number of teenage mothers—was a major reason, along with lack of job opportunities, for the widening of the overall income gap between the races.

Organized Labor

In spite of the fact that, in the early 1980s, 33 percent of black workers—compared to 26 percent of white workers— were card-carrying union members, the number of black union leaders remained disproportionately small. Recent gains in this arena notwithstanding, the historic problem of Blackamericans seldom having an effective voice in organized labor remains unresolved.

From 1955 to 1974, A. Philip Randolph, president of the Brotherhood of Sleeping Car Porters and vice-president of the AFL-CIO, was one of a handful of black union leaders. Until very recently, the tradition in even the more liberal unions was to elect white executives who then appointed Blacks to lesser offices. Black union members were seldom on the boards or in the offices of power.

The United Auto Workers broke with tradition in the 1960s by electing Nelson "Jack" Edwards to its executive board. Edwards joined Randolph and Frederick O'Neal, president of Actors Equity, as the only black labor representatives in positions of influence. Despite the large numbers of black members, there were no Blacks on the board of the Teamsters' union, or that of the International Ladies Garment Workers Union, or in the steel or mining unions, or in the craft trades.

Another breakthrough came in 1972 with the election of William "Bill" Lucey as secretary-treasurer of the American Federation of State, County, and Municipal Employees. Lucey continued to hold that office into the 1980s and served as well as president of the Coalition of Black Trade Unionists, which he founded. In addition, Marc Stepp became an officer of the United Auto Workers in 1974. But organized labor had a long way to go before its black membership would have adequate representation where meaningful decisions are made.

By the early 1980s the situation was changing. Leon Lynch was vice-president of the United Steelworkers; Brad

William Lucy, International Secretary-Treasurer of the American Federation of State, County and Municipal Employees, AFL-CIO.

Upshaw was president of the Professional Football League; Robert L. White was president of the National Alliance of Postal and Federal Employees; L. Calvin Moore had become vice-president of the Oil, Chemical, and Atomic Workers International Union; and seven Blacks had been installed as vice-presidents of the American Federation of Teachers.

Although in the early 1980s most evidence of formal overt discrimination had disappeared, bias remained, having only become more subtle. Black workers still found it difficult to realize their fair share of union leadership positions. As of 1983, only two of thirteen AFL-CIO department heads were black, as was only one of the directors of the federation's seven regions. Of the 101 unions affiliated with the AFL-CIO, only one was headed by a black executive, while the thirty-five-member AFL-CIO executive council included but two Blacks. In comparison, Blacks constituted 23 percent of the AFL-CIO's 15 million members.

Occupations and Professions

Blacks in white-collar jobs and in the skilled trades increased by about 70 percent between 1960 and 1970, and Blacks holding professional jobs increased by 131 percent. During the same period, there was a 56 percent decrease in the number of Blacks in farm-related work, and 28 percent of the Blackamericans engaged in domestic work found other kinds of jobs or left the labor market altogether. From 1970 to 1980, the proportion of Blacks holding white-collar jobs showed an additional 54 percent increase, while black farm and domestic workers continued to decline.

According to the 1980 census, there were 9.3 million black people employed in the United States—about 9 percent of the total work force. Blacks, however, constituted nearly 12 percent of the total population, and they continued to be underrepresented in the better-paying professions while being greatly overrepresented in lower-paying, unskilled jobs. Over 25 percent of all cleaning workers, janitors, cab drivers, garbage collectors, nurse's aides and welfare aides were black, for example, while fewer than 5 percent of all engineers, lawyers, doctors, and bank officials were black. The search for parity was more encouraging in such occupations as registered nursing, elementary school teaching, mechanics, clerical work, and police work, where from 7 to 10 percent of the work force was black.

In short, Blacks were earning more than they once were but considerably less than they should. In addition to still being underrepresented in the professions, they were underemployed in many categories where they did work, and sometimes paid less for doing the same job even when equally well prepared in terms of education and ability. As evidence of the depth of the problems, the U.S. Steel Corporation was forced to pay $2.1 million to settle a lawsuit filed by five hundred workers and former workers who had been passed over for promotion because of race.

Unemployment

The big problem of the early 1980s was unemployment, which hit a high of 20 percent for Blacks in 1982. Unemployment for young black males was a staggering 50 percent. In fact, more blacks were out of work in 1983 than in 1963.

Black employment in government has traditionally been a weathervane of the status of Blacks overall, and that continues to be the case. In 1970 the federal government employed more Blacks—15 percent of its total labor force—than any other single industry. But they were concentrated in the lower-paying grades, with only 2 percent holding jobs in upper brackets (G.S. 16 or above). Those statistics changed dramatically during the administration of President Carter, when large numbers of Blacks were promoted and appointed to supervisory and managerial positions. By 1980, 5 percent of all employed Blacks worked for the federal government. The trend was reversed by the Reagan administration, however, when the shift from domestic to defense spending along with massive federal workforce reductions eliminated three Blacks for every two whites; the rule of "last hired, first fired" continued to reign supreme.

Black unemployment was aggravated not only by government policy but by a new trend of the 1970s that saw private industry moving out of the cities and sometimes out of the country. This shift has meant a decrease in the number of jobs available in urban centers where Blacks are most heavily concentrated. The problem has been further compounded—and doubtless will be for years to come—by the growth of automated, high-technology industries requiring advanced levels of education and specialized skills while reducing the number of jobs with less stringent qualifications. The dilemma for Blacks today is not merely one of "catching up," but of preparing for a radical shift in the character of the world of work. If Blacks are to be reasonably represented in the economic forces shaping the future, it will require drastically improved preparation in areas of learning and technical skills that have as yet barely touched the black experience.

Line winds around block as unemployed wait to receive surplus food from government depots.

The Ballot and its Blessings

Some of the 22 members of the Congressional Black Caucus meet. From left: George Crockett, Augustus Hawkins, Julian Dixon (chairman), Harriet Pritchett (executive director), Charles Rangel, Walter Fauntroy.

Following the student sit-ins and Freedom Rides of the late 1950s and early 1960s, a wave of voter registration drives swept across the South, but not without strong and often violent resistance. In many cities attempts by black people to exercise the right of franchise were met with mob threats, the bombing of churches, the dynamiting of homes, and murder. Southern school boards fired many teachers who took part in voter registration. Whole communities of black tenant farmers were evicted in rural Tennessee. Tuskegee, Alabama, the site of Booker T. Washington's famous institute, so gerryman-

dered its voting districts in 1957 as to eliminate black voters almost entirely. In Bessemer, Alabama, a black union leader received six months on the chain gang for ordering a poster with the legend, VOTE TODAY FOR A BETTER TOMORROW.

During a voting drive in Georgia in 1962, eight black churches housing voter registration meetings were bombed or burned by terrorists. In the town of Albany, more than a thousand black citizens were arrested for peaceful demonstrations for voting rights.

New Faces in Public Office

Only one percent of American public officials in 1983 were black, but Blacks were 12 percent of the population. Black communities organized drives to get people to register and vote.

In spite of such violent opposition, some progress in the exercise of the right to vote was made. In 1962, aided by a Supreme Court—ordered reapportionment of voting districts, black voters in Georgia elected a Blackamerican, Leroy R. Johnson, to the state senate for the first time in more than fifty years. This victory encouraged campaigners for black voter registration to redouble their efforts everywhere in the South.

In the North, too, Blacks began to realize the power of the ballot. By 1965 there were five black representatives in Congress: William L. Dawson, Illinois; Adam Clayton Powell, New York; Charles C. Diggs, Michigan; Robert N. C. Nix, Pennyslvania; and Augustus F. Hawkins, California.

In state legislatures and in elective and appointive positions in counties and cities throughout the North and West, other Blacks served in important posts. During the Kennedy administration, Robert C. Weaver became administrator of the Housing and Home Finance Agency; Carl T. Rowan became an assistant deputy secretary of state; and Thurgood Marshall was appointed a judge of the second circuit, United States Court of Appeals, in New York. Moving up through the congressional seniority system, Adam Clayton Powell of New York became chairman of the powerful House Education and Labor Committee.

Transition in the Ranks

The 1962 elections made Otis M. Smith auditor general of Michigan and Edward M. Brooke attorney general of Massachusetts. In Connecticut Gerald A. Lamb was elected state treasurer, and in New York Edward Dudley became borough president of Manhattan.

Those were the brave years of the early 1960s. A hundred years after freedom and seventy-five years after Reconstruction, Blackamericans were seriously determined to exercise the full rights of franchise and to enjoy the full benefits of citizenship. Since then millions of new black voters have been added to the rolls, and black people have new expectations and a new sense of power, brought about in no small part by the passage of the 1965 Voting Rights Act.

By the 1970s many of the well-known names had moved on. Dawson of Chicago and Powell of New York were dead. Gone from the Washington scene were Robert Weaver and Carl Rowan. Thurgood Marshall had become associate justice of the United States Supreme Court. The "Great Society" under President Lyndon Johnson had been succeeded by the cautiously conservative administration of President Richard Nixon, who adopted a policy of benign neglect toward Blacks.

Nevertheless, as 1972, a national election year, ended, Georgia could count thirteen black state representatives, a record exceeded only by Illinois with fifteen and Maryland with fourteen. Michigan and Missouri also had thirteen each. In all, 209 Blacks sat in the legislatures of thirty-seven states—including Mississippi and Alabama in the Deep South, and Nevada and New Mexico in the Far West.

In the 1972 elections, Georgia elected its first black congressman since Reconstruction. He was Andrew Young, a former aide to Martin Luther King, Jr. Two black women, Yvonne Burke of Los Angeles and Barbara Jordan of Houston, joined Shirley Chisholm of Brooklyn in the U.S. Congress.

As the black population continued to shift from the South to the North and West, and from the farm and small town to the big cities of America, black mayors, once a rare phenomenon in America, became commonplace. Los Angeles, Cleveland, Detroit, Washington, Newark, Gary, and Chicago found themselves with black leadership, as did numerous smaller towns and cities. Two black lieutenant governors were elected in 1974, the first since Reconstruction—George Brown of Colorado and Mervyn Dymally of California. On the

Political parties in the 1980s began to highlight educational issues and to seek the support of black delegates at political conventions.

The Carter Appointments

The black vote was the decisive factor in the election of Jimmy Carter in 1976. During his tenure President Carter appointed Andrew Young as U.S. ambassador to the United Nations. When Young resigned, Mr. Carter appointed another black statesman, Donald McHenry. Carter appointed Patricia Harris secretary of Housing and Urban development and later secretary of Health, Education and Welfare. He also appointed Clifford Alexander secretary of the army. Carter appointed more blacks to senior government positions than any other president. He nominated forty Blacks to the federal judiciary, more than double the number of all previous presidents combined. His appointments included Drew Days, assistant attorney general, civil rights division of the Justice Department; Ernest Green, assistant secretary of labor and employment; Eleanor Holmes Norton, chairwoman, Equal Opportunity Commission; Wade McCree, solicitor general; and Louis Martin, special assistant to the President.

national level, the five congressmen of the early 1960s had become sixteen, while Edward Brooke of Massachusetts had become the first black senator since Reconstruction.

The consequences of these electoral gains were both symbolic and tangible. Governmental units were no longer able to withhold vital information from black communities or to make decisions in private detrimental to their welfare. For the first time Blacks had representatives *inside* the system who knew their problems, their needs, their priorities—and who argued and voted accordingly. As a result of their presence, black businesses received contracts, black men and women gained jobs through affirmative action programs, black youth gained a new contingent of role models, and Blacks and whites alike gained affirmation that Blacks could govern as competently and as compassionately as their colleagues.

The 1970s also brought new uncertainties. President Nixon was reelected in 1972, carrying every state in the Union but one. However, the Watergate scandal brought on his resignation before his new term was fairly under way, and his successor, former congressman Gerald Ford, made few changes of consequence during the three years he was in office.

President Reagan's Appointments

In the 1980 election President Carter received 90 percent of the black vote, but was handily defeated by Ronald Reagan who got only 8 percent. President Reagan proved considerably more conservative in his approach to racial understanding and immediately upon assuming office set about dismantling the social programs developed or maintained by President Carter. Reagan's black appointments included: Samuel R. Pierce, Jr., secretary of Housing and Urban Development; Clarence Pendelton, first black chairman of the U.S. Civil Rights Commission; Melvin Bradley and Dan Smith, senior policy advisers to the president; Thaddeus Garrett, Jr., adviser to Vice-President Bush; Steven Rhodes, special assistant to the President; and Thelma Duggin, deputy special assistant to the President.

Reaganomics

President Ronald Reagan's early assertion that Blacks "would be appreciably better off today" if the social programs of the 1960s and 1970s had never been inaugurated left most Blacks highly apprehensive about his position on civil rights. As a result, the early 1980s were marked by increased black political concern. Numerous conventions were held to develop strategies for securing equality of opportunity and attacking the complex political and economic problems that confronted the country. These meetings attracted a diverse group of black citizens, including businessmen, elected officials, clergymen, and even the unemployed. What they had in common above all else was the uncomfortable feeling that Reaganomics boded ill for the common interests of black people, and that they must unite on an agenda to improve the situation. In 1980, the National Black Independent Political Party was organized under the leadership of Ron Daniels, Ron Walters, Manning Marable, and Ben Chavis.

Harold Washington, elected first black mayor of Chicago in 1983.

Blacks in Public Office

By 1982, as compared to the past, the number of Blacks in public office was impressive indeed. For example, in 1964 there were 280 black elected officials; in 1982 there were 5,038, with 61 percent of them in the South. In 1970 there were 50 black mayors; in 1982 there were 205, twenty-seven of whom were women. Harold Washington became the mayor of Chicago in 1983 after a hotly contested primary. Tom Bradley, two-term mayor of Los Angeles, won the Democratic primary for governor of California in 1982 but was defeated in the general election. Three Blacks have served as speakers of the House in the state legislatures in recent times: the Reverend S. Howard Woodson, New Jersey (1973); K. Leroy Irvis, Pennsylvania (1977); Willie Brown, California (1980).

Although Senator Edward Brooke of Massachusetts was defeated in his 1978 reelection bid, by 1982 the membership of the Congressional Black Caucus had increased to twenty-one. Though still a small minority in the total Congress, the Black Caucus speaks aggressively as a voice for justice and equality in all deliberations on national policy matters. While continuing the civil rights advocacy of their earlier years,

caucus members have become increasingly skilled in legislative procedures and were responsible in the 1970s for the passage of the Humphrey-Hawkins Full Employment Act. By the 1980s, Black Caucus members held important committee assignments and subcommittee chairmanships across the entire spectrum of congressional activity, with four members chairing full committees. They have been among the representatives most adamant in opposing Reaganomics, and each year have introduced an "alternative" budget placing priority on the domestic needs of America's poor and disinherited.

Through the efforts of the National Coalition on Black Voter Participation, which annually sponsors Operation Big Vote, black voter participation has continued to increase. The proportion of the total voting age population that votes has declined in the past five presidential elections, but the proportion of eligible Blacks voting in 1980 increased by 2 percent over 1976. In 1980, 67 percent of all eligible Blacks were registered to vote; 51 percent of those registered actually voted, compared to 59 percent of registered whites who voted.

War . . .

and Its

Aftermath

On Friday, January 27, 1973, the war in Vietnam was formally brought to a close with the signing of a cease-fire agreement in Paris. It was the longest war in American history, having lasted something more than twelve years with a direct cost of more than $110 billion. It was also the most unpopular war, and the most controversial. Not many Americans agreed upon what they were fighting for, or whether our goals had been realized when the armistice was signed. There was almost universal agreement, however, that it was time, indeed long past time, to get our men out and go home.

A disproportionate number of the men fighting in Southeast Asia were Blackamericans. They were the poor and the jobless conscripts who inevitably fell heir to the uniforms rejected by the white middle-class youth, who, if their traditional insulation of class, education, and profession proved insufficient to protect them from physical involvement in the war, could quit the country in protest to live in Canada or Sweden.

The war was a difficult and shattering experience for most black soldiers. They could not "opt for Canada" as could educated white youth of the American establishment. America would eventually forgive its white dissidents, and they could come home again to jobs and families and positions. Bitter experience has taught Blackamericans that what is protest for some may well be considered treason for some others. (It was only in 1972 that the federal government finally cleared 167 black soldiers of the all-black First Battalion of the 25th Infantry, who were dishonorably discharged by President Theodore Roosevelt for protesting their mistreatment in Brownsville, Texas, in 1906—sixty-six years earlier!) The burden of the war, then, fell upon Blacks as a caste, the poor as a class, and the professional military. Many of the last two categories, ironically, came from the southern United States, making for improbable military comradeship with black soldiers. Inevitably, as the war dragged on, racial incidents at American bases in Asia (and in occupied Europe) increased. At the front, black casualties were disproportionately high, suggesting the possibility of bias in military assignments. There were riots involving black and white sailors aboard American warships and between the races at training camps in America and at army cantonments abroad. Off duty, black soldiers and sailors frequented one section of town, whites another. Reflecting the growing sense of black ethnicity at home, Blacks in the military began to find new pride in their identity. They also demanded that recognition be given their traditional culinary, recreational, and cosmetic preferences, instead of continuing the traditional assumption that what white soldiers preferred to eat, the music they enjoyed most, or the way they liked to cut their hair was necessarily good for or acceptable to Blacks. By the war's end, relationships between the races in the military services had seriously deteriorated and a series of formal investigations had been called for.

The return of the war veterans posed critical problems of adjustment. Jobs were hard to find. Rehabilitation to civilian life was not automatic or easy, and the public was either hostile or apathetic. Many soldiers had been brutalized by combat, drugs, and racial experiences.

The demand for a volunteer army eliminated the draft, although it was reinstituted by President Reagan. But the American establishment does not want its sons ever again to be faced with the choice of serving in a war like the one in Vietnam or expatriating themselves to avoid conscription. Reagan's draft efforts seem to have foundered before his term was half over. The American commitment to an all-volunteer Army remained strong. The expectation is that, if the pay is attractive enough, under the established cadre of professional officers, the Blacks and the poor will be Hessians to the nation, with little inconvenience to the rest of America. Black enlistees are primarily concerned about getting off the streets and getting off the dole. The military seems the surest way. Should the prevailing unemployment and underemployment differentials between whites and Blacks continue, the American army of the future could well be the largest black military force in the world.

However, there remains a strong opposition that would like to see the number of Blacks already in the military reduced. Some worry about the efficiency of black high school dropouts in a high-technology military machine. Others worry more about the increasing number of black officers in control of large contingents based near our racially volatile cities at home.

The Power in the Armed Forces

By the early 1980s Blacks made up 20 percent of United States armed forces personnel and 33 percent of the Army alone, a fact that reflected high black unemployment in civilian life as well as the traditional willingness of black people to fight for their country. Most Blacks were still assigned to the infantry, tank crews, and other duties that risked high exposure in combat, a fact that contributed to the disproportionate rate of black casualties in the Vietnam War. Of the approximately half million Blacks in the military services, about 2 percent were women.

Sharing the power as commissioned officers were twenty-seven generals in the Army, ten generals in the Air Force, one brigadier general in the Marine Corps, and one admiral and two commodores in the Navy. Altogether, as of 1982, there were more than seventeen thousand commissioned black officers in the four branches of the U.S. Armed Forces. The highest-ranking general officers were one general and one lieutenant general in the Army, and one rear admiral in the Navy.

Top Brass

The first black four-star general, Daniel "Chappie" James, Jr., was named commander-in-chief of the North American Air Defense Command in 1975. He died in 1978. Roscoe Robinson, Jr., became the first black four-star general in the U.S. Army in 1982. Samuel Lee Gravely earlier became the first black U.S. Navy admiral (1971), and Frank E. Peterson, the first black Marine Corps general (1972). By 1983, there were 2,254 black female officers in the services, including one brigadier general and eight colonels in the Army, three colonels in the Air Force, and two captains in the Navy. Hazel Johnson was appointed brigadier general in the U.S. Army Nurses' Corps in 1982.

Sharing the Power at the Corporate Level

A small but increasing number of Blacks now sit on the boards of some of America's most powerful and prestigious corporations At first such appointments were for public relations purposes and a single, highly visible black personality would be chosen without regard to other qualifications. While visibility is undoubtedly still important, black corporate directors are increasingly men and women of proven competence in areas of vital significance to free enterprise. A few Blacks like Andrew Brimmer, Vernon Jordan, Jewel Lafantant, and Jerome Holland hold seats on a number of corporate boards. Others such as John H. Johnson, Earl Graves, and Jesse Hill are corporate executives in their own right, bringing with them the expertise of both training and experience. While it is improbable that black appointments to corporate boards will automatically mean more and better jobs for other Blacks in the ranks, such appointments are valuable in themselves, and as they increase will undoubtedly provide some degree of leverage where previously there was none at all.

In 1970, Joseph L. Searles, III, became the first Black to hold a seat on the New York Stock Exchange, and in 1972 Jerome H. Holland was the first Black to be named to the board of directors of the New York Stock Exchange.

Black Enterprise

Blackamericans earned about $126 billion in 1980, more money than all but twelve of the 158 nations of the world. Since Blacks are high consumers, one might expect this extraordinary income to be reflected favorably on the balance sheets of black business. That is not the case. Traditionally, black business has been the small, family-type, service-oriented undertaking with high risks, low profits, and poor management skills. Generally, adequate financing has been all but unavailable, and the rate of failure has been high and predictable. That picture, too, is slowly changing as Blacks with better management skills and increased available capital pool their resources for more favorable investments in black enterprise. While about 95 percent of all black businesses are still sole proprietorships, or mom-and-pop types, by 1979 the top hundred black enterprises were doing more than $1.25 billion worth of business per year.

At the top of the heap was Motown Industries of Hollywood, $64.8 million; followed by Johnson Publishing of Chicago, $61 million; Fedco Foods, Bronx, New York, $45 million; H. J. Russell Construction of Atlanta, $41 million; and Johnson Products, Chicago, $35.4 million. In addition, the thirty-nine black insurance companies (led by North Carolina Mutual of Durham with $5.1 billion) had $13.5 billion worth of insurance in force. Forty-eight black banks had total deposits of a billion dollars in 1979, with assets totaling $1.18 billion. The leading black-owned bank was Independence Bank of Chicago, with assets of $98.3 million.

There are now about 130 black-owned radio stations, compared to only 50 in 1978. Still, approximately 99 percent of all TV news editors and station managers are white. With few exceptions, such as the National Black Cable Network, Blacks have been unable to control cable franchises in urban areas with a majority black population. In Boston, WCVB Channel 7 became one of the first CBS affiliates with significant black stockholders and a black general counsel, treasurer, and vice-president. WLBT in Atlanta is probably the most prominent black TV station at this time.

Some of the success of black enterprise at the top has been due to changing attitudes and policies of some of America's more progressive corporations, who discovered that black business is good business for everybody. Hence, many white corporations make sizable deposits in black banks, carry on affirmative action programs for training black managers, arrange insurance coverage through black insurance companies, buy goods and services from black vendors, support black radio stations and newspapers, and elect Blacks to their corporate boards. In 1982, four black insurance companies, led by North Carolina Mutual, contracted together to provide $300 million worth of group life insurance to the giant R. J. Reynolds Industries.

Another source of support for black enterprise is government contracts. In 1982, Soñicraft, Inc., of Chicago, which manufactures communications equipment, was awarded a contract by the U.S. Air Force that could be worth $268 million over the eight-year life of the agreement.

Sharing the Glory

The plaudits of the crowd have seldom been lavished on black talent, except for strictly defined roles that were almost always demeaning. Blacks could sing and dance, for example, but they could not sing opera. If occasionally they were permitted minor stage or cinema roles, they played those stereotypes that whites would not or could not accept. In sports they could not compete against whites. Once black jockeys were prominent in horse racing—until they began to win derbies. Then the doors were closed to them.

Despite the fact that racial prejudice is still a strong factor in sports and entertainment, Blacks have managed to set the pace consistently in some areas of personal achievement and have won many distinctions for themselves and for their country. Increasingly they share the honor and the glory that is the proper recognition of inherent genius and superb performance: from the Sports Hall of Fame to Oscars, Emmys, and Tonys in entertainment, and from poet laureate to the Pulitzer, American Book Award, and the Nobel prizes.

Adolf Caesar *(right)* and Larry Reilly in *Soldiers Play*, produced by the Negro Ensemble Company.

The Brownsville Raid, a Negro Ensemble production.

Blackamericans in Arts and Letters

Scene from *The River Niger*.

Where the contributions of Blackamericans to the cultural life of America are cited, it is traditional to limit the citations to sports and entertainment. Most Americans have heard of Louis Armstrong, Willie Mays, Muhammad Ali, and Nat "King" Cole. Not so many can identify Jacob Lawrence, Benjamin Quarles, or Dorothy Porter. America has always produced black athletes and black singers and musicians who were either great in actual accomplishment or in potential, although the opportunities for them to be seen or heard were usually minimal. There were no Blacks in "organized" baseball until 1947. Many of the best black

entertainers still have difficulty getting exposure commensurate with their abilities—a case in point being Eubie Blake, whose talents were not fully appreciated until the late 1970s and early 1980s as he was approaching a hundred years of age. Yet Blacks in the worlds of sports and entertainment are accepted. America, it is said, knows them and approves them.

But America does not know much about the black contingent in the worlds of arts and letters. Scholars like W.E.B. Du Bois, Alain Locke, Carter Woodson, Charles Wesley, and John Hope Franklin are either little known to the average American or are assumed to be white. Richard Wright, Paul Robeson, and Imamu Amiri Baraka are just names unless, like DuBois, they become news not because of their artistic and scholarly accomplishments, but because of their politics. The tragedy is that Blackamericans, until quite recently, were as ignorant of the *scope* of black attainment as were whites. We are habituated to a dependence upon the prevailing opinions for our judgments and upon traditional sources for our information. As a result, our understanding of the black experience in arts and letters is as limited as our sources and as parochial as our borrowed norms. One of the significant contributions to the incentives of black youth has been making black achievement in arts and letters more visible.

This visibility was in no small part a product of the black-consciousness movement of the 1960s. Any myth of nonachievement was then shattered with the 1969 organizing of a Black Academy of Arts and Letters by a collectivity of personages that included John O. Killens, Lerone Bennett, Duke Ellington, Adelaide Hill, Harry Belafonte, Charles White, Vertis Hayes, and John Hope Franklin. Active for nearly a decade, the Black Academy provided impetus for the election of black fellows to the membership of the prestigious if staid old American Academy of Arts and Sciences. The Black Academy was instrumental as well in bringing recognition to the historic works of persons such as Henry O. Tanner, Frederick Douglass, and Ira Aldridge, and to contemporary works such as Samuel Yette's *The Choice* and *Soledad Brother: The Prison Letters of George Jackson.*

Indeed, the very remembrance of nearly forgotten black artists seemed to serve as a catalyst for exciting new expressions of black life. While James Baldwin was undoubtedly the most widely read social critic and novelist of the 1960s, he was joined in that decade and the one following by other artists—writers, such as Maya Angelou; poets, such as Nikki Giovanni; playwrights, such as Lorraine Hansberry; choreographers, such as Alvin Ailey. And this tradition of creative expression of the black experience is being carried on in the 1980s by new talents such as Toni Morrison.

It nevertheless remains the case that it is not always easy for a black artist to reach public attention via conventional means in America. Henry O. Tanner was only one of many painters who had to go to Europe for recognition. The French government bought his *Resurrection of Lazarus* in 1896, and he was awarded the Medal of Honor at the Paris Exposition four years later. Since Tanner's time (he died in 1937), only a handful of black artists' works have been shown or purchased by any of America's important galleries. Among those best known

Leona Mitchell, soprano, has sung leading roles with the Metropolitan, the San Francisco, the Houston, the Cologne, and the Covent Garden opera companies.

Kathleen Battle, soprano, has been a regular guest artist with the orchestras of New York, Boston, Cleveland, Philadelphia, and Chicago, and sings often at the major opera houses.

Wilhemina Fernandez, singer, has also starred in the film *Diva*.

to the American public are Horace Pippin (who, after years of productive struggle, was finally "discovered" in the late 1930s), Romare Bearden, Charles White, and Jacob Lawrence.

The younger black artists did not wait for the established galleries to introduce them to America—they went directly to the people. In the 1960s and 1970s, the bleak walls of tenements and stores and schools in black communities across the country became the canvases of a new generation of painters determined to be seen *and* heard. Called "Walls of Respect" or "Walls of Black Dignity," these public galleries often featured serious works of political or cultural significance. In Chicago, Boston, Detroit, and Watts, the works of young artists such as Don McIllraine, Dana Chandler, Bill Walker, and others of their generation became well known in the black community.

If black art as a dimension of cultural nationalism has moderated in the 1980s, it nevertheless has stabilized at a new plateau. It now enjoys sufficient respect to serve as an important medium of inspiration, opportunity, and expression for today's generation of black youth.

James Earl Jones stars often on Broadway and in Hollywood films in roles ranging from contemporary comedy and tragedy to Shakespeare.

After a long career as film star, Sidney Poitier now produces and directs movies.

Lou Gossett, Jr., in his Academy Award role in *An Officer and a Gentleman.*

The Black Screen

The American movie industry has traditionally excluded authentic elements of the black experience from its productions, yet the history of America is replete with authentic black heroes (Crispus Attucks, Nat Turner, Harriet Tubman, to name a few). Certainly, there are enough colorful black political figures in our history—Frederick Douglass, Henry McNeal Turner, David Walker, Adam Clayton Powell—as well as military heroes, scientists, educators, and religious leaders to make questionable the conspicuous absence of films about black people in the history of American filmmaking. When the film industry did, on the rarest of occasions, deign to depict black people and black life on the screen, it was almost always in caricature or stereotype. Blacks were either clowns in the Mantan Moreland or Stepin Fetchit tradition, or they were stereotyped as maids, janitors, or fieldhands. There are millions of Americans who, until quite recently, never saw black people kiss, shake hands, or even cry on the screen (except over the death or discomfiture of some white character to whom they were servilely attached). Only white folks were supposed to have authentic emotions. Their black retainers could only share those emotions vicariously. In *Casablanca*, when Humphrey Bogart fell into a sentimental slough over a beautiful girl, it was Sam, the piano player, who, sensing the white man's mood, sat down at the piano and expressed the white man's feelings. *Gone With the Wind*, another American classic, cast scores of Blacks, but they were members of the environment, the scen-

ery, the background. Like the beautiful horses, the elegant carriages, the handsome magnolias, the Blacks were a part of the setting surrounding the white actors and giving *them* authenticity. There *were* some films about black people—not many—among them, *The Birth of a Nation, Sambo,* and *The Wooing and Wedding of a Coon,* but none of these were calculated to enhance the dignity or self-respect of Blackamericans. Two notable exceptions were *The Emperor Jones* (starring Paul Robeson) in 1933, and *Green Pastures* (starring Rex Ingram) in 1936.

If there was no place for the black experience in American films, then, of course, there was no place for black actors, producers, writers, technicians, or directors. With the occasional exception of a Sidney Poitier or Lena Horne, charged with representing to the millions of black moviegoers the impossible aspirations of thousands of black would-be actors, writers, directors, etc., the American film industry was lilywhite.

And so it remained until the early 1970s, a period when the industry was in serious trouble. The affluent whites had fled to the suburbs, leaving the scores of theaters in the central cities (some of them quite elaborate and expensive to maintain) standing empty. Blacks, who now represented 40 percent of the American movie audience and who had become increasingy self-conscious about identity, were not anxious to keep paying high prices to see white actors perform in roles irrelevant to the black experience. Suddenly they began

Richard Pryor.

Diana Ross.

Billy Dee Williams.

to experiment with black movies, but not without trepidation.

In 1970, Ossie Davis produced *Cotton Comes to Harlem*, starring Godfrey Cambridge and Raymond St. Jacques. *Cotton* grossed more than $9 million and made it quite clear that black people would pay to see black actors on the screen. The next year, Melvin Van Peebles, a very talented young black writer, wrote, produced, directed, distributed, and starred in *Sweetback*, a low budget picture apparently designed for even lower sensibilities. But the *Sweetback* formula was an instant commercial success. It pitted a black man against the white establishment and *permitted him to win!* *Sweetback*, which grossed $15 million in a few months, and *Superfly*, which made a hero of a successful dope pusher, were financed by blacks. Not so the rash of black movies, featuring a new kind of escape, that raced them for the hard-to-come-by black dollars. *Buck and the Preacher; Come Back, Charleston Blue; The Legend of Nigger Charley; Shaft; Sounder; Melinda; Blacula; Slaughter; Skin Game* were but the vanguard of a seemingly endless succession.

By early 1973, one quarter of the two-hundred-odd films being produced annually were black-oriented. Most of them, with the notable exceptions of *Sounder* and *Buck and the Preacher*, were ill-disguised exploitations of the seamier side of the black experience: crime, sexual crudeness, violence, drug involvement, and preoccupation with material ends and immediate visceral gratification. But Blacks lined up by the millions to see them. And while there were some mercifully

consigned to oblivion, others of the same genre found their targets in the romantic fantasies of the millions whose dreams are shaped by their desperation. For months the trade journals showed the black films to be grossing millions of dollars. Civil rights leaders and others protested the one-dimensional characterization of Blackamerica but they found the box office a difficult character to reason with.

Dozens of black actors did find lucrative employment in the 1970s where before there were few or none at all: Jim Brown, Ron O'Neal, Fred Williamson, Cicely Tyson, Richard Rountree, and Rosalind Cash. A few black directors, Gordon Parks (both Sr. and Jr.), Ossie Davis, Hugh Robertson, Christopher St. John, Maya Angelou, and Wendell Franklin were working. Black writers like Lonne Elder III, whose versatility created both *Sounder* and *Melinda*, became known. And one or two talented and daring mavericks, or independently wealthy individuals like Sidney Poitier, began producing films for their own companies.

But, as if on cue, once Hollywood had exhausted the exploitation theme and the true depths of black talent and story material began rising to the fore, the black experience again faded from the images projected to the American public via film. In spite of the emergence of such artists as Lou Gossett, James Earl Jones, Diana Ross, and Billy Dee Williams, scripts to accommodate their talent were scarce after 1980. Richard Pryor was among the few who seemed able to command steady employment.

Blacks On TV

Hank Brown, cameraman for ABC-TV network news.

The importance of the medium of television in shaping the public image of Blacks can hardly be overstated. No less important than its impact on white attitudes is its influence on Blacks themselves—and particularly black children—who, percentagewise, are heavier viewers of television than nonminorities.

A black presence on television is now almost taken for granted—a dramatic change from the early days of broadcasting in the 1940s and 1950s when Blacks, if they appeared at all, were cast only as servants and fools. Yet progress is always relative, and black participation in the medium is far from ideal, both in terms of quantity and quality.

Perhaps the earliest program to move away from the stereotypical "Amos 'n' Andy" (1951–53) syndrome to a more positive and realistic portrayal was Nat "King" Cole's show in 1956. Aside from guest appearances of black entertainers with TV hosts such as Steve Allen, Ed Sullivan, and Arthur Godfrey, however, substantive change awaited the dramatic serialization of the civil rights movement on TV via the newsrooms.

In 1965 Bill Cosby appeared in "I Spy" as the first non-racially typed black performer in a dramatic series, to be followed in 1968 by Diahann Carroll as "Julia." Black comedy—featuring such personalities as Flip Wilson, George Kirby, Nipsey Russell, Moms Mabley, and Godfrey Cambridge—dominated in the 1970s, leading the way to situation comedies such as "The Jeffersons," "Sanford and Son," and "Good Times."

At the same time, Blacks began to appear in commercials, as game show contestants, as sports announcers and newscasters. Tony Brown appeared on PBS as host/producer of "Black Journal," which continues today as "Tony Brown's Journal," while black commentators such as Carl Rowan and Julian Bond have hosted or participated regularly in issues analysis programs. Increasingly throughout the seventies, local stations featured community-oriented programs addressing black cultural, political, and economic issues and concerns.

The dramatization of "Roots" continues to hold the record for television audience participation. Other made-for-television movies of a positive vein have included "The Autobiography of Miss Jane Pittman," "A Woman Called Moses," "Paul Robeson," and "I Know Why the Caged Bird Sings." On the other hand, "Beulah Land" was aired with some revisions only after considerable protest, led by the NAACP, as a consequence of the film's negative and stereotypical characterizations of Blacks.

Black dramatic series continue to have a difficult time gaining acceptance: Alex Haley's "Palmerstown, U.S.A.," "The Lazarus Syndrome," "White Shadow," and "Paris" all enjoyed only brief runs. "Fame" represents a further effort to reverse this trend. Fewer than thirty black actors and actresses appeared regularly in TV series in the fall of 1981, and these rarely in starring roles. During the early 1980s Blacks were to be seen in supporting roles in such shows as "Little House on the Prairie," "WKRP in Cincinnati," "Hill Street Blues," "Barney Miller," and "The Love Boat." The situation comedies, casting Blacks in what many consider pejorative images, continued in the form of "Diff'rent Strokes," "Benson," and "Gimme a Break."

The problem of fair and accurate representation of black life on the television screen is a reflection of deeper problems behind the scenes. Of the more than four thousand members of the Writers Guild/West, fewer than one hundred are black writers. Almost 90 percent of all black comedy shows on TV are written by whites. At the beginning of the decade, only 2 of 132 top network TV executives were black; of one thousand TV directors, only five were black and only one of those produced for prime-time television. Until Blacks gain wider acceptance in the industry as writers, producers and technicians, the underrepresentation and misrepresentation of Blacks in television will undoubtedly continue.

Max Robinson, anchorman for ABC-TV network news.

Sports . . . and the Cinderella Syndrome

When Jackie Robinson joined the Brooklyn Dodgers in 1947, an era of racial exclusiveness in sports died. Racism did not die with dignity and grace, and, indeed, its pale ghost still hovers about the front offices, the coaches' boxes, and the managers' lockers of professional baseball. But the overt phenomenon is dead; and the speed, the skill, and the dignity of Jackie Robinson did more to lay it to rest than those of any other single individual. Before Robinson gave it the lie for all time, the legend was that Blacks and whites would never play together as a team. Individual Blacks might run track (Jesse Owens), or excel in the ring (Joe Louis), or perform any number of feats by themselves, but they could never command the respect that would make white athletes want to play with them. That is all history now.

When Jackie circled the bases for the last time, on October 24, 1972, the rich, the poor, the great, and those who pursue their presence filled Riverside Church in New York City to say good-bye to one of the most respected men in sports. It had been twenty-five years since Jackie Robinson first strolled onto the baseball diamond to face the cheers, the jeers, the doubt, the hope, and the cold hatred that pervaded Ebbetts Field and organized baseball. And it had been fifteen years since he had ended his playing career as one of the most popular and accomplished heroes ever to wear the uniform. Black athletes were now major forces in baseball. And in football. And in basketball. And, of course, boxing. Blacks were the highest paid athletes in the country in at least two sports, but there were no black managers (with the sole exception of Wilt Chamberlain in basketball), no Blacks in the front offices, no Blacks among the owners of the franchises, which passed freely from city to city and owner to owner. In short, black athletes were still essentially performers.

The irony was that, no matter how superbly they performed, no matter how much better they were than the competition, when their performing days were over, they were not invited to stay on as coaches or managers to illuminate the sports with their experience and expertise. They could only expect to retire to their chicken franchises or contracting businesses or some other enterprise not related to the sports that had claimed their professional years and to which they had contributed so much in the superior way in which they played the game.

The Jackie Robinson era brought new hopes and new dreams to millions of Blackamericans who had little enough reason to hope or to dream. Their hopes and dreams had to do with escape—escape and survival. Escape from the painful and brutalizing circumstances of poverty and its consequences, from hunger, disease, addiction, fear, and inconsequence. Escape from the ghetto, the *black ghetto*. Escape and survival. Survival in a world of fashionable clothes, television sets, luxury automobiles, suburban homes, and a system of values that tended to write off as nonpersons those in, but not of, that world. In sports there was the possibility of instant riches—instant escape, instant survival. Thanks to Jackie Robinson, a Willie Mays, a Kareem Abdul-Jabbar could rise from obscurity to certain fame and fortune. The color bar seemed broken.

Sugar Ray Leonard, world junior middleweight and welterweight champion, scores another victory.

O. J. Simpson, pro-football rushing champion.

Kareem Abdul-Jabbar, NBA scoring champion.

Hank Aaron, baseball's all-time home-run champion.

Larry Doby, Chicago White Sox manager.

Frank Robinson, San Francisco Giants manager.

The illusion was enhanced as Muhammad Ali, three-time world heavyweight boxing champion, became a living legend for a new generation of youth, and Sugar Ray Leonard charmed the world with his welterweight and junior middleweight championship feats before retiring in 1982. True, the color bar was lowered slightly in other sports. Lee Elder became the first Black to play in the celebrated Masters' Golf Tournament, and Arthur Ashe won the Wimbledon's men's singles championship. In team sports, Ron Mitchell became the first black head coach at a major white university when he took over Boston University's basketball team. Frank Robinson became the first black manager of a major league baseball team—the Cleveland Indians—in 1975, and subsequently manager of the San Francisco Giants. In the meantime, Larry Doby became manager of the Chicago White Sox, and Maury Wills, manager of the Seattle Mariners. Eric Gregg was hired as the lone Black umpire out of fifty-six in professional baseball. But these remain notable exceptions; the color bar is still high. In the meantime, the exhibition of black superstars continues to make untold millions for their owners.

Even more important is the hard, cold fact that fame and fortune in professional sports is far from certain for any dreamer, black or white. The few hundreds of men who make up the rosters of professional sports constitute a superelite club, with a very limited number of memberships available. Actually, the odds against joining this elite group are quite formidable, and the number of black youngsters who can "run, hit, throw, and use a glove," or who can "handle a basketball," but who will never escape via the sports route must be legion. Organized baseball, football, and basketball seem much bigger than they are. Blacks dominate the player rosters, true, but the mathematics of professional sports are quite simple. Nine men make a team in baseball, eleven in football, and only five in basketball. Each sports has but so many teams, including reserves, and only a *few* in any sport make the fabulous salaries of the superstars.

Out of the hopes and yearnings of the Jackie Robinson era there emerged a sort of Cinderella syndrome, which encouraged every black boy in the slums of America to see himself as a potential Jackie. He could escape. The practical solution to the needs of kids in the ghetto was to give them a pair of sneakers and a basketball (or glove), and nature would do the rest. That is an illusion. Sometimes it is the cruelest of hoaxes. The future of Blackamerica is in keeping black boys (and girls) in school and graduating them with dependable skills. If they have athletic talent in addition, so much the better. The Cinderella syndrome requires perspective even as it needs understanding.

Arthur Ashe, captain of U.S. tennis team winning the Davis Cup.

Evelyn Ashford, national champion in the 100-meter-dash.

Maury Wills, manager of the Seattle Mariners.

Where Blackamericans Live

According to the U.S. Census Bureau, the population of Blacks in the United States in 1980 was 26,624,000. Adjusting for an estimated undercount of 4.8 percent, or 1.3 million, the black population was approaching a total of 28 million. Even this adjusted count is probably conservative.

From 1970 to 1980 more Blacks moved into the South than left, reversing the trends of perhaps every decade since the Civil War. The outmigration of Blacks peaked in the early 1970s, when fully half of all Blackamericans lived outside the South; by 1980, the Southern population had risen again to 53 percent. Another 20 percent lived in the North Central states, while 18 percent resided in the Northeast and 9 percent in the West. Fifty-eight percent of the Black population resided in just ten states: New York (9.1 percent), California (6.9 percent), Texas (6.5 percent), Illinois (6.3 percent), Georgia (5.5 percent), Florida (5.1 percent), North Carolina (5.0 percent), Louisiana (4.7 percent), Michigan (4.5 percent), and Ohio (4.1 percent).

For years, Blacks had left the plantations and farms looking for a better life—better jobs, better schools, better housing, better chances for themselves and for their children. The places they found did not always come up to their expectations—jobs were not always easy to come by, even in the North or in California. Housing was as likely to be segregated in New York or Omaha as it was in Atlanta or Memphis. Still, the North and the West beckoned. They were traditional havens of escape from the traditional expectations of life in the South.

Chances were better in the cities. So by 1970 a third of all Blackamericans lived in just fifteen American cities. Five million of them lived in New York, Chicago, Philadelphia, and Detroit alone. That was more black people than made up the entire population of Senegal, and four times the 1970 population of Liberia. There were more Blacks than whites in Atlanta, and Washington, D.C., had become over 70 percent black. Sixteen American cities had more Blacks than whites, but Blacks made up only about 5 percent of the suburban population.

As the economic situation deteriorated in the North in the late 1970s and early 1980s and as new opportunities developed in the South, the life chances for many Blacks began to appear as good in one region as the other, and a substantial number opted to return. At the same time, those Blacks who had risen to the upper income brackets intensified a second trend of migration—from the central cities to the suburbs. The black population of the suburbs almost doubled from 3.6 million in 1970 to nearly 6.2 million in 1980. Percentagewise, at the end of the 1970s, the black population was growing more rapidly outside the central cities than inside. In 1980 about a fourth of the black population lived in the suburbs, while somewhat more than half lived in central cities. Less than a fifth of all Blacks lived in nonmetropolitian areas or on farms.

Although more than 40 percent of Blacks owned their own homes in 1970—an important factor in family stability and well-being—more than half of the homes occupied by rural Blacks were substandard, and the odds against black home ownership in the cities were quite formidable. Blacks had to buy at grossly inflated prices in a market of least attractive homes in neighborhoods that were run down or otherwise undesirable. Mortgage loans to finance homes were more difficult for Blacks to obtain from traditional lending institutions.

While discrimination in housing was less blatant and widespread in the early 1980s, high interest rates discouraged many middle-class Blacks from buying homes. Blacks in the central cities were still the worst-housed segment of the nation, with the situation deteriorating as the Reagan administration virtually eliminated new construction of subsidized housing. The supply of housing for the poor further decreased with the return of middle-class whites to inner-city neighborhoods, and the conversion of rental units to condominiums.

Getting an Education—
Problems in the Public Schools

Despite Southern evasion and resistance, thirty years after the 1954 Supreme Court decision outlawing segregation in public schools, there was more segregation in *Northern* schools than in the schools of the once solidly segregated South. While the South, under pressure from the courts, black citizens, and world opinion, moved reluctantly to dismantle her dual school system that had existed *de jure*, the North slipped almost imperceptibly into quite as vicious a system of *de facto* segregation of the schools. The encrusted patterns of segregated housing and the gerrymandering of school districts managed to keep black children confined to all-black ghetto schools in Chicago and New York and New Haven quite as effectively as Jim Crow had for generations kept black children out of white schools in Birmingham, Alabama, and Atlanta, Georgia, and Jackson, Mississippi. Inevitably, the focus on school desegregation shifted to the North.

For decades American school children have been bused for miles to attend consolidated schools in the North and in the South, but previously, busing was done on a racial basis that maintained segregation. As a tactic for integrating schools, busing became one of the more crucial issues of the Presidential election of 1972. Incredibly, Richard Nixon, then President of the United States, asked the courts to declare a "moratorium on busing," and pledged himself to do whatever he personally could to minimize or end the practice!

In the meantime, the more critical school problems of racial violence, drug addiction, sexual abuse, underachievement, the arbitrary placement of black teachers in integrated schools, discontinuance of free lunch programs for poor children, and the inadequacy of school curricula drew little public attention. It was as if all the problems of public education would go away if only black children would stay off the public school buses and in their segregated neighborhoods. Many schools became racially polarized. Black children felt they were not wanted; whites felt "their" schools had been in-

vaded. In Boston the violence-plagued, segregated school system was placed under direct supervision of a federal judge for more than ten years.

In the early 1980s more black children attended racially isolated schools than in 1954 because of "white flight" and, in some cases, the falling white birth rate. The level of racial integration is expected to rise in the public schools as more whites return to the cities. This process, called gentrification, has already increased the white public school population in the downtown areas of Boston and a few other places where the inner cities had been abandoned to black migration.

Blacks made up about 12 percent of the population of the United States, but in public education they were grossly underrepresented in administrative posts. For example, of the sixteen thousand school districts in the country, there were fewer than one hundred black school superintendents. Black educators held only 8.7 percent of the total administrative positions at all levels.

The Black Colleges

In 1960 fully 65 percent of the 170,000 black college students attended black colleges. In 1970 only 34 percent of the 500,000 black college students were in black colleges. By the early 1980s the number of black college students had risen to 1.1 million, but the proportion attending predominately black colleges had dropped to less than 25 percent. Yet of all Blacks graduating from college, more than 50 percent still received their degrees from black institutions—a reflection of the high attrition rate of black students at white colleges and universities. The statistics tell two stories: one, of the continuing importance of the black colleges; another, of their struggle for survival.

The drain on the 103 historically black institutions of higher education began with the 1954 Supreme Court decision outlawing school desegregation as college-bound blacks took advantage of opportunities to attend white universities. Since the early 1970s, in what some see as a deliberate strategy to destroy black institutions, compulsory integration of black colleges has become a heated public policy debate. Proponents argue that the requirement of integration cuts across the board; opponents point out that black schools never had a policy of discriminating against whites.

The central issue in the maintenance of black colleges is the crucial role they play in preserving the black heritage, instilling pride in black youth, and training black leadership. The very fact that such a disproportionate number of black students entering white colleges fail to graduate provides a powerful argument for the psychological and social dimension found at black colleges that is so crucial to achieving academic success.

In spite of the vigorous objections of the black community, however, the trend is toward consolidation of the forty previously all-black state-supported colleges with the larger state university systems, some of which now have more white students than black.

Meanwhile, the continued existence of the sixty-three private colleges is threatened by falling enrollments, inflated operating costs, and competition with the more affluent white institutions for their better-qualified teaching and administrative personnel. The situation was aggravated in the 1970s by the decline in support from philanthropic organizations, precipitated in part by the presumption that black colleges were no longer needed, and in part by changes in tax laws adversely affecting foundations. The Ford Foundation stood out as an exception, committing $100 million to the support of ten black colleges. The precarious status of black institutions was further aggravated in the 1980s by the Reagan administration's cutbacks in federal educational grants and loans on which black colleges had become heavily dependent. The full impact of these cuts remains to be seen. The United Negro College Fund, a fundraising agency of the private black colleges, is a chief means of individual and corporate support for the colleges. In its appeal for help, the UNCF reminds Americans, "A mind is a terrible thing to waste!"

On the brighter side, a small number of black administrators now head traditionally white institutions: Clifton Wharton, Jr., is chancellor of the State University of New York, Randolph W. Bromery is chancellor of the University of Massachusetts, and Jewel Plummer Cobb is president of Fullerton State University in California.

Students from black colleges in Alabama march to the state capital to protest cutbacks in funds for their schools.

The Search for Identity— Black Studies

The search for identity has long been a popular theme for fiction writers and social scientists trying to interpret the black man's response to his peculiar place in the American social structure. The question of his political status was resolved, at least in theory, by the Fourteenth Amendment; but no document, political or otherwise, has ever been able to help him establish his cultural identity or, in a large sense, his "ethnic" status.

Blackamericans have been understandably ambivalent about ethnic identity. For most of their history as citizens, they have been so intent upon being Americans that relatively little consideration was given to any previous cultural identity. The mother country of most Blackamericans is Africa—generally speaking, West Africa. We cannot be more precise than this, because no one thought it important to keep records on the tribal or geographic derivations of a slave. No one anticipated that one day the Blackamerican, like his white counterpart, might long to know more about his ancestry, his history, his culture, the piece of earth identified with the significant experiences of his people—the sources of his understanding of who he is. Our textbooks and other standard sources of information have not helped to resolve the problem. They have either grossly distorted the history and the cultural attainments of the West African civilizations, or omitted West Africa altogether as a section of the world worth the attention of American education—even the education of Americans whose forefathers came from West Africa only a few generations ago!

The pride in being American has always been properly characteristic of the Blackamerican. Indeed, the desire to be *fully* American, and to be taken as such, has been the organizing focus of most group efforts and an extraordinary amount of personal effort throughout the black experience in America. Americanism was always taken for granted. Ambivalence always arose with the question of "American, *but what else?*" America never answered *that!*

To many Blackamericans, the logical way to respond to the unanswered questions seemed to be to return to origins—to go back to the Old Country, to Africa—looking for clues. For others the return to origins need not be physical; it could be intellectual. It could be accomplished through the study of the African peoples in Africa and abroad at colleges and universities right here in America. But alas, the college catalogues were replete with courses in European studies, Russian studies, Chinese studies, and the like, but studies about

Africans or people of African descent were scarcely represented. Even in black colleges, there was often not more than an occasional course in Negro History. Indeed, it was widely assumed by (and sometimes taught to) American schoolchildren that "Negroes have no history; they are just here."

The 1960s generation of young Blacks would not and did not accept such an absurdity. They demanded—sometimes through confrontation—and got Black Studies introduced at some level at most American institutions of higher learning. The hope was that the Black Studies movement would help answer the perplexing questions of status and identity, that Black Studies departments would provide opportunities for black students to engage one another in serious dialogues of mutual interest, and that the programs would eventually produce the research and exposition that the search for identity requires.

As the 1970s progressed, it quickly became apparent that this hope was to be frustrated. Many Black Studies departments were established with inordinate haste and without the care, planning, or personnel normally required for serious academic enterprises. Only a few programs were incorporated as an integral part of the host college or university; an equally small number established the same high standards of academic excellence required of other departments in the institution. The discipline was never given the opportunity to mature and was never granted comparable status with other ethnic studies.

As the momentum of the Black Revolution dissipated, so too did the always marginal support for Black Studies. By the early 1980s Black or Afro-American Studies programs were offered at only a handful of universities; on most campuses the discipline had become a dead issue. That development, however, is a commentary on the blindness and recalcitrance of the white educational establishment. Black Studies are needed now more than ever. Indeed, it can well be argued that Black Studies are more important than many areas of study that continue to enjoy priority attention and are even more important for whites than for Blacks.

It is one of the ironies of history that nobody thought the black experience significant until yesterday. It is one of the certainties of the present that it is significant. The failure to recognize its importance and to incorporate it in America's program of higher education may well prove to be one of the tragedies of the future.

Afro-Americans and Africa

The 1976 publication and subsequent televising of Alex Haley's celebrated *Roots* intensified the interest in African affairs and Blackamerican relationships with Africa that had developed during the Black Revolution of the sixties.

The black African states attaining independence after World War II had important meaning for Blackamericans, partially because the stirrings of nationalism that culminated in self-determination for most of black Africa were significantly influenced by Marcus Garvey and his Universal Negro Improvement Association of the 1920s and by the Pan-African Movement of W. E. B. DuBois. But the ongoing struggle for civil rights in the United States has always been a constant reminder that, despite tremendous change, black Africa, like black America, is still not completely free. South Africa, the last white colonial power, keeps millions of native Africans hostage in their own land. American Blacks are sensitive to this situation and find it unacceptable. Blackamerica's sense of identification with Africa is strong, but the more romantic notions about Africa have given way to a kind of cultural sophistication that brings Africans and Afro-Americans together for more serious interests. The thousands of Blackamericans who now visit Africa each year do not go to see the country so much as they go to establish meaningful relationships with the African peoples. Hundreds of Blackamerican students are studying or visiting in Africa, and Blackamerican business interests in Africa are substantial and growing.

The first black president of the Ford Foundation, Franklyn A. Thomas, has helped set up special development grants for African education and agricultural projects. Blacks are increasingly involved as consulting teams for African governments and in business partnerships with African businessmen. Blackamericans such as Mayor Andrew Young of Atlanta, publisher John H. Johnson, and Dr. Adelaide Hill Gulliver of Boston University are frequent consultants to African governments; attorney Rita Senna Fritz-Jaguillard is a special assistant to Prime Minister Robert Mugabe of Zimbabwe. In 1982, Garland Enterprises, a black-owned company in Columbus, Ohio, signed a contract to build a $43 million steel mill in Anambra, Nigeria. Russell Construction Co. of Atlanta was one of the first Blackamerican firms to take on multimillion-dollar projects on the African continent.

The fact that many Blackamericans have mastered one or more African languages and have a firsthand knowledge of African culture—including African religions, art, history, and economics—suggests the seriousness with which Africa is today considered a major force in the black experience in America. Similarly, Africans in America are no longer hesitant to identify with their black counterparts. A large number of African students study at black colleges, and many African professors teaching in American colleges and universities are active in the affairs of their black constituents. Blackamerican music and literature are popular in all the black African countries, while African art in various forms has found new appreciation in black communities in the United States.

Dr. Henry M. Mitchell, dean, School of Theology, Virginia Union University.

Bishop John Hurst Adams, African Methodist Episcopal Church.

Dr. Gayraud S. Wilmore, Dean of Black Church Studies Program, Colgate Rochester/Bexley Hall/Crozer Theological Seminary.

Dr. Williams R. Jones, Director of Black Studies and Professor of Religion, Florida State University.

The Black Church

What is the Black church? It is 20 million Americans of African descent who are formally associated with each other as Christians in America. At least another 6 to 8 million Blacks are considered under the general oversight of the Black church, or consider themselves to be nominal Christians within the family of black churches. Within this family more than 100,000 ministers give full- or part-time effort to the spiritual and practical needs of the black community in some seventy-five to eighty thousand churches, with a real value in excess of $10 billion. The Black church is the genesis and the prime expression of the black subculture, tracing its roots to colonial times, and beyond.

The struggle for dignity that marked the late 1960s reached deep into the religious structures of the American society. The kneel-ins and pray-ins at the white churches of the South were countered with lockouts, arrests, and violence. Scores of black churches were bombed or burned. Sometimes they were rebuilt by the labor and contributions of white Christians, and white clergymen often participated in freedom rides or in other demonstrations on behalf of human rights for Blackamericans. But the churches in America remained essentially segregated. In fact, the history of the church in America is the history of American segregation. And the history of black religion is in part the record of the black Christian's attempts to deal with the phenomenon of racism.

The ways in which black people have expressed themselves religiously have always been a rich and distinctive aspect of the Blackamerican subculture. Religion provides a direct relationship between man and what he understands to be the Cause and Master of his being, introducing meaning and purpose into his life. The way in which individuals or groups *express* their religion, that is, the peculiar emphases their rituals and creeds assume, may reflect in turn a body of experiences that are peculiar to the individual or group in question. Because the black experience in America is a unique experience, the religious expressions of black people are often independent of those of white America.

Religious fidelity appears as one of the most impressive and most consistent characteristics of the black experience. As slaves, black people worshipped in secret, under fear of punishment and death, or they developed their own churches under the watchful eye of the white master. But, through highly allegorical preaching and praying and through the clever use of "spirituals," they managed to present God's Word and to hear God's Word in a way the slavemaster had never intended. God would deliver, and God *did* deliver. When physical bondage was ended, black religion made the continuing social bondage bearable, while at the same time

Dr. James H. Cone, Charles A. Briggs Professor of Systematic Theology, Union Theological Seminary.

Dr. J. Deotis Roberts, President, Interdenominational Theological Center, Atlanta, Georgia.

Dr. Joseph R. Washington, Jr., Professor of Religious Studies, University of Pennsylvania.

fashioning an instrument for its defeat. Martin Luther King, Jr., was not an accident of history. He was the logical flowering of a religious tradition that had learned to depend on the triumph of God's moral intentions over the entrenched perfidy and selfishness of man. The Black church is the formal institutionalization of black religion, and the Black church has always been a prime instrument of black freedom. It is paradoxical that in his role as "magnificent intruder," Martin Luther King, Jr., became the most significant, most celebrated voice in the whole history of American Christianity.

As if fate had so designed it, the martyrdom of Martin Luther King, Jr., was overlapped by the emergence of a school of black theologians whose role it was to broaden and to clarify theologically the moral identity of black people implicit in Dr. King's philosophy of love and nonviolence. Led by James Cone of Union Theological Seminary, this new phalanx of church scholars included such thinkers as Major Jones and DeOtis Roberts of the Interdenominational Theological Seminary, Gayraud Wilmore of Colgate-Rochester Divinity School, Henry Mitchell of Virginia Union, William Jones of Florida State University, and Joseph Washington, Jr., of the University of Pennsylvania. In the Catholic church the "black theology" thrust of these Protestant scholars has been echoed by a small handful of black clergymen, including Father Moses Anderson, who was elected auxiliary Bishop of Detroit in 1983, and Father Clarence Joseph Rivers of Cincinnati. Father Anderson, who was only the seventh Black-american bishop to be named in the history of the Catholic church, was highly instrumental in helping black Catholics achieve identity in the European-oriented structures of American Catholicism.

Other movements of significance were astir in black religion. Among the most exciting was the election in 1982 of Dr. T. J. Jemison as president of the National Baptist Convention, U.S.A., Inc., which is the largest organized body of black Protestants in the world. The Reverend Jemison succeeded Dr. J. H. Jackson, of historic Olivet Baptist Church in Chicago. Jackson, whose conservative views about civil rights had troubled the Black church for years, had been president of the National Baptist Convention since 1953.

At its annual meeting in New York City in December 1982, the Congress of National Black Churches formally announced its existence. The Congress had been organized in Atlanta four years earlier when Bishop John Hurst Adams of the AME Church called together a group of denominational church leaders and scholars to consider the role of the Black church in the future. Concerned that the resources of the Black church, including an estimated billion dollars in annual membership contributions alone, were not sufficiently reflected in the overall welfare of the black community, the conferees organized the Congress of National Black Churches. It is a coalition of the seven major black denominations having national (rather than local or regional) constituencies. Included in the CNBC are the African Methodist Episcopal Church; the African Methodist Episcopal Zion Church; the Christian Methodist Episcopal Church; the National Baptist Convention of America; the National Baptist Convention, U.S.A., Inc.; the Progressive National Baptist Convention, Inc.; and the Church of God in Christ. Other denominational groups may become members of the congress upon proof of national constituences.

Some goals of the congress include better and more extensive theological training for black clergymen and the reconstruction of theological education in Black church seminaries to reflect more realistically the peculiar needs of the communities it serves. Another goal is economic development, in which the local churches combine their buying power for the good of the community, organize credit unions, and develop insurance programs. And to become more politically active is another interest of the Black church.

My People

The night is beautiful,
And so the faces of my people.

The stars are beautiful,
So the eyes of my people.

Beautiful, also, is the sun.
Beautiful, also, are the souls of my people.

LANGSTON HUGHES

372

INDEX

PICTURE CREDITS

The pictures on pages not listed below are from the personal collections of the authors. Key to picture position: t—top; c—center; b—bottom; l—left; r—right. Combinations: br—bottom right, etc. The following are some of the abbreviations used for picture sources:

American Antiquarian Society........AAS
Associated Press ....AP
Boston Public Library...............BPL
Mathew Brady ....Brady
Chicago Historical Society..........CHS
Columbia Broadcasting System.....CBS
Columbia University
  (Gumby Collection) ....Gumby
CORE C
Culver Service ....Culver
Currier & Ives ....C & I
Farm Security Administration........FSA
Harper's Weekly ....HW
Harvard University, Widener
  Library ....HCL
Historical Society of Pennsylvania....HSP
  (Leon Gardiner Collection) ..HSP(LG)
Illustrated London News...........ILN
Frank Leslie's Illustrated Weekly......LW
Library of Congress, Prints and
  Photographs ....LOC
Massachusetts Historical Society......MHS
F. H. Meserve Collection........Meserve
Metropolitan Museum of Art....Met. Mus.
National Archives
National Association for the Advance-
  ment of Colored People........NAACP
New York Historical Society........NYHS
  (Landauer Collection) .....NYHS(LC)
New York Public Library..........NYPL
  (Arents Collection) ....NYPL(AC)
  (Picture Collection) ....NYPL(PC)
  (Schomburg Collection) ...NYPL(S)
  (Stokes Collection) ....NYPL(St)
  (Theater Collection) ......NYPL(TC)
Society of California Pioneers......SOCP
Southern Patriot ....SP
Southern Christian Leadership
  Conference ....SCLC
Underwood and Underwood.......U & U
United Nations ....UN
United Press International...........UPI
U. S. Army Air Force...........USAAF
U. S. Army Signal Corps.........USASC
U. S. Military Academy...........USMA
U. S. Navy ....USN
Wide World ....WW
Works Projects Administration.....WPA

PART ONE: 3: tl—Bernard Cole; bl—Roger Caban. 4: Bernard Cole. 5: tl—Bernard Cole; tc—Barbara Handwerke; tr—Bernard Cole. 7: tl—Baltimore Museum of Art; tr—Museum of Primitive Art, New York. 8: Yale University Art Gallery. 9: tr—Bulloz-Art Reference Bureau. 10: tl—New York Historical Society. 12: CHS. 13: NYPL. 14: NYPL. 15: tl, r—NYPL (AC): bl—NYPL. 16: NYPL. 17: t, c—NYPL (PC). 18: NYPL (PC). 19: t—*Ballou's Pictorial;* c—CHS; b—HW. 20: t—NYPL; c, b—W. H. Brown, *History of the First Locomotive in America.* 21: t—NYPL; bl—AAS; br—SOCP. 22: NYHS. 24: NYHS (LC). 25: t—ILN; bl, br—NYHS (LC). 26: b—CHS. 27: NYHS (LC). 28: l—C & I; r—Mrs. Byron Dexter. 29: t—Culver; b—NYPL (PC). 30: HCL. 31: l—NYPL (PC); r—AAS. 32: tl, tc, tr—J. W. Giddings, *Exiles of Florida;* b—NYPL (PC). 33: NYPL. 34: l—NYPL (PC). 35: t—NYPL, NYPL (PC), P. Runes, *Selected Writings of Benjamin Rush,* NYPL (PC); c—*Life and Times of Frederick Douglass;* b—NYPL. 37: tl—NYPL (S); bl—Brown Bros. 38: tr—NYPL (PC). 39: HSP. 40: tr—Met. Mus. 42: LOC. 43: NYPL (PC). 44: t—BPL; c—Met. Mus.; b—NYHS. 45: t—St. Hist. Soc. of Wis. b—LOC. 46: t—J. T. Adams, *March of Democracy.* 47: t, br—Meserve; c—Richard-

son, *Beyond the Mississippi;* bl—Kans. St. Hist. Soc. 48: NYPL (PC). 49: br—Kans. St. Hist. Soc.; c—NYPL; t—Richardson, *Beyond the Mississippi.* 50: HCL. 51: tc—Brady; tr—NYHS; b—Lincoln U. Lib.

PART TWO: 53: CHS. 54: l—NYPL (S); r—MHS. 56: LOC. 57: t—Old Print Shop, NY; bl—NYPL (S); br—NYPL (PC). 58: NYPL (PC). 59: t—NYHS; b—C & I. 60: Mother Bethel AME Church, Phila. 61: t—NYPL (St). 63: tr—NYPL (S); bl—HSP; br—NYPL (PC). 67: tl—NYPL (S); tc—HSP; r—NYPL (PC). 68: NYPL (PC). 69: t—Old Print Shop, NY; bl—NYPL (PC); br—NYPL. 70: t—NYPL. 71: t—BPL; b—HCL. 73: tl, tr, cr—HCL; bl—NYPL. 74: NYPL (TC). 76: t—NYPL (S). 77: bl—Mrs. A. Bowser; bc—NYPL (S); br—W. Still, *Underground Railroad.* 80: l—NYPL; r—Calif. Hist. Soc. 81: t—Bancroft Lib., U. of Calif.; b—NYPL. 82: NYPL (S). 83: bl—HCL; br—HSP.

PART THREE: 86: t, b—NYPL. 87: c—NYPL; b, first, second, third—NYPL. 88: NYPL (PC). 89: NYPL. 90: blc, brc—NYPL (S). 91: bl, r—NYPL (S). 92: tl, tr, bl—NYPL (S). 93: tl, tr—AAS; b—Smith Col. Lib.; bl—J. W. Coleman, Jr., *Slavery Times in Kentucky;* br—Drury, *Midwest Heritage.* 94: t—AAS; c—Smith Col. Lib. 95: t—Smith Col. Lib.; *Gleason's Pictorial,* NYPL (PC). 96: b—NYPL (S). 97: tr, b—Smith Col. Lib. 98: r—NYPL. 99: tl—HCL. 100: t—HW; c, b—NYPL. 101: t—Nat. Portrait Gall.; b—Smith Col. Lib. 102: from top, counterclockwise, last four—Meserve. 103: counterclockwise, second—LW; fourth, fifth—Meserve. 104: NYPL (PC). 105: r, downward, second, fourth—Brady; third—Meserve; l, downward—Meserve, NYPL (PC), NYPL (PC), Brady. 106: c—NYPL; b—Smith Col. Lib. 107: t—AAS; c, b—R. Nye, *Fettered Freedom.* 108: tl—Cornell U. Lib.; c—NYPL. 109: HCL. 110: J. W. Barber, *History of Amistad Captives.* 111: t—New Haven Colony Hist. Soc.; b—J. W. Barber, *History of Amistad Captives.* 112: t—New Haven Colony Hist. Soc.; bl—Yale U. Art Gall.; br—J. W. Barber, *History of the Amistad Captives.* 113: Met. Mus. 114: Smith Col. Lib. 115: *Life and Times of Frederick Douglass.* 116: *Narrative of Frederick Douglass.* 118: t—Met. Mus.; b—AAS. 119: t—NYPL (S); c—*Life and Times of Frederick Douglass;* b—AAS. 120: t—NYPL; b—LOC. 121: t—Swarthmore College Lib.; b—AAS. 123: tr—LOC; bl—R. Nye, *Fettered Freedom;* br—NYPL. 124: t—Meserve; b—HCL. 125: tl—LOC; tc—*Charles Sumner;* b—A. Shaw, *A. Lincoln.* 126: t—Mus. Mod. Art (PC), NY; bl—Brady; bl, br—LOC. 127: b—C & I. 128: Smith Col. Lib. 129: LOC. 130: tl—Mrs. A. Bowser; tr—NYPL. 131: t—NYHS; l—Swarthmore; r—NYPL. 132: tr, tl, c—NYHS; b—Detroit Pub. Lib. 133: third, fourth, fifth, seventh, eighth, ninth, tenth, eleventh—W. Still, *Underground Railroad;* first—NYPL; sixth—Meserve. 134: b—NYPL. 135: c—NYPL; b—HW. 136: BPL. 137: bl—Onondaga Hist. Soc. 138: *Gleason's Pictorial.* 139: tl—*Gleason's Pictorial;* tr—Mother Bethel AME Church Mus., Phila.; b—NYPL (PC). 140: t—BPL; others—NYPL. 141: t—R. Nye, *Fettered Freedom;* cr—Meserve. 142: NYPL (S). 143: NYPL (S). 144: tl—CHS; tr—Met. Mus.; b—Gumby. 145: bl—

NYPL (TC); br—Gumby. 146: tl—NYHS. 147: b—ILN. 148: l—LOC; r—NYPL. 150: LW. 151: LW. 152: t, br—LW; bl—Oberlin Coll. Lib.; bc—LOC. 153: l—LOC; r—BPL. 154: b—*Abe Lincoln and His Times.* 155: b—LOC. 157: t—HW. 158: HSP. 159: t—LW; br—NYHS. 160: LW. 161: LW. 162: t, c—LOC; b—Brady. 164: t—Met. Mus.; c—Culver. 165: b—Culver. 166: tl, b—LW; c—NYHS. 167: t—NYHS. 170: LOC. 171: LOC. 172: c—LOC; bl, r—NYHS. 173: t—HSP (LG). 174: t—Brady; bl, r—CHS. 175: t—LOC; r—CHS; cl, bl—Brady. 176: bl—NYPL (S); br—Howard U. (Moorland Coll.). 177: tl—Meserve; b—LOC. 178: b—NYHS, Quarles, *Negro in the Civil War.* 179: l—Quarles, *Negro in the Civil War.* 180: LW. 181: l—NYPL; br—HW. 182: LOC. 183: b—Argosy Gall. 184: LW.

PART FOUR: 187: Culver. 188: t—Mrs. Byron Dexter Coll.; b—NYPL. 189: t—NYHS; b—NYPL; r—NA. 190: b—LOC. 191: b—Smith Coll. Lib. 192: tl—NYPL; tr—E. King, *Southern States;* b—NYHS. 193: bl—NYHS; br—NYPL. 194: t—Howard U. (Moorland Coll.); b—NYPL (PC). 195: t, c—NYPL; b—J. T. Trowbridge, *The South.* 196: t—Meserve; bl—LOC; br—J. T. Trowbridge, *Picture of Desolated States.* 197: t—Meserve; bl, r—LW. 198: NYPL. 199: tl, r, c, br—NYPL; bl—Meserve. 200: b—NYPL. 201: b—NYPL. 202: LOC. 203: t—J. L. Trowbridge, *Picture of Desolated States;* c—LW; b—NYPL. 204: Confed. Mus., Richmond, Va. 205: Confed. Mem. Coll., New Orleans, La. 207: t—*Every Saturday;* b—LW. 208: t—Meserve; b—NYPL (S). 209: t, b—first, NYPL; bl, second—NYPL (S); bl, fourth—HSP. 210: t—*Life and Times of Frederick Douglass;* first—Mrs. A. Bowser, second—LW; fourth—HW. 211: b—NYPL. 212: t—HW; b—LW. 213: t—HW; b—LOC. 214: t, b—LW. 215: tl, b—LW; tr—Meserve. 216: t—HW; b—NYPL. 217: t, c—Kans. St. Hist. Soc.; b—NYPL. 218: l—Kans. St. Hist. Soc.; r—NYPL. 219: t—NYPL. 220: l—Culver; cr—NYPL. 221: b—Meserve. 222: tc, tr, c—E. King, *Southern States.* 224: t—AAS; bl—NYPL; br—E. King, *Southern States.* 225: t—NYPL (S); cr—Mrs. Byron Dexter Coll.; b—NYHS. 228: NYHS. 229: Mrs. Byron Dexter Coll. 230: LOC. 231: tl—Culver; tr, b—LOC. 232: second and third, NYPL; fourth, Yale U. Lib. 234: NYPL (PC). 237: tl, r—E. King, *Southern States.* 238: tl—Culver. 239: Culver. 240: NYPL. 241: U & U. 242: tl, c—U & U; bl—Culver; r—Culver. 243: U & U. 244: tl—Mrs. A. Bowser; tr—HCL; b—HW. 245: LOC. 246: t—USMA; b—NYPL. 247: t—LOC.

PART FIVE: 249: *Voice of the Negro.* 250: NYPL. 251: bl—NYPL; br—NYPL (S). 253: tr, c, b—NYPL (TC). 254: tl—NYPL (S); trc, tr—NAACP. 255: tl, r—NAACP, bl—Dodd, Mead. 257: tl—HCL; br, l—NYPL. 259: t—NAACP; b—NYPL (S). 260: NAACP. 261: tl—NAACP; tc, r—Urban League. 262: NA. 263: NA. 264: NA. 265: NA. 266: Gumby. 268: b—NAACP; tr—Gumby. 269: b—U & U; others—Gumby. 271: UPI.

PART SIX: 273: NAACP. 274: bl—J. L. Allen; bc—AP; br—NAACP. 275: b—W. Reiss, *New Negro.* 276: fourth—NYPL (TC). 277: b—NYPL (TC). 278: bl, r—

Scurlock. 280: t—NYPL (S); b—NAACP. 281: t—NYPL (S); b—NAACP. 282: WW. 283: tl—WW; tr—UPI; b—NAACP. 284: t—WPA (Fed. Theater); c—FSA; b—WW. 285: t—NAACP; b—WW. 286: t—WPA (Fed. Arts Proj.); c—NA. 287: t—WPA (Fed. Arts Proj.); b—NA. 288: NAACP. 289: NAACP. 290: t—WW; b—NAACP. 291: tl, r, cr—NAACP; b—Scurlock.

PART SEVEN: 292: UN. 294: t—USAAF; others—USASC. 295: t—USASC; c—M. Palfi; b—USAAF. 296: tl—USN; tr—NAACP; c—Weber. 297: tr—UPI; b—WW. 298: John Vachon for *Look*. 299: John Vachon for *Look*. 300: bl—WW; br—UPI.

301: tl—UPI; c—NAACP; bl, r—WW. 302: c, bl—UPI; br—WW. 303: WW. 304: UPI. 305: UPI. 306: WW. 307: WW.

PART EIGHT: 310: t—UPI; bl—UPI; br—UPI. 311: l—WW; r—WW. 312: t—WW; bl—SP; bc—UPI; br—UPI. 313: tl—UPI; tr—UPI; b—C. 315: WW. 316: t—SP; c—SP; b—SP. 317: t—WW; c—C; b—C. 318: tc—C; tr—C; b—C. 319: tl—WW; tr—WW; bl—C; br—WW. 321: tl—WW; tr—WW; bl—C; br—WW. 322: Bob Adelman. 323: WW. 324: tr—UPI; br—UPI. 325: WW. 326: t—WW; b—WW. 327: t—WW; l—WW; b—WW. 328: tl—WW; tr—WW; c—WW; b—WW. 339: t—SP; b—W.

PART NINE: 330: Photo Researchers, Inc., Bettye Lane. 332: t—National Urban League; b—NUL. 336: t—NUL; b—PR. 337: PR. 338—39: WW. 340: PR. 341: PR. 342: PR, Bettye Lane. 343: PR. 344: t—USAF; b—USN. 345: t—USA. 346: t—USN. 347: b—Maro Lynchard. 348: t—PR; b—PR. 349: t—PR; b—PR, Bettye Lane. 350: t—Bart Andrews; b—Bert Andrews. 351: Bert Andrews. 354: l—National General Pictures. 355: tr—Paramount: c—Paramount. 356: ABC News. 358: WW. 359: tl—George Sullivan; r—George Sullivan. 360: t—WW; b—WW. 361: tl—WW; bl—WW. 362 Rapho/Photo. 363: PR. 364: PR. 365:—PR; b—PR. 366: PR. 371: r—Jules Schick. 372: t: Arlene Boehm; bl—PR; br—Rapho/Photo. 373: t—Chester Higgins, Jr.; bl—PR; br—Rapho/Photo.